The Sacraments

A Practical Guide

Christian Heritage Rediscovered

The Series, as the name suggests, is meant to focus on Christian Faith & Living vis-à-vis topics like Literature & Poetry, Indigenous Philosophizing, Ethical response towards Agriculture, Health & Healing, Science & Technology, Ecofeminist Theology, Sociological approach towards Human Rights, Law & Politics, Arts, History of Ideas, Ancient Civilizations, Cultural Contiguity, Religious Cosmologies & Mysticism, Footsteps of famous Theologians, World Peace & Harmony, Global Capitalism, Network Marketing, Cybertheology, Population & Demographics, Epigraphic Studies, Contextualized Education, and many others. We welcome a Mss. on any topic/s mentioned, whether they are original works, scholarly monographs, collections of conference papers, revised dissertations, or translations of historical documents. Through the Series we, the Publishers, are striving to put forward published works that may help Institutions, Academic Bodies, Researchers, Scholars and the World at large in furthering their respective knowledge and understanding on the concerned subject. We welcome your comments on our efforts and further suggestions on how we can foster the upcoming thoughtful theologically grounded books.

Christian Heritage Rediscovered - 22

The Sacraments

A Practical Guide

Jeffrey A. Truscott

CWI

Christian World Imprints™

First Published in 2016 by

Christian World Imprints(TM)
Christian Publishing & Books from India
H-12 Bali Nagar, **New Delhi-110015**
info@christianworldimprints.com
www.ChristianWorldImprints.com
Phone: +91 11 25465925

ISBN: 978-93-5148-076-1 (HB) ISBN: 978-93-5148-077-8 (FB)

Cataloging in Publication Data--DK

Courtesy: D.K. Agencies (P) Ltd. <docinfo@dkagencies.com>

Truscott, Jeffrey A., 1962- author.
The sacraments : a practical guide / Jeffrey A Truscott.
pages cm. -- (Christian heritage rediscovered ; 22)
Includes index.
ISBN 9789351480761 (HB)
ISBN 9789351480778 (FB)

1. Sacraments. 2. Baptism. 3. Lord's Supper. 4. Reformation. I. Title. II. Series: Christian heritage rediscovered ; 22.

DDC 234.16 23

All Scripture quotations are taken from the New International Version of the Bible (NIV).

Printed at Replika Press Pvt. Ltd.

The Book

The Sacraments: A Practical Guide seeks to foster a recovery of worship in both Word *and* Sacrament among Protestant Christians, especially those in Asia. Classical Protestant understandings are seen as the basis of a contemporary liturgical piety centered on the sacraments. This book aims to encourage Protestants to rediscover their traditional sacramental theologies and practices in order that they might recover their distinctive identities and revitalize their witness in the world. To know and understand a church's sacramental faith and practice is to find the heart of its theology and faith.

Practical in nature and pastoral in its outlook, this handbook for sacramental practice focuses on baptism and the Lord's Supper with much attention given to practical matters such as the physical requirements and pastoral issues surrounding the two sacraments. This book is intended for pastors and other church leaders who want to renew the worship life of their churches by rediscovering the sacraments, particularly the sacramental theologies and practices of their own ecclesial traditions.

The Author

Jeffrey A. Truscott is an ordained minister of the Evangelical Lutheran Church in America, currently serving as Lecturer in Liturgy and Worship at Trinity Theological College, Singapore, where he is also the Chaplain. Prior to that, he was Associate Professor and Dean of the Chapel at Japan Lutheran College and Theological Seminary in Tokyo. He holds degrees from two Lutheran seminaries in the United States and a Ph.D. in liturgical studies from the University of Notre Dame, Indiana, USA.

Introduction

It seems as though the sacraments have little place in Protestant faith and practice today. In many churches, the Lord's Supper is celebrated at only a few Sunday services per year, while baptism is often administered outside the Sunday service with only a few regular churchgoers in attendance. For most Protestants, the sermon is the real center of the Sunday service, and it can often occupy a sizable portion of the service time, in some cases, even 60 minutes! Given that the sacraments exist on the liturgical periphery for many Protestants, why would anyone want to write a book on the sacraments for a Protestant audience? The answer is two-fold:

First, Protestants need to find their distinctiveness. It seems that Protestantism has become an undifferentiated mass of Christians despite the great variety of denominations and traditions. Few churches embrace the distinctive teachings and practices of their founders. Service orders vary little from one another, particularly among those churches that have employed the practices and models of so-called contemporary worship. Protestant preaching seems to rely on conventional homiletical clichés and conventions propounded by church growth experts ("Keep it positive!" "Meet a need!"). One rarely hears a preacher who evidences familiarity with (or a passion for) a major Protestant reformer and who challenges listeners to take their church's confessions and liturgical traditions seriously. Such a lack of historical grounding is puzzling not only to Roman Catholic and Orthodox Christians who do take tradition seriously, but also to the postmodern mind that wonders what a church's or preacher's particular "angle" is. To the world, Protestant churches almost seem to have been produced on an assembly line!

Thus, one goal of this book is to encourage Protestants to rediscover their traditional sacramental theologies and practices in order that they might recover their distinctive identities and revitalize their witness in the world. To know and understand a church's sacramental faith and practice is to find the heart of its theology and beliefs. In a word, sacraments are a window into the soul of a tradition, and it is one worth looking through! Revisiting Protestant sacramental theology is a particularly fitting task as we approach the 500th anniversary of the Reformation in 2017. Knowing where we came from helps us to set trajectories for the future. While some might argue that focusing on Protestant particulars is anti-ecumenical, I would argue the opposite: one cannot engage in serious and authentic ecumenical dialog with others unless one knows one's heritage. You cannot find common ground with another if you don't know who *you* are! To think that ecumenicity is all about putting aside the distinctive teachings of a tradition is at best to misunderstand the nature of the ecumenical task and, at worst, to foster a false, *ersatz* ecumenicity.

Second, Protestants need to renew the liturgical life of their churches. The last decades of the twentieth century witnessed the so-called "worship wars" over "traditional" versus "contemporary" music and other liturgical practices. In many cases the conflict resulted from the attempt to wed the Praise and Worship approach of Charismatic/ Pentecostal churches characterized by a movement to the "inner sanctuary," with the traditional/liturgical "ordo" of mainline churches, characterized by an emphasis on setting forth the means of grace. Unfortunately, the "wedding" was a mismatch, and churches today are looking for peaceful ways to move forward. Indeed the way forward is *backward* – through a rediscovery of the sacramental center of the Sunday liturgy that is the legacy of the early church *and* the Protestant Reformers themselves (as we will see). Furthermore, in a post-modern world, with its emphasis on seeking "experiences," what could be more experiential than the sacramental encounter with Christ in the water of the font or the bread and wine of the table? Thus, Protestants already have the spiritual food that can feed hungry souls of today, and so it is only a matter of finding renewed zeal for the means of grace that Christ himself gave to the church. To restore the sacraments to a more prominent role in the liturgy is *not* to detract from the proclamation of the Word, but to express its transformative power through embodied means. The sacraments renew each *individual* by offering a tangible assurance of the mercy and love of God proclaimed in readings and preaching. They also renew the church by reinforcing our common baptismal/eucharistic identity and so lead us forth into mission as unified people – much like preaching does. The Protestant goal is rightly worship in Word *and* Sacrament.

This book is intended for pastors and other church leaders who want to renew the worship life of their churches by rediscovering the sacraments, particularly the sacramental traditions of their own churches. Obviously, it would take many volumes to describe and analyze even one Protestant tradition's approach to the sacraments. Accordingly, I offer only an *overview* of the baptismal and eucharistic theologies of major Protestant traditions. Readers are therefore encouraged to undertake their own study of the sacraments, particularly through the reading of primary sources. Furthermore, historical and theological material is not discussed here for its own sake but to serve as vital background to sacramental practice. If nothing else, this overview of Protestant sacramental theology will help explain why a particular tradition has certain practices and avoids others. Indeed, the bulk of this book is devoted precisely to sacramental practice – hence the title, *The Sacraments: A Practical Guide.*

The organization of this book revolves around baptism and the Lord's Supper, the two actions designated as sacraments by a majority of Protestants. Chapter 1 endeavors to define "sacrament," show the biblical basis of sacraments and sacramentality, and summarize Protestant understandings concerning which liturgical actions do and do not constitute sacraments and why. The baptismal chapters begin with an overview of Protestant baptismal theologies and practices (ch. 2). The following chapter (3) explores baptism from a ritual studies perspective. Chapters 4 through 7 deal with practical matters: the relationship of baptism to time (ch. 4), physical needs/baptismal architecture (ch. 5), the participants (ch. 6), and the baptismal rite itself (ch. 7). The relationship of baptism to the whole Christian life is taken up in ch. 8. The final chapter on baptism (ch. 9) offers an exploration of the theological and practical challenges that remain before us.

The discussion of the Lord's Supper begins with an overview of Protestant eucharistic theologies and practices (ch. 10). Then follow "practical" chapters on the Lord's Supper and liturgical time (ch. 11), physical requirements/architecture (ch. 12), matters pertaining to the participants (ch. 13), the meaning and practice of the eucharistic liturgy (ch. 14), and a chapter on the relationship of the Lord's Supper to justice (ch. 15). The concluding chapter of this book (ch. 16) explores the sacramentality of the occasional rites (healing, marriage, ordination, funeral) and their relationship to baptism and the Supper.

The reader should note several points about word usage. When referring to those persons gathered for the church's Sunday worship, "assembly" rather than "congregation" is used, since the entire congregation of a local church is unlikely to be present at every Sunday service. "Liturgy" refers to the public worship service of a church, as opposed to the "order of service." When discussing the first main section of the Sunday service devoted to the reading of Scriptures and preaching, "word" is used, while "Word" (upper case) refers to the Word of God. Although the sacrament of Holy Communion has many names (Sacrament of the Altar, Eucharist, Meal, Service of Word and Table), "Lord's Supper" is the preferred word here because of its biblical basis (cf. 1 Cor. 11:20) and because it best sums up the essence of the experience as an encounter with the risen Lord himself (cf. Luke 24:30-31). Some readers may find it helpful to read my *Worship: A Practical Guide* (Genesis, 2011) in order to familiarize themselves with my style and way of expression.

The translations of quoted material from ancient and medieval sources are all taken from existing works, usually ones cited in Johnson's *Documents of the Baptismal Liturgy* or his *Sacraments and Worship: The Sources of Christian Theology.* Since most pre-Reformation documents are found in numerous editions, I cite volume, chapter, and section numbers rather than specific page numbers (see Kate L. Turabian, *A Manual for Writers* [8th ed], p. 188).

This book owes much to the assistance and support of various individuals and organizations, whom I must thank: Trinity Theological College, Singapore, especially the Academic Dean, Dr Tan Kim Huat, for granting me a sabbatical leave during the first half of 2014 in order to pursue the writing of this volume; the Global Mission unit of the Evangelical Lutheran Church in America and its East Asia Director, Dr Y. Franklin Ishida, for allowing my study leave for the same purpose; Dr. Frank C. Senn, Chicago, Illinois, for reading draft chapters and making many insightful and helpful comments; Jennie Smith, for proofreading drafts of the manuscript; my mother, Anna Truscott, for once again graciously permitting me to use our home in Chicora, Pennsylvania, as a library and office; and the people of Holy Trinity Lutheran Church, Chicora, Pennsylvania, for their love and support during the project. All of the aforementioned have my deepest gratitude.

Soli Deo Gloria
Jeffrey Truscott
Singapore

Abbreviations

AR	*Articles of Religion* (Anglican Church)
BC	*The Book of Concord: Confessions of the Evangelical Lutheran Church*, ed. Robert Kolb and Timothy J. Wengert (Minneapolis: Fortress Press, 2000).
BCP	*Book of Common Prayer*
BCP *Texts*	*The Book of Common Prayer: The Texts of 1549, 1559, and 1662,* ed. Brian Cummings (Oxford: University Press, 2011).
BCP 1979	*The Book of Common Prayer and Administration of the Sacraments and Other Rites and Ceremonies of the Church Together with the Psalter or Psalms of David* (New York: Seabury Press, 1979).
BCW	*Book of Common Worship* (Louisville/London: Westminster John Knox Press, 1993).
BEM	World Council of Churches, *Baptism, Eucharist and Ministry*, Faith and Order Paper No. 111 (Geneva: World Council of Churches, 1982).
BT	*Baptism Today: Understanding, Practice, Ecumenical Implications*, ed. Thomas F. Best, World Council of

Churches Faith and Order Paper No. 207 (Collegeville: Liturgical Press, 2008).

CIRP J. D. C. *Fisher, Christian Initiation: The Reformation Period* (Chicago: Hillenbrand Books, 2007).

CW *Common Worship: Services and Prayers for the Church of England* (London: Church House Publishing, 2000).

CWMS *The Complete Writings of Menno Simons*, ed. and tr. J. C. Wenger (Scottdale, PA: Herald Press, 1956).

DBL E. C. Whitaker, *Documents of the Baptismal Liturgy*, rev. exp. Maxwell E. Johnson (Collegeville: Liturgical Press, 2003).

DSSB *Diocese of Singapore Service Book* (1995).

ELW *Evangelical Lutheran Worship Leaders Desk Edition* (Minneapolis: Augsburg Fortress, 2006).

JWPB *John Wesley's Prayer Book: The Sunday Service of Methodists in North America* (Maryville, TN: OSL Publications, 1991).

LBW *Lutheran Book of Worship Ministers Desk Edition* (Minneapolis: Augsburg Publishing House; Philadelphia: Board of Publication, Lutheran Church in America, 1978).

LCC *Library of Christian Classics.*

LW *Luther's Works*, 55 vols., gen. eds. Jaroslav Pelikan and Helmut T. Lehmann, (St Louis: Concordia; Philadelphia: Fortress Press, 1955-86).

LWC *Liturgies of the Western Church* (Philadelphia: Fortress Press, 1980).

PEER R. C. D. Jasper and G. J. Cuming, *Prayers of the Eucharist: Early and Reformed*, 3rd ed. (Collegeville: Liturgical Press, 1987).

SW	*Sacraments and Worship: The Sources of Christian Theology*, ed. Maxwell E. Johnson (Louisville: Westminster John Knox Press, 2012).
UMBW	*United Methodist Book of Worship* (Nashville: United Methodist Publishing House, 1992).
UMG	Evangelical Lutheran Church in America, *Use of the Means of Grace: A Statement on the Practice of Word and Sacrament* (Minneapolis: Augsburg Fortress, 1997).
WJW	*The Works of John Wesley*; begun as "The Oxford Edition of The Works of John Wesley" (Oxford: Clarendon Press, 1975-1983); continued as "The Bicentennial Edition of the Works of John Wesley" (Nashville: Abingdon Press, 1984-); 26 of 35 vols. published to date.

Contents

CHAPTER 1

The Meaning of Sacraments

The purpose of this chapter is to provide a general background to the sacraments. Since many Christians are unfamiliar with the word "sacrament," we begin by defining it and other sacramental terminology. Because Protestant sacramental theology today is grounded in earlier understandings, we will provide a brief historical overview of how sacraments "in general" were understood, giving most of our attention to the Protestant Reformers of the sixteenth century. As we will see, the approach of our Protestant forebears is one of both continuity and discontinuity with the preceding fifteen centuries. Finally, we will look at the sacramental approach of two modern theologians, the Dominican Edward Schillebeeckx and the Methodist James F. White.

What is a Sacrament?

Although a term of common usage in the church, "sacrament" may be somewhat obscure to many Christians today. In the ancient Roman milieu, it referred to a soldier's solemn oath of loyalty and obedience to commanders and to the state. The term therefore conveys the sense of a sacred covenant enacted between two parties. Throughout the period of the early church, there was great variation as to the number of sacraments and what was to be included in that category. The medieval Western church settled on seven sacraments: baptism, confirmation, the Lord's Supper, penance (private confession), extreme unction ("last rites"), ordination, and marriage. Protestants consider only baptism and the Lord's Supper to be "sacraments." Mainline churches prefer the word "sacrament," and view the sacraments as "means of grace" which God uses to convey certain spiritual benefits (forgiveness, healing). Protestants of the "free church" tradition, such as Baptists, Pentecostals, and Holiness Christians, speak of baptism and the Lord's Supper as "ordinances," that is, actions performed in obedience to a command. Rather than conveying grace, the "ordinances" signify or point to divine grace and serve as memory aids.

The term "sacrament" will be used throughout this book, and it is defined as a *rite whose words and actions are bound up with God's saving activity in and through the church.* This definition needs further clarification. First, the sacraments are meant to sanctify by fostering the recipient's sense of belonging to God and to the Christian community. They draw us closer to God *by* drawing us more deeply into our Christian community. Second, the sacraments are integral to the life of the church and thus there are no sacraments outside of the church and its intended use of the sacraments. One does not baptize one's *self* in private. Rather, a person is baptized into a Christian community and so must be baptized by a representative of that community in order to demonstrate the theological relationship between baptism and church life.[1] Similarly, one cannot administer "Holy Communion" to one's self in private, since the Lord's Supper signifies and realizes the *community* that is the body of Christ (cf. 1 Cor. 10:17). One can no more celebrate "communion" alone than

---

[1] Although persons have long been baptized outside of public worship due to illness or impending death, such baptisms are normally reported to the church and there will be an official ratification of that baptism in a public worship setting.

one could play football alone! The celebration of communion with home-bound, hospitalized, or imprisoned individuals is normally administered by ordained clergy or by lay ministers sent out by the church as its representatives. In some cases, ordained and duly-appointed lay sacramental ministers may even commune the "absent" with elements from a previous public celebration of the Lord's Supper, thus making clear the relationship between a "private" communion and participation in the church's fellowship. Because the sacraments are bound up with the life of the church, they are above and beyond purely individualistic (and hence idiosyncratic) celebrations.

The word "sacramental" refers to rites that possess the character of sacraments, but do not possess all the qualities of a sacrament. While Roman Catholics might say that confirmation and marriage are "sacraments," Protestants are inclined to say that these rites only possess a sacramental character because they merely point to or illustrate something sacred. In Protestant thought, confirmation and other sacramental ceremonies lack either a divinely-appointed sign, or a divinely-given promise of sanctifying grace. Even then, such "sacramental" ceremonies are not rejected as unnecessary or unimportant, but are regarded as helpful for maintaining good order in the church or as useful in proclaiming the gospel.

Finally, what the Protestant and Roman Catholic Churches call "sacraments," Eastern Orthodox Churches call "mysteries." The Greek word *mysterion* does not mean something unknown or information that cannot be revealed, but refers to a reality beyond human comprehension, something of God. "We declare God's wisdom, a mystery that has been hidden and that God destined for our glory before time began" (1 Cor. 2:7). Theologians such as Aquinas, Luther, and Calvin, all had to admit that some aspects of the sacraments could not be explained or involved the miraculous. If we flavored our understanding of the sacraments with "mystery," we could avoid reducing them to human actions and knowledge such that we put God entirely out of the picture. Any view of the sacraments completely devoid of the presence and work of God is inconsistent with both the Christian Scriptures and the writings of early theologians.

Sacramental Actions in the Hebrew Scriptures

The Bible in fact depicts God using physical means to relate to human beings. James White observes that Christian sacramental understanding owes much to the Jewish Scriptures.[2] Expanding somewhat on White's work, I would note that the Hebrew Bible knows four types of actions wherein God's activity is connected to a physical thing or action. First, God uses physical things as a means of *personal theophany*, that is, to make self-revelation to an individual or to the community of Israel. In Exodus 3, God appears to Moses in the "burning bush" to announce his plan to rescue Israel from slavery. During the Exodus event itself (13:21), God goes before the Israelites as a pillar of cloud by day and a pillar of fire by night, leading them to the promised land. Second, there are *sacramental* actions performed by God's representatives that confer blessings or power on individuals or on Israel as a whole. After the grumbling Israelites were afflicted with snake bites, Moses raises a bronze serpent on a pole so that those who gaze upon it are healed (Num. 21:4-9). When David is anointed by Samuel the Spirit of the Lord comes "powerfully" upon him from that very day (1 Sam. 16:13). In all these cases, the relationship between God and the "thing" or action is mysterious. God might have been "in" the bush, cloud and fire, but nothing suggests that God *is* these things. Far from having any association with the presence of God, the bronze serpent and the oil used to anoint David only serve as focal points for God's healing or sanctifying activity. As White points out, the Hebrew Scriptures know of a tension between the disclosure of God's will through events and objects versus the affirmation that these things are not to be confused with the Deity.[3]

Third, sacrifices are instituted by God and partake of some of the qualities of Christian sacraments, namely, by atoning for sin (Lev. 9) expressing thanks to God (Lev. 7:11-21), and by facilitating communion between God and the faith community and within

[2] James F. White, *Introduction to Christian Worship*, third rev. exp. ed. (Nashville: Abingdon, 2000), 177-78.

[3] White, *Introduction*, 177.

that community. Other similarities include (1) the pattern whereby the victim is presented by the people and slaughtered by the priests (cf. Lev. 9:2,3); and (2) the understanding that the sacrificed animals are eaten in the very presence of God (Deut. 12:6-7, 18). The most important sacrificial meal in the Old Testament is the Passover (Ex. 12; Lev. 23:5), which is the yearly commemoration of the Israelites' deliverance from slavery in Egypt. Other ancient cultures certainly knew of sacrifices: ancient Canaanite shepherds offered lambs to their gods, and farmers likely offered some of the first fruits of the grains to their harvest gods. Yet, for Israel sacrifice was not entirely about trying to "appease" God – a "something for something" exchange meant to provoke God into favorable action. Rather, Israel's sacrifices celebrated the mercy of God both in the past and in the present, and manifested Israel's identity as God's redeemed people. The Passover especially brings out the commemorative and identity-building aspects of sacrifice for Israel, as we see in Ex. 12:24:

> Obey these instructions as a lasting ordinance for you and your descendants. When you enter the land that the Lord will give you as he promised, observe this ceremony. When your children ask you, "What does this ceremony mean to you?" then tell them, "It is the Passover sacrifice to the Lord, who passed over the houses of the Israelites in Egypt and spared our homes when he struck down the Egyptians.

The Passover Haggadah (ritual, order of service) makes clear that the Passover has implications for Jewish people of all times and places:

> ...we were slaves unto Pharaoh in Egypt, and the Eternal, our God, brought us forth thence with a mighty hand and an outstretched arm. And if the Most Holy ... had not brought forth our ancestors from Egypt, we and our children and our children's children would still be in bondage to the Pharaohs in Egypt.[4]

---

[4] *Passover Haggadah* (n. p. 2000), 10.

More than just the remembrance of a past historical event, the Passover celebration is a manifestation of God's saving power for the people of Israel *today*. Thus, sacrifices and sacrificial meals allow Jewish people to participate in a vital relationship with God.

Fourth, the Hebrew Scriptures mention spontaneous symbolic actions, which White refers to as "*prophetic symbolism*," i.e., actions that illustrate a particular point. Examples include Jeremiah's making a yoke to symbolize how Judah will serve the king of Babylon (Jer. ch. 27), and his smashing a clay pot to symbolize Judah's coming destruction (Jer. ch. 19). These actions anticipate and participate in the event that they symbolize, "and thus have potency to fulfil God's will."[5] While we tend to associate the Hebrew prophets with spoken and written words, these examples remind us that prophetic communication was by no means limited to verbal communication. Jeremiah affirms God's use of material things for spiritual purposes.

Jesus and Sacraments

The gospels depict Jesus himself using physical means to reveal spiritual truth.The very fact that Jesus heals bodies and in one case uses physical means (saliva and mud) to do so (John 9:6) affirms the material world as a means for God's power to impact human lives. Like the acts of prophetic symbolism in the Old Testament, Jesus' riding into Jerusalem on a donkey (Mark 11) is a visible depiction of a divine reality, namely, the coming of God's messiah to Israel. An *al fresco* meal involving 4,000 participants also becomes a manifestation of his messianic identity (Mark 8:1-10). Jesus shared a meal with his disciples that points to his impending death, reveals his nature as a suffering servant (Luke 22:27), and anticipates the final consummation of God's kingdom (Mark 14:25). In John's gospel, Jesus' action of washing his disciples' feet becomes a symbol of servanthood and anticipates his greatest act of servanthood on the Cross. We cannot help but see a connection between Jesus' use of material things and actions and his own identity as the *incarnate* Son of God: the Word made flesh (1:14) uses physical, embodied means

[5] White, *Introduction*, 178.

of communicating the gospel. Thus, any community that grounds its very identity in him is necessarily one that likewise uses physical means to proclaim the gospel and administer its gifts.

Traditionally, Protestants have viewed the church's sacraments as grounded in authoritative commands of the Lord Jesus, specifically, Matt. 28:19 (cf. Mark 16:15-16) in the case of baptism, and 1 Cor. 11:24-25 (cf. Luke 22:19) in the case of the Lord's Supper. But we must also recognize a certain authority in Jesus' own *example*. Besides being a recipient of John's baptism (Mark 1:9), Jesus himself *may* have been a "baptizer" of others according to John 4:1 – that is, if we take the contradictory statement in John 4:2 as a later interpolation.[6] If Jesus did in fact baptize, there would be a clear line of continuity in practice: the baptism of repentance given by John, was received by Jesus, administered by him and his apostles, and then passed onto the primitive Christian communities that arose after the resurrection. As noted above regarding meals, the Lord himself participated in numerous meals/feedings, and the feeding of the five thousand uses language that parallels the Last Supper (cf. Luke 9:10-17 and 22:19), thus creating a correspondence between an account containing "only" the example of Jesus and one with the authoritative "do this" command for the church. Simply put: Jesus himself "did" what he "commanded," and so *both* the Lord's command and example have authority for the church.

Sacraments Elsewhere in the New Testament

In fidelity to the example and will of the Lord Jesus, early churches initiated converts by means of a ritual bath. The Book of Acts depicts baptism as *the* way by which converts were grafted into the church (see Ch. 3 "Baptism as a Process of Initiation"). Paul, who himself received baptism (Acts 9:18), speaks of administering baptism (1 Cor. 1:14, 16) and appeals to baptism while making an important argument in his letter to the Roman Church (Rom. 6) – a fact that assumes the importance of baptism for both Paul and his addressees.

---

[6] See Maxwell E. Johnson, *The Rites of Christian Initiation: Their Evolution and Interpretation*, rev. exp. ed. (Collegeville: Liturgical Press, 2007), 17-20.

Elsewhere, we find an oblique reference to baptism in John (3:5) that seems to depict baptism as a type of rebirth. This connection is more certain in the Letter to Titus (3:5). These apostolic churches certainly did not invent ritual bathing; precursors can be found in the ritual purification bath of the Essene community at Qumran, the baptism of repentance administered by John (Mark 1:1-8; Matt. 3:1-12; Luke 3:1-20), and possibly in Jewish proselyte baptism.[7] Distinctive about Christian baptism is its administration by another person as opposed to being self-administered (as in the Essene community), and, unlike John's baptism, it ritualized not only repentance, but the very gift of the Holy Spirit (Acts 2:38).

Besides bathing, ritual meals were also important in the apostolic church. The Book of Acts depicts a post-Pentecost community whose life centered on meals and instruction on apostolic teaching (2:42). Paul participated in a meal gathering during which he delivered a long discourse (20:7-12). As we know from Paul's correspondence with the church in Corinth, Christians there gathered for a meal that included ritual actions with bread and cup, which unfortunately was subject to abuse and misunderstanding (ch. 11). Early Christian communal life therefore reflects the customs of other ancient social groups and religious societies who gathered for a meal proper followed by a time of discussion or entertainment known as the *symposium*.[8] It would not be an exaggeration to say that the apostolic church was in large part a meal fellowship, or supper club.[9]

Finally, anointing is also mentioned in the New Testament. In James 5, sick persons are to be anointed and prayed over (vv. 13-16). In other words, oil was used as a physical sign of the healing promised by the gospel. Elsewhere, in the New Testament references to anointing are used in metaphorical ways, as an image for knowledge of the truth (1 John 2:20), God's "ownership" of the Christian and

---

[7] *Interpreters Dictionary of the Bible*, s. v. "Proselyte."

[8] See Dennis E. Smith, *From Symposium to Eucharist: The Banquet in the Early Christian World* (Minneapolis: Fortress, 2003).

[9] See Gordon W. Lathrop, *The Four Gospels on Sunday: The New Testament and the Reform of Christian Worship* (Minneapolis: Fortress, 2011).

reception of the Holy Spirit (2 Cor. 1:21-22), and true sight (Rev. 3:18). Whether or not the actual practice of anointing lies behind these references is unclear, but they nevertheless connect a physical element with the reception of a spiritual blessing.

The biblical witness therefore offers a strong basis for the church's sacraments. If the triune God desires to communicate with us and convey blessings through physical means, then the church's own way of communicating the will and love of God can do no less. While recognizing the fallen and corruptible nature of the material world, Christians cannot be opposed to the material world or the use of material things in worship. As White puts it: "…Christians need to remember that they are not called to be more spiritual than God; the path to the spiritual leads through many material realities."[10] Indeed, we might argue that a healthy appreciation for the sacraments is what it means to be "spiritual."

Sacraments Prior to the Protestant Reformation

As we mentioned above, the New Testament contains no sustained studies or arguments specifically about baptism or the Lord's Supper. Rather, it has only brief references to these and a few other sacramental actions. It is only in the early church that writers begin defining and explaining the sacraments at greater length. In the medieval period, we find systematic and detailed discussions that undergird the sacramental "system" that defined the church of that time. What follows is a survey of early and medieval writers on the topic of "sacraments in general," this is, the nature and meaning of "sacraments."

Bishop Augustine of Hippo (354-430 CE) was the first patristic theologian to offer a systematic reflection on the sacraments. He defines a sacrament this way: "the Word is joined to the element and the result is a sacrament, itself becoming, in a sense, a visible Word as well."[11] This definition will influence medieval theologians as well as Protestant Reformers such as Luther and Calvin. Augustine

---

[10] White, *Introduction*, 178.

[11] Augustine of Hippo, *Treatise on the Gospel of John* LXXX.3 (ca. 416).

distinguishes between the "visible sacrament" and the "invisible grace" worked by the Holy Spirit, and it is the latter that makes a sacrament efficacious (able to produce certain saving effects).[12] He also distinguishes between sacraments of the "old covenant" (i.e., in the Hebrew Scriptures) and those of the new covenant. While the former can only promise a Savior, the latter give salvation.[13] Against the rigorist Donatists who argued that sacraments, especially baptism, administered by apostate clergy were invalid (defective), Augustine insists that because the sacraments are bound up with the Word of God baptism given by a "misguided man" is still holy and beneficial for the recipient. Baptism received by an unholy, perverse person, while valid, will ultimately not benefit the recipient. Yet, baptism administered in such instances does not need to be repeated if and when the perverse individual repents and makes amendment of life.[14] We might note that in Augustine's day, the number of sacraments was still not fixed, and the great bishop could apply the term "sacrament" to the giving of salt at baptism, using ashes for penitents, reciting the creeds and Lord's Prayer, the baptismal font, and observing the *Pascha* (Easter). While the observance of Christmas was, in his view, merely the observance of an anniversary, the Pascha has to do with the saving reality of our own death and resurrection, thus making this observance especially holy.[15]

Medieval theologians continued to refine the definition of sacraments. Hugh of St Victor (1096-1141) speaks of sacraments as having three components: (1) a "similitude" (likeness, resemblance) to the thing signified; (2) an authoritative command or institution to make this signification; and (3) the ability to confer the thing signified on the recipient.[16] Peter Lombard (ca. 1096-1164) was the first western European theologian to list seven sacraments: baptism, confirmation, the Lord's Supper, penance (i.e., confession and

---

[12] Augustine of Hippo, *Questions on the Heptateuch* III.84 (ca.410).

[13] Augustine of Hippo, *Commentary on the Psalms* LXXIII.2 (ca. 416).

[14] Augustine of Hippo, *On Baptism Against the Donatists* IV.12 (ca. 400).

[15] Augustine of Hippo, *Letter 55 to Januarius* 1.2.

[16] Hugh of St Victor, *On the Sacraments of the Christian Faith* I.9 (1140).

absolution), extreme unction (anointing of the dying), ordination, and marriage. Some of these, e.g., baptism, offer a remedy for sin and confer grace, while others (e.g., marriage), only offer a remedy for sin. The others (e.g., Lord's Supper and ordination) strengthen with grace and power. All of the sacraments receive their power from the death of Christ and therefore could not have been instituted before Christ, such as immediately after the fall of Adam.[17] The choice of seven, which eliminated some things, reflects the traditional equation of that number with completion or perfection. Lombard's list will be authoritative in Western Christianity until the Reformation, and remains in effect for the Roman Catholic Church. Expanding on Augustine's idea that a sacrament is "the visible form of an invisible grace," Lombard distinguishes between the *form* or *sign* of a sacrament, e.g., the bread and wine of the Lord's Supper or the water of baptism, and the *res* or "thing." The *res* consists of (1) what is contained and signified, e.g., the flesh of Christ in the case of the Lord's Supper; and (2) what is signified but not contained, viz., "the unity of the Church in those who are predestined, called, justified and glorified" (Rom. 8:30).[18]

The pinnacle of medieval sacramental theology is found in the thought of the Dominican Thomas Aquinas (1225-74). The discussion of the sacraments in his *Summa Theologica*, structured as a series of question and answers, remains a basic text on the subject. An important contribution is his affirmation that the sacraments are causes of grace in the sense that they contain an "instrumental power of bringing about the sacramental effects."[19] Like previous theologians, he holds that only the sacraments of the New Covenant are causes of grace and that "sacraments" of the Old Covenant contained no such power. He speaks of some sacraments (baptism, confirmation, and ordination) as imprinting a certain character on the soul which can never be removed. Only God, he says, could institute a sacrament, since the power of the sacraments comes from

[17] Peter Lombard, *The Sentences* 4.II.1(ca. 1152).

[18] Lombard, *The Sentences* 4.VIII.6-7.

[19] Thomas Aquinas, *Summa Theologica* III.61-65 (ca. 1271).

God alone. Like Augustine, he views the power and efficacy of the sacraments as independent of the moral and spiritual disposition of the ministers, i.e., a "true" sacrament is conferred even by wicked and faithless ministers. Following Lombard, he identifies seven sacraments, and states that they were given to remedy the defects caused by sin and to perfect humans spiritually. The greatest of the sacraments, he says, is the Eucharist (Lord's Supper) since it (1) contains Christ substantially; (2) is the end (or perhaps "goal") of all the other sacraments; and (3) is the ritual termination of nearly all the other sacraments.[20]

As a leading theologian of the medieval church, Aquinas cast a long shadow. Some of the Protestant Reformers would not question his assertions about the divine nature of various sacraments, the difference between the sacraments of the "old" versus the "new" covenant, and the independence of sacramental efficacy over and against the disposition of the minister and/or recipient. Just about all would reject his notion of "indelible character" and the enumeration of seven sacraments. Yet for the Roman Catholic Church, his thought would continue to be a bulwark for sacramental theology.

Having adopted the Lombardian list of seven sacraments, the Council of Florence, in its "Decree for the Armenians" (1439), succinctly defines the purpose of each sacrament while seeking to express the relationship that sacraments have to one another:

> Through baptism we are spiritually reborn; through confirmation we are made to grow in grace and are strengthened in faith. When we have been reborn and strengthened, we are sustained by the divine nourishment of the Eucharist. But if through sin we incur sickness of the soul, through penance we are made healthy; we are healed, spiritually and physically according as the soul needs, through extreme unction. Through ordination, the Church

[20] We might note, for example, how in the early church the newly baptized almost immediately received their first communion.

> is governed and increased spiritually, through marriage it grows physically.[21]

According to the Council, essential to each of the sacraments is (1) the proper form or words (rite); (2) the proper matter or "things"; and (3) the proper intention of the minister to do what the church rightly does with the sacrament. Following Aquinas, baptism, confirmation and ordination are deemed as imprinting an "indelible" character on the soul and are thus unrepeatable for a particular individual. The other sacraments are repeatable.

Medieval sacramental theology was both blessing and bane. On the one hand, it made the sacraments coherent and rational, and its definitions created a system that guided Christians from birth to death, assuring them of eternal salvation. But on the other hand, this very "neatness" was somewhat limiting. White questions whether this "system" with its precise definitions and distinctions did not in fact remove the element of mystery from the sacraments by saying too much.[22] Furthermore, medieval thinking seemed to put the sacraments in the realm of abstract philosophical categories, with theologians reflecting on the sacraments almost in isolation from their liturgical setting. The ontology or "thingy-ness" of the sacraments preoccupied theologians and very little attempt was made to relate sacraments to the Christian life in ways that were vital, challenging, or refreshing. While sacraments had an important place in medieval systematic theology, there was lacking a *pastoral* theology of the sacraments with the potential to energize the life and mission of the church. This kind of renewal would have to wait several centuries.

Sacraments in Protestant Thought

The Protestant Reformation needs to be viewed against the backdrop of its historical and social milieu. Reform was already in the air before the early-sixteenth century. The English theologian John

---

[21] Council of Florence, "Decree for the Armenians" (1439), SW, 11-12.

[22] White, *Introduction*, 187.

Wycliffe (ca. 1320-84) challenged the authority and necessity of the papacy, and stressed the authority of the Bible. Jan Hus (1369-1415) promoted views of the church, papacy, and Lord's Supper that were influential in his native Prague (Czech Republic) and anticipated the views of later Protestant Reformers. Intellectually, the seeds for the Reformation had been sown in the Renaissance beginning in the fourteenth century, with its advocacy of classical literature and renewed interest in classical languages. Erasmus of Rotterdam (1466-1536) prepared new Greek and Latin editions of the New Testament. Important Reformation figures such as Martin Luther, Philip Melanchthon, and John Calvin were all biblical expositors who were well-versed in biblical languages. The Reformation emphasis on the Bible as the sole determinant of doctrine and church life – the principle of *sola scriptura* ("Scripture alone") – reflects the humanistic emphasis on classical languages and literature that emerged in the century prior to the Reformation.

Martin Luther viewed the Bible as central to enumerating and defining the sacraments. As far as he was concerned, the New Testament witnesses to only *one* sacrament, namely, Christ himself (cf. 1 Tim. 3:16) and three sacramental signs: baptism, the Lord's Supper, and penance.[23] The traditional enumeration of seven sacraments lacks validity because a true sacrament needs to have both God's promise and a divinely instituted sign, that is, an earthly element (water, bread, wine) as witnessed to by the Bible. Confirmation contains no (biblical) word of promise, and marriage lacks both a divinely instituted promise and sign. Ordination has no divine promise and indeed receives no mention at all in the New Testament. While extreme unction might have a biblical basis in the New Testament Letter of James, no apostle, he maintains, has the authority to institute a sacrament. Hence, Luther identifies only baptism and the Lord's Supper as sacraments for only they have divinely instituted signs and promise the forgiveness of sins. While initially willing to consider "penance" (individual confession and absolution) a sacrament, he eventually excluded it from the list

[23] Martin Luther, *The Babylonian Captivity of the Church* (1520), LW 36, 18.

of sacraments because it lacked a "sign" (material element) and was really only a way of reappropriating the essence of baptism.[24]

For Luther, the divine promise is crucial. Only such a promise, as clearly stated in a biblical text, can evoke the faith that receives God's promise. Faith then places the person in a right relationship with God, i.e., "saves" that person, and thus Luther's sacramental theology is the working out of his doctrine of justification by grace through faith. Only baptism and the Lord's Supper, with their scriptural promises, are of saving significance and hence true sacraments. For Luther, a conscience troubled by sin and beset by spiritual doubts needs that kind of assurance. Although the other traditional sacraments of the church lack this saving significance and were either inventions of the church (e.g., confirmation, ordination), or, in the case of marriage, a universal ordinance wrongly classified as a sacrament, Luther does not reject these as rites of the church. Confirmation, he says, could be practiced as a "sacramental ceremony" that "sanctified" a person in accordance with 1 Tim. 4:4-5, specifically, when pastors examined the faith of children and then laid hands on them. Luther even prepared vernacular rites for marriage and ordination (see ch. 16). Still, he says, "these things cannot be called sacraments of faith, because they have no divine promise connected with them, neither do they save; but the sacraments do save those who believe the divine promise."[25]

It was precisely his doctrine of justification that led Luther to reject the traditional tendency to denigrate "sacraments of the old covenant" as lacking in saving significance and to extol those of the new covenant for possessing precisely that quality. The sacraments of the new covenant, Luther argues, do not differ from those of the old in their effectiveness. Divinely instituted "signs" like circumcision and Noah's rainbow (Gen. 9:13) involve promises that required faith on the part of the recipients. Hence, the sacraments of both covenants are "signs or sacraments of justification, for they are sacraments of justifying faith and not of works."[26] Luther is careful

[24] Luther, *Babylonian Captivity*, LW 36, 18-123.

[25] Luther, *Babylonian Captivity*, LW 36, 92.

[26] Luther, *Babylonian Captivity*, LW 36, 65.

to state, however, that it is not the sacramental act that justifies, but *faith*.[27] Even though the ability of the sacrament to produce an effect (its "efficacy") is tied to the recipient's faith, Luther holds that a true sacrament is administered even to an unbelieving recipient, for it is still bound to God's Word rather than to the recipient's faith.[28]

Furthermore, Luther does not spiritualize faith so as to drive a wedge between faith and the material sign of a sacrament. The sacramental element is quite important for him, and this becomes especially apparent in his discussions about baptism. Over and against more radical reformers who rejected or downplayed baptism because of its outward, physical nature, Luther argues that faith needed something to "cling to," namely the water, in order to appropriate the spoken promises that are connected to that sacrament. One could not reject baptism because of its external nature since it "*must* be external so that it can be perceived and grasped by the senses, and thus brought into the heart, just as the entire gospel is an external, oral proclamation."[29] Not surprisingly, the celebration of baptism should make full use of the sacramental sign. Hence, he advocates baptismal immersion in order to do justice to the meaning of the word baptism, or in German *Taufe*, which he understood as connoting that the recipient be "plunged deeply into the water."[30] His German baptismal rites directed the minister to *dip* the infant into the font.[31] Today we would say that Luther had an appreciation for the "sign-value" of sacraments, and thus his thinking anticipates the modern liturgical renewal movement's attention to the signifying power of sacramental signs.

---

[27] See Jeffrey A. Truscott, "Luther's Pastoral Approach to Baptism," in *A Living Tradition: On the Intersection of Liturgical History and Pastoral Practice*, eds. David Pitt, Stefanos Alexopoulos, and Christian McConnell (Collegeville: Liturgical Press, 2012), 139-40.

[28] Cf. Martin Luther, *Large Catechism* (1529), BC, 463.53.

[29] Luther, *Large Catechism*, BC, 460.30. Emphasis added.

[30] Martin Luther, *The Holy and Blessed Sacrament of Baptism* (1519), LW 35, 26.

[31] Martin Luther, *The Order of Baptism* (1523), LW 53, 100.

Important discussions about the sacraments are found in confessional documents prepared by Luther's associate in Wittenberg, Philip Melanchthon (1497-1560). The *Augsburg Confession* (1530) defines the church with reference to the sacraments, namely, as "the assembly of saints in which the gospel is taught purely and the sacraments are administered rightly" and declares that true unity is found not when there is liturgical uniformity, but when there is agreement on the administration of the sacraments.[32] Following Luther, baptism and the Lord's Supper are the presumed sacraments,[33] although "private absolution" is highly commended.[34] In the *Apology of the Augsburg Confession* (1531), the necessary constituents of a sacrament are the divine "commands and promises," and for Melanchthon, "command" is another way of saying a commanded *rite* or sign, which means that he and Luther essentially had the same sacramental criteria. Yet for Melanchthon confession and absolution and even ordination can properly be considered "sacraments" since they too are associated with divine commands and promises, thus taking a somewhat broader view than Luther.[35] As long as the church does those things commanded by God which have divine promises connected with them, there is really no point in quarreling about the number of sacraments.[36]

Theologians of the Reformed tradition approached the sacraments in an entirely different manner than the Lutherans. According to Ulrich Zwingli (1484-1531), the Reformer of Zurich, God does not use material things for spiritual purposes because "it is clear and indisputable that no external element or action can purify the soul."[37] Additionally, he fears that any view in which the sacraments caused or imparted grace necessarily placed a limitation

---

[32] *Augsburg Confession*, Art. VII, BC, 43.2.

[33] *Augsburg Confession*, Art. IX, BC, 43.1-2, Art. X, BC, 44.1-2.

[34] *Augsburg Confession*, Art. XI, BC, 44.1.

[35] *Apology of the Augsburg Confession* (1531), Art. XIII, BC, 219.4.

[36] *Apology of the Augsburg Confession*, Art. XIII, BC, 221.17.

[37] Ulrich Zwingli, *Of Baptism* (1525), in *Zwingli and Bullinger*, ed. G. W. Bromiley (Philadelphia: Westminster Press, 1953), 156.

on the Spirit's freedom to work where and when he pleases.[38] Zwingli therefore prefers to emphasize the inward working of the Holy Spirit. For him, the emphasis came to be placed on the human side of the sacraments, rather than on the divine side. Accordingly, he defines sacraments as ceremonies and badges of faith by which one identifies one's self as a Christian: "In baptism we receive a token that we are to fashion our lives according to the rule of Christ; by the Lord's Supper we give proof that we trust in the death of Christ...."[39] Like Luther, Zwingli recognizes only baptism and the Lord's Supper as sacraments. The other traditional "sacraments" are to be considered as mere ceremonials since they do not serve in any way to identify members of the Christian community, as do baptism and the Lord's Supper.

John Calvin (1509-64) the Reformer of Strasbourg and Geneva, defines a sacrament as an "outward sign by which the Lord seals on our consciences the promises of his good will toward us in order to sustain the weakness of our faith; and we in turn attest our piety toward him in the presence of the Lord and of his angels and before men."[40] Calvin understands the sacraments as an expression of divine condescension where by God uses the means most appropriate for our capacity. "Our merciful Lord so tempers himself to our capacity that he condescends to lead us to himself even by these earthly elements and to set before us in the flesh a mirror of Spiritual blessing."[41] For Calvin, like Augustine and Luther, the sacraments are only efficacious for those who receive them in faith. A somewhat unique emphasis in Calvin, one with affinities to Eastern Orthodox theology, is his insistence that the sacraments have their power only by the working of the Holy Spirit; without the Spirit's agency the

---

[38] Ulrich Zwingli, *Commentary on True and False Religion* (1525), in *The Works of Huldreich Zwingli*, ed. Clarence H. Heller, tr. Samuel M. Jackson, (Philadelphia: Heidelberg Press, 1929), 183.

[39] Zwingli,*Commentary on True and False Religion*,184.

[40] John Calvin, *Institutes of the Christian Religion* (1559) IV.14.1, ed. John T. McNeill, tr. Ford Lewis Battles, in LCC, 21(Philadelphia: Westminster Press, 1960), 1277.

[41] Calvin, *Institutes* IV.14.3, LCC 21, 1278.

sacraments are empty. In and of themselves, the sacraments do not confer any divine grace, but only announce it. Yet, God truly brings about what is signified and promised in the sacraments, although only believers receive the sacraments to their benefit.[42] By affirming that the sacraments are instruments of divine activity, Calvin rejects the Zwinglian reduction of sacraments to mere identity badges; by acknowledging the objective nature of that activity such that mercy and grace are *offered* to all regardless of their spiritual disposition, he aligns himself with Luther. Like both Luther and Zwingli, Calvin recognized only baptism and the Lord's Supper as true sacraments, and like Melanchthon, he had a very high regard for ordination.

Calvin's influence spread beyond Switzerland and Germany to the Netherlands and to the British Isles. The sixteenth-century Church of Scotland echoes Calvin's idea of sacraments as "seals" of God's promises to the elect, and as a clear rejection of Zwinglianism, declares that it "utterly damn[s] the vanity of they that affirm sacraments to be nothing but naked and bare signs."[43] The Puritan *Westminster Confession of Faith* (1647), drawing on an understanding that goes back to Augustine, affirms that the efficacy of a sacrament does not depend on the "piety or intention" of the minister, but on the "work of the Spirit and the word of institution."[44]

In treating the subject of sacraments, the Church of England's *Articles of Religion* (1563), emphasizes "effectual signs":

> Sacraments ordained of Christ, be not only badges or tokens of Christian men's profession; but rather they be certain sure witnesses, and effectual signs of grace, and God's good will toward us, by which he doth work invisibly in us, and doth not only quicken, but also strengthen and confirm our faith in him.[45]

---

[42] Calvin, *Institutes* IV.14.7, LCC 21, 1282.

[43] Church of Scotland, *The Scottish Confession of Faith* (1560), SW, 19.

[44] *Westminster Confession of Faith* (1647), Chapter III, SW, 22.

[45] Church of England, *Articles* of Religion (1563), Art. XXV, in *Book of Common Prayer* (Oxford 1784), SW, 20. For a modern Prayer Book containing the Articles see BCP1979, 872.

Baptism and the Lord's Supper are true sacraments; confirmation, penance, ordination, marriage, and extreme unction are either corruptions of apostolic teaching or "states of life" allowed by the Scriptures that lack the requisite divinely instituted visible sign. Only "worthy" recipients receive the sacraments to their benefit, while the "unworthy" receive them to their damnation. This article, in a slightly modernized and revised version, was included by John Wesley in his *Sunday Service* book.

As for the Anabaptists and free-church traditions, authors usually do not give systematic treatments of the "ordinances" in their theological works. Instead, they comment on baptism and the Lord's Supper in sections devoted to these topics, and these reflections will be covered in the chapters on baptism and Lord's Supper later in this book.

As the above discussion demonstrates, classical Protestant thinking on the sacraments is far from monolithic. All agree that there are two sacraments – baptism and the Supper – but there is some disagreement about proper terminology. There is also diversity of thought regarding the nature of the sacraments. Lutherans, Calvinists, and Anglicans understand sacraments as "means of grace" to be received in faith, but Zwinglian theology, which is prominent among the "free-churches," rejects the idea that material things can serve as channels of divine blessings such as forgiveness and the sanctification of the human person. Instead, the latter churches accord that power to the proclaimed Word of God alone. Protestants agree that the sacraments are to be received in faith, but as we shall see later in our discussion of the Lord's Supper, not all agree that Christ and his gifts are received by "unworthy" recipients. Insisting on the literality and unconditionality of the Lord's promise "this is my body," Luther affirms that even "unworthy" communicants receive the very body of Christ – although not to their benefit. Because of these significant differences in sacramental theology, we cannot say that there is a *single* Protestant theology of the sacraments. Hence, those with teaching responsibilities in churches are advised to provide careful and complete instruction on sacramental theology.

Sacraments in the Modern Era

The "modern era" essentially begins with the Enlightenment, an intellectual movement of the late-seventeenth and eighteenth centuries in Europe. It stressed reason over tradition and challenged traditional assumptions about government, religion and science, and was to have a profound impact on the church's sacramental life. It regarded God as a creator who preferred to watch over the creation from afar rather than intervene directly in its affairs. Essentially, the Enlightenment posited a "desacralized" universe devoid of the presence of God. Consequently, Enlightenment thinkers rejected the idea that sacraments supernaturally infused divine grace into the human soul or involved the personal presence of God. Rather, sacraments were considered merely inducements to good moral behavior, holiness, or love.[46] We can see this understanding especially in the thought of the Prussian philosopher, Immanuel Kant (1724-1804). For him baptism is not holy in and of itself, but only *aimed* at something holy, namely, the recipient's development into a "citizen of the divine state." The Lord's Supper is merely a means of forming a moral community characterized by brotherly love. The view that communion is a means of grace is really an illusion that works against the spirit of true religion by fostering clericalism, due to the important role that clergy played in the sacraments.[47]

The Enlightenment's rationalism and rejection of supernaturalism, however, did not lead to a rejection of the sacraments, which were still viewed as having divine authority. Rather the sacraments were simply downplayed. The Lord's Supper in Lutheran and Anglican Churches was celebrated less frequently and served only to incite personal introspection and good behavior. Especially in the Lutheran church, confirmation gained greater importance spiritually and liturgically, since, as a public confession

---

[46] See James F. White, *Protestant Worship: Traditions in Transition* (Louisville: Westminster John Knox Press, 1989), 52-53.

[47] Immanuel Kant, *Religion within the Limits of Reason Alone* (1793), tr. Theodore M. Green and Hoyt H. Hudson (New York: Harper and Row, 1960), 187-88.

of faith, it constituted the individual's rational and mature response to the gospel and personal acceptance of the church's faith. As the role of the sacraments declined, preaching – usually focused on issues of morality – took on greater importance. Essentially, then, the Enlightenment transformed the church from the mystical body of Christ constituted and sanctified by its sacraments to a school for moral improvement. Only early Methodism with its renewed emphasis on the Lord's Supper challenged this trend.

A reaction against Enlightenment rationalism, revivalism with its emphasis on personal, subjective religious experience, arose in the early-nineteenth century. The earliest origins are traced to "camp meetings" in the sparsely-populated American wilderness that gathered mostly unchurched people for worship services that culminated in baptism and the Lord's Supper. The "revival" worship that developed from the camp meetings was eventually popularized and systematized by Charles G. Finney (1792-1875) for use in mainline churches. Geared for the making of converts, Finney's revival techniques included protracted meetings (over several days), emotionalistic preaching that stressed conversion, special seating for potential converts that made them the focus of congregational prayer, and specialized counseling for those uncertain of their spiritual state.[48] Finney believed that there was no divinely-appointed means (or "measures") of making converts and that it was up to the church of every age to find the means that best suited the local context. He rejected traditional practices that seemed ill-suited for this purpose and retained only those that supported it. For him, "tradition" in and of itself could not be considered a proper guide to practice since no form of worship or liturgical practice was normative. He noted, for example, how churches differed significantly in their use of choirs, instrumental music, and assembly posture during prayer. For Finney, the real test of legitimacy was whether something effectively drew crowds and made converts. While Finney's pragmatic approach remains influential today, the underlying argument is flawed because it merely highlighted a diversity of non-essential elements while

[48] White, *Protestant Worship*, 176.

overlooking universals such as the word-meal core of the liturgy that is evident in the New Testament itself.

Revivalist worship developed its own traditional liturgical structure or "ordo," despite the tradition's anti-traditionalism. Still in use in Protestant churches today, that ordo consists of (1) singing and other "preliminaries"; (2) sermon; and (3) harvest of souls (aka "altar call," "altar ministry," "invitation"). As White notes, this structure reflects the revivalistic approach of "warming up" the assembly (song), calling potential converts to conversion (sermon) and "reaping the results in calling those converted to come forward for baptism" ("harvest," altar call).[49] Two things are obvious from this structure. First, everything in revival worship leads to the harvest, which is the culminating action. Second, the personal experience of salvation (conversion) is central, which contrasts with "liturgical" worship that is based on the celebration of the objective means of grace, as well as Enlightenment-influenced worship that seeks to produce moral behavior and responsible citizenship.

But the goal of individual religious experience did not mean the displacement of the sacraments in churches influenced by revivalism. For them the "ordinances" were divinely mandated and so could not be discarded.[50] Rather, these took on a more subjective meaning, that is, a role related to the all-important personal religious experience. Among those churches that arose in the heyday of American revivalism (Baptist, Disciples of Christ), the baptism of believers continues to be practiced, not as a supernatural act of regeneration, but as a way for "saved" individuals to demonstrate obedience to the divine command and to express visibly their personal conversion experience. For revivalist churches, the Lord's Supper is a way of remembering Christ, rather than a way of receiving divine blessings. For these churches the sacraments reinforce the sermon by serving as aids to memory.

While revivalism emphasized subjective personal experience, twentieth-century approaches to the sacraments sought to locate

---

[49] White, *Protestant Worship*, 178.

[50] White, *Protestant Worship*, 181.

"experience" objectively in the sacraments themselves. The Dominican scholar, Edward Schillebeeckx (1914-2009), whose work influenced the liturgical reforms of the Second Vatican Council, viewed the sacraments as "personal encounters" with God, a notion that became popular among Protestants. Schillebeeckx begins with the affirmation that Jesus is the "primordial" (original) sacrament (cf. 1 Tim. 2:5) and that any encounter with him is an encounter with God, or in his words, Christ is the "sacrament of the encounter with God."[51] Since Jesus embodies the saving power of God, his saving actions are the bestowal of divine grace in visible form: "they cause what they signify; they are sacraments...."[52] As the earthly "prolongations" of Jesus' "glorified bodiliness," the church's sacraments are not "things," but encounters with Jesus that make his saving power available to humanity in visible form.[53] Thus, Schillebeeckx effectively defines sacraments as "the visible realization on earth of Christ's mystery of saving worship."[54] The sacraments serve to give us participation in Christ's own saving worship, in the mystery of his Passover (death and resurrection) and Pentecost (Spirit-sending). The church ultimately becomes the visible manifestation of the saving mystery of Christ himself.

The sacramental theology of Schillebeeckx is helpful in two ways. First, by speaking in terms of "personal encounter," his approach transcends the philosophical categories of "substance" and "accidents" that lie behind transubstantiation, a theory of the eucharistic presence of Christ that has proved divisive since the Reformation. As such, Schillebeeckx's notion of "personal encounter" is of great ecumenical value; even Protestants of Zwinglian and free-church sacramental thinking can relate to the idea of personally encountering/knowing Jesus. Second, precisely by framing the sacraments in terms of the existentialist category of "encounter," Schillebeeckx's theology allows

---

[51] Edward Schillebeeckx, O. P., *Christ the Sacrament of the Encounter with God* (New York: Sheed and Ward, 1963), 15.

[52] Schillebeeckx, *Christ the Sacrament of the Encounter with God*, 17.

[53] Schillebeeckx, *Christ the Sacrament of the Encounter with God*, 44.

[54] Schillebeeckx, *Christ the Sacrament of the Encounter with God*, 45.

us to relate the sacraments to the life of the church and to personal spirituality. Admittedly, classical Protestant sacramental theology, to some extent, made the sacraments *impersonal* infusions of divine grace. With Schillebeeckx we can appreciate how the church – the visible manifestation of Christ's saving power mediated through the sacraments – has both a sacramental *life* and a life that is *sacramental.* His view allows individual Christians to understand sacraments in terms of the person of Christ, rather than as abstract doses of grace or object lessons about events that happened long ago and far away. Schillebeeckx reminds us that we meet the incarnate *Christ* in the sacraments and we meet him *today*.

The Methodist liturgical historian James F. White also emphasized human experience in the sacraments.[55] For him, the sacraments are both *anthropological* and *theological*, and thus require human analogies to explain their meaning. "Self-giving" is the most apt anthropological category for explaining human experience in the sacraments, for self-giving is the quintessential way of expressing love. God's self-giving love is expressed through both the words and actions of Christian worship. The words of worship, whether spoken from God to us, from us to God, or between us, are all means of God's own self-giving to us. Noting that the action of giving a gift is ultimately the giving of the self ("the gift is the giver"), White argues that human *actions* in worship – "sign acts" – are also a means of God's self-giving. Actions such as making an offering or giving a benediction are sign acts, but they are not sacraments. Only those actions in which both God and humans act together can properly be called sacraments. Drawing on Luther, White states that "human beings perform the outward actions, the visible sacrament, but it is God who acts in self-giving to give the inward fruit that makes it a sacrament and not just another sign act."[56] As a continuous mode of God's self-giving, a sacrament requires an inherently human action because, as Calvin noted, God desires to temper the manifestation

[55] James F. White, *Sacraments as God's Self-Giving* (Nashville: Abingdon Press, 1983), 14-33.

[56] White, *Sacraments as God's Self-Giving*, 21.

of his love to our capacity to receive it. White avoids placing Word and Sacrament in competition or opposition, affirming that Christ is given in both Word and Sacrament, which makes the two liturgical components complementary.

While acknowledging the necessity of the traditional sacramental categories of *validity* (conditions for proper celebration), *regularity* (celebrating according to church law), and *efficacy* (how the effect is produced), White also stresses the *quality* of the sacramental celebration. Because the sacraments are experienced in a community and communicate meaning to that assembly, attention must be paid to the "fullness" of the sign act such that, for example, baptism should be administered with more than a thimble full of water. As human events, sacraments need to be adequate and meaningful expressions of God's self-giving love.

White also takes up the question of the number of sacraments – an especially troublesome question during the Reformation. But rather than enumerating sacraments, he groups sacraments under three "levels of authority": *dominical*, *apostolic*, and *natural*. For White, baptism and the Lord's Supper are dominical sacraments not because of literal commands from the Lord Jesus himself, but because biblical evidence suggests that baptism and the Lord's Supper were practiced in the apostolic church in obedience to the Lord's example of receiving baptism and celebrating meals.[57] *Apostolic* sacraments – forgiving, healing, and ordaining – are based on Jesus' actions that were imitated by the apostles in fulfilment of the intentions and actions of Jesus. In the case of ordination, the dominical action was Jesus' electing persons and then sending them out in ministry (cf. Mark 1:16-20, 6:7-13). Christian marriage and burial are *natural sacraments*, rites common to all people, but ones that the Church nevertheless sees as avenues of God's ministry through the church to people making important life transitions. White concedes that other rites might be included in each of these categories and that other categories might be recognized. But ultimately, he prefers to leave open the question of the number of sacraments, since the

[57] White, *Sacraments as God's Self-Giving*, 72.

number was not fixed during the first twelve centuries of the church's existence.[58]

White's work offers an important contribution to our sacramental discussions today. The stress on the humanness of the sacraments and the "quality" of celebration can help Protestants appreciate the difference between theological questions about the sacraments and practical, liturgical ones. *What* the sacraments are and *how* we do them, although related, are distinct questions, and Protestants have tended to neglect the latter question. If we can stress clear and proper communication of the Word in preaching, then the same should be true for the celebration of the sacraments. White is right: a thimbleful of water does not adequately communicate that a person is drowned or that sin is washed away in baptism. Yet "quality of celebration," a human category, needs to be held in tension with the divine origin of the sacraments. It is difficult to think that God *only* acts through "good" celebrations of the sacraments or that God does more *if* we do more. If that were true, the sacraments would not be expressions of the gospel because they would not offer God's self-giving love *unconditionally*. We can aim for a "quality" celebration that makes full use of the sacramental sign – a good washing in baptism, a good loaf of bread at the Lord's Supper – yet we do these things while acknowledging that God may use even a poor quality celebration for his saving purposes. Otherwise, the sacraments could be overshadowed by constant worries that our celebrations are qualitatively inferior and perhaps that a repetition is required to "get it right."

White's three-fold categorization is also significant because it transcends the neuralgic question of the number of sacraments. White highlights the Christological character of all the sacraments/sacramental rites. It is especially important to acknowledge the Christological grounding of marriage and the funeral, lest those two rites become exercises in practical monotheism, with little reference to Christ! Yet, it is difficult to see marriage and the funeral as expressions of God's self-giving in quite the same way as in baptism

[58] White, *Sacraments as God's Self-Giving*, 72-75.

and the Lord's Supper. The latter are so bound up with the person and presence of Christ and with his gospel promises that Paul can speak of "putting on Christ" in baptism and participating in Christ's body and blood in the Lord's Supper. Certainly, marriage points to Christ's self-giving to the church and visibly embodies that reality, but there is no *saving promise* attached to marriage. A funeral can certainly proclaim God's promises to those who die in the faith of Christ, but there is no visible *sign* of those promises that evoke faith. If we want to transcend questions about the number of sacraments, rather than White's three-fold *categorization*, we might substitute the following three-fold sacramental *affirmation*:

1. There is a *single* sacrament or one "primordial" sacrament, Christ (as in Luther and Schillebeeckx).
2. There are two sacramental signs, baptism and the Lord's Supper.
3. There are various other ceremonies celebrated by the church for the sake of good order and for proclaiming the gospel of Christ.

While I agree with Melanchthon that quarreling over the number of sacraments is pointless – and likewise quarreling over the classification of sacramental actions – White's attempt to enhance the sacramental status of marriage and burial of the dead may be less than helpful, especially after many centuries of Protestant thinking that went in the opposite direction. For many Protestant churches, grounding the various ordinances more Christologically and relating them to baptism may be sufficient theological advancements.

Conclusion

The church's thinking on the sacraments was a slow evolutionary process, and it continues to be such. No theologian has ever had the "last word" on the sacraments, and most likely contemporary sacramental thinking will seem unsatisfactory to future generations of Christians. Yet we can be grateful for the contributions of past theologians: to Augustine for providing the basic sacramental language and highlighting the divine nature of the sacraments; to medieval theologians for explaining the sacraments in rational, intelligent terms; to the Reformers for accenting the grace-filled nature of the sacraments and for putting them back into the hands of the liturgical assembly; and to modern theologians for reminding us that sacraments, like so many events in the Hebrew Scriptures, are personal meetings with God, as opposed to abstract things.

Equipped with an understanding of the nature of the sacraments, we can now begin to explore the meaning of those two sacraments that stand at the heart of the Sunday worship assembly – baptism and the Lord's Supper.

For Further Reading

Colwell, John E. *Promise and Presence: An Exploration of Sacramental Theology*. Milton Keynes, UK: Pater Noster, 2005.

Cross, Anthony R. *Baptist Sacramentalism*. Eugene, OR: Wipf and Stock, 2007.

Macquarrie, John. *A Guide to the Sacraments*. London: SCM Press, 1997.

Rowell, Geoffrey. *The Gestures of God: Exploration in Sacramentality*. London: Continuum, 2000.

Senn, Frank C. *A Stewardship of the Mysteries*. New York: Paulist Press, 1999.

Staples, Rob L. *Outward Sign and Inward Grace: The Place of Sacraments in Wesleyan Spirituality*. Kansas City: Beacon Hill Press, 1991.

Vander Zee, Leonard J. *Christ, Baptism, and the Lord's Supper: Recovering the Sacraments for Evangelical Worship*. Downer's Grove: IVP, 2004.

Webber, Robert E. *The Sacred Actions in Christian Worship*. Nashville: Star Song, 1994.

White, James F. *The Sacraments in Protestant Practice and Faith*. Nashville: Abingdon Press, 1999.

CHAPTER 2

Baptismal Meaning Among Protestants

For many people history is merely the irrelevant past. Certainly, advances in technology can make it seem that way: as citizens of the twenty-first century, we no longer get from one place to another by steam locomotive or horseback. Those days are long gone and forgotten! Yet, at the same time, we know that our own individual and family histories have a big impact on our lives and our personal identities today. For example, the immigrant experience of struggling to make new lives in a new country – whether in Singapore or North America – can ultimately define a people and their ethos. When we look carefully at our lives and the life of our nation, we realize that history is not just the past, but is part of our present. We share attitudes and sensibilities with our ancestors, not to mention a common religion. We live *from* history, and history defines who and what we are. History shapes our identity.

Christians are inherently an historical people. Our story begins with the story of ancient Israel, whose messiah came in the person of the first-century rabbi Jesus of Nazareth. His ministry and redemptive death inaugurated a new age in history to which the church has given continual witness. The christological and trinitarian doctrines hammered out at the ecumenical councils of the fourth and fifth centuries (Nicaea, Constantinople, Ephesus, and Chalcedon) continue to define the church's faith and worship. For Protestants the lives and writings of the great sixteenth-century Reformers are studied by both clergy and laity alike, and the Protestant confessions of Augsburg, Schleitheim, and Westminster, as well as the *39 Articles of Religion* of Anglicanism and the Methodist *Book of Discipline,* are second only to the Bible and ecumenical creeds in authoritativeness. But the church is not concerned about past history out of nostalgia or romanticism ("If things could just be like they were back then!"). Rather, the church studies its history in order to gain perspective on its mission in the present and to keep in mind the end of all things in God's future, when Christ will come again in glory as the world's final judge.

Today, the church needs the past more than ever. In our pluralistic and relativistic postmodern age, it is easy to lose our focus and become confused especially when it comes to liturgical practice. With a diversity of baptismal practices and theologies, for example, worship leaders might ask: *How* should I baptize? What are the essential actions? What *is* baptism? Besides attention to the Scriptures, a systematic review of our own Protestant liturgical-theological traditions, I believe, will enable us to answer these important questions. But note: we should not study the Reformers' teaching on baptism in order to duplicate their practices exactly. That would make little sense, since their context is completely different from our own. In contrast to the Reformers of the sixteenth century, Christians today need not be so concerned about pairing rites down to their bare essentials in order to bring clarity; we have more and better means of clarifying the meaning of the sacraments than they did. The point of studying early Protestant baptismal practice and theology is to be *instructed* by it, rather than to *imitate* it. What our Protestant forebears can teach us are the *essentials* of baptism. Equipped with this grounding in our own traditions, we can then baptize with integrity, as opposed to following our own individual (and perhaps idiosyncratic) ideas or doing what other Christians do, regardless of whether that makes sense for our own tradition. The goal for ordained worship leaders who read this book is to develop a baptismal practice that is faithful to their traditions, but also relevant for today's pastoral and ecclesial context.The point is to *renew* liturgical practice, not just reclaim tradition for its own sake – although our context may dictate reclaiming practices that the Reformers laid aside. Thus, this book seeks to foster a pastoral liturgical leadership that is both historical and contextual in orientation.

This chapter will offer a brief overview of the baptismal theologies and practices that emerged in four sixteenth-century reform movements (Lutheranism, Reformed-Calvinism, Anglicanism, and Anabaptism), as well as in two later movements, namely Methodism and Pentecostalism. (A similar method will be followed in Chapter 10 on the Lord's Supper.) Space does not permit an exhaustive study of each tradition, so it is hoped that readers will engage in a more in-depth study of their own tradition's teaching on baptism in order to deepen their understanding and enrich their practice.

Martin Luther

For Dr. Martin Luther (1483-1546), baptism was not a matter of ecclesiastical abuse but neglect. The church of his time had failed to extol it as a gift of divine grace and source of spiritual comfort. Accordingly, much of his writing on the subject – mostly in German – sought to lift up the theological and pastoral importance of baptism, and draw out the practical implications for liturgy and spirituality. One of the clearest expressions of Luther's baptismal theology is found in his *Large Catechism* (1529). Drawing on the Augustinian definition of a sacrament as God's Word added to a natural element, Luther stresses baptism's foundation on God's command (Matt. 28:19) and promise (Mark 16:16). Indeed, it is really *God* who baptizes, although the rite is administered by human hands. The effect of baptism is to *save* by delivering from sin, death, and the devil, and granting entrance into Christ's kingdom. These benefits are received by faith alone; and without faith, baptism is useless.[1]

Although baptism has a "once for all" and saving character, it is not simply done and then forgotten. To the contrary, baptism has continuing significance, for it signifies the ongoing struggle of dying to sin and rising to new life. Put another way: baptism initiates one into an ongoing life of repentance, which means that all acts of confession and repentance are but practical ways of working out the implications of baptism.[2] Because baptism is related to the repentant life whereby sin is continually subdued, it anticipates one's death, which is the end of the struggle against sin (cf. Rom. 6:7).

For Luther, spirituality is rooted in baptism. In the first place, a Christian can take comfort from baptism when assailed by spiritual doubts, for

> ...we must regard baptism and put it to use in such a way that we may draw strength and comfort from it when our sins or conscience oppress us, and say "But I am baptized! And if I have been baptized, I have the promise that I shall be saved and have eternal life, both in soul and body."[3]

Second, as mentioned above, the remembrance of baptism leads to a life of continual repentance:

> Therefore, let all Christians regard their baptism as the daily garment that they are to wear all the time. Every day they should be found in faith and with its fruits, suppressing the old creature and growing up in the new. If we want to be Christians, we must practice the work that makes us Christians.... As Christ, the mercy seat, does not withdraw from us or forbid us to return to him even though we sin, so all his treasures and gifts remain. As we have once obtained

---

[1] Martin Luther, *Large Catechism* (1529), BC, 457.3-460.34.

[2] See Martin Luther, *Small Catechism* (1529), BC, 360.12, and *Large Catechism*, BC, 465.74.

[3] Luther, *Large Catechism*, BC, 462.44-45.

> forgiveness of sins in baptism, so forgiveness remains day by day as long as we live, that is, as long as we carry the old creature around our necks.[4]

Luther defends the baptism of infants on several grounds including the analogy with circumcision in the Hebrew Scriptures and "infant faith." But his central argument rests on baptism's grounding in the Word of God, both its command and its promise. If baptism takes place primarily *because* of the purported faith of the recipient, then it rests on something uncertain, for human faith – which for him is more than mere cognitive knowledge – can never be quantified and is discernable only by God. As noted in the previous chapter, a recipient's lack of faith does not invalidate baptism in Luther's view. Rather than constituting the basis for baptism, faith is the means of "appropriating" or receiving baptism, for one believes the biblical promises that pertain to baptism. That very faith is imparted through baptism, as well as the Lord's Supper and the proclaimed Word of God.[5] Thus, the church does not baptize because a person has faith, but so that he/she may obtain faith. Since baptism rests on the saving initiative of God, which is especially apparent when baptism is conferred on an infant who brings no decision, efforts, or works to the sacrament, Luther's baptismal theology serves as a corollary to his doctrine of justification by grace through faith.[6]

Infant baptism was likewise defended in Lutheran confessional documents of the sixteenth century, especially the *Augsburg Confession* and its *Apology*. Since baptism is the only means of saving from the damnatory effects of original sin,[7] and since the biblical mandate (Matt. 28:19) and promise concerning baptism apply also to children, the sacrament is appropriately administered to infants

---

[4] Luther, *Large Catechism*, BC, 466.86.

[5] Luther, *Large Catechism*, BC 355.6. See *Augsburg Confession* (1530), Art. V, BC, 41.1.

[6] See Maxwell E. Johnson, *The Rites of Christian Initiation: Their Evolution and Interpretation*, rev. and exp. ed. (Collegeville: Liturgical Press, 2007), 321.

[7] *Augsburg Confession*, Art. II, BC, 39.2.

and small children.[8] The church's very existence demonstrates that God himself approved of the practice, for otherwise, there would have been no impartation of the Holy Spirit to sustain the church over the centuries.[9] Such an argument makes perfect sense within a theological framework that understands baptism as an effective sacramental action of God to save and sanctify the recipient.

In 1523, Luther prepared a German baptismal rite.[10] A very conservative revision of the Latin rite in use in northern Germany at the time of the Reformation, it kept many of the traditional baptismal ceremonies. The Reformer hoped that a German-language service would enable those in attendance to participate more intelligently and sincerely. Indeed, sponsors and other lay persons present are admonished to listen to the prayers of the priest and pray them inwardly. The priest is encouraged to pray slowly and deliberately. Such earnest participation, Luther says, is far more important than secondary ceremonies such as making the sign of the cross and anointing.[11]

In broad outline, the 1523 rite unfolded as follows:

Exsufflation
Sign of the cross (forehead and breast)
Opening prayers
Giving of salt
Flood Prayer
Exorcisms
Mark 10:13-16
Lord's Prayer (with laying on of hands)
Ephphatha
Renunciation
Creedal questioning
Anointing

---

[8] *Apology of the Augsburg Confession* (1531), Art. IX, BC, 184.2.

[9] *Apology of the Augsburg Confession*, Art. IX, BC, 184.3.

[10] Martin Luther, *The Order of Baptism* (1523), LW 53, 96-103.

[11] Luther, *Order of Baptism*, LW 53, 101-2.

Washing
Postbaptismal anointing
Peace
Conferral of baptismal robe
Conferral of baptismal candle

Luther's liturgical conservatism is evident in the retention of the exsufflation (blowing in the face of the child), exorcisms (rites for expelling Satan), ephphatha (opening of the senses), marking with the sign of the cross, anointings before and after the washing, as well as the two-part structure with the preliminary rites (1-9) performed at the church door and the remaining rites at the font. The Reformer's conservatism owed to his belief that too many changes and deviations from the traditional rite would prompt the criticism that he was instituting a new baptism and was thereby calling into question the legitimacy of baptisms performed with older rites.[12] A possible original contribution was the so-called Flood Prayer (*Sintflutgebet*), with its typological images of the Great Flood (Gen. 6), the Exodus, and Jesus' own baptism in the Jordan River, which is understood as consecrating all water for baptism. Most likely, Luther's prayer was a translated and edited version of one used for the blessing of baptismal water.[13] Because this prayer was incorporated into other sixteenth-century Protestant baptismal rites that are discussed later in this chapter, I provide the text:

> Almighty eternal God, who according to thy righteous judgment didst condemn the unbelieving world through the flood and in thy great mercy didst preserve believing Noah and his family, and who didst drown hardhearted Pharaoh with all his host in the Red Sea and didst lead thy people Israel through the same on dry ground, thereby prefiguring this bath of thy baptism, and who through the baptism of thy dear Child, our Lord Jesus Christ, hast consecrated and set apart the Jordan and all water as a salutary flood and a

[12] Luther, *Order of Baptism*, LW 53, 103.

[13] Johnson, *Rites of Christian Initiation*, 323.

> rich and full washing away of sins: We pray through the same thy groundless mercy that thou wilt graciously behold this *Name* and bless him [sic] with true faith in the spirit so that by means of this saving flood all that has been born in him from Adam and which he himself has added thereto may be drowned in him and engulfed, and that he may be sundered from the number of the unbelieving, preserved dry and secure in the holy ark of Christendom, serve thy name at all times fervent in spirit and joyful in hope, so that with all believers he may be made worthy to attain eternal life according to thy promise; through Jesus Christ our Lord. Amen.[14]

Luther's baptismal rite is noteworthy in three respects. First, there is no advice or directions about preferred days or times for administering baptism, e.g., baptizing on major liturgical feasts or at the main Sunday service. Luther likely assumed that baptism would be administered "on demand," which in most cases would have been soon after birth.[15] Second, and related to the previous point, Luther did not assume the public celebration of baptism, since only the priest, candidate, and godparents are mentioned. Given the importance that Luther attached to baptism for all Christians, it is somewhat surprising that he did not encourage the celebration of baptism within a public worship service when all present could have been reminded of their baptism. Perhaps his pastoral conservatism prevented him from pressing the matter with a community long accustomed to private celebrations of the sacrament.

Third, while the direction to "dip" the child into the font is not an extraordinary feature for its time, the emphasis that Luther gives the action is. In a 1519 sermon on baptism, Luther advocates baptismal immersion as a way of expressing the true meaning of the German word for baptism, "*Taufe*," which is related to the word "deep" ("*tief*"). For him, this etymology implies that what is *baptized*

[14] Luther, *Order of Baptism*, LW 53, 97.

[15] Luther himself was baptized on 11 November 1483, the day after his birth.

is to be plunged *deeply* under the water. He writes: "For baptism, as we shall hear, signifies that the old man and sinful birth of flesh and blood are to be wholly drowned by the grace of God. We should therefore do justice to its meaning and make baptism a true and complete sign of the thing it signifies."[16]

Because it seemed that many of the symbolic ceremonies contained in the 1523 rite obscured the essentials, Luther revised the baptismal service in 1526, pruning away many of the secondary features.[17] Retained was the first marking with the sign of the cross, the opening prayer and Flood Prayer, the second of the two exorcisms, the gospel reading, the Lord's Prayer, renunciation, creedal questioning, and washing with the triune formula (still by dipping). The traditional postbaptismal formula was modified to accompany the conferral of the baptismal robe. Arguably, the removal of rites and gestures that Luther deemed non-essential allowed the washing itself to stand out as the central action of baptism, something the Reformer undoubtedly desired given that his preferred Romans 6 death and resurrection theology is most aptly portrayed by plunging the candidate under the water (=death) and then drawing him/her out again (=resurrection).

Luther's followers used both rites described above, although the German Lutheran Church Orders of the sixteenth and seventeenth centuries were more dependent on the 1526 rite. These church orders were to influence Lutheran baptismal practice into the twentieth century. It is also noteworthy that Lutherans since the Reformation have practiced the so-called "emergency baptism" (*Nottaufe*) of persons in danger of dying. In such cases, baptism could be performed even by a lay person, although some form of public acknowledgement and ratification of the baptism has been deemed necessary.[18] The practice

---

[16] Martin Luther, *The Holy and Blessed Sacrament of Baptism* (1519), LW 35, 29.

[17] Martin Luther, *The Order of Baptism Newly Revised* (1526), LW 53, 106-9.

[18] See *Occasional Services: A Companion to Lutheran Book of Worship* (Minneapolis: Augsburg Publishing House; Philadelphia: Board of Publication, Lutheran Church in America, 1982), 16-22, and Commission on Worship, The

reflects the Lutheran understanding that baptism is necessary for salvation (cf. *Augsburg Confession*, Art. II).

Ulrich Zwingli

Ulrich Zwingli (1484-1531) developed a theology of baptism that was completely different from Luther's. For Zwingli, material things and outward actions cannot mediate spiritual realities or "cause" the grace that sanctifies the human person. The inward working of the Holy Spirit to bring about faith in a person is more decisive than an outward rite.[19] Thus, baptism does not save, justify or spiritually purify. However, this emphasis on inward faith does not mean that infants and small children could not receive baptism. Like circumcision in the Old Testament, baptism is a covenant sign, and children born to Christian parents rightly receive it, since they are also children of God.[20] Parents and sponsors "dedicate" children to God in baptism, which serves as a sign that these children have been "engrafted" into Christ and his church.[21]

Zwingli is associated with two baptismal rites. The first, composed by Zwingli's associate, Leo Jud (1482-1542) in 1523, was a slight revision of Luther's first baptismal rite with many of the traditional baptismal ceremonies retained. Significant differences from Luther were the design of the rite for *public* administration of baptism and the omission of the postbaptismal anointing and candle ceremonies.[22] In 1525, Zwingli himself produced a drastic revision of Jud's rite that removed all gestures and ceremonies that he

---

Lutheran Church—Missouri Synod, *Lutheran Service Book* (St Louis: Concordia, 2006), 1023.

[19] Ulrich Zwingli, *Commentary on True and False Religion* (1525), in *The Works of Huldreich Zwingli*, ed. Clarence H. Heller, tr. Samuel M. Jackson (Philadelphia: Heidelberg Press, 1929), 187.

[20] Zwingli, *Commentary on True and False Religion*, 197.

[21] Ulrich Zwingli, *Of Baptism* (1525), in *Zwingli and Bullinger*, ed. G. W. Bromiley, LCC XXIV (Philadelphia: Westminster Press, 1953), 145-46.

[22] Leo Jud, "A Short and Public Form for the Tender in Faith for the Baptism of Children" (1523), CIRP, 126-29.

believed to be without biblical foundation. The rite consisted simply of questions to the godparents, the Flood Prayer (omitting the phrase "this saving flood"), Mark 10:13-16, a second set of questions to the godparents, the baptismal washing (with no reference to dipping), robe, and concluding peace.[23]

For Zwingli, baptism is entirely a human action, the operative words being "pledge" and "dedicate"– actions that of course have the human person as their subject. While any sacramental sense involving divine activity is absent from Zwingli's baptismal thinking, he did bring out the ecclesial dimension of baptism – something absent in Luther's thinking. Connecting baptism with discipleship and church membership is an emphasis that resonates well into the twentieth and twenty-first centuries, even among churches that would disagree with much of Zwinglian baptismal theology.

John Calvin

John Calvin (1509-1564), the Reformer of Geneva and Strasbourg, espoused a baptismal theology somewhere between those of Luther and Zwingli. He held that baptism signifies initiation into the church or "engrafting" into Christ, as well as the forgiveness of sins.[24] Further, it signifies mortification of the flesh and "rebirth into newness of life and into the fellowship of Christ."[25] Thus, in contrast to Zwingli, Calvin believed that baptism is more than an outward sign that a person is a Christian. But Calvin's tendency to speak of baptism as *signifying* grace was much different from the Lutheran emphasis on baptism as a means of *conveying* grace. For Calvin, baptism expresses or points to forgiveness and reception of the Holy Spirit, while for Luther it *is* these things. Also, Calvin came to a different conclusion about "emergency baptism." Since baptism is a solemn reception

[23] Ulrich Zwingli, "The Second Revision of the Zurich Order of Baptism" (1525), CIRP, 130-31.

[24] John Calvin, *Institutes of the Christian Religion* IV.15.1 (1559), ed. John T. McNeill, tr. Ford Lewis Battles in LCC XXI (Philadelphia: Westminster Press, 1960), 1303-4.

[25] Calvin, *Institutes* IV.16.2, LCC XXI, 1325.

into the church, it is especially holy to seek baptism from a duly-appointed minister. But because the grace of God is not bound to baptism, the omission of baptism conferred by an ordained minister does not prevent the reception of God's grace, which could also come to one who received the proclaimed Word in faith.[26] This position effectively rules out "emergency" baptism, something that Lutherans allowed and even practiced as a badge of orthodoxy.

Calvin produced a baptismal rite for use in Geneva that was included in *The Form of Prayers and Ecclesiastical Chants with the Manner of Administering the Sacraments and Solemnizing Marriage according to the Custom of the Ancient Church* (1542). This rite, which bore little resemblance to those of Luther and Zwingli, took the following shape:

Opening sentence (Ps. 124:8)
Presentation of the child
Instruction
Prayer
Admonition to parents
Baptism with trinitarian formula

Three aspects of this rite are notable. First is the participation of the assembly. Owing to the nature of baptism as incorporation into the church, the rite was to be celebrated at the Sunday liturgy in the presence of the congregation.[27] The minister was to speak audibly using the vernacular, so that the congregation may be edified. All secondary ceremonies (e.g., anointing, candle) were eliminated because they neither edify the assembly nor contain any biblical warrant. Second is the emphasis on instruction and formation: parents are exhorted to teach the child the Christian faith and guide the child in proper Christian living. This emphasis is a reflection of Calvin's association with Martin Bucer of Strasbourg (1491-1551),

---

[26] Calvin, *Institutes* IV.15.22, LCC XXI, 1323.

[27] John Calvin, *The Form of Prayers and Ecclesiastical Chants with the Manner of Administering the Sacraments and Solemnizing Marriage According to the Custom of the Ancient Church* (1542), CIRP, 113.

who, in response to the challenge of Anabaptism, stressed the need for instructing those baptized in infancy so that they would lead godly lives.[28]

Third, and most significantly, is the manner in which Calvin's rite illumines his overall approach to infant baptism. As Maxwell Johnson points out, while the language of the exhortation does speak of spiritual gifts (e.g., forgiveness of sins) being conferred by God in baptism, the subsequent prayer of invocation makes it seem as though an infant is being baptized for a *future* faith and repentance that depends on *future* instruction in the Christian faith:

> Lord, God, Father eternal and almighty, since it has pleased thee by thine infinite mercy to promise us that thou wilt be our God and the God of our children, we pray thee that it may please thee to confirm this grace in the present infant, born of a father and mother whom thou hast called into thy church, and, as he is *offered* and *consecrated* to thee by us, that thou wouldst receive him into thy holy protection, declaring thyself to be his God and Saviour, remitting to him the original sin of which the whole lineage of Adam is guilty, and then afterwards sanctifying him by thy Spirit, so *that when he comes to the age of understanding*, he may know and adore thee as his only God, glorifying thee all through his life, so as to obtain evermore from thee remission of sins. And so that he can obtain such graces, may it please thee to incorporate him in the fellowship of our Lord Jesus Christ to be partaker of all his benefits, as one of the members of his body. Grant us, Father of mercy, that the baptism which

---

[28] In an introduction to the baptismal rite used in Strasbourg, 1525-1530, Bucer writes "...you shall explain and present the whole of baptism as an initial sign of faith and an entry into the Christian life, whereby the parents testify before the church that they will bring up their child to the glory of God and will teach and explain to him what happened at his baptism, so that he may remember to order his life in a Christian manner and not to live like a heathen" (CIRP, 35).

> we minister to him according to thine ordinance may bring forth its fruit and virtue.[29]

In that case, baptism is depicted as a solemn "pledging" or "dedicating" of an infant to God, and "an outward sign of what was true internally on other grounds, and…there was no necessary causal relationship between the two."[30] Only for the elect, Johnson concludes, can baptism be said to "perform what it signifies."[31] Yet, all church members must obediently receive baptism, since the identity of the elect is known only to God. Thus, the "ambiguity" of Calvin's baptismal theology is brought into focus when viewed against the backdrop of his theology of divine election.

Thomas Cranmer

The principal architect of the earliest Anglican baptismal services in the BCP 1549 and BCP 1552 was Archbishop Thomas Cranmer (1489-1556). He produced no systematic treatise on baptism, and his thinking about sacraments in general and baptism in particular is scattered throughout a number of writings. Bryan Spinks maintains that Calvin's doctrine of predestination was decisive for Cranmer, which necessarily meant that the sacraments do not convey grace. Like Calvin, Cranmer could only affirm that the sacraments *signify* grace:

> *Although the sacramental tokens be only significations and figures*, yet doth Almighty God effectually work in them that duly receive his sacraments, those divine and celestial operations which he hath promised, and by the sacraments be signified. For else they were vain and unfruitful sacraments, as well to the godly as to the ungodly.[32]

---

[29] Calvin, *Form of Prayers*, CIRP, 115-16 (emphasis original).

[30] Johnson, *Rites of Christian Initiation*, 337.

[31] Johnson, *Rites of Christian Initiation*, 337.

[32] Thomas Cranmer, "Answer to Stephen Gradiner's Explication," in *Writings and Disputations of Thomas Cranmer Relative to the Sacrament of the Lord's Supper*, ed. J. E. Cox (Cambridge: Parker Society, 1844), 3, as cited in Bryan D. Spinks,

On the question of infant baptism, Cranmer holds that since infants were circumcised under the old covenant, they are rightly baptized under the new covenant in Christ. The promises to Abraham and his seed, as well as various New Testament passages that speak about "children" (e.g., Mark 10:13-16), prove that infant baptism is scripturally grounded.[33]

In compiling the baptismal rite for the first Prayer Book, Cranmer drew on a number of sources, including: (1) the Latin Sarum rite; (2) a baptismal rite developed for Cologne at the behest of the reform-minded Roman Catholic Archbishop, Herman von Wied (1477-1552);[34] (3) the (Lutheran) Brandenburg-Nuremburg rite (1533); and (4) a Gallican/Mozarabic blessing for the baptismal font.[35] Cranmer's basic approach was summarized in a short explanation at the conclusion of the BCP 1549, which states that certain ceremonies were dropped because they fostered superstition and served the greedy purposes of unscrupulous Christians, while others were retained because they could serve good order and discipline and would not likely be abused.[36] The shape of the rite was:

Introductory words
Flood Prayer
Sign of the cross
Prayer
Exorcism
Mark 10:13-16

Reformation and Modern Rituals and Theologies of Baptism: From Luther to Contemporary Practices (Aldershot: Ashgate, 2006), 67. Emphasis added.

[33] Thomas Cranmer, *Confutation on Unwritten Verities* (n. d.), CIRP, 87-88.

[34] "A simple and religious consultation of us Hermann by the grace of God Archbishop of Cologne…" also known as the *Consultation*. CIRP, 54-69.

[35] Spinks, *Reformation and Modern Rituals and Theologies*, 67.

[36] "Of Ceremonies: Why Some Be Abolished and Some be Retained," in Church of England: *Book of Common Prayer* (1549), Society of Archbishop Justus, http://justus.anglican.org/resources/bcp/1549/Of_Ceremonies_1549.html[accessed 22 December 2013].

Lord's Prayer
Creed
Renunciation of the devil
Creedal interrogation
Baptism
Baptismal robe
Anointing of the head
Admonition to godparents[37]

Like the first baptismal rites of Luther and Zwingli, the 1549 rite of Cranmer was a conservative attempt at reform. While many of the traditional symbolic ceremonies were discarded, a few were retained, e. g., the signing on the forehead, exorcism, anointing of the head, and the conferral of the baptismal robe.[38] Cranmer also retained the custom of celebrating the first part of the service (1-8) near the church door, and then moving to the font for the renunciation and following ceremonies (9-14). Theologically, baptism is still viewed as a remedy for original sin, initiation into the church, regeneration, the forgiveness of sins, and the conferral of the Holy Spirit. At the same time, following continental Reformers, baptism is to be celebrated at the liturgy of Sunday or one of the holy days (feasts) so that assembly members can be reminded of their own baptism. The Reformation emphasis on instruction and formation is seen in two exhortations to the godparents, one placed before the renunciation/profession and a longer one placed after the postbaptismal anointing. Johnson suggests that Cranmer's conservative approach to the crafting of this rite represents the classically Anglican attempt to steer a middle course (*via media*) between Protestantism and Roman Catholicism.[39]

A unique contribution of Cranmer in the 1549 baptismal rite was his use of Spirit-language. An adapted version of the traditional postbaptismal anointing formula speaks of God's anointing the newly baptized with the "unction of the Holy Spirit," which thereby

---

[37] CIRP, 89-95.

[38] Spinks, *Reformation and Modern Rituals and Theologies*, 67.

[39] Johnson, *Rites of Christian Initiation*, 348.

associated presbyteral anointing and the conferral of the Holy Spirit in a manner unheard of in Western Christianity. Johnson suggests that this innovation was influenced by Eastern liturgical sources.[40] Similarly, drawing on ancient Spanish (Mozarabic) and French (Gallican) sources, Cranmer included a prayer for the blessing of the baptismal font (usually done once a month) that called upon the Spirit to "sanctify" the font.[41]

Following the publication of the BCP 1549, the Strasbourg reformer, Martin Bucer (1491-1551), came to England in 1549 and wrote a critical assessment of the Prayer Book which came to be known as the *Censura*.[42] Although generally approving of the baptismal rite, Bucer nevertheless rejects the following: the postbaptismal robe and anointing because they promote superstition; language in the Flood Prayer suggestive of a general consecration of water by Christ's baptism in the Jordan; the exorcism because such an action rightly pertains only to those possessed by demons; the creedal interrogation since it was directed to an infant who cannot rationally understand what is being done; and, for a similar reason, the formula used for the signing with the cross. Bucer also objects to the consecration of the baptismal font, since it implies that a spiritual blessing is being imparted to a thing when in fact God's blessings (e.g., forgiveness of sins, eternal life) can only be imparted to people.[43] Bucer's overall approach is dominated by a desire to avoid abuse and superstition and an emphasis on rational understanding – a position commensurate with more radical reformers in England, as well as with Cranmer himself who had doubts concerning the legitimacy of traditional baptismal ceremonies.

---

[40] Johnson, *Rites of Christian Initiation*, 344.

[41] Johnson, *Rites of Christian Initiation*, 345.

[42] Martin Bucer, *The Judgment of Martin Bucer Upon the Book of Sacred Rites or of the Ordering of the Church and Ecclesiastical Ministration in the Kingdom of England Written at the Request of the Reverend Archbishop Thomas Cranmer*, ix, in Bucer, *Scripta Anglicana* (Basel, 1577), 477-81 (CIRP, 96-105).

[43] Bucer, *Judgment of Martin Bucer* (*Censura*), CIRP, 104.

Bucer's *Censura* had a significant impact on the baptismal rite that was produced for a revised edition of the Prayer Book in 1552. In line with Bucer's suggestions, Cranmer removed the exorcism, the postbaptismal vesting and anointing rites, and eliminated the preliminary service at the church door, placing the entire rite at the font. Additionally, the renunciation and creedal interrogation were redirected toward the godparents, rather than the child candidate. Yet, Cranmer did not follow Bucer's suggestion to revise the Flood Prayer. The signing with the cross was placed immediately after the washing, and the one and only naming of the child takes place prior to the washing.[44] The rubric pertaining to the washing was simplified (no longer referring to three "dippings"). Interestingly, the 1552 rite included a series of petitions from the font blessing prayer in the BCP 1549, as well as the final (collect) prayer from that blessing rite, although the original language suggestive of a "consecration" or blessing of baptismal (font) water was removed, following Bucer's suggestion.[45] The traditional theological emphases (forgiveness, reception of the Holy Spirit, and incorporation into the church) remained in the 1552 rite. But regeneration was treated in a more subtle manner: while the revised Flood Prayer dropped language that ties regeneration directly to the baptismal act (viz., "that by this wholesome laver of regeneration…"), a new prayer of thanksgiving used regeneration language in a way suggestive of a *future* event: "grant that he…*may* crucify the old man…" "…he *may* be a partaker of [Christ's] resurrection…" and "…he *may* be inheritor of thine everlasting kingdom"[46] – as with the baptismal theology of John Calvin. Thus, it appears that the 1552 baptismal rite attempted to appease both sides in the debate over baptismal regeneration.[47]

---

[44] "The Ministration of Baptism," BCP 1552, CIRP, 110.

[45] "The Ministration of Baptism," BCP 1552, CIRP, 109. See n. 2.

[46] "The Ministration of Baptism," BCP 1552, CIRP, 111.

[47] "The Ministration of Baptism," BCP 1552, CIRP, 110-11. Phraseology "See now, dearly beloved brethren, that these children be regenerate and grafted into the body of Christ's congregation…" and "We yield thee hearty thanks, most merciful Father, that it hath pleased thee to regenerate this infant with thy Holy Spirit…"

Like their Lutheran contemporaries, early Anglicans practiced "emergency baptism." A rite entitled "Of Them That be Baptized In Private Houses in Time of Necessity" appeared in the BCP 1549, and it was unchanged in the BCP 1552.[48] The rubrics stressed that the baptism of infants should not be delayed any longer than the Sunday after the child's birth and that the child should only be baptized in the home when there is great necessity. The rite was simple: after the Lord's Prayer and the naming of the child, water was to be poured on the child using the traditional trinitarian formula. If the child survived, he or she was brought to the church so that the priest/curate could ascertain whether the child had been lawfully baptized, a process for which the Prayer Book provided a form. If the baptism had been performed correctly, the priest/curate certified the previous actions and then proceeded with the reading of Mark 10:13-16, the exhortation, the Lord's Prayer, the renunciation and creedal interrogation, prayer of thanksgiving, and final exhortation. If the in-home baptism was performed incorrectly or uncertainty surrounded the action, the priest was to baptize the child. Emergency baptism continues to be practiced among Anglicans, with many contemporary Prayer Books providing ritual forms.[49]

What is perhaps most striking about Cranmer's reform of baptism is its ecumenicity. In an era without Internet or other forms of instant communication, and long before the twentieth-century ecumenical movement, Cranmer was knowledgeable of older Western European rites and Eastern rites, as well as contemporary developments in Christian initiation among Lutheran and Reformed churches on the continent! One rite influencing another rite was nothing new in liturgical history, but the ecumenical intentionality of Cranmer seems unprecedented and in some ways anticipated the liturgical reform movement of the twentieth century, which was

---

point in the direction of baptismal regeneration without specifically connecting that reality to the water baptism.

[48] "Of Them That be Baptized In Private Houses in Time of Necessity," BCP 1549, CIRP, 144-47.

[49] See "Emergency Baptism," BCP 1979, 313.

inherently ecumenical. Cranmer's work challenges worship leaders today to think ecumenically about the liturgy and its renewal, lest we be limited by our own liturgical myopia.

Yet, we may not want to imitate all aspects of Cranmer's reform of Christian initiation. Like other Reformers, Cranmer was beset by questions surrounding the symbolic rites, their number, meaning, and propensity to engender abuse. We cannot doubt that at a time in Christian history when spiritual formation of the laity was insufficient, secondary rites obscured the meaning of baptism and opened the way to abuse and misunderstanding. But whether churches today should adopt the "reform by deletion" approach of Cranmer or a ritual minimalism is highly questionable. To begin with, ministers today are better educated than their Reformation-era counterparts and thus more capable of communicating the meaning of baptism and its rituals through preaching, catechesis (instruction), printed matter, and electronic media. Second, the twentieth century has seen a renewed interest in symbols and ritual, and the social sciences have helped Christians to understand that these are an inherent part of human culture. In an age when people seem starved for symbols and often improvise symbols and rituals to express emotions that are nearly inexpressible (e.g., grief, outrage), the church's treasury of symbols, if used carefully and sensitively, can potentially enliven and enrich the baptismal experience of each and every Christian.

Menno Simons

With its origins in sixteenth-century Switzerland, Southern Germany, and the Netherlands, the Anabaptist movement is to be distinguished from the so-called "magisterial" reform movements (Lutheran, Reformed, Anglican) by its insistence that the church is a purely voluntary community and that those who join it through baptism must be capable of an explicit confession of faith and commitment to Christian discipleship. Infant baptism was rejected as a distortion of the Christian Scriptures and a sign of the church's corruption. As James F. White writes: "Baptism was an important issue [to Anabaptists] because it came to be the means of distinguishing between a pure church of known believers, visible to all, and a mass of people indiscriminately baptized as infants, a church that included good and bad alike."[50] Although "Anabaptist" means "one baptized again," early members of the movement did not consider themselves "re-baptized" since their initial (infant) baptism was, in their view, really no baptism at all. Despite brutal persecution early on by Reformed, Lutheran, and Roman Catholic Christians, the movement lives on today in Mennonite, Amish, and Brethren churches around the world.

Although a number of early Anabaptist theologians such as Balthasar Hubmaier (1480-1528), Hans Hut (1490-1527), and Melchior Hoffman (1495-1543) wrote on the topic of baptism, the most important was the former priest, Menno Simons (1496-1561), whose *Foundation of Christian Doctrine* (1539) is a classic Anabaptist text. The section on baptism is devoted to the author's objections to infant baptism, the first being that it is unscriptural. The verbal sequences "teach...baptizing" in Matt. 28:19 [sic] and "preach...believe...baptize" in Mark 16:16 indicate that cognitive understanding and faith must precede baptism, which rules out the baptizing of uncomprehending infants.[51] Furthermore, one's death to sin (Col. 2:11-12; Rom. 6:3-4) and regeneration are both contingent on a cognitive faith which means that baptism cannot confer these things on infants. 1 Peter 3:21 indicates that the inward working of the Spirit is of primary and saving significance, while baptism is only an outward sign of faith of secondary importance.[52] Second, those baptized in infancy in actuality do not live authentic Christian lives, but dissolute ones.[53] Indeed, faithful living is important, since baptism is not a sacramental cleansing from sin but rather

[50] James F. White, *Protestant Worship: Traditions in Transition* (Louisville: Westminster John Knox Press, 1989), 82.

[51] Menno Simons, *Foundation of Christian Doctrine* (1539), CWMS, 120.

[52] Simons, *Foundation*, CWMS, 124.

[53] Simons, *Foundation*, CWMS, 127-28

> … a sign of obedience, commanded of Christ, by which we testify, when we receive it that we believe the Word of the Lord, that we are sorry for, and repent of our former life and conduct; that we desire to rise with Christ unto a new life; and that we believe in the forgiveness of sin through Jesus Christ.[54]

Third, infant baptism lacks legitimacy because baptismal practice following the apostolic period was subject to constant change regarding timing, mode, and accompanying rituals; the fact that a pope (Innocent I) had to "confirm" infant baptism undermines any contention that baptism is grounded in God's Word!

All of the traditional arguments for baptizing infants, such as analogies to circumcision in the Old Testament, the baptism of households in the New Testament, and the purported "faith" of infants are rejected by Simons.[55] An important theological basis for baptizing infants, the supposed damnatory effects of original sin, is denied since children are subject to God's grace:

> And although infants have neither faith nor baptism, think not therefore that they are damned. Oh no! They are blessed; for they have the Lord's own promise of the kingdom of God; not through any elements, ceremonies and external rites, but only by grace, through Jesus Christ, Matt. 19:13-15. And therefore, we do truly believe, that they are under grace, acceptable to God, pure, holy, heirs of God and eternal life, and on account of this promise, all sincere, Christian believers, may assuredly rejoice and comfort themselves in the salvation of their children.[56]

The above statement, however, seems at odds with his contention that faith (rather than baptism) saves:

---

[54] Simons, *Foundation*, CWMS, 125.

[55] Simons, *Foundation*, CWMS, 132-36.

[56] Simons, *Foundation*, CWMS, 135.

> The Lord commanded his gospel to be preached to every creature, so that all who believe and are baptized may be saved. Where there is faith, which is called the gift of God by Paul, there also are the power and fruits of faith....
>
> Had Noah and Lot not believed the word of the Lord, they would have fared ill. Had Abraham not believed, he would not have obtained such glorious promises; but they believed, and did right, and became heirs of righteousness (Heb. 11:8).[57]

Thus, it appears that Simons envisioned a two-fold salvation: infant salvation through the promise of Christ, and adult salvation through faith. Baptism is conferred on the latter as a sign of that faith and its resulting obedience.

Since liturgical matters for Anabaptists centered on following the Word of God rather than prescribed liturgies (deemed unnecessary and potentially idolatrous),[58] there are no extant baptismal services from early Anabaptist communities. For these, baptism would have involved pouring water over the head of the kneeling candidate, and in at least one case the baptismal "vessel" was a milk pail![59] As the requirement of full baptismal submersion only emerged with English Baptists in the seventeenth century, the practice was unknown among early continental Anabaptists.

In general, early Anabaptists spoke of three baptisms:

1. Baptism in water (a sign of the forgiveness of sins).
2. Baptism of the Holy Spirit (releases gifts for ministry that build up the church).
3. Baptism in blood (suffering, hardship and death for the sake of the gospel).

---

[57] Simons, *Foundation*, CWMS, 130-31.

[58] White, *Protestant Worship*, 81.

[59] See James F. White, *A Brief History of Christian Worship* (Nashville: Abingdon Press, 1993), 114.

Given the persecution that Anabaptists have endured over the years, the third of these has been particularly meaningful for Anabaptist communities around the world.[60]

The significance of the Anabaptist movement lies not only in its distinctive approach to Christian initiation, but also in its influence on the baptismal practices of other Christians. Its critique of infant baptism and emphasis on conscious faith and responsible discipleship led other early Protestants, especially Reformed, to craft baptismal rites that included exhortations and parental promises about instructing children and encouraging them to lead godly lives. It is hard not to see the influence of Anabaptism behind the statement in the World Council of Churches' *Baptism, Eucharist and Ministry* (1982) document that "personal commitment is necessary for responsible membership in the body of Christ."[61] Indeed, one doubts whether twentieth-century churches would have even been concerned about so-called "indiscriminate baptism" (baptizing without the expectation of faith or commitment) had it not been for the critical influence of Anabaptism.Thus, the movement has made a positive contribution to the ecumenical church.

Yet, Anabaptist baptismal theology will be challenged by churches with strong doctrines of grace. While acknowledging that faith and baptism go together and that the former is necessary to benefit from God's saving gifts, Lutheran and Reformed Christians would question whether faith can be insisted upon such that salvation and incorporation into the church seem to be contingent upon human action rather than the divine initiative. Is not faith the means by which Christians *receive* the divine promises and gifts rather than a kind of down payment for them? Even if Anabaptists and others insist that a prebaptismal faith is a gift of the Holy Spirit, in practice it is difficult, if not impossible, to ascertain the genuineness of such faith. Put bluntly: in the case of "believer's baptism," how can we be absolutely sure that we baptize on the basis of more than wishful

---

[60] Rebecca Slough, "Baptismal Practice among North American Mennonites," BT, 91.

[61] BEM, 3.

thinking, peer pressure, or even self-deception? Anabaptists and other "believer-baptizing" churches therefore have as difficult an apologetic task as those churches that baptize infants.

John Wesley

A priest of the Church of England with a profound love for the *Book of Common Prayer*, John Wesley (1703-1791) led an evangelical reform movement in England that sought to reach people neglected and forgotten by the established church during the early stages of industrialization in England. Wesley's significance for the movement lay in his abilities as both organizer and preacher.

Based on a section from his father Samuel's *The Pious Communicant* (1700), Wesley's most important writing on Christian initiation is *A Treatise on Baptism* (1756). He defines baptism as the initiatory sacrament by which one enters into a covenant with God. Following Reformed theologians, he likens it to circumcision as a sign of God's covenant. As the New Testament does not enjoin any particular mode, baptism may be administered by washing, dipping, or sprinkling the person while pronouncing the trinitarian formula.[62] The benefits of baptism include the remission of the guilt of original sin, entrance into a covenant with God, admission to the church and membership in Christ, regeneration as a child of God, and becoming an heir of the kingdom of God.[63]

A good portion of the *Treatise* is devoted to defending infant baptism. To begin with, children are proper candidates for baptism because they carry the guilt of original sin.[64] Second, the Hebrew Scriptures show that children can be included in covenants (cf. Deut. 29:10-12), and "the infants of believers, the true children of faithful Abraham, always were under the gospel covenant."[65] Baptism takes the place of circumcision for Christians as the new

---

[62] John Wesley, *Treatise on Baptism* (1756) I.2, in *The Works of John Wesley*, Vol. X (Grand Rapids: Zondervan, 1958), 188.

[63] Wesley, *Treatise on Baptism* II.1-5, *Works of Wesley* X, 190-92.

[64] Wesley, *Treatise on Baptism* IV.2, *Works of Wesley* X, 193.

[65] Wesley, *Treatise on Baptism* IV.4, *Works of Wesley* X, 194.

seal of the covenant. Third, infants are properly brought to Christ and admitted to the church through a solemn dedication (cf. Matt. 19:13-14), i.e., through baptism.[66] Fourth, the Apostles most likely baptized infants since the Jews baptized and circumcised infant children of converts (proselytes). Finally, since infant baptism has been a universal practice, it can hardly be contrary to the mind of Christ or the Apostles. Wesley concluded that infants not only can be baptized but *ought* to be baptized.[67]

Perhaps most controversial is Wesley's two-fold concept of regeneration, which he acquired from the Moravians, a central-European Protestant movement that stressed personal prayer and worship, communal living, and generosity with possessions.[68] On the basis of the implied theology of the Anglican Prayer Book, Wesley holds that infants are regenerated by baptism. Yet, actual sin means that adults who were baptized as infants, as well as many persons baptized as adults, need to be "born again." This "new birth" is neither the same as baptism nor does it necessarily accompany baptism.[69] It is a divinely-produced transformation whereby

> ...the love of the world is changed into the love of God; pride into humility; passion into meekness; hatred, envy, malice into a sincere, tender, disinterested love for all mankind [sic]. In a word, it is that change whereby the earthly, sensual, devilish mind is turned into the "mind which was in Christ Jesus."[70]

Furthermore, the "new birth" is necessary for the attainment of holiness (i.e., having the divine imprint on one's being), salvation, and for personal happiness.[71] The new birth serves as the initial

[66] Wesley, *Treatise on Baptism* IV.6, *Works of Wesley* X, 195-96.

[67] Wesley, *Treatise on Baptism* IV.10, *Works of Wesley* X, 198.

[68] Spinks, *Reformation and Modern Rituals*, 108.

[69] John Wesley, "The New Birth" (1760) IV.2,WJW 2, 197.

[70] Wesley, "The New Birth" II.5, WJW 2, 194.

[71] Wesley, "The New Birth" III.1-3, WJW 2, 194-96.

step in the process of becoming holy: "When we are born again, then our sanctification, our inward and outward holiness, begins; and thenceforward we are gradually to 'grow up in Him who is our Head.'"[72] This growth in holiness reflects Wesley's rejection of Calvinistic predestination and his adoption of Arminianism, with its free-will assent to and cooperation with God's saving actions.

In 1784, Wesley published *The Sunday Service of the Methodists in North America with Other Occasional Services,* which contained two baptismal rites: one for infants and the other for adults.[73] Both were based on the baptismal rites in the BCP 1662. The infant rite consisted of:

Exhortation
Flood Prayer
Prayer of invocation
Mark 10:13-16
Prayers for the child
Baptismal washing with trinitarian formula
Sign of the cross
Prayers of thanksgiving[74]

Spinks notes several interesting features: (1) the use of "regeneration" language only before the washing in the exhortation and prayer of invocation (such language being omitted from the final thanksgiving prayer); (2) the omission of the renunciation/profession of faith as well as the promises made by godparents; (3) the replacement of the term "godparents" with the phrase "friends of the Child"; (4) the deletion of the phrase "the mystical washing away of sin" from the British version of rite; and (5) the substitution of the phrase "admitted into the visible body of Christ's church" for "grafted into

[72] Wesley, "The New Birth" IV.3, WJW 2, 198.

[73] The Prayer Book's rite for "private baptism" was not included by Wesley, which suggests that all baptismal services were to take place during public worship services.

[74] John Wesley, "The Ministration of Baptism of Infants" (1784), JWPB, 139-43.

the body of Christ's church" – perhaps to suggest that infants may not be part of the invisible church. Spinks maintains that Wesley's restriction of regeneration language to a prebaptismal context reveals his qualms about equating the *signum* and *res* of baptism, i.e., suggesting that regeneration necessarily occurs in baptism.[75] Rather than baptismal regeneration, the emphasis in Wesley's infant rite was on (1) initiation, as suggested by phrases like "received into Christ's holy church" (exhortation) and "incorporate him [sic] into the holy Church" (thanksgiving prayer); and (2) the subduing of sin, as suggested by the words "being dead to sin and living unto righteousness" (thanksgiving prayer).

Wesley's adult rite differed from the infant rite in the following respects: (1) the use of John 3:1-8 instead of Mark 10:13-16; (2) the inclusion of a creedal interrogation of the candidates and a pledge of obedience; and (3) the omission of the postbaptismal sign of the cross.[76] Interestingly, Wesley omitted the word "now" that occurs before "born again" in the 1662 postbaptismal prayer ("Give thy Holy Spirit to these persons, that being now born again and made heirs of everlasting salvation…"), thereby suggesting that "rebirth" is a future reality, rather than one brought about by the baptismal act itself.[77] This amendment reflects Wesley's desire to avoid suggesting the coincidence of baptism and rebirth. Overall, Wesley's adult rite, like the infant rite, emphasized the forgiveness of sins, striving against sin, and incorporation into the church, whose fellowship was crucial for the living of a holy life according to Wesleyan thinking.

Liturgical scholar Karen Westerfield Tucker summarizes the legacy of Wesleyan baptismal theology with its accent on the two "new births":

> The consequence for Methodists has been generally the absence of a strong understanding of baptismal regeneration

---

[75] Spinks, *Reformation and Modern Rituals*, 110.

[76] Wesley, "The Ministration of Baptism to Such as are of Riper Years," JWPB, 143-49.

[77] Wesley, "Baptism of Riper Years," JWPB, 149.

> in infants, since emphasis came to be placed on the profession of personal assurance. Compounding this were other theological and social factors present in the American and European environments of the nineteenth century, such as a stress on the individual and his or her personal liberty, and a positive view of human nature, ability and achievement (and with it a questioning of original sin). The language of regeneration was further reduced or eliminated from some Methodist baptismal rites, while baptism as a sign of adoption and an action of initiation was accentuated. Thus, baptized infants became members of the "universal church" in what was often perceived as a dedication service; rites were developed (later popularly called "confirmation" in some Methodist denominations) that granted membership in the local congregation following public profession.[78]

Westerfield Tucker concludes that these developments led to the subordination of divine grace to human decision and that world Methodism therefore experiences confusion and uncertainty about (1) what is implied by designating baptism a "sacrament"; (2) what baptism accomplishes; and, (3) how it fits into the Christian life. Classic Methodist texts, she says, do not alleviate this confusion.

Pentecostalism

Unlike the Protestant reform movements that emerged in Europe during the sixteenth through the eighteenth centuries, Pentecostalism arose in twentieth-century America. With initial beginnings in the work of Charles F. Parham (1873-1929) at Bethel Bible College, Topeka, Kansas, USA, and later William J. Seymour (1870-1922) at the Apostolic Faith Gospel Mission, in Los Angeles, California, USA, the movement spread throughout the United States and eventually to countries in Europe, Latin America, Africa, and

---

[78] Karen B. Westerfield Tucker, "The Initiatory Rites of the United Methodist Church," BT, 100-1.

Asia.[79] Denominational embodiments of Pentecostalism include the Assemblies of God, the Church of God in Christ, the Church of God (Cleveland, Tennessee, USA), and the Church of the Foursquare Gospel. In the 1960s, the influence of Pentecostalism came to be felt in both Protestantism and Roman Catholicism through the "charismatic renewal" movement.

Theologically, the roots of Pentecostalism are in the Holiness movement, which was an outgrowth of the Wesleyan focus on holiness and perfection. While the Holiness movement emphasized the personal assurance of salvation by the indwelling of the Holy Spirit (i.e., "baptism in the Holy Spirit" or "the second blessing"), it did not seek or demand the outward manifestation of that experience in the form of speaking in tongues. The Pentecostal movement, however, does consider speaking in tongues as requisite evidence of baptism in the Holy Spirit.

Since the most important personal experience in Pentecostalism is the reception of the Holy Spirit, baptism in water is of secondary importance. Many Pentecostals would consider it part of the "first stage" of salvation, which involves conversion, justification, and water baptism. Groups differ as to what then follows, whether a second stage consisting of baptism in the Holy Spirit and a sanctified life, or the sanctified life as second stage, followed by a third stage consisting of baptism in the Holy Spirit.[80] Water baptism is not considered a sacramental means of grace, but rather an ordinance carried out in obedience to the New Testament. The vast majority of Pentecostal churches baptize adult candidates only, usually by immersion. Some Pentecostals baptize only in the name of Jesus, while others use the traditional trinitarian formula.[81]

According to Daniel Albrecht, Pentecostal baptismal practice is guided by the core beliefs that baptism (1) is for adults only; (2) constitutes an outward sign of an inward change (the latter occurring prior to the former); (3) is preceded by changes in lifestyle

[79] White, *Protestant Worship*, 194-96.

[80] White, *Protestant Worship*, 201-2.

[81] White, *Protestant Worship*, 202.

that symbolize conversion; and (4) serves as a public testimony of identification with Christ's church.[82] Although Pentecostal liturgical practice is marked by spontaneity and improvisation, there is nevertheless a discernible shape, which in broad outline is:

Pastoral introduction
Candidate's testimony (in the water)
Pastoral questions
Address and prayer
Baptismal formula and washing
Signs of the Spirit
Congregational response
Pastoral words (outside the water)[83]

If not performed in a tank-type baptismal pool located in a congregation's main worship space, baptism is likely to be administered at an outdoor venue either out of necessity or to make the service an evangelistic opportunity. The pastoral introduction will normally serve as a transition to the baptism, as well as provide words of instruction about the meaning of the ordinance. The entire baptismal rite is viewed in terms of a journey into and out of the waters. Upon entering the waters, the candidates testify to their faith and conversion experience. The plunging into the waters and rising up again itself symbolizes the candidates' transformation through emotional and/or physical healing. The rising up is also a moment of congregational celebration for God's work in the newly baptized. The exit from the baptismal pool marks a return to the world where the newly baptized will be Christ's witnesses.[84]

Perhaps Pentecostal baptismal practice, with its focus on journeying from world to water and from water back to the world, could serve to enrich the practice of mainline churches, especially those that invest baptism with deep sacramental meaning. At the

[82] Daniel Albrecht, "Witness in the Waters: Baptism and Pentecostal Spirituality," BT, 148.

[83] Albrecht, "Witness in the Waters," BT, 149.

[84] Albrecht, "Witness in the Waters," BT, 152-57.

same time, perhaps the theology of mainline churches could help Pentecostals to appreciate the sacramentality of baptism, even if they would prefer to avoid such language.

Conclusion

In this chapter, we have given a brief overview of the baptismal theologies and practices of several Protestant traditions. Our hope, once again, is not that readers will copy the early practices of their traditions, but appreciate the core baptismal beliefs of their traditions more profoundly so that they develop a living liturgical tradition – a practice that is at once grounded in tradition, yet responsive to the needs of worshippers today. Additionally, it is hoped that this chapter will enable readers to appreciate the uniqueness of their own traditions against the backdrop of the wider ecumenical church and perhaps gain helpful insights from other traditions that will renew the baptismal practice of their own churches.

The remainder of this section will consider baptismal *practice.* As we will see, the twentieth century witnessed the emergence of an ecumenical consensus about baptism that continues to shape the theology and practice of many Protestant churches today.

For Further Reading

Felton, Gayle Carlton. *This Gift of Water: The Practice and Theology of Baptism Among Methodists in America.* Nashville: Abingdon Press, 1993.

Old, Huges Oliphant. *The Shaping of the Reformed Baptismal Rite in the Sixteenth Century.* Grand Rapids: Eerdmans Publishing, 1992.

Stevenson, Kenneth E. *The Mystery of Baptism in the Anglican Tradition.* Harrisburg, PA: Morehouse Publishing, 1998.

Trigg, Jonathan D. *Baptism in the Theology of Martin Luther.* Leiden: E. J. Brill, 1994.

CHAPTER 3

Baptism as a Process of Initiation

For many Christians the word "baptism" refers to the ritual washing that marks a person's conversion to the Christian faith and incorporation into the Church. But in fact, baptism, if understood only in this narrow sense of a washing, does not do justice to what it means to become a Christian. In the first place, becoming a Christian is not merely a matter of submitting to a washing, but rather it is about being *initiated* into the church, for baptism is inherently related to membership in the church, the body of Christ (cf. 1 Cor. 12:13). Analogously, we think of how a person is "initiated" into other social bodies, e.g., an academic society at a university or a professional society. Thus, it is more accurate to speak in terms of "Christian initiation" rather than "baptism" if we are referring to the reality of becoming Christian. Second, rather than a one-time ritual action (baptism), Christian initiation is a *process* involving distinct phases and rituals that occur over time. It is like the process of becoming a soldier with its initial induction, time of indoctrination and training, and, finally, full incorporation into the ranks of the fighting force. This chapter will argue for the *practice* of an initiatory process, and describe how both ancient and modern Christians alike have made new Christians through a process known as the baptismal catechumenate.

"Immediate" Baptism versus a Process of Initiation

Thinking in terms of a "baptismal process" may be difficult for some churches in Asia, especially independent churches without a long history of baptismal practices and disciplines. Churches may perceive an urgency to baptize converts, perhaps even at the same service as their first confession of faith. Arguments in favor of this immediate initiation are that (1) baptism will be received with more appreciation and joy if administered at the time of initial spiritual fervor; (2) a striking and meaningful testimony is offered to the church if baptism is administered at the height of the convert's enthusiasm; and (3) delaying baptism could result in a convert's being dissuaded from baptism. Further supporting this approach are those accounts in the Acts of the Apostles in which baptism is apparently conferred almost immediately following the recipients' positive response to apostolic preaching or instruction, or in the case of Saul, shortly following an encounter with the Lord Jesus himself. These baptismal accounts include:

1. The Day of Pentecost (2:41)
2. The Samarians (8:12)
3. The Ethiopian eunuch (8:38)
4. Saul of Tarsus (9:18)
5. Gentiles (10:48)
6. Lydia (16:15)
7. The jailer and his family (16:33)
8. Ephesians (19:5)

However, the conferral of baptism immediately after a person's initial response to the gospel is undesirable for biblical, pastoral, and historical reasons. First, while the accounts in Acts 10 and 16 (Gentiles, jailer and family) refer to persons with no biblical/spiritual formation other than a single apostolic sermon, in all other cases, the persons mentioned did have biblical and moral formation in *Judaism*. Those who heard Peter's Pentecost sermon were Jews, "devout men from every nation under heaven" (2:5). The Samarians, descendants of the Northern tribes of Israel, would have been familiar with the Pentateuch. The Ethiopian, who had come to Jerusalem to worship the God of Israel and was reading the prophet Isaiah when discovered by Philip, obviously had some knowledge of and commitment to Judaism. Saul was a Pharisee, and Lydia was probably a Jewish proselyte. The Ephesians, referred to as "disciples" who had received the baptism of John (sans the Holy Spirit), were probably persons cultivating a life based on the Baptizer's teaching, if not Judaism in addition. Because of their background in Judaism, most recipients of apostolic baptism described in Acts already had the biblical knowledge necessary to make sense of the Christian gospel, as well as the ethical formation to live as Christian disciples. We cannot discount the importance of the Jewish background of such persons, especially given the fact that Christianity was, at least initially, a *Jewish* messianic movement, or, put another way, a particular *way* of being Jewish. Thus, these early baptismal accounts from Acts cannot serve as a justification for contemporary churches to baptize persons who have had little or no baptismal preparation. If anything, they point to the need *for* prebaptismal formation! Interestingly, Acts also hints of *post*baptismal formation when it states that members of the early community "devoted themselves to the apostles' teaching and to fellowship, to the breaking of bread and to prayer" (2:42). It would appear that, as far as the primitive church was concerned, newly-baptized persons needed further strengthening through ongoing instruction and liturgical formation.

Second, baptizing those with little or no formation and instruction is highly questionable from a pastoral point of view. If the church baptizes in order to take advantage of a person's purported initial fervor, it baptizes on the basis of *emotions* rather than theological grounds or even on the basis of genuine Christian commitment. We note that believer-baptizing churches normally expect evidence of conversion and commitment to discipleship, realities that may take some time to develop and to exhibit themselves! Indeed, administering baptism too hastily may prevent a "seeker" from adequately considering his/her readiness for leaving behind an old life and adopting a new one; in other words, a too hastily administered baptism could prevent converts from "counting the cost of discipleship" (Luke 14:25-35). Arguably, the likelihood of inadequately prepared individuals lapsing is high. Such a scenario would hardly be edifying to the church, nor would it inspire confidence in the church's pastoral office.

Third, any urge to baptize converts as soon as possible must be tempered by the recognition that a baptismal *process* emerged early on. The narratives from Acts cited above suggest an embryonic baptismal "shape" or structure, consisting of (1) proclamation of the gospel; (2) conversion and faith by those who hear the gospel; (3) water baptism; and (4) communal living that centered on listening to apostolic teaching and living out its ethical implications.[1] Following the apostolic period, the baptismal process received elaboration. A regulative document or "church order" from the late-first or early-second century, the *Didache*, prescribes prebaptismal instruction focusing on the Ten Commandments and Christian morals (chs.1-6), as well as a period of fasting for baptismal candidates and ministers (ch. 7). The baptismal process envisioned in the *Didache* apparently led to the inclusion of the newly baptized in the community's eucharistic celebrations.[2] The *First Apology* of a Roman Christian named Justin (d. 165 CE) speaks of prebaptismal instruction for candidates and also a fast involving both the candidates and the entire Christian community, the lengths of which are not specified.[3] It is clear in Justin's writing that the baptismal process *culminates* in the candidates' reception of their first communion with the whole Christian community (ch. 65). Eventually, during the patristic era, "baptism" develops into a complex set of rites and structures

---

[1] Aidan Kavanagh, *The Shape of Baptism: The Rite of Christian Initiation* (New York: Pueblo, 1978), 20-23.

[2] The *Didache* 9.5 (late-first or early-second cent.).

[3] Justin the Martyr, *First Apology* 61 (ca. 155).

collectively known as the "catechumenate,"[4] and Christians in the twentieth century revived the catechumenal process in order to meet the needs and challenges of their own day.

The Rites of Passage

We cannot appropriate the meaning and understand the significance of the baptismal catechumenate without considering both its ancient roots and its anthropological role as a rite of passage. Although it may seem strange to discuss anthropology in a book on liturgical practice, such a discussion will be beneficial in two ways: first, by helping us to appreciate the *humanness* of baptism. The church certainly did not invent the rites of passage or initiation; the need to initiate people into new social statuses or new social groups is something that Christianity shares in common with the rest of humanity. Furthermore, we do see some similarities between early Christian initiation and initiatory practices in the surrounding culture, e.g., the administration of a washing, the withholding of certain teachings until candidates are fully initiated, etc. An awareness of these similarities can foster a humility that is beneficial for mission and evangelism. This is not to suggest, however, that Christian initiation, as a rite of passage, was simply borrowed from other ancient religions and is therefore merely a cheap "knock off." The eminent historian of religion, Mircea Eliade, devoted an entire section in his *Rites and Symbols of Initiation* to arguing for the distinctiveness of Christian initiation as compared to the initiatory processes of the ancient mystery religions.[5] Indeed, Christian initiation does not seek to accomplish the same things as the initiatory rites of other ancient religions. It is not merely the ritualization of physical or social "maturity," entrance into a secret society, or the consecration of those persons who are especially

---

[4] From the Greek "*katecheo*" which means to "echo in the ear." Thus catechumens or "hearers of the word" were those "trainees" who attended the service of the Word at the Sunday Eucharist and special teaching sessions as part of their instruction in the Christian faith.

[5] Mircea Eliade, *Rites and Symbols of Initiation: The Mysteries of Birth and Rebirth*, tr. Willard R. Trask (Woodstock, CT: Spring Publications, 1995), 115-21.

spiritual or religiously dedicated. Rather, it ritualizes *repentance* (not maturity); it initiates into a *public* community (not an exclusive one); and it is for all who respond to the gospel (not only for those with special religious vocations). Insofar as it is bound up with the Christian gospel, Christian initiation is unique and irreducible.

Second, anthropological studies of initiation can enable us to appreciate the *symbolism* and symbolic nature of initiatory rites. Protestant Christianity, unfortunately, has lost touch with the symbolic dimension of the Christian faith, preferring instead to rely on propositional logic, rational proofs, and legalistic formulas. It therefore lacks an appreciation for symbols, rituals, and art, those things that are necessary for expressing the inexpressible. This is ironic given the inherently symbolic nature of many scriptural texts and indeed of Christ himself who is the visible icon of the Father (Col. 1:15). Anthropological studies of initiation focus on explicating initiatory symbols and their meaning, and, in considering such studies, we come to appreciate the symbolic dimension of Christian baptism, which is not simply a bath, but rather a symbolic washing that offers participation in something greater than bodily cleansing. Arguably, anthropology can deepen our understanding of Christian initiation by helping us to pass from an exclusively right-brain understanding to a more rounded, holistic left-brained understanding. While anthropological studies might point to similar symbolic motifs, e.g., "death and resurrection," I would stress that Christian initiatory symbols do not necessary point in the same *direction* as the initiatory symbols of other religions. The Christian "dies" in baptism not to be reborn as a "pure" member of a closed, righteous community, but to become one who identifies with society's marginalized persons. Reflecting on the anthropological significance of humanity's rites of passage, especially initiation, will help us to discover the uniqueness of Christian initiation.

As we noted above, baptism as it emerged in the primitive church was not so much a single ritual action, but a *process*. Concerning any process, we might ask: what does it seek to accomplish? What is its purpose? In their baptismal services, ancient churches sought to ritualize a change from one state of mind to another, that is, to actualize the repentance of those who heard and accepted the gospel.[6] In this case "repentance" does not mean merely feeling sorry for sins and misdeeds, but adopting an entirely new mindset or perspective on life, as is implied by the Greek word *metanoia*.[7] Thus, baptism into Christ means changing from one kind of person to another, forsaking one set of allegiances and adopting another set, and leaving behind one faith community and being united with another. Essentially, baptism is about making a significant life *transition*.

Throughout history, human societies developed ritual structures for people to navigate through the difficult life transitions associated with birth, illness, puberty, and death (mourning). Cultural anthropologists refer to the complex of rites and practices associated with these transitions as "rites of passage," which typically involve three distinct phases:

1. **Separation.** A person is identified by the community as someone undergoing a life transition and is grouped with others going through that same transition.
2. **Transition.** The initiates receive intentional training in the ways and mores associated with the new status (e.g., adulthood).
3. **Incorporation.** The transitional stage completed, those entering the new life stage (aka "neophytes") are reintroduced into the society as full-fledged members of the community with all the rights and privileges of that community.

A pioneer in the study of rites of passage was the early-twentieth century anthropologist Arnold Van Gennep (1873-1957), who noted that each of the three phases can itself involve rites for separation, transition, and incorporation, and the purpose of these rites is to lessen harm to the individuals and society (e.g., due to anxiety, sense

---

[6] See Acts 2:38 and Mark 1:15 "The kingdom of God has come near. Repent and believe the good news!"

[7] Under "3340. Metanoeó," Biblos.com, http://biblehub.com/greek/3340.htm [accessed 31 December 2013].

of loss, etc.).[8] He likens the passage from one status to another (or one group to another) to a person's making a journey from one world to another, which involves movement through "neutral territory."[9] In initiation, the period of the novitiate has both negative and positive aspects. The negative ones usually take the form of prohibitions and restrictions (taboos) and are intended to mentally and physically weaken the novice so that he/she forgets about the past life.[10] The positive ones take the form of instruction in social laws and customs, participation in religious ceremonies, and recitations of religious stories.[11] Van Gennep interprets rites of passage in terms of the death and resurrection metaphor, with the novice being put to death through harsh treatment (e.g., beatings, seclusion, intoxication), in order that he/she might be resurrected and taught how to live in accordance with the mores of the new social position toward which he/she is journeying. While Van Gennep's analysis of the ancient (Roman) Christian catechumenate in terms of this model is insightful,[12] modern liturgical scholars might question the accuracy of some of his descriptions, and would caution us to avoid generalizing about ancient Christian initiation based solely on Van Gennep's analysis of initiation in the *Roman* church.

The Roumanian historian, Mircea Eliade (1907-86), drew attention to the ordeals of the transitional phase and how these rites reactualized a community's sacred story. By ordeals he means things like sleep deprivation, fasting, the knocking out of teeth, and circumcision.[13] These all signify a ritual death that is followed by a resurrection or new birth.[14] The initiatory death provides a clean slate on which is written the faith community's sacred history, and the

---

[8] Arnold Van Gennep, *The Rites of Passage*, tr. Monika B. Vizedom and Gabrielle L. Caffee (Chicago: University Press, 1960), 11-13.

[9] Van Gennep, *Rites of Passage*, 15-19.

[10] Van Gennep, *Rites of Passage*, 8-9, 75.

[11] Van Gennep, *Rites of Passage*, 75.

[12] Van Gennep, *Rites of Passage*, 93-96.

[13] Eliade, *Rites and Symbols of Initiation*, 13.

[14] Eliade, *Rites and Symbols of Initiation*, xii.

result is the formation of a new person. Because the rites of initiation have been received from the ancient ancestors from time immemorial, they reactualize the community's sacred story, making it present for the contemporary community, and thus revitalizing it.[15] Christian liturgists would see a similarity between Eliade's reactualization and the technical liturgical term *anamnesis* (to remember, re-present) which is especially important for eucharistic theology.

The British anthropologist Victor Turner (1920-83) devoted much of his work to describing and interpreting the transitional or "liminal"[16] phase of the rites of passage. During this phase, he says, the initiate is "neither here nor there [but] betwixt-and-between all fixed points of classification, [and] passes through a symbolic domain that has few or none of the attributes of his past or coming states."[17] The initiate, having been stripped of all attributes of his [sic] previous social position, is set apart from the rest of society and secluded in a lodge or camp where he is reduced to an equal status with his fellow initiates. What then emerges is a state of *communitas* where the normal social distinctions are temporarily suspended and egalitarian cooperation is emphasized.[18] Within this state the initiates submit to the guidance and teaching of various "elders."[19] The liminal state with its *communitas* offers the initiates the opportunity to contemplate the issues facing humanity and how predecessors in the community have sought to deal with those questions.[20] *Communitas* is indispensible to society because it allows people to be fully together with one another, rather than segregated into separate social "cells." Traditionally in "revivalistic religions" (especially in Protestantism), *communitas* has restored the social bond of adherents to that which

[15] Eliade, *Rites and Symbols of Initiation*, 4.

[16] Latin, *limen*, "threshold."

[17] Victor Turner, "Passages, Margins and Poverty: Religious Symbols of *Communitas*," *Worship* 46:7 (1972), 393.

[18] Turner, "Passages, Margins and Poverty," 398.

[19] Victor Turner, *The Ritual Process: Structure and Anti-Structure* (New Brunswick, NJ: Aldine Transaction, 2011), 96.

[20] Turner, "Passages, Margins and Poverty," 402.

was experienced when the movement first came into existence. The value of *communitas*, furthermore, is that when people are removed from their normal social structure into liminal situations, they return to the normal social structures and situations revitalized – and presumably able to revitalize those structures and situations.[21] Although no society can function without this dynamic, Turner warns that if *communitas* is exaggerated in religious or political movements, there can be abuses such as "despotism, over-bureaucratization or other modes of structural rigidification."[22] Ultimately, *communitas* will require structure if the physical and material needs of a movement are to be met – but any maximization of structure will lead to a longing for *communitas*.

The Baptismal Process in the Early Church

The early church was aware of the difficulties involved in conversion and the resulting needs of those who desired to become Christians. So it developed a process for new converts to make the transition from paganism to Christianity. This rite of passage became known as the "catechumenate." Although the catechumenate in its full embodiment eventually disappeared from the ancient church, it would eventually be resurrected by twentieth-century Christians, who drew inspiration from ancient catechumenal patterns and practices. What follows is a summary of the catechumenal process according to three ancient Christian sources.

The *Apostolic Tradition of Hippolytus*, which contains material dating from as early as the year 217 CE,[23] describes a baptismal process that could last for up to three years (ch. 17). Persons ("seekers") are admitted to the catechumenate following an examination of their

---

[21] Turner, *Ritual Process*, 129.

[22] Turner, *Ritual Process*, 129.

[23] Many scholars today would *not* attribute authorship of this document to the Roman presbyter Hippolytus, nor would they hold that all of the material is necessarily Roman or from the early-third century. See Paul F. Bradshaw, Maxwell E. Johnson, and L. Edward Phillips, *The Apostolic Tradition: A Commentary*, Hermeneia Commentary Series (Minneapolis: Fortress, 2002).

motives and conduct.[24] The catechumens are permitted to participate in the service of the Word at the Sunday liturgy, but are separated from the assembly in order to pray by themselves (ch. 18) and are forbidden to share in the kiss of peace – obvious signs that they are not considered full-fledged Christians. Following the prayers, the teacher lays hands on the catechumens, prays for them, and then dismisses them. Based on their moral conduct and commitment to performing Christian good works, those deemed worthy are later *selected* to receive baptism (ch. 20). These persons experience daily exorcisms, that is, special prayers for the expulsion of evil, and those deemed impure, i.e., incapable of hearing the gospel, are rejected. A period of immediate baptismal preparation begins with the candidates bathing themselves on the Thursday prior to the Sunday designated for baptism (presumably to prevent the baptismal font from being fouled!). They fast on the following Friday and on Saturday they undergo a number of rites at the hand of the bishop: exorcism, exsufflation (blowing in the face of the candidate to symbolize the Holy Spirit), and marking with the sign of the cross on the forehead, ears, and nose.[25] That night is spent in a vigil consisting of biblical readings and commentary by the teachers. The rites of initiation (ch. 21) take place early the next morning ("when the cock crows"). The candidates are baptized nude, beginning with children followed by the men and finally the women. After renouncing Satan, a candidate is anointed with the oil of exorcism and then descends into the font. Baptism is administered by triple immersion, i.e., the candidate is dunked into the water after each affirmative response to three creedal questions. The candidate emerges from the water and receives a second anointing with the "oil of thanksgiving." After all have been baptized, the candidates clothe themselves and are

[24] *The Apostolic Tradition Ascribed to Hippolytus of Rome* 15 (ca. 217).

[25] The document does not say whether these are the first two days of the Paschal Triduum (Maundy Thursday and Good Friday), so we should not conclude that the *Apostolic Tradition* is describing an *Easter* baptism, as some have been tempted to do in the past.

escorted into the church where the bishop says the following prayer while laying hands on each of the newly baptized:

> Lord God, you have made them worthy to receive remission of sins through the laver of regeneration of the Holy Spirit: send upon them your grace, that they may serve you according to your will, for to you is glory, to Father and Son with the Holy Spirit in the holy Church, both now and to the ages of ages. Amen.[26]

The bishop then anoints the newly baptized on the head while saying "I anoint you with holy oil in God the Father Almighty and Christ Jesus and the Holy Spirit."[27] Following a signing on the forehead (with the cross, presumably), the bishop and the newly baptized greet each other with a kiss. From this point, the new Christians are permitted to pray and exchange the peace with the rest of the liturgical assembly. Later in the service, the newly baptized receive their first communion as well as a cup of milk and honey, signifying entrance into the promised land.

The baptismal process outlined in the *Apostolic Tradition* is echoed in the diary entries of a fourth-century Spanish nun known as Egeria, who describes the final baptismal preparation period observed by the ancient church in Jerusalem.[28] At the beginning of an eight-week long Lent, catechumens who seek baptism formally present themselves to church officials who examine their morals and conduct with the help of the catechumens' spiritual mentors ("mothers and fathers"). Similar to the *Apostolic Tradition*, only those deemed spiritually and morally fit are permitted to enter the final phase of initiation (ch. 45). Throughout this period, those chosen for baptism, the baptismal "elect,"[29] undergo regular exorcisms and receive instruction from the bishop. The exclusionary practices of

[26] *Apostolic Tradition* 21 (translation from DBL, 8).

[27] *Apostolic Tradition* 21 (translation from DBL, 8).

[28] *Egeria's Travels* 45-47.

[29] Cyril of Jerusalem (313-386 CE) referred to these persons as the *photizomenoi* or "ones to be enlightened."

the *Apostolic Tradition* are echoed in the prohibition against other catechumens attending these instruction sessions devoted to the Bible and core teachings, especially the doctrine of the resurrection. During the fifth week of Lent, the creed is orally given to the baptismal elect and, after committing it to memory, they repeat it back to the bishop verbatim during the week before Easter ("Great Week"). Baptism itself takes place at the Easter (Paschal) Vigil where the newly baptized receive their first communion (ch. 38). The theology of baptism is not explained to them until after their baptism, that is, during the week after Easter. Catechumens are likewise excluded from hearing this explanation (ch. 46).

Finally, Bishop Augustine of Hippo (354-430 CE), in his various writings, alluded to a baptismal catechumenate with similarities to those described by the *Apostolic Tradition* and Egeria. Like the *Apostolic Tradition*, Augustine mentions rites for the making of a catechumen, which in the North African Church included a lengthy address on the Bible and the nature of the Christian faith, after which candidates were asked if they believed what had just been expounded. Those who answer affirmatively were signed on the forehead with the cross, a gesture suggestive of ownership. During the Eucharist, the catechumens received salt to signify sanctification. Exorcism, in the form of exsufflation, and the laying on of hands also appear to be part of the rites for making a catechumen.[30] Like the *Apostolic Tradition* and Egeria, Augustine also describes a final preparation period for baptism, which likely involved scrutinies (severe questions about morals and conduct), exorcisms, and vigils.[31] In addition to the giving of the creed, Augustine's church also delivered the Lord's Prayer to the baptismal candidates during Lent, although it was only the creed that had to be repeated back (returned) to church officials, apparently because it was rarely used in the liturgical services of North Africa at that time.[32] On Maundy Thursday, the candidates

[30] Augustine, *De Catechizandis Rudibus* 20; *De Peccatorum Meritis et Remissione* 2.26.42.

[31] Augustine, *De Fide et Operibus* 6.9.

[32] Augustine, *Sermon* 58.

had their feet washed, not to portray the action in John 13, but because they were simply dirty![33] The baptismal service, celebrated at the Easter Vigil, included the returning of the creed, prebaptismal questioning (renouncing the devil and turning to God), and then later a postbaptismal anointing, laying on of hands, and invocation of the seven-fold Spirit.[34] In a particularly evocative passage, Augustine uses culinary images to describe the process of baptism:

> Remember, you did not exist, and you were created: you were carried to the Lord's threshing floor . . . when you were set aside as catechumens you were stored in his barn. You gave in your names: you began to be ground with fasting and exorcism. After that you came to water, were moistened and made one. You were cooked then, when the ardour of the Holy Spirit came near, and now have been made the Lord's bread.[35]

These ancient sources suggest an initiatory structure similar to the pattern described by anthropological studies of the rites of passage. Essentially, the rituals for the making of a catechumen (*Apostolic Tradition*, Augustine) *separate* converts from the world and incorporate them into the "order" of catechumens. The period of the catechumenate itself serves as the *transitional* phase with its emphasis on instruction and conferral of the creed (Egeria, Augustine) and the Lord's Prayer (Augustine) that symbolize the initiate's reception of the new community's faith and mores. The liminal, "neither this nor that" quality of the catechumenal phase is evident in the practice of allowing initiates to attend the Sunday liturgy of the community, but not permitting their full participation in it.[36] *Incorporation* into the new community at baptism is ritualized through the following:

---

[33] Augustine, *Epistle* 54.7.

[34] Augustine, *Sermon* 324; *Miscellania Agostiniana* 1.490.

[35] Augustine, *Miscellanea Agostiniana* 2.6-19.

[36] The ambiguity of this liminal period is also attested to by the ancient understanding that catechumens who died as martyrs could be given a full Christian burial, since they were "baptized in their blood."

prebaptismal anointing, suggestive of the attainment of a new status or way of being (cf. 1 Sam. 16:13); the giving of salt (= purification); the postbaptismal anointing and handlaying by the bishop (*Apostolic Tradition*, Augustine), the latter also suggestive of new status (cf. 1 Tim. 4:14); and the first communion of the newly baptized with the whole community (*Apostolic Tradition*, Egeria). Some aspects of the catechumenate could be given dual interpretations: the enrollment for baptism could be seen as both an *incorporation* into a new order (the elect), as well as a *separation* from the rest of the catechumens; the baptismal washing could be interpreted as either an act of separation – a cleansing from a past life – or as an act of incorporation since it carries overtones of new birth.

In line with Van Gennep's observations, ancient Christian initiation had both positive and negative aspects. The latter is seen in the segregation of the initiates from the rest of the church, prohibitions against receiving communion until after baptism, fasting (*Apostolic Tradition*, Egeria), vigils (*Apostolic Tradition*) and the renunciation of Satan. The exorcisms and scrutinies – the intense examination of conduct – serve as "ordeals" meant to "weaken" the evil in candidates and draw them away from their former lives (i.e., served as rites of separation).[37] Yet, if all of these negative actions ritualized the initiate's "death," baptism in the nude followed by an anointing (reminiscent of actions done to newborns), and the giving of a cup of milk and honey to the newly baptized (traditionally given to newborns) suggest a *rebirth*.

Thus, we can see that the ancient catechumenate shares a similar structure, distinction of rites, and the positive-negative polarity found in the rites of passage of all human societies. But this does not mean that the ancient catechumenate is reducible to one among many similar sociological phenomena. After all, there is something deeply spiritual about it. First, the ancient catechumenal process is punctuated with *prayer*, which, in a broader sense, included

[37] In Augustine's church, the period of final preparation for baptism may have included *public* exorcistic rites during which the initiates stood naked on goat skins! See Augustine, Sermon 216.

the various exorcisms. To pray for a catechumen and request the expulsion of evil by invoking the divine name is to acknowledge that the initiatory process is a divine work, not merely a human one. It is more than a person's works-righteous, self-justifying approach to God, but rather God's work of grace for that person. Second, the ancient initiatory process included *spiritual discernment.* While the individuals may have "decided" to become catechumens, much more was involved than personal choices and decisions. Ultimately, they were *permitted* to become catechumens after examination and were later *chosen* to receive baptism. Making baptism a matter of communal discernment could help the contemporary church overcome the effects of individualism, especially the privatization of the Christian faith. Finally, the ancient catechumenate was *holistic* in that its rites and gestures were directed to the human body, and it employed natural elements (salt, water, oil), and the reckoning of time. The catechumenal process thereby affirmed the goodness of God's creation. If that aspect were to be recovered in Christian initiation today, the church would go a long way toward shaping Christians who are responsible stewards of God's creation. These factors alone suggest that we seriously consider adopting the catechumenate as *the* way of making and forming adult Christians in our churches.

The Catechumenal Process Today

Late in the twentieth century, the baptismal catechumenate experienced a revival. In response to the need to baptize numerous adult converts in Africa, the Roman Catholic Church produced its *Rite of Christian Initiation of Adults* (RCIA).[38] Yet RCIA has proven useful elsewhere in the world, as in the Roman Catholic Archdiocese of Singapore, where 962 converts were baptized at Easter Vigil services in 2013.[39] In returning to an ancient model that makes *adult* conversion and baptism the initiatory norm, RCIA is nothing short

[38] *Rite of Christian Initiation of Adults* in *The Rites of the Catholic Church* (New York: Pueblo, 1983), IA, 13-181.

[39] Darren Boon, "1,000 to Join Church this Easter," *Catholic News*, March 10, 2013.

of revolutionary. Undoubtedly influenced by RCIA, North American Protestants including Lutherans, Episcopalians, and Methodists developed their own catechumenal rites (see the conclusion of this chapter for bibliographical references).

Protestant catechumenal rites share four features in common. First, like ancient catechumenal rites, they are *holistic* in their approach in that they seek to incorporate baptismal candidates into the life of the church through words and actions, sights and sounds, and reflection and social action. Second, Protestant rites are *congregational* in that the whole church is involved in the welcome, formation, baptism, and integration of candidates into the life of the church. Besides pastors, the catechumenal process recognizes the need for sponsors (mentors), catechists (teachers) and others to accompany candidates on their baptismal journey. Third, Protestant catechumenates are *liturgical*, that is, focused on the Sunday liturgy as the venue for prayer and other rites that support the catechumens. Fourth, Protestant catechumenal rites are *missional* in that their goal is the fulfillment of the great commission rather than any narrow liturgical goal. By involving the entire congregation and its public worship, the catechumenate puts the making of disciples at the heart of congregational life; by drawing together worship, pastoral care, and mission, it integrates aspects of congregational life that might otherwise be disconnected and remote from the experience of many Christians. By doing these things, the catechumenate offers a model of Christian formation with strong advantages over traditional models of initiation that focus on the impartation of cognitive knowledge and make little mention of the candidates to the church before the actual day of their baptism. Thus, the adoption of the baptismal catechumenate offers the hope of renewal not only to baptismal candidates, but also to the whole Christian community.

Protestant catechumenal processes today involve four stages punctuated by four public liturgies:

Stage 1: Inquiry. Persons with little or no background in the church ("seekers") begin to show an interest in the Christian faith because a family member, friend, or other person intentionally shared the gospel or perhaps because of the seeker's own growing interest in spirituality. Inquirers may have questions such as Who is God? What is salvation? How do Christians pray? How would being a Christian help me to be spiritual? During this time of initial encounter, the Christian community needs to be open to such questions even as it helps inquirers to reflect on their readiness to make the changes and commitments necessary for being Christian disciples.

Inquirers will meet regularly for Bible study and discussion with teachers and sponsors. During such meetings inquirers share their faith stories and reflect on how the biblical narratives relate to their personal journeys. Each inquirer is assigned a sponsor who guides the inquirer through the baptismal process, answers questions, models the Christian life, and prays with the inquirer. In a sense, the sponsor becomes a spiritual mentor for the inquirer. Teachers share information, answer questions and help inquirers to connect Bible and doctrine with their personal spirituality. Through study, personal sharing, and one-on-one encounters, this period assists inquirers (and the church community) to discern whether they will continue on the journey that leads to baptism and discipleship.

Rite 1: Welcome to the Catechumenate. After a period during which the inquirer becomes familiar with the church and its faith, he or she may decide to make a more formal and public commitment to the church, specifically, by requesting baptism. At this point, the inquirer enters the catechumenate through a rite known as "Welcome to the Catechumenate" or "Admission of Catechumens," which corresponds to the ancient rites for the "making of a catechumen" (*Apostolic Tradition* 15, 16, Augustine). Because the catechumenate stresses the corporate nature of the church and baptism, the Welcome/Admission rite is celebrated at any Sunday liturgy during the year. During the gathering, either after the opening hymn or after the collect (prayer of the day),[40] the inquirers are formally presented to

[40] The rite may even take place after the sermon. See Office of Evangelism Ministries, The Episcopal Church, *The Catechumenal Process: Adult Initiation and Formation for Christian Life and Ministry* (New York: The Church Hymnal Corporation, 1990), 242.

the worship assembly, each being introduced by name. Following that the minister will ask two questions of the inquirers: What do you ask of God's church? and What do you seek from God's Word? In the first instance the inquirers respond "To hear the Word of God with you," and in the second "Faith and fullness of life." Then follow questions concerning the commitment of the inquirers to hearing the Word faithfully, as well as questions to the sponsors and the assembly about their intention to support the inquirers and (in the case of the assembly) their sponsors. The outward verbalizing of commitments helps to make the transition into the catechumenate a concrete reality for the inquirers, even as it names a goal toward which they are to strive. Likewise, the verbalizing of the assembly's commitment to catechumens and sponsors concretizes its intended course of action.

Following the gospel and sermon the catechumens have the sign of the cross marked on their foreheads as a symbol of God's love and their commitment to following Christ. In some cases, the sign of the cross may be made over various body parts to symbolize different aspects of Christian faith and discipleship, e.g., "Receive the + cross on your ears, that you may hear the gospel of Christ, the Word of life."[41] The catechumens are each presented with a Bible and a special prayer of blessing may be prayed over them – gestures of incorporation. With the public celebration of these rites at the Sunday liturgy, the catechumens not only receive the support of the assembly, but also come to realize that hearing the Word of God and reflecting on its meaning is communal in nature, rather than merely individual.

In some cases, a catechumen may need or desire to renounce a former way of worship whose practices are incompatible with Christianity, e.g., those involving idolatry, magic, or the occult. An appropriately worded statement may be read by the catechumen before or after the question "What do you seek?" to express this renunciation. Care must be taken that such a statement does not

[41] *Welcome to Christ: Lutheran Rites for the Catechumenate* (Minneapolis: Augsburg Fortress, 1997), 11.

appear to attack other religions, especially in social and political contexts where religious harmony is highly valued.

Stage 2: The Catechumenate. With the twin goal of fostering conversion and forming a Christian character in the catechumens, this phase is devoted to study, good works (social action), and worship, and thus serves as a transitional period between the time of inquiry and the attainment of full membership in the church. Catechumens meet regularly with teachers, sponsors, and pastors to discuss the lectionary readings and sermons and to learn about the church's history and its response to social problems. In many churches, catechumenal instruction will focus on the catechisms (e.g., Luther's *Small Catechism* and the Reformed *Heidelberg Catechism*), which explore the meaning of the Ten Commandments, Lord's Prayer, and creed by means of a question and answer format. Because these three "symbols of the faith" are components of the Sunday liturgy, their presentation enables the catechumens to link their personal faith with the church's faith and worship.[42] It is appropriate that all instructional sessions with the catechumens conclude with prayer by the teacher who might lays hands on each candidate, if that gesture is culturally appropriate.[43] Ideally, catechumens gain experience in Christian charity by visiting nursing homes and prisons and helping with social ministries, such as food pantries and soup kitchens. Catechumens are in regular attendance at the Sunday liturgy, learning how to participate in its rituals and appreciate its symbols. Following the ancient custom, most churches do not permit catechumens to receive communion. Through their participation in public worship and with individual guidance from teachers and sponsors, catechumens learn how to shape their personal prayer lives.

The catechumenal phase is characterized by two central qualities, the first being *flexibility*. Throughout this time, teachers, sponsors, pastors, and the catechumens themselves are discerning whether the

---

[42] For a fine discussion of the role of the catechisms in catechumenal instruction, see Simon Chan, *Liturgical Theology: The Church as Worshipping Community* (Downer's Grove: IVP Academic, 2006), 108-15.

[43] See *The Catechumenal Process*, 245.

catechumens are growing in faith and commitment, and consequently whether they are ready to take the next step of *publically* declaring a desire for baptism. Since some catechumens may not be ready to do so, and some may *never* be ready, the catechumenate is "open-ended" by allowing the deferment of baptism or withdrawal from the process entirely – a decision that is treated with respect. Because of the need for flexibility, most Protestant resources do not specify a length of time for the catechumenate, preferring instead to follow the *Apostolic Tradition* by making spiritual readiness, rather than time, the deciding factor in advancement to the next stage.

Second, the catechumenal phase is characterized by a *liminality* that has implications for both the catechumens and the whole Christian community. Sharing an identity as persons who are neither worldlings nor full Christians, the catechumens form an interpersonal bond whereby they recognize each other as equals in the Lord Jesus Christ (cf. Gal. 3:26-28). This experience of *communitas* has the potential for flavoring the whole Christian community, such that established Christians easily accept the "new recruits" as equals and integrate them into the life of the church. The liminality of the catechumenate also reawakens a sense of the church's existence "betwixt and between" the first and final comings of the Lord Jesus Christ – in other words, that it is a pilgrim people making its way to the final consummation of the redemptive reign of God, as opposed to being a community tied to this world and its sinful ways and structures. Thus, the catechumenate can spiritually renew the whole Christian community.

Rite 2: Enrollment for Baptism. This rite serves as an official statement of intentions by the baptismal candidates, and marks the beginning of their final and most intensive preparation for baptism. With "death and resurrection" (Rom. 6) as the central baptismal paradigm, many churches baptize adult catechumens at the Easter Vigil and officially enroll them for baptism at the beginning of Lent following practices mentioned by Egeria (*Travels* 45) and Augustine (*Sermon* 132.1). If baptism is to take place at the Epiphany or the

Baptism of our Lord, the enrollment takes place on the First Sunday in Advent.

The enrollment rite is relatively simple and may be celebrated between the sermon and creed (or response hymn and creed). After the candidates are introduced, questions of intention are put to candidates, sponsors, and the assembly. In some churches, sponsors and teachers are questioned about the Christian conduct of the catechumens.[44] The names of the candidates are read out and then written in a special book, either by the candidates themselves or by the sponsors. Finally, the presiding minister offers a special blessing prayer for the candidates. It is also possible for the date of baptism to be announced during the enrollment rite.

Stage 3: Candidacy for Baptism. While ancient churches used this final preparation period to "root out" residual evil in candidates through public examinations ("scrutinies") and exorcisms, modern churches use this time for the "examination of conscience."[45] Gathered in groups, the candidates reflect on areas of life still burdened by sin – weaknesses, addictions, unhealthy allegiances – and pray for God's continued guidance and strengthening in the conversion process. At the same time, the candidates give thanks for their strengths and areas of growth.

Public rites are celebrated during the final three Sundays in Lent (or Advent). On the Third Sunday, candidates might receive a copy of the creed or the catechism, in imitation of the ancient rite of handing over the creed (*traditio symboli*). This action may be followed by the personal testimony of the candidates.[46] Somewhat in imitation of ancient exorcistic rites, the Fourth Sunday in Lent may

---

[44] See *The Catechumenal Process*, 246.

[45] See Daniel T. Benedict, Jr., *Welcome to the Waters: Baptism and Our Ministry of Welcoming Seekers and Making Disciples* (Nashville: Discipleship Resources, 2000), 107.

[46] Some churches provide alternative materials for the celebration of these candidacy rites at other times during the liturgical year. See *Welcome to Christ*, 26.

include prayer for the overcoming of evil.[47] On the Fifth Sunday, a worship book may be presented to the candidates as a sign of their commitment to corporate worship and special intercessory prayers may be made for the candidates. The Lord's Prayer may be "given" to the candidates as a sign of their vocation to corporate prayer. For each of these services, the candidates and their sponsors are invited to gather before the assembly. During the special intercessory petitions on the Fifth Sunday, it is appropriate for sponsors to lay hands on the shoulders of the candidates who may kneel or simply bow their heads. All the candidacy rites conclude with the presiding minister offering a blessing for the candidates. Although some churches provide materials appropriate for all three lectionary years, others suggest using the lectionary readings for year A whenever there are adult baptismal candidates, since these readings have traditionally been understood as containing images for baptism.[48]

Rite 3: Baptism (The Rites of Christian Initiation). Baptism marks the culmination of the catechumenal process and formal incorporation into the church. The candidates are now sacramentally joined to Christ in his death and resurrection (cf. Rom. 6) and become fellow members of the body of Christ. Because conversion itself is a process of dying to the old and becoming a new person in Christ, the baptism of adult candidates most appropriately takes place at the Great Vigil of Easter, although baptism on other great liturgical festivals is appropriate and meaningful. The advantage of "Paschal" (Easter) baptism is that the images of the Vigil readings express the meaning of baptism as: re-creation (Gen. 1-2), a cleansing flood (Gen. 7-8), a response to God's call (Gen. 22), deliverance

[47] The prayer in *Welcome to Christ* ("Fourth Sunday in Lent") is "Lord God, you promised that the ancient evil of the serpent would be vanquished on the cross of your Son. We ask you: Crush the power of the devil. Protect your people from the evils of the world. Preserve us from sin and error, that with saints and angels we may live in the joy of your goodness and truth, through Jesus Christ our Lord" (28). It is also possible to include such petitions within the intercessions for the day, as in *The Catechumenal Process* (249).

[48] *The Catechumenal Process*, 250.

from death (Ex. 15), the water of life (Is. 55), reception of the life-giving Spirit (Ezek. 37), and a rescue from a fiery ordeal (Dan. 3). It is therefore desirable to celebrate baptism immediately following the Old Testament readings in the four-fold Vigil structure (e.g., Service of Light, Service of Readings, Baptism, Service of Word and Meal), although celebrating baptism after the gospel and sermon is now considered the normal position.[49] The liturgy of the Lord's Supper at the Vigil enables the newly baptized to experience the full meaning of initiation, namely, a participation in the risen Lord and fellowship with his people. (A detailed consideration of the baptismal liturgy will follow in a subsequent chapter.)

Stage 4: Baptismal Living. As noted earlier in this chapter, some ancient churches did not explain the meaning of the sacraments (baptism, Lord's Supper) to the newly baptized during their early baptismal formation. This withholding of information may have been a way of heightening the impact of the baptismal process by creating an aura of secrecy, or perhaps it represents a pedagogical assumption that the explanation of highly symbolic sacramental rites is best suited for those who have first experienced them. Accordingly, there developed in some ancient churches a postbaptismal period of *mystagogy* ("study of the mysteries") for reflection on the meaning of the sacraments (Egeria, *Travels* 47). The early church has left us examples of mystagogical sermons (lectures), including those of Cyril of Jerusalem and Ambrose of Milan.[50]

Modern churches with a baptismal catechumenate see the importance of continued formation after baptism and so recognize a time of "baptismal living" dedicated to reflection on the practical implications of baptism. This essentially transitional period is particularly crucial because it demonstrates that baptism is not so much a graduation from the catechumenate as entrance into a new phase of Christian living. It is at this point that discipleship comes into view: the newly baptized are invited and challenged to think

[49] See "Resurrection of Our Lord: Vigil of Easter," ELW, 652.

[50] See DBL, 30-33, 181-83.

about how they will live out their baptism as faithful members of the priestly people of God. It is fitting when this period coincides with the Fifty Days of Easter, since lectionary readings from Acts highlight the work and faith of the earliest disciples. If baptism is conferred on the feast of the Baptism of our Lord, the period of "baptismal living" ("mystagogy") occurs during the time after Epiphany and concludes on the Transfiguration (Sunday before Ash Wednesday). Teachers, sponsors and the newly baptized meet for discussions that consider both the nature of the sacraments and how the newly baptized will use their gifts for ministry both in the church and in daily life.

Rite 4: Affirmation of the Vocation of Christians in the World. At the conclusion of this time of postbaptismal reflection, a rite of "Affirmation of Vocation of the Baptized in the World" may be celebrated to mark the transition into intentional baptismal living (discipleship).[51] The service is set within that part of the Sunday liturgy most closely related to mission and service in the world, namely, the "Sending." After the post-communion prayer, the presider addresses the newly baptized, encouraging them to carry out their vocations ("callings") in the world, having been made members of the priesthood in Christ through baptism. A brief description of each person's areas of service in the church and world is read to the assembly, and each is questioned about their commitment to patterning their whole life after Christ. After a short prayer, the "affirmers" are charged to go into the world to love and serve God. The benediction and dismissal follow. Because participation in the life of the church and service through its ministries is how baptism is lived out, catechumenal leaders will strive to integrate the newly baptized into existing church groups and ministries, e.g., Christian education, choir, young adults, etc.

The Baptismal Process for Children and Parents

This chapter has argued for recognizing and practicing baptism as a process, as opposed to a single event. Although the discussion so far

[51] *Welcome to Christ,* 59-61.

has only made reference to the baptism of adults, it is also possible to think in terms of a baptismal process for children.

Currently, the Christian initiation of infants and children involves a series of un-integrated times and rites, some of which are lacking in baptismal associations. Typically, a few months after birth, a child will be baptized at a Sunday service or other time. Often the choice of day depends on the availability of grandparents and other relatives. In the years following the baptism, the child might be sent to the church's Sunday School in fulfillment of parental promises, but in reality little about the Sunday School curriculum relates to baptism. Because many Protestants perceive a need for the church to minister to adolescents, a young person of approximately age 14, the age of puberty, will be sent to confirmation classes. These classes culminate with the *rite* of confirmation, which for many Protestants, amounts to first reception of Holy Communion and thus "joining church." This overall pattern involves distinct rites of passage, one for ritualizing birth and the other for puberty, and lacking is a sense of an organic process that grows out of baptism, the foundational rite of Christian initiation.

Arguably, however, the above scenario of infant baptism followed by adolescent confirmation can be reframed and reconfigured as a baptismal process, one that draws together both of these psycho-social experiences. Rather than a quick session on the logistics of baptizing an infant, a pastor could offer prebaptismal preparation of parents that extends into something of a parental mini-catechumenate whose instructional component covers the meaning of baptism (as described in the denomination's official catechism or other symbolical books), the structure and nature of the baptismal rite (itself a document of baptismal theology), and concludes with a discussion of parental obligations regarding the Christian instruction and formation of their baptized child. Ideally, this instruction would serve not only to prepare parents for their child's baptism, but also renew their own understanding of baptism, possibly leading to their public renewal of baptism (i.e., in a rite of affirmation of baptism). The instruction of children in Sunday School could be viewed as not merely the learning of Bible stories, but as learning the faith into which the child was baptized. As a sign of the baptismal and ecclesial orientation of Christian instruction for children, Sunday School curriculum could cover baptism and the Lord's Supper (and possibly first communion instruction), and children's messages in the Sunday liturgy could expound the meaning of baptism, especially on liturgical feasts of baptismal significance (e.g., Baptism of our Lord, Pentecost). Additionally, when baptism is celebrated in the Sunday liturgy, children could be invited to gather around the baptismal font or pool to observe the rite and be reminded of their own baptism. Thus, the Christian instruction of children could serve as a type of catechumenate.

Likewise, confirmation could be given a more baptismal orientation. Instruction might focus not only on doctrines but also on the connection between doctrine, personal faith, and discipleship, such that participants come to appreciate how baptism is lived out. For example, the doctrine of creation could be related to stewardship of the earth and instruction could be tied to an environment-oriented project such as clearing rubbish from a body of water or stretch of public land. Rather than "joining church," a rite of confirmation could be celebrated as an *affirmation of baptism* in which the young persons say "yes" to their baptism by acknowledging God's baptismal gifts and committing themselves to active discipleship in the world and service to the church. Confirmation instruction/affirmation of baptism would then become analogous to the mystagogical period of the catechumenate. Of course, care must be taken so that the affirmation of baptism does not compete with or overshadow baptism. This impression is avoided if it is understood that affirmation of baptism is not the attainment of something new, but the celebration of what God did for the child in baptism and continues to do. Appropriately, then, baptized children are permitted to receive Holy Communion as their baptismal birthright prior to confirmation/affirmation of baptism. This pattern dispels any sense that a new status is conferred in confirmation/affirmation of baptism. Thus, the traditional rites of initiation – baptism, confirmation, and first communion – can be celebrated as a process in the case of children.

Conclusion

Christian history teaches us to treat baptism as a process. Indeed, in the third and fourth centuries, we see the emergence of a baptismal process that has much in common with the rites of passage known and practiced in societies from time immemorial. Like all rites of passage, the baptismal catechumenate aimed to help people make a difficult transition, namely, from one spiritual community to another. Christians in the twentieth century have recognized this process as an invaluable missional tool, not only because of its usefulness in the conversion process – a particular concern of the early church – but also because it fosters discipleship and faithful Christian living – a particular concern of the modern church, whose members are distracted by media, entertainment, work, leisure, etc. The ancient catechumenal process and its modern incarnations also help us to reimagine the baptism of infants as a process, albeit one staged out over the years following baptism. The catechumenate reminds all Christians that discipleship is a continual journey in the grace of God that finds it fulfillment only in our initiation into God's eternal kingdom that lies on the other side of death.

Resources for the Adult Catechumenate

Benedict, Daniel T., Jr. *Come to the Waters: Baptism and Our Ministry of Welcoming Seekers and Making Disciples.* Nashville: Discipleship Resources, 2000.

Evangelical Lutheran Church in America. *Welcome to Christ: A Lutheran Catechetical Guide.* Minneapolis: Augsburg Fortress, 1997.

___________. *Welcome to Christ: Lutheran Rites for the Catechumenate.* Minneapolis: Augsburg Fortress, 1997.

Living Witness: The Adult Catechumenate. Division for Parish Life: Evangelical Lutheran Church in Canada, n. p., 1992.

Office of Evangelism Ministries, the Episcopal Church. *The Catechumenal Process: Adult Initiation and Formation for Christian Life and Ministry.* New York: The Church Hymnal Corporation, 1990.

Webber, Robert E. *Liturgical Evangelism: Worship as Outreach and Nurture.* Harrisburg: Morehouse Publishing, 1986.

CHAPTER 4

Baptism and Time

Christians do not simply *endure* time; we *observe* time because of its sacred character. On the one hand, God is above and beyond time, since God's eternal being is without beginning or end. Yet, on the other hand, we believe that God acted in history by rescuing the people of Israel from slavery in Egypt and by sending His Son, Jesus, to save all people. Thus, Christians observe a *ritual calendar* whose days and seasons point to God's saving activity.

In observing time, Christians do something very human, for human activity in general revolves around time. The progression of the natural seasons dictates times for planting and harvesting or, at another cultural level, when particular sports are played. The rhythm of human life has times for birth, schooling, marriage, military service, raising families, and finally death. Secular society has its special times, e.g., for honoring the founders of the nation, remembering those who died in military service, and marking national anniversaries associated with independence, wars, or perhaps even national tragedies. In recalling past events in a nation's history, a people are reminded of who they are and the values to which they are to subscribe (e.g., freedom, equality). This "reminding" is concretized through rituals such as parades, singing the national anthem, saluting the national flag, and visiting graves and other places of national interest. In remembering Christian sacred history, believers are likewise reminded of their identity in Christ and are re-formed in the values of the Christian community through the various ritual actions of the liturgy.

The observance of sacred time is something that Christianity has in common with other world religions, most especially, Judaism. The Hebrew Scriptures witness to a rather developed "liturgical calendar" centered on three annual observances: Passover (Ex. 12:14-16), the Feast of Weeks or Pentecost (Ex. 34:22-23), observed 50 days after the first day of Unleavened Bread, and the Feast of Booths (Lev. 23:33-36). The one and only regular fast day commanded in the Hebrew Scriptures, the Day of Atonement or *Yom Kippur*, focuses on repentance and the confession of Israel's sins (Lev. 16). The Jewish week was marked by the Sabbath day (beginning Friday at sundown and extending to Saturday sundown), which was used for rest and worship (cf. Gen. 2:2). The day was punctuated with prayer at three times (Psalm 55:17). For the Jews, sacred time had to do with identity and faith formation: the Passover and harvest-related festivals called to mind deliverance from slavery and the gift of the Promised Land, while the Sabbath and daily prayer times reminded them that they were God's covenantal people, bound to obey the Torah.

Christian sacred time likewise revolves around salvation history. Specifically, the Christian calendar focuses on events in the life of Jesus Christ: his birth, baptism, ministry, death, resurrection, Spirit-sending, and promised return. The observance of the feasts and seasons associated with Christ is not just about remembering historical events for their own sake – a religious nostalgia for the past. Rather, the events in Christian history have significance for all time, and our ritual observance of them signifies Christ's presence with us and calls us to faith. Maxwell Johnson states that Christmas, for example, does not merely concern the birth of the baby Jesus in Bethlehem; rather, it concerns "our rebirth in the adult Christ today [who] is born anew in us through the Spirit who brings glad tidings of salvation...."[1] We might add that Easter is really about *our* resurrection, and the Day of Pentecost celebrates *our* life in the Holy Spirit today. These and other observances of the Christian calendar make us aware of who we are as Christians. Since a full treatment of the history and theology of the liturgical calendar is not possible here,[2] I will provide only a brief overview as background to this discussion about sacred time and baptism.

The Christian year is comprised of two overlapping cycles of time. The *temporal cycle* (from Latin *tempora*, "seasons") consists of Sundays, feasts (e.g., Christmas, Easter), holy days (e.g., Ash Wednesday) and the various seasons centered on the life of Christ and is itself comprised of two phases, namely, the *Easter* and *Christmas cycles*, each with their own respective feasts. While Christmas is always on 25 December, the dates of Easter and its related days change every year, depending on the occurrence of the first full moon of spring in the Northern Hemisphere. The temporal cycle also has two "in-between" spans of time referred to as "Ordinary Time," which have traditionally been designated by ordinal numbers (e.g., the Second Sunday after Epiphany, the Third Sunday after Pentecost). The temporal cycle unfolds as follows:

Christmas Cycle

Advent

First Sunday of Advent
Second Sunday of Advent
Third Sunday of Advent
Fourth Sunday of Advent

[1] Maxwell E. Johnson, ed., *Between Memory and Hope: Readings on the Liturgical Year* (Collegeville: Liturgical Press, 2000), xii.

[2] For a more thorough explanation and description of the Christian calendar, see my book *Worship: A Practical Guide* (Singapore: Genesis, 2011), chs. 7 and 8.

Christmas

Christmas (The Nativity of our Lord)

Christmas Eve

Christmas Day

First Sunday of Christmas

Second Sunday of Christmas

Epiphany of Our Lord (January 6)

Time after Epiphany (Ordinary Time)

Baptism of Our Lord

Sundays after Epiphany

The Transfiguration of Our Lord (Last Sunday after Epiphany)

Easter Cycle

Lent

Ash Wednesday

First Sunday in Lent

Second Sunday in Lent

Third Sunday in Lent

Fourth Sunday in Lent

Fifth Sunday in Lent

Holy Week: Palm Sunday, Monday, Tuesday, Wednesday

The Three Days

Maundy Thursday

Good Friday

Easter (Resurrection of Our Lord)

Vigil of Easter

Easter Day

Easter

Second Sunday of Easter

Third Sunday of Easter

Fourth Sunday of Easter

Fifth Sunday of Easter

Sixth Sunday of Easter

Ascension of Our Lord
Seventh Sunday of Easter
The Day of Pentecost

The Time after Pentecost (Ordinary Time)
The Holy Trinity (First Sunday after Pentecost)
Sundays after Pentecost
Christ the King (Last Sunday after Pentecost)

Running concurrent with the temporal cycle is the *sanctoral* (Latin, *sanctus*, "holy") *cycle*, with its commemorative days for apostles, gospel authors/compilers ("evangelists"), saints, martyrs, and other Christians.

Christians have long made connections between the liturgical calendar (the "church year") and baptism. The connection is by no means absolute nor have Christians historically been of one mind on the matter. Nevertheless, we will explore this topic in the belief that designating certain days for baptism can enhance baptism spiritually and liturgically for both baptismal candidates and the worship assembly.

Baptism and Sacred Time: An Historical Overview

The New Testament offers no evidence that the earliest Christians prescribed certain times for baptizing. According to Acts 2:41, about 3,000 people were baptized on the Jewish feast of Pentecost in response to Peter's sermon about Jesus. However, nothing in this narrative hints that baptizing on Pentecost is to be normative. The author of Acts seems more concerned with describing the primitive church's faithfulness *in* baptizing and its faith *about* baptism, especially its associating baptism with the gift of the Holy Spirit (cf. Acts 2:38). All other instances of baptism in Acts (8:12-13, 8:26-40, 9:18 [cf. 22:16], 10:48, 16:15, 16:33) contain no references to Jewish festivals. Elsewhere in the New Testament there are references to baptism that contain overtones to feasts that eventually emerge in Christianity, e.g., the "new birth" image in John 3:7/Titus 3:5 and its link to the feast of the Lord's Baptism, and the "death and resurrection" image of Rom. 6:1-12 with its Paschal (Easter) associations. However, these texts do not include any prescriptions concerning preferred baptismal times, nor do they offer any evidence that they actually reflect first-century baptismal practice. Although the apostolic church viewed baptism as integral to its life and mission, it accorded no significance to the timing of baptism, as far as we can discern from the New Testament.

The earliest post-apostolic sources for baptism say little about prescribed baptismal days. A late-first century/early-second century document of Syrian origins, the *Didache*, only makes prescriptions concerning the mode of baptism (preferably in running water, *perhaps* using a trinitarian formula), prebaptismal fasting, and reserving communion for the baptized only.[3] In his *First Apology*, a Roman Christian named Justin (d. 165 CE), provides a number of important details about the baptismal practice of his Christian community, but makes no explicit references to sacred time. Intriguingly, Justin associates baptism with Christ's own baptism in the Jordan River, which perhaps hints of the administration of baptism on the observance day of our Lord's Baptism, which is also known as the *Theophany* (Greek: "manifestation of God").[4] But it is unlikely that this feast was celebrated by Justin's community, since the first sure evidence for the *Theophany* is offered by Clement of Alexandria (150-215 CE), who wrote several decades after Justin, namely, around 200 CE. As noted in the previous chapter, the *Apostolic Tradition*, attributed to Hippolytus of Rome (ca. 217 CE), does offer a specific timing for Christian initiation whereby the baptismal elect bathe on Thursday, fast on Friday, and receive baptism and other initiatory rites early on Sunday morning following an all-night vigil. While it is tempting to conclude that these are the days of the *Paschal Triduum*, i.e., Maundy Thursday, Good Friday, and the Great Vigil of Easter, the document does not explicitly say this.[5] In his treatise

[3] The *Didache* 7.1, 9.5 (late-first or early-second cent.).

[4] Justin Martyr, *Dialogue with Trypho* 88 (ca. 160).

[5] Because some extant texts of the *Apostolic Tradition* are much later than the third century CE and because some of the baptismal practices described in chapters

On Baptism, the North African theologian Tertullian (160-225 CE) mentions two days that are appropriate for baptism: the Passover (i.e., Easter), because Christians are baptized into the Lord's death, and the Pentecost – by which he means all 50 days following Easter – because of the Lord's post-resurrection appearances during that time and because the grace of the Holy Spirit was given on the Day of Pentecost. Tertullian goes on to state, however, that *any* day, hour, or season is suitable for baptism because it is the same grace given, regardless of the time.[6] Thus, it appears that the idea – if not the practice – of reserving certain days for baptism, began to emerge in the late-second or early-third centuries.

From the fourth century on, sources indicate the conferral of baptismal rites during the pre-Easter preparatory season of Lent and at the Great Vigil of Easter itself. In the late-fourth century, the pilgrim Egeria describes a Lenten prebaptismal preparation period in Jerusalem that involved fasting, exorcism, and instruction. The baptismal candidates "return" (repeat back) the creed to the bishop during Holy Week, are baptized at the Easter Vigil, and receive instruction on the *mysteries* (the sacraments) during the week following Easter.[7] Lectures on the meaning of baptism given by John Chrysostom at Antioch (388, 390 CE) also suggest a prebaptismal preparation period that took place during Lent.[8] References to death/burial and resurrection in the late-fourth century *Apostolic Constitutions* hint of a Paschal baptism, e.g.:

> 1. Baptism…is given in the death of the Son, the water [is] in place of the entombment, the oil [is] in place of the Holy Spirit, the seal [is] in place of the cross, and the chrism confirms the confession. 2. The Father is commemorated as

17-21 find parallels only in the *fourth century*, we cannot be absolutely certain that what is described in these chapters necessarily reflects baptismal practice in *pre-Nicene* Rome.

[6] Tertullian, *De Baptismo* 19 (late-second cent.).

[7] *Egeria's Travels* 42 (ca. 381-84).

[8] "St. John Chrysostom (editor's introduction)," DBL, 40.

> author and sender, and together with him the Holy Spirit as witness. 3. Descent [into the water is] the dying together [with Christ], the ascent [from water is] rising together [with him].[9]

North African churches of the late-fourth and early-fifth centuries certainly knew of a final preparation period during Lent, for as Augustine declares: "Lo, the Paschal season has come, give in your names for baptism."[10] As we mentioned earlier, other prebaptismal rites in Augustine's church were associated with the Lent-Easter cycle: the washing of the candidates' feet on Maundy Thursday, the return of the creed on Easter eve by the candidates, and baptism at the Easter Vigil (see ch. 2). A century later, Ferrandus, a deacon of Carthage (520-47), writing to bishop Fulgentius concerning the salvation of a man who, due to sudden illness, could not reply to the creedal question within the baptismal rite, clearly indicates the paschal timing of Christian initiation in North Africa:

> This man, then, is handed over to the church to receive the Church's sacraments: he becomes a catechumen in customary fashion: after a short time, with the approach of the Paschal solemnities, he is offered among the *competentes* [baptismal elect], enrolled, instructed. Then, when he knows and understands the universal and venerable mysteries of the Catholic religion, the scrutiny is celebrated and he is delivered by exorcism from the devil. Moreover, he confesses the exact words of the holy creed from memory in a clear voice in the presence of the faithful: he receives the pious rule of the Lord's Prayer. Knowing now both what he should believe and what he should pray, he is ready to be baptized, when suddenly he is afflicted with a severe fever....[11]

---

[9] The *Apostolic Constitutions* III.17 (ca. 381).

[10] Augustine, *Sermon* 132.1.

[11] Ferrandus to Fulgentius, *Letter* (ca. 520-47).

Conciliar statements from the West in the sixth century and later attempt to *enforce* Paschal baptism. Noting a tendency for candidates to seek baptism at other times in the church year, the Council of Gerona (517 CE), restricts baptism to Easter and Christmas.[12] The Seventeenth Council of Toledo (732 CE), forbids the conferral of baptism during Lent, stating that bishops are to seal baptisteries shut at the beginning of Lent, and that they are only to be opened again on Maundy Thursday![13] The fact that church authorities had to *restrict* baptism to Easter suggests that baptism was in fact being administered at other times, even during Lent.

Western liturgical books of the late-patristic and medieval eras assume the conferral of baptismal rites in association with the Easter cycle. Reflecting Roman liturgical practice of the early-sixth century, the *Gelasian Sacramentary* contains baptismal rites that take place within Lent, e.g., scrutinies of the baptismal elect for the Third, Fourth, and Fifth Sundays in Lent. Other Lenten rites include the taking down of the names of the elect, the conferral of salt, and the delivery of the gospels, creed, and Lord's Prayer to the baptismal elect. The rites of initiation take place on Holy Saturday, beginning with the return of the creed (by the infants!) during the morning.[14] The tenth-century *Ambrosian Manual* provides rubrics and spoken formulas for dismissing catechumens during the first three weeks of Lent, rites for the delivery of the creed on the Second Saturday in Lent, and the rites of initiation on Holy Saturday.[15] Interestingly, the rubrics refer to "infants," an indication that adults are no longer the normal baptismal candidates.

Yet, we cannot ignore the cautions advocated by the eminent liturgical scholar Paul Bradshaw on the matter of Paschal baptism in the ancient church. Based on an analysis of available sources,

---

[12] The Council of Gerona (517), Canon 4.

[13] The Seventeenth Council of Toledo (732), Canon 2.

[14] *The Gelasian Sacramentary* (seventh century) I.XXVI-XLIV, ed. H. A. Wilson (Oxford: 1894).

[15] *The Ambrosian Manual,* in M. Magistretti, *Monumenta veteris liturgiae Ambrosianae*, Vol. 3 (Milan: 1904).

Bradshaw has argued that prior to the Council of Nicaea (325 CE), Easter baptism was only a *preference* expressed by sources such as Tertullian in North Africa and a *Commentary on Daniel*, which is an undisputed work of the Roman presbyter Hippolytus (170-235 CE).[16] Even then, the possibility of baptism taking place on other days was not excluded. Furthermore, after the Council of Nicaea, Easter baptism seems to become only a universal *ideal* in both the Christian East and West, for sources indicate that baptisms also took place on other important days in the liturgical calendar (e.g., Epiphany). Bradshaw therefore casts doubt on whether Easter baptism was ever the normative practice of the ancient church that some people assume it to be.[17]

Indeed, baptismal rites were also celebrated in connection with Epiphany (*Theophany* or Baptism of Our Lord) in the ancient church. Evidence suggests that ancient Egyptian churches knew of a forty-day fast that *followed* the Epiphany, and culminated with the conferral of baptism on the sixth day of the sixth week of this fast.[18] It seems that candidates were required to fast after the celebration of the Lord's baptism, in imitation of the gospel sequence of events. Interestingly, Ambrose of Milan (337-397 CE) speaks of the enrollment of the baptismal elect (the *competentes*) taking place on the Epiphany, which according to Johnson, may represent a connection with the Epiphany focus in Egypt.[19] In a sermon from the year 381 CE, Gregory of Nazianzus speaks of *not delaying* baptism until Epiphany, Pentecost, or Easter, thereby giving indirect witness to the conferral of baptism

---

[16] Gustave Bardy and Maurice Lefévre, *Hippolyte: Commentairesur Daniel*, Sources chrétiennes 14 (Paris: 1947), 100.

[17] Paul F. Bradshaw, "'*Diem baptismo sollemniorem*': Initiation and Easter in Christian Antiquity," in Maxwell E. Johnson, ed. *Living Water, Sealing Spirit: Readings on Christian Initiation* (Collegeville: Liturgical Press, 1995), 137-47.

[18] Maxwell. E Johnson, *The Rites of Christian Initiation: Their Evolution and Interpretation*, rev. exp. ed. (Collegeville: Liturgical Press, 2007), 68.

[19] Ambrose of Milan, *In Expos, Ev. Luc.* 4.76; see Johnson, *Rites of Christian Initiation*, 170.

on all three of these feasts.[20] Furthermore, Leo I mentions that baptism is conferred on the Epiphany in Sicily during his time.[21]

We should also be aware of the likelihood that Easter and other major feasts became preferred baptismal days not so much because of their inherent theological connections to baptism itself, but because of *fasting practices*. Noted previously were those documents such as the *Didache* and the writings of Justin that mention prebaptismal fasting for candidates, ministers, and the entire Christian community. Fasting therefore seems to have become a standard feature of prebaptismal preparation in the ancient church. As it happens, major feasts in the early church were generally preceded by fasts. It may well be, therefore, that Easter and other feasts commended themselves as baptismal times because fasting was already being observed by the church. In other words, pastoral convenience may have played a role in the rise of preferential days for baptism.[22] Nevertheless, it cannot pass unnoticed that the preferred days for baptism make reference to important biblical themes surrounding baptism: adoption, death and resurrection, new life, and reception of the gift of the Holy Spirit.

The relationship between baptism and any liturgical feast, however, was eventually to break down, especially in the West. In response to Pelagianism, the theological position that humans have the "free will" to reject evil and choose good and thereby merit eternal salvation, Augustine argued that humans are in fact "turned in" on themselves and seek only to gratify their own needs. This sinful condition, inherited from Adam, can only be remedied by the help of the divine grace given in baptism, and those who die unbaptized are not saved. For Augustine, the baptism of infants demonstrated that infants, conceived and born in sin were in need

---

[20] *In Sanctus Baptisma* 2:4, as cited in Johnson, *Rites of Christian Initiation*, 137. See also Bradshaw "'*Diem baptismo sollemniorem*,' Initiation and Easter in Christian Antiquity," 145.

[21] Johnson, *Rites of Christian Initiation*, 210.

[22] See Paul F. Bradshaw and Maxwell E. Johnson, *The Origins of Feasts, Fasts, and Seasons in Early Christianity* (Collegeville: Liturgical Press, 2011), 76.

of the forgiveness of sins offered by baptism. Although Augustine actually viewed infant baptism as a kind of proof of original sin, his rationale was turned around such that people came to believe that original sin *necessitated* the baptism of infants – a practice well known even before Augustine. Eventually, infants became the normal baptismal candidates and, in the Middle Ages, many parents sought to have their children baptized as soon as possible after birth out of fear that a child who died unbaptized was damned.[23] In other words, parents were not inclined to delay the baptism of their children until Easter, Pentecost, or other feasts. Although initiating children during the Lent-Easter cycle was something that literally remained on the books through the Middle Ages, *quamprimum* baptism (as soon as possible) was to be the norm inherited by Reformation-era churches and continues as such in many churches today.

Protestant reformers varied when it came to advocating specific days for baptism. Luther and Zwingli prescribed no particular days for baptism, undoubtedly due to the assumption that baptism would be administered soon after birth. In Bucer's Strasbourg, baptism was to be conferred at the services held on Sundays and Wednesdays so that the rite could be witnessed by the liturgical assembly.[24] Similarly, Calvin's 1542 baptismal rite prescribes "Sundays or other … days at the sermon" as times for baptizing.[25] The *Consultation* of Hermann von Wied,[26] the reforming archbishop of Cologne, and Cranmer's BCP 1549[27] and BCP 1552[28] all advocate baptism at Easter and

---

[23] For a discussion of Augustine's teaching on original sin and its implication for baptism, see Johnson, *Rites of Christian Initiation*, 194-97.

[24] See "A Rite of Baptism, Used at Strasbourg, 1525-1530," CIRP, 35, 37, and "The Strasbourg Order of Baptism after 1537," CIRP, 38.

[25] John Calvin, *The Form of Prayers and Ecclesiastical Chants with the Manner of Administering the Sacraments and Solemnizing Marriage According to the Custom of the Ancient Church* (1542), CIRP, 113.

[26] Hermann von Wied, "Consultation" (1543), CIRP, 55.

[27] "Of the Administration of Public Baptism to be Used in the Church," BCP 1549, CIRP, 89.

[28] "The Ministration of Baptism to be Used in the Church," BCP 1552, CIRP, 106.

holy days. Both archbishops, however, realized the difficulty in maintaining this ancient "custom." Early Anabaptists, for whom baptism was a sign of conversion and commitment, did not link baptism to the church year.

Later Protestants gave little emphasis to baptizing on liturgical feasts. The BCP 1662 mentions only Sundays and other holy days for baptizing.[29] The baptismal rites of John Wesley, modeled on those in the BCP 1662, make no mention of specific baptismal days.[30] For early American Methodists, Presbyterians, Baptists, and other Christians, revival camp meetings that drew thousands of un-churched seekers, became the prescribed time for baptism.[31] Believer-baptizing churches that arose well after the Reformation, e.g., Baptists, Disciples of Christ, and Pentecostals, who might only observe Christmas and Easter, have traditionally not tied baptism to major feasts, although they, along with modern Mennonites, do baptize at the Sunday service so that baptism can be a testimony to the church.[32]

Despite a long history during which baptism was by no means conferred exclusively on major feasts, late-twentieth century churches sought to designate such days, especially Easter, as preferred times for baptism. The Roman Catholic Church's *Rite of Christian Initiation of Adults* or RCIA (1972), discussed in the previous chapter, envisions the following as the normal pattern: baptismal "election" and final preparation of candidates during Lent, baptism at the Easter Vigil,

[29] "The Ministration of Publick Baptism of Infants to be Used in the Church" (1662), BCP *Texts*, 408.

[30] John Wesley, "The Ministration of Baptism of Infants" and "Baptism to Such as are of Riper Years" (1784), JWPB, 139-49.

[31] See James F. White, *Protestant Worship: Traditions in Transition* (Louisville: Westminster John Knox Press, 1989), 173.

[32] See the following in BT: Keith Watkins, "Baptismal Understanding and Practice in the Christian Church (Disciples of Christ)," 110; Paul Fiddes, "The Baptism of Believers," 74, and Rebecca Slough, "Baptismal Practice among North American Mennonites," 92.

and a period of mystagogy during the weeks following Easter.[33] Lutheran, Anglican/Episcopal, Methodist, and Presbyterian worship books from the late-twentieth and early-twenty-first centuries also make provision for baptizing at the Easter Vigil, either following the Old Testament readings or the sermon.[34] The catechumenal materials of these denominations prescribe either Lent or Advent for the final preparation of candidates and provide for baptism on either the Baptism of Our Lord or the Easter Vigil. Except for the Presbyterian *Book of Common Worship*, all of the above-mentioned Protestant books, along with the World Council of Church's *Baptism, Eucharist and Ministry* statement,[35] suggest the Baptism of Our Lord, the Day of Pentecost, and All Saints Day as other appropriate times for baptism. If there are no baptismal candidates, the services on these feasts may include a rite of affirmation of baptism or renewal of baptismal vows for the entire liturgical assembly.[36]

Toward a Rationale for Preferred Baptismal Days in Contemporary Churches

Obviously, a certain amount of ambivalence and pastoral challenge surround the use of prescribed baptismal days. Yet, I nevertheless offer the following points in support of reserving baptisms for the above-mentioned liturgical days, i.e., celebrating baptismal festivals:

---

[33] *Rite of Christian Initiation of Adults* in *The Rites of the Catholic Church* (New York: Pueblo, 1983), IA, 62-50.

[34] See "Resurrection of Our Lord: Vigil of Easter," ELW, 643-53; "The Great Vigil of Easter," BCW, 294-314; "The Great Vigil of Easter," BCP 1979, 284-314; and "Easter Vigil or The First Service of Easter," UMBW, 368-76.

[35] See "Notes on the Services," ELW, 27; "Additional Directions (Holy Baptism)," BCP 1979, 312; "Services of the Baptismal Covenant (Introduction)," UMBW, 84; BEM, 7.

[36] See "Affirmation of Baptism" and "Resurrection of Our Lord: Vigil of Easter," ELW, 596-600, 652; "The Great Vigil of Easter" and "Reaffirmation of the Baptismal Covenant for a Congregation," BCW, 310, 464-71; "The Great Vigil of Easter" and "Holy Baptism," BCP 1979, 290-92, 312; "Services of the Baptismal Covenant (Introduction)" and "The Baptismal Covenant IV," UMBW, 84, 111-14.

Baptismal festivals integrate baptism more deeply into the church's liturgy. As noted, many churches celebrate baptism within the Sunday service to underscore the connection between baptism and life in the church, and to remind all present of their own baptism. Unfortunately, baptism can be experienced as an interruption in the Sunday service when preaching, song choices, and the corporate prayers of intercession lack reference to baptism. By contrast, when celebrated on great liturgical feasts (Baptism of Our Lord, Easter, Pentecost, All Saints), baptism is more easily integrated into the liturgy since the calendar and lectionary carry baptismal overtones that can be exploited by worship planners and leaders. On the Baptism of Our Lord, the sermon can suggest that our baptism, much like Jesus' baptism, is both a divine affirmation and a commissioning into the *missio Dei*. On Easter day (or at the Great Vigil) the sermon can meaningfully expound how baptism is (or signifies) the candidates' own death and resurrection with Christ, i.e., a dying to sin and rising to new life. Baptism on the Day of Pentecost can be enhanced by a sermon that proclaims the candidates' baptism as another outpouring of the Holy Spirit. On All Saints Day, the preacher can declare that the baptismal candidates are joining the whole company of God's holy ones through baptism. We might note how liturgical prayer can enhance the baptismal celebration by likewise bringing out the baptismal significance of the day, as in the following from the BCP 1979:

> Father in heaven, who at the baptism of Jesus in the River Jordan proclaimed him your beloved Son and anointed him with the Holy Spirit: Grant that all who are baptized into his Name may keep the covenant they have made, and boldly confess him as Lord and Savior; who with you and the Holy Spirit lives and reigns, one God, in glory everlasting. *Amen.* (Baptism of our Lord)
>
> O God, who made this most holy night to shine with the glory of the Lord's resurrection: Stir up in your Church that Spirit of adoption which is given to us in baptism, that we,

> being renewed both in body and mind, may worship you in sincerity and truth; through Jesus Christ our Lord, who lives and reigns with you, in the unity of the Holy Spirit, one God, now and forever. *Amen.* (Easter Vigil)[37]

The baptismal experience can be deepened by liturgical hymns with baptismal overtones, or by baptismal hymns that are appropriate for use on liturgical feasts. The meaning of baptism can be expressed through liturgical resources, thus integrating the baptismal celebration into the service and overcoming the sense that baptism "interrupts" the service. Because of the pastoral advantages of celebrating baptism on liturgical feasts, churches that normally do not observe the Baptism of Our Lord or Pentecost are encouraged to consider expanding their liturgical calendars.[38]

Baptismal festivals highlight the ecclesial meaning of baptism. Christians today are challenged to move beyond individualistic understandings of baptism, whereby baptism is viewed as merely a mark of an adult's conversion experience, or serves as an infant's "christening" (official naming). In both cases, the meaning of baptism is diminished. But in recent times many churches have endeavored to connect baptism with broader ecclesial issues such as discipleship, membership in the body of Christ, participation in the church's mission, and they have tried to relate baptism to the reception of Holy Communion, which is participation in the corporate body *par excellence.* When baptism is conferred on days in the *church's* liturgical calendar – which is to say, *reserved* for these days – it is clearer that baptism is about more than one's personal faith, choices, and decisions. The juxtaposition of baptism to great church festivals suggests that baptism involves one's receiving the faith of the universal church and joining one's self to the worldwide fellowship that confesses the crucified and risen Lord who is God's beloved Son, Sender of the Spirit, and Chief Cornerstone of the church. There will always be (and should be) an

[37] "Collects: Contemporary," BCP 1979, 214, 222.

[38] For suggestions on "expanding and refreshing" a church's observance of the liturgical calendar, see my *Worship: A Practical Guide*, 118-20.

individual dimension to baptism, insofar as God's promises apply to each and every individual recipient and each individual is invited to respond in faith. But that aspect of baptism needs to be balanced with the ecclesial dimension baptism, which can be symbolized through a celebration connected with the church's observance of sacred time.

Baptismal festivals integrate baptism and church life. When celebrated apart from the Sunday worship assembly, or only occasionally at the Sunday liturgy, baptism seems to have little relevance for the church. But when baptism punctuates Easter, Pentecost, and other festivals and becomes a part of these observances, the perception of baptism is changed entirely. Not only is its inherent theological importance symbolized by juxtaposition to these liturgical days, but so is its importance to the church for the making and forming disciples (cf. Matt. 28). In other words, the rhythm of regular baptisms on liturgical feasts demonstrates that baptism is integrally part of the church's life and mission and thus something to which the church must attend with all seriousness and energy. The prominence given to baptism reminds each Christian to reach out to potential seekers so that they might ultimately be joined to the church through baptism. Thus, while baptismal festivals demonstrate that baptism is about the church, they also symbolize how the church needs to be about baptism.

But undoubtedly, the above proposals could meet with resistance. To begin with, churches long accustomed to baptizing at public services other than those held on Sunday (e.g., Saturday evening), or who confer baptism at regularly-scheduled baptismal services that do not coincide with the great liturgical feasts or perhaps on feasts with not-so-obvious connections to baptism (e.g., on Christmas) may find it difficult to shift baptismal celebrations to Baptism of Our Lord, Easter, Pentecost, or All Saints Day. Certainly, a change in initiatory patterns would require significant pastoral explanation as well as revision of printed and electronic resources. Additionally, parents might be anxious about delaying the baptism of their children due to (unfounded) fears about their unbaptized children living without the blessing of God, or the presence of family members at a baptismal service takes precedence over the church's calendar in some minds. "Storing-up" baptism for particular days may indeed bring practical conflicts.

In response to the issues raised above, I would point out the benefits of baptismal festivals. As mentioned previously, baptism can be better integrated into a service liturgically on feasts of baptismal significance, which means less of a struggle in planning worship and ultimately providing a service that is more meaningful to the assembly. Furthermore, if the catechumenate were adopted, there is potential for transforming the life of the church entirely, because the church's baptismal mission would take on a more prominent role in public worship, education, and pastoral care. The focus on supporting catechumens in their conversion process and preparing them for baptism would remind assembly members not only of their own need for ongoing conversion, but also of the role of each Christian to make disciples (Matt. 28). Thus, any disruption caused by reconfiguring baptismal practice to fit the rhythms of the church calendar is offset by the promise of renewing and reinvigorating the church.

As for the concerns families might have, pastoral instruction through preaching and church communications could make clear that baptism is neither a "vaccination" against tragedy and suffering nor a kind of insurance against eternal damnation. Those churches that baptize infants certainly believe that saving promises are made to infants, but they baptize in the hope that children will receive those promises in faith and grow up to become faithful disciples. They baptize for life, not for death! Furthermore, pastoral care can and should help families to appreciate how baptism is much more than a family event that just happens to take place in the church. Scheduling their child's baptism at a time of significance for the church is how parents live out their obedience to the church and model faith and discipleship for their children. The following, although written with the North American context in mind, can equally apply to the Asian context, where cultural values are increasingly influenced by American and European societies:

> Scheduled baptismal festivals suggest that the rhythm of the church's life and worship take precedence over individual and family preferences. In our highly individualized society, many look upon baptism as *their* day. Baptizing several candidates on the same occasion suggests that God's action in water and Word is bigger than any individual and that what for many is a family celebration is, in fact, a celebration of God's entire family. Scheduling baptism in a way that encourages proper preparation and mutual commitment challenges the consumerism that encourages people to get what they want when they want it. In subtle ways baptismal festivals reflect the baptismal renunciation of "the powers of this world that rebel against God" and the distinctive nature of baptismal living.
>
> People may be helpfully encouraged to consider a family celebration of the baptism at another time if they are not able to gather on the scheduled baptismal festival, perhaps using elements from an order for the anniversary of a baptism.[39]

In encouraging such baptismal festivals during which (perhaps) several people are baptized, I certainly do not want to commend a new legalism whereby the practice is considered necessary for salvation. Baptizing on particular days must be viewed as a matter of freedom – something the church may do or not do, and, if the former, is free to lay aside in situations where pastoral necessity requires it. We might therefore think of baptismal festivals as a means of achieving good order (1 Cor. 14:40), that is, a way of achieving a well-regulated and intentional baptismal practice that edifies the church and glorifies God. In that case, baptismal festivals would be similar to prescribed times for ordination, the Annual General Meeting, or a church's anniversary celebration.

[39] Dennis L. Bushkovsky and Craig A. Satterlee, *The Christian Life: Baptism and Life Passages,* Using *Evangelical Lutheran Worship*, Vol. 2 (Minneapolis: Augsburg Fortress, 2008), 54.

Conclusion

The earliest Christian sources offer no prescriptions for baptizing on certain days. In the third century, it appears that the Epiphany (Baptism of our Lord) was given baptismal significance in the East, while baptizing at Easter became a preference in the West, although Paschal baptism certainly never attained absolute dominance over other times for baptizing. With the demise of the catechumenate and the rise of *quamprimum* baptism in the case of infants, the connection between initiation and the liturgical year broke down almost entirely – at least in practice. Reformation churches took different approaches, with some giving the matter no emphasis, others stressing the need to baptize at the Sunday liturgy, and others holding out for Easter and other holy days. The matter was given very little consideration thereafter until the twentieth century with the liturgical renewal movements in Roman Catholicism and Protestantism. For those churches that have revived the catechumenate, initiation and sacred time have been integrated in a way unknown since ancient times. While there is no justification for pastoral insistence on the catechumenate or so-called "baptismal festivals," both have potential for renewing the meaning of baptism and the life of the church.

Appendix: Preparing for a Baptismal Festival

The following is offered as a checklist in preparation for a baptismal festival.

Logistics

1. 90 days prior to festival: announce date of upcoming baptismal festival to congregation; schedule times for (adult) inquirers to meet for study and reflection
2. 40 days prior to festival: enrollment of candidates during the Sunday liturgy and preparation of items needed for catechumenal rites
3. 40 days prior to festival: pastors begin meeting with parents of infants/small children to discuss meaning of baptism,

service logistics, parental obligations for Christian formation of children

Preaching

Preachers need to keep in mind that the liturgy is also part of the context of preaching. The seasons of the church calendar and other aspects of the liturgical *ordo* will need to be factored into the sermon. Also, it is desirable that the preacher consider the homiletical implications of celebrating baptism in the service. When baptism is celebrated on a major liturgical feast, the preacher may want to ponder the following questions.

1. *Baptism of Our Lord*: What does the Jordan event reveal about Jesus? What does it imply about Christian baptism? What does Christian baptism have to do with the candidate's relationship to God the Father? With the anointing of the Spirit? Consider how baptism brings a person into a special relationship with the triune God. Also, consider the connection between Jesus' baptism and his temptation. Does Christian baptism initiate us into a life of struggle against evil as well as a life of service and mission?
2. *Easter*: How is Christian baptism a death and resurrection? See Rom. 6:3-11 and Col. 3:1-4. What dies when one is baptized? What is raised up in baptism? What does the Rom. 6 text imply about baptism and ongoing life as a Christian?
3. *Pentecost*: What is the connection between Acts 2 and Christian baptism? (See Acts 2:38 especially.) How might the images and promises of John 7:37-39 (Lectionary Year A) connect with our baptismal experience? See also John 14:8-17, 25-27 (Year C), and John 15:26-27, 16:4-15 (Year B).
4. *All Saints*: How is our identity as God's "holy ones" connected to baptism? Revelation 7:9-17 (Year A) mentions those clad in white robes, which either reflects or gave rise to the practice of clothing the newly baptized in white robes immediately

after their baptism. Consider how baptism includes each of us in the multitude of those clad in white robes. John 11:32-44 (Year B) is the story of Lazarus' receiving new life. How is baptism a sign/conferral of new life? Revelation 21:6 (Year B) speaks of water for the thirsty. Consider how baptism is a thirst-quenching water and how it meets the deep spiritual needs of each of us. For All Saints Lectionary Year C, consider the relationship between baptism and the Holy Spirit and the inheritance of an eternal kingdom (Eph. 1:11-23).

Liturgy and Music

Denominational liturgical books contain prayers for feasts that are especially appropriate when baptism is celebrated. Some of these prayers could also be used at other times when baptism is celebrated. Additionally, certain hymns in these books or the related books are appropriate when baptism is celebrated.

1. American Lutheran

   a. Collect Prayers of Baptismal Significance in *Lutheran Book of Worship* and *Evangelical Lutheran Worship*

      1) Baptism of our Lord (Years A, B, C)
      2) Easter Day (Years A, B, C)
      3) Easter Vigil: Fourth (ELW, p. 648), Fifth (ELW, p. 650) and Twelfth (ELW, p. 652) readings
      4) Sundays in Lent 3A and 4C (especially appropriate for the catechumenate)

   b. Hymns of Baptismal Significance

      1) LBW 188/ELW 450 I Bind Unto Myself Today (esp. for Baptism of Our Lord)
      2) LBW 191/ELW 458 Praise and Thanksgiving Be to God (Easter, Pentecost)
      3) LBW 194/ELW 442 All Who Believe and Are Baptized (Easter, Pentecost)

4) LBW 195/ELW 448 This is the Spirit's Entry Now (Pentecost)

The following are found only in *Lutheran Book of Worship*:

1) 83 From God the Father Virgin Born (Epiphany)
2) 190 We Praise You, Lord (Easter)
3) 192 Baptized into Your Name Most Holy (Easter)

2. Hong Kong Lutheran: *Hymns of Praise*
   a. 252 Dearest Jesus, We are Here (General)
   b. 253 All Who Believe and are Baptized (Easter or Pentecost)
   c. 254 Cradling Children in His Arms (General)

3. North American Episcopal/Anglican
   a. Prayers of Baptismal Significance in BCP 1979
      1) The First Sunday after Epiphany (Baptism of Our Lord)
      2) Easter Day ("O God, who made this holy night to shine…")
      3) For All Baptized Christians (pp. 252-53)
      4) At Baptism (p. 254)
   b. Hymns of Baptismal Significance in *The Hymnal 1982*
      1) 120 The Sinless One to Jordan Came (Baptism of Our Lord)
      2) 121 Christ, When for Us You Were Baptized (Baptism of Our Lord)
      3) 139 When Jesus Went to Jordan's Stream (Baptism of Our Lord)
      4) 294 Baptized in Water (Pentecost)
      5) 296 We Know that Christ is Raised (Easter)
      6) 297 Descend, O Spirit (Pentecost)
      7) 299 Spirit of God Unleashed on Earth (Pentecost)

4. Church of England
    a. Collect Prayers of Baptismal Significance in *Common Worship* (CW)
        1) The Baptism of Christ (p. 383)
        2) Easter Eve (p. 399)
        3) Second Sunday of Easter (Post-communion, p. 401)
    b. *Times and Seasons*
        1) The Eucharist on the Festival of the Baptism of Christ (pp. 170ff), may include the celebration of baptism itself.
5. American Methodist
    a. Prayers of Baptismal Significance in *United Methodist Book of Worship* (UMBW)
        1) Easter Vigil: Collect for Fifth Reading (p. 374)
    b. Hymns of Baptismal Significance *United Methodist Hymnal* (UMH)
        1) UMH 252 When Jesus Came to Jordan (Baptism of Our Lord)
        2) UMH 465 Holy Spirit Truth Divine for (Pentecost)
6. *Book of Common Worship* (BCW) and *The Presbyterian Hymnal*
   BCW contains an especially good collection of prayers that are appropriate when baptism is celebrated.
    a. Epiphany of Our Lord
        1) Eucharistic Thanksgiving, pp.194-95
        2) Prayer of Thanksgiving (non-eucharistic), p. 197
    b. Baptism of Our Lord
        1) Collect 1, p. 198
        2) Collect 2, p. 199
        3) Litany for Baptism of Our Lord, pp. 199-200 (including collect on p. 200)
        4) Prayer of Confession, p. 200
        5) Prayer of Thanksgiving, p. 204

c. Lent
    1) Prayer 3 (Lent I, Years A, B, C), p. 243
    2) Prayer 2 (Lent III, Years A, B, C), p. 245

d. Easter Vigil
    1) Collect for Second Reading, p. 305
    2) Collect for Fourth Reading, p. 306
    3) Collect for Fifth Reading, p. 306
    4) Collect for Eighth Reading, p. 308
    5) Collect of the Day, p. 309

e. Pentecost
    1) Litany C, pp. 342-43
    2) Great Thanksgiving (Eucharistic Prayer), pp. 343-47
    3) Thanksgiving Prayer (non-eucharistic), p. 347

f. The baptismal service in BCW contains resources that are appropriate on liturgical feasts
    1) Scripture Sentence 1, p. 403 (Pentecost, All Saints)
    2) Scripture Sentence 4, p. 404 (Easter)
    3) Thanksgiving Over the Water 1 (Baptism of Our Lord, Easter, Pentecost)

g. BCW has a list of "additional resources" for use when Affirmation of Baptism is celebrated, some of which might be used in connection with liturgical feasts.
    1) Opening Sentence 3, p. 472 (Easter)
    2) Opening Prayer 1, p. 472 (Baptism of Our Lord)
    3) Opening Prayers 2 and 3, p. 473 (Pentecost)

h. Hymns of Baptismal Significance in *The Presbyterian Hymnal* (1993)
    1) 70 Christ When for Us You Were Baptized (Baptism of Our Lord)
    2) 492 Baptized in Water (Pentecost)
    3) 494 Out of Deep Unordered Water (Easter Season)
    4) 495 We Know that Christ is Raised (Easter)

CHAPTER 5

Baptism and its Physical Requirements

The longevity of a liturgical space is by no means assured. Some Christian communities have worshipped in a space for hundreds of years. Others might use several spaces over a 50-year period – either because they outgrow spaces or other factors necessitate the construction of new spaces. All churches face the possibility of needing to renovate or rebuild due to damage from natural disasters, fires, or other calamities. Intentional changes in liturgical norms and laws by a denomination may also necessitate architectural renewal. Thus, planning a new liturgical space is a distinct possibility for many churches. A new worship space will likely include a new or refurbished baptismal space, and the design of the latter will require study, reflection, and discussion with architectural and liturgical experts.

This chapter is intended as a guide for congregations and committees seeking to renew their baptismal space and vessel, as well as a source of general information on baptismal architecture. The goal is to help churches make informed decisions by providing an overview that integrates baptismal architecture, history, and theology. Regarding nomenclature, "font" refers to an above-ground structure, such as the traditional pedestal (wine glass) font, or any kind of tub or tank. "Pool" refers to an in-ground or "at-grade" structure, especially one that can accommodate the immersion (submersion) of a candidate who descends into the water. Recognizing the diversity of baptismal architecture in the church, I will use "font/pool" when referring to baptismal vessels in general. "Baptistery" refers to a distinct architectural structure that houses the baptismal space and vessel, a feature that was especially characteristic of ancient church architecture.

Any discussion of baptismal architecture needs to take a theologically balanced view. Baptism does not necessarily require *any* vessel at all, since the action could take place in a river, lake, or stream (cf. Acts 8:36). However, if a liturgical tradition (e.g., Reformed or Anglican) requires that baptism be administered when the greatest number of church members can be present, which normally means during the liturgy of Sunday morning or a major feast, then having a font/pool located in the liturgical space is a necessity. We also have to acknowledge that from the theological perspective of some traditions (e.g., Lutheran), the baptismal *action* and the recipient's response of faith are more important than baptismal architecture. Sacramental efficacy is not dependent on the size or quality of the font/pool! Yet, the latter can serve as a *symbol.* Like great artworks, a national flag, or a memorial that marks a significant historical event, baptismal architecture visually portrays ideas, images, and values of a transcendent nature. A baptismal font/pool symbolizes our baptismal death/resurrection, and thus aids the ongoing conversion process that was begun in baptism. In that case, baptismal architecture takes on great importance and the sacrament (ordinance) is really done a great *disservice* by architectural minimalism. Balancing theology, practicality, and symbolism will be the task of those charged with designing a new baptismal space for their church.

This chapter will begin by discussing two simple principles that serve as starting points for baptismal architecture. Following that, we will consider the "givens" that inform the design of baptismal architecture. Less obvious perhaps, but equally important for our discussion, are recent theological trends with implications for baptismal practice. We include a brief survey of contemporary baptismal architecture, not with the hope that these trends will be followed slavishly, but rather that this state of the question overview (of sorts) might inform building committees about what is appropriate and possible.

Toward a Good Beginning

Many human endeavors are guided by maxims, such as "play to win" (sports), or "the customer is always right" (retail business). The same should be true for churches and committees that are tasked with designing new baptismal spaces. The two principles that I propose do not necessarily guarantee satisfying spaces and structures, since that will depend on many factors, including a church's original specifications, the abilities of the designers and builders, and the quality of the materials used. Rather, the two fundamentals mentioned below will help to avoid the blind alleys that lead to unsatisfying or disastrous structures.

First: *form follows function*. We might restate this by saying that the design of something should reflect its basic purpose. If we are designing a place for baptism, we begin with the recognition that it is for *baptizing people*. That of course seems obvious, but sometimes in our fervor to create, we forget the obvious. So we ask: *Where* do we envision baptism taking place? *How* do we envision it being administered? *How many* people will be involved in the baptismal action? By keeping functionality in mind, we can avoid a structure that we have to work *around* rather than *with*.

Second: *less is more*. This principle reminds us of the desirability of understatement. Liturgical appointments need not be massive in proportion or rich in decoration to be both beautiful and effective. The amply-scaled and sparsely-adorned baptismal font located inside the west entrance of St. Andrew's Cathedral, Singapore, is an impressive reminder of baptism to those who enter the holy space. Many of the fonts/pools discussed in this chapter are likewise modest (but ample) in proportions and yet beautiful and functional. The idea "less is more," however, does not justify architectural minimalism or the use of cheap materials. Rather, it means balancing all other design factors with a certain amount of restraint. Such restraint, I maintain, along with a clear sense of purpose for the intended structure, will result in baptismal architecture that functions well and glorifies God.

Determining Baptismal Architecture: "Givens"

The design of baptismal architecture is not a matter of guesswork. There are certain obvious ideas and practical examples – "givens" – that can guide us. The following are offered not as an exhaustive list, but as a foundation for reflection.

Given #1: Baptism is a bath. In initiating converts by means of a ritual bath, Christians (like Judaism and other ancient Mediterranean religions) use an everyday cultural action (bathing, washing) to express and enact spiritual realities. It is analogous to the religious use of meals to define and constitute a fellowship of believers/adherents and manifest divine power. For Christians, the outward cleansing that takes place with baptismal water points to (symbolizes) the inner cleansing/purification enacted and empowered by the Holy Spirit. If baptism is a bath, washing, or cleansing, then *water* is necessarily important. Thus, a structure that contains sufficient water for a bath – or a good washing – is necessary. Ruled out is a minimalistic structure (a finger bowl), or something so highly stylized and "artistic" that its purpose as a vessel for washing is obscured. Only when the font/pool can be recognized as a place of washing will the meaning of baptism be transparent to the worshipping community.

Given #2: Baptism is a sacrament. Most mainline Protestants refer to baptism as a "sacrament," that is, a means by which God's personal presence sanctifies and equips us for participation in the *missio Dei* (see ch. 1). Most Protestant baptismal liturgies contain language of sacramental significance, as we see in the extracts below:

> God, who is rich in mercy and love, gives us a new birth into a living hope through the sacrament of baptism. By water and the Word God delivers us from sin and death and raises us to new life in Jesus Christ. We are united with all the

baptized in the one body of Christ, anointed with the gift of the Holy Spirit, and joined in God's mission for the life of the world. (*Evangelical Lutheran Worship,* 583)

Our Lord Jesus Christ suffered death on the cross and rose again from the dead for the salvation of mankind. Baptism is the outward sign by which we receive for ourselves what he has done for us: we are united with him in his death; we are granted forgiveness of sins; we are raised with Christ to new life in the Spirit. (*Diocese of Singapore Service Book,* 49)

Our Lord Jesus Christ has told us that to enter the kingdom of heaven we must be born again of water and the Spirit, and has given us baptism as the sign and seal of this new birth. Here we are washed by the Holy Spirit and made clean. Here we are clothed with Christ, dying to sin that we may live his risen life. As children of God, we have a new dignity and God calls us to fullness of life. (*Common Worship,* 349)

Through the Sacrament of Baptism we are initiated into Christ's holy Church. We are incorporated into God's mighty acts of salvation and given new birth through water and the Spirit. All this is God's gift, offered to us without price. (*United Methodist Book of Worship,* 87)

In baptism God claims us, and seals us to show that we belong to God. God frees us from sin and death, uniting us with Jesus Christ in his death and resurrection. By water and the Holy Spirit, we are made members of the church, the body of Christ, and joined to Christ's ministry of love, peace, and justice. (*Book of Common Worship,* 404-405)

Clearly, Protestant baptismal theology ties baptism to the saving activity of God. Even churches that do not have a "high" or "sacramental" understanding of baptism view it as the biblically-mandated means of initiating converts into the church and as a sacred testimony to the work of the Holy Spirit in the lives of new converts. For them, baptism has, at least, a sacramental *quality* about it. Ideally, then, Protestant baptismal theology would find expression in baptismal fonts/pools of sufficient size and quality to suggest the importance of baptism. The location of the font within the liturgical space should do likewise.

Simply put: a weighty baptismal theology deserves a weighty baptismal architecture. A font barely larger than a finger bowl or a candy dish hardly proclaims the saving activity of God. Insignificant baptismal architecture ultimately undermines baptism theology. We might consider, by way of analogy, how the architecture of a country's presidential palace (e.g., the Istana in Singapore), legislature building, or supreme court are usually grand and elegant, not for the sake of ostentation but rather for the sake of symbolism. The grand, eye-catching architecture of such places is meant to suggest the importance of the activities associated with them, namely, the enactment, enforcement, and interpretation of laws – activities that are to be respected. Government architecture, in other words, is a statement of national values, particularly the high regard that democratic countries have for the rule of law. Thus, baptismal architecture is how we express our faith in the saving activity of God in baptism and invite all to share that faith.

Given #3: Baptism is interpreted in the Bible. Baptismal architecture can also draw inspiration from the Bible. The New Testament does not offer a complete systematic theology of baptism, but some passages do offer brief "interpretations" of the meaning of baptism. Maxwell Johnson summarizes these as follows:

1. forgiveness of sins and the gift of the Holy Spirit (Acts 2:38)
2. new birth through water and the Holy Spirit (John 3:5; Titus 3:5-7)
3. putting off the old self and putting on the new, i.e., being clothed in the righteousness of Christ (Gal. 3:27; Col. 3:9-10)

4. initiation into the one body of the Christian community (1 Cor. 12:13; cf. Acts 2:42)
5. washing, sanctification, and justification in Christ and the Holy Spirit (1 Cor. 6:11)
6. enlightenment (Heb. 6:4, 10:32; 1 Peter 2:9)
7. being anointed and/or sealed by the Holy Spirit (2 Cor. 1:21-22; 1 John 2:20, 27)
8. being sealed or marked as belonging to God and God's people (2 Cor. 1:21-22; Eph. 1:13-14, 4:30; Rev. 7:3)
9. being joined to Christ through participation in his death, burial, and resurrection (Rom. 6:3-11; Col. 2:12-15).[1]

According to Johnson, early Christian sources speak of fonts as either *wombs* (John 3:5), *tombs* (Rom. 6), or both, and "such a theology will give rise architecturally to how fonts themselves will come to be shaped: tomb-like appearance; eight-sided reflecting the entrance into the eighth day or first day of the new creation; quatrolobe to suggest the shape of the cross; six-sided to suggest the Passion; and circular to suggest a womb."[2] It only makes sense that baptismal architecture today would draw on these interpretations, especially if that architecture is a means of forming people whose faith is grounded in the New Testament.

Given #4: Baptism is interpreted by early church architecture. Many ancient fonts are indeed suggestive of a "womb" or "tomb," and following is a list of representative fonts/pools that express these characteristics. Readers will find photographs of the structures referred to in the works cited.

1. *Cruciform.* The "original" font of the Memorial of Moses Church (Mt. Nebo, Dead Sea), which dates from the year 531 CE, contains a font in the shape of a Greek cross (equal-

[1] Maxwell E. Johnson, *The Rites of Christian Initiation: Their Evolution and Interpretation*, rev. exp. ed. (Collegeville: Liturgical Press, 2007), 37.

[2] Johnson, *The Rites of Christian Initiation*, 38. Some scholars today are cautious about generalizing with regard to the shapes of ancient baptismal fonts. See Everett Ferguson, *Baptism in the Early Church: History, Theology, and Liturgy in the First Five Centuries* (Grand Rapids: Eerdmans, 2009), 819-20.

length arms). This font, which is sunk approximately one meter below floor level, is entered via internal steps in three of the "arms."[3]

2. *Tomb*. The earliest known baptismal font used by Christians is found in the famous Dura-Europas house church structure that was converted for Christian use in approximately the year 240 CE. Lying under a columned canopy, the sarcophagus-like structure (resembling a modern bath tub) could accommodate the submersion of a candidate who knelt in the water. The font is surrounded by wall paintings of various biblical scenes.[4]
3. *Octagonal*. St. Ambrose of Milan (ca. 339-97) himself had a hand in the design and construction of the font in the San Giovanni alle Fonti baptistery that is connected to the church of St. Thecla in Milan. Dating from the time of the bishop himself, the octagonal font is sunk into the ground and has a diameter of 5.16 m, making it ample for immersions.[5]
4. *Womb*. Constructed during the late-Romanesque period and standing nearly two meters high, the poured-bronze font in St. Maria im Kapital, Cologne, Germany, suggests a womb by its round, bulbous shape. It is inscribed with Ezek. 36:25-28.[6]
5. *Hexagonal*. An oil painting from around 1450 CE depicts the baptism of St. Ursula, with a bishop apparently preparing to dunk the infant into a hexagonal font. Another medieval painting depicts the baptism of five adults – the companions of St. Ursula – in another large hexagonal font.[7]

---

[3] Regina Kuehn, *A Place for Baptism* (Chicago: Liturgy Training Publications, 1992), 41. See illustration 37.

[4] See Ferguson, *Baptism in the Early Church*, 441. See illustration 13.

[5] Ferguson, *Baptism in the Early Church*, 637. See illustration 20.

[6] Kuehn, *A Place for Baptism*, 7-8. See illustration 6.

[7] Kuehn, *A Place for Baptism*, 69-70. See illustrations 67 and 68.

6. *Tub/Tank-shaped.* This particular shape correlates with New Testament interpretations of baptism as a washing or cleansing (Titus 3:5-7). Wooden tubs may have been used for baptism as far back as the eleventh century CE, and iconography suggests that the candidates sat or knelt in the font and were immersed either by having water poured on them or by being pushed forward. Some metals tubs from the Romanesque period still survive.[8]

The point of sharing the above examples is not to encourage their imitation. Rather, it is to point out that ancient and medieval fonts were constructed so as to suggest biblical understandings of baptism. Undoubtedly for early Christians, baptismal structures were used to teach baptismal meanings, just as stained glass was used to teach important biblical narratives. Churches today might want to imitate this *method* by pondering how a new font or pool can become a means of expressing New Testament baptismal motifs.

Determining Baptismal Architecture: Recent Theological/ Liturgical Trends

Drawing on the insights of theologians such as Edward Schillebeeckx[9] and Karl Rahner,[10] late-twentieth century churches have given greater attention to the "sign value" or symbolic dimension of sacraments and sacramental rites. Concretely this meant making fuller use of the sacramental elements (water, wine, bread) and avoiding any minimalism that might obscure the meaning and nature of the sacramental sign. *Environment and Art in Catholic Worship* (1978), a document prepared by the Roman Catholic Bishops' Committee on the Liturgy (USA), calls for the "opening up of our symbols, especially the fundamental ones of bread and wine, water, oil, [and] the laying

[8] Kuehn, *A Place for Baptism*, 80-81. See illustrations 76 and 77.

[9] Edward Schillebeeckx, O. P., *Christ the Sacrament of the Encounter with God* (Franklin, WI: Sheed and Ward, 1963).

[10] See Karl Rahner, "Theology of Symbol," in *Theological Investigations*, Vol. 4 (London: Darton, Longman and Todd, 1961-1992), 221-52.

on of hands, until we can experience all of them as authentic and appreciate their symbolic value."[11] Applying this principle to both the mode and architecture of baptism, *Environment and Art* states that:

> To speak of symbols and of sacramental signification is to indicate that *immersion* is the fuller and more appropriate symbolic action in baptism. New baptismal fonts, therefore, should be constructed to allow for the immersion of infants, at least, and to allow for the pouring of water over the entire body of a child or adult. Where fonts are not so constructed, the use of a portable one is recommended.[12]

While not delving into architectural implications, the World Council of Churches' *Baptism, Eucharist and Ministry* document similarly advocates immersion as an appropriate way of symbolically expressing the meaning of baptism:

> In the celebration of baptism the symbolic dimension of water should be taken seriously and not minimalized. The act of immersion can vividly express the reality that in baptism the Christian participates in the death, burial, and resurrection of Christ.[13]

Obviously influenced by this attention to the symbolic aspect of baptism, the sacramental practices statement *Use of the Means of Grace* (UMG, Evangelical Lutheran Church in America) states that water is to be used "generously," and lists immersion among the various modes of baptism.[14] Accordingly, Lutheran congregations

[11] National Conference of Catholic Bishops, Bishops' Committee on the Liturgy, *Environment and Art in Catholic Worship* (Chicago: Liturgy Training Publications, 1993), par. 15. Henceforth EA.

[12] EA, par. 76. Emphasis added.

[13] BEM, 6.18.

[14] UMG, 26, 26A. See also ELW, 28, and Dennis L. Bushkofsky and Craig A. Satterlee, *The Christian Life: Baptism and Life Passages,* Using Evangelical Lutheran Worship, Vol. 2 (Minneapolis: Augsburg Fortress, 2008), 69.

"may consider the creation of fonts of ample proportions filled with flowing water, or baptismal pools which could allow immersion."[15] *United Methodist Book of Worship* suggests several modes of baptism, including immersion, noting how it signifies burial with Christ in accordance with Rom. 6.[16]

Developments in ecclesiology also have had repercussions for baptismal architecture. In the late-twentieth century, churches rediscovered the importance of the church as a corporate body of believers – that is, as a *priestly* people – who minister to each other and to the world. This revived interest in the doctrine of the priesthood of all believers contrasts with more clerical forms of leadership that had dominated since the Reformation, and also reflects rising social egalitarianism in Europe and America throughout the twentieth century. These developments translated into greater importance being given to the participation of the whole assembly in the Sunday liturgy. *Environment and Art* states that "among the symbols with which liturgy deals, none is more important than the assembly of believers" and that the "primary demand" on a space is to provide a place for the assembly to celebrate its liturgy.[17] An emphasis on the assembly's participation is also evident in the following statements from UMG:

> The assembled congregation participates in proclaiming the Word of God with a common voice. It sings hymns and texts of the liturgy. It confesses the Nicene or Apostles' Creed.
>
> Candidates for Holy Baptism, sponsors, and an ordained minister called by the Church gather together with the congregation for the celebration of Baptism within the corporate worship of the Church.
>
> The gathered people of God celebrate the sacrament. Holy Communion, usually celebrated within a congregation,

---

[15] UMG, 27A.

[16] "Services of the Baptismal Covenant (Introduction)," UMBW, 81.

[17] EA, 28, 40.

> also may be celebrated in synodical, churchwide, and other settings where the baptized gather....[18]

These statements imply that assembly members – those gathered for the church's public worship or liturgy – are not merely passive observers, but participants in the liturgy in an inherent way. Put another way: the liturgy is the work of the gathered people of God, rather than of ordained ministers alone. This renewed appreciation for the role played by the entire liturgical assembly was expressed not only through liturgical responses in a service, but also through new roles for lay members in the Sunday liturgy, such as lectors (Scripture readers), cantors (song leaders), sacramental ministers (especially for the distribution of the cup at the Lord's Supper), intercessors (prayer leaders), and other assistants.

Renewed attention to the assembly's role in the liturgy has important implications for baptismal architecture. Since the congregation is an important participant in the baptismal liturgy – symbolized in many services by the assembly's words of welcome to the newly baptized – the font/pool is best located where the assembly can see and hear the baptismal service. Ideally, sufficient space is allotted *around* the font/pool such that the minister(s), candidate(s), sponsors, parents, and other members of the baptismal party can gather near the font/pool. Sufficient baptismal space is also crucial if children in the assembly are regularly invited to stand near the font to obtain a better view of the baptismal action. Because water is a symbol for the *assembly's* sake, it is logical that the design and placement of the font makes water visible and *available* to the assembly, especially if assembly members are encouraged to touch the baptismal water (and make the sign of the cross) as they enter the worship space. A placement of the font/pool near the main doors of the liturgical space would best facilitate this action.

---

[18] UMG, 10, 21, 39.

Current Trends in Baptismal Architecture

In determining the baptismal architecture of a church, it is important to be aware of what contemporary churches have actually done, in order to know what is practically feasible and pastorally meaningful. We must be aware, however, that what "works" in one locale – even if that is merely two city blocks away – may not necessarily work in our own church. Thus, the goal of considering recent trends is to be guided and instructed by the efforts of others, learning both from their architectural successes and (possibly) their failures.

A quick browse of recent books on baptismal architecture covering the modern era, such as Kuehn's *A Place for Baptism*[19] or S. Anita Stauffer's *On Baptismal Fonts: Ancient and Modern*[20] reveals that contemporary churches have employed a variety of shapes and sizes in their baptismal architecture. Hence, we cannot say that any one shape has become dominant in recent decades. That is undoubtedly due to the diverse cultures, theologies, and liturgical traditions of churches. We can only generalize that newer fonts tend to express the biblical images discussed above (as we might have expected), and that many recent fonts/pools permit baptismal immersion for infants and adults. Even churches not historically associated with baptismal immersion (e.g., Roman Catholic, Lutheran, Anglican/Episcopal) have installed immersion fonts and pools. St. Mary of the Angels Roman Catholic Church, Bukit Batok, Singapore, for example, has a massive tomb-shaped immersion font located in the center of the assembly seating space, suggesting the centrality of baptism in the life of the church.[21] Immersion pools have been constructed for a number of Anglican churches in Singapore, including St. Andrew's Cathedral (near the west entrance), and the Church of the True Light, Little India (at the back of the assembly space). In some cases, European and American churches that traditionally used smaller pedestal-type

---

[19] See note 3 above.

[20] S. Anita Stauffer, *On Baptismal Fonts: Ancient and Modern* (Bramcote/Nottingham: Grove Books, 1994).

[21] For photographs of this font, go to http://stmary.sg/about-us/art-architecture/.

fonts have retrofitted their liturgical spaces with immersion pools that place the upper "bowl" portion of the older pedestal font atop the outer edge of the new immersion pool, such that water from the former can flow into the latter.[22] Although incorporating sections of an older font into a new structure is a commendable way of affirming the church of the past and its baptismal practice, care needs to be taken that the result is balanced, harmonious, and attractive.

At the same time, contemporary baptismal architecture has seen unique designs. As one enters the large gathering space or "plaza" on the first level of St. James' Anglican Church, Holland Village, Singapore, one encounters a fish-shaped immersion pool, which recalls the famous words of Tertullian: "but we, little fishes, after the example of our big fish (ΙΧΘΥΣ), Jesus Christ, are born in water, nor have we safety in any other way than by permanently abiding in the water…".[23] One of the most famous baptismal structures in North America is the circular pool at St. Benedict the African Roman Catholic Church in Chicago, Illinois, which is partly surrounded by a curved, sloping walkway that leads downward from the church entrance to the main level. The entire space of St. Benedict suggests an African hut, which reflects the African American heritage of the church and the surrounding community.[24]

Both above- and at-grade structures are common today, although preference seems to be for raised structures that offer more visual impact and less risk of accidental falls into an at-grade pool. The massive tomb-shaped immersion font in St. Mary of the Angels, Singapore, is entirely above-grade, measuring 3 m long by 1.5 m wide and 80 cm deep. One step leads to the upper edge of this font, and three lead to the inner bottom, where candidates will be immersed. St. John's Chapel Anglican, Bukit Timah, Singapore, and Wesley Methodist Churches, Singapore, both have pools that are built into the floor. At St. John's Chapel the pool is located at the right corner of the "stage" area, just in front of the assembly's seating area, giving

[22] See Kuehn, *A Place for Baptism*, 70. See illustrations 69 and 70.

[23] Tertullian, *De Baptismo* 1 (ca. 200).

[24] See Kuehn, *A Place for Baptism*, 45-50.

the assembly good visibility. At Wesley, the at-grade pool was placed in an additional seating area located next to the old assembly space. In both cases, the pool is filled for each baptismal service, drained afterwards, and then covered over. Adjacent to a ramp leading to the main entrance, the square baptismal pool of Covenant Presbyterian Church, Little India, Singapore, located entirely outdoors, is sunk into the ground. The flagstone-lined pool, embellished with a cross in the center, permits the immersion of candidates who descend several submerged steps. As the water is drained after each service, Covenant's pool presents no safety hazard. A cruciform immersion pool, with steps on three sides, is located on the grounds of Yishun Christian Church, Singapore, beside the worship hall. The tile-lined pool is surrounded by a metal railing to prevent entry when the pool is not in use.

The location of the font/pool has been a bigger issue for contemporary churches compared to ancient ones. For ancient churches, modesty dictated baptizing nude candidates in separate buildings. Since both Roman Catholic[25] and Protestant[26] churches now emphasize the public nature of baptism and the role of the baptismal liturgy itself in the spiritual formation of the assembly, separate baptismal spaces are neither desirable nor required. This changed situation poses both opportunities and challenges for churches because of the numerous options available for locating the font/pool. Since the "solution" taken by one church might not necessarily work at another, we will discuss below some of the more common options.

Many Christian communities have placed the font/pool somewhere in the main liturgical space itself. Especially in newly

---

[25] The *First Instruction for the Right Implementation of the Constitution on the Sacred Liturgy of the Second Vatican Council* states only that the font's placement should facilitate the assembly's participation (99). http://fdlc.org/Liturgy_Resources/Liturgy_Documents_files/LITURGYInterOecumenici.htm. [accessed 31 January 2014]. EA suggests placing the font either near the entrance to the liturgical space or in the midst of the liturgical assembly (77).

[26] See UMG: "A baptismal font filled with water, placed in the assembly's worship space, symbolizes the centrality of this sacrament for faith and life" (27).

designed spaces, a location near the doors leading into the liturgical space suggests that one "enters" the church by means of baptism.[27] This location also helps assembly members to be reminded of their baptism as they prepare to worship. We have alluded above to fonts/pools with such a placement, and we might also note the Church of St. Ignatius, Singapore, where a shallow pool is located at the back of the main liturgical space, just inside the doors. Other examples include Trinity Lutheran Seminary, Columbus, Ohio, USA,[28] and St. Peter's Lutheran Church, Citicorp building, New York City, USA.[29] Similarly, locating the font/pool in the gathering area of the church (i.e., the narthex) also suggests that baptism is the means of initiation into the church.[30] In some cases, such as St. Mary of the Angels, mentioned above, the font/pool might be located within the main assembly area in proximity to the altar-table and other liturgical centers.[31] This location highlights baptism's role as a means of grace.

A tropical climate opens up the possibility of placing the font/pool outdoors. Trinity and Charis Methodist Churches in Singapore have sizeable immersion pools located on the perimeter of outdoor plazas (open gathering areas). This placement allows a worship assembly to gather about the font in order to witness the baptismal action and alleviates the need to mop up any displaced water. Although the symbolism of baptism as "entrance" into the church or being baptized *into* the corporate body of the church might be lost, the location of the font/pool in an open outdoor area – possibly visible from the public street (like with St. James' Anglican Church in Holland Village) – enables the baptismal liturgy to become a public witness. Thus, in choosing the location of a font/

[27] For other examples of this type of placement for the font/pool, see Kuehn, *A Place for Baptism*, 111-12. See illustrations 115, 116, and 117.

[28] For images of the font at Trinity Lutheran Seminary, see Walter C. Huffman and S. Anita Stauffer, *Where We Worship* (Minneapolis, Augsburg, 1987), 19.

[29] See Huffman and Stauffer, *Where We Worship*, 22.

[30] See Kuehn, *A Place for Baptism*, 112. See illustration 118.

[31] See Kuehn, *A Place for Baptism*, 114-15. See illustrations 124 and 125.

pool, a building committee and congregation will need to discern and weigh theological, liturgical, and pastoral priorities and most likely will have to accept some compromises.

Of course, locating a font in a separate building or structure altogether is by no means unheard of in recent times. An architecturally distinct baptistery or baptismal chapel symbolically heightens the importance of baptism as a sacrament or ordinance of the church. Further, it suggests the mystery of baptism, insofar as there is an element of seclusion to the action when it is performed in a space separated from the main assembly area. While a detached baptistery might hamper or rule out the celebration of baptism at a public liturgy, it is still possible to build one that symbolizes entry into the church, e.g., when it is situated between the gathering area (narthex) and the main liturgical space. Even a baptistery placed adjacent to the main liturgical space suggests an integral relationship between baptism and the ongoing worship life of the church.[32]

One common feature today is the provision of ample space about the baptismal vessel. As noted above, ministers, sponsors, family members, and others need space for gathering around the font or pool, as would children from the assembly if they are invited to witness the baptism. It is difficult to prescribe precise measurements for the area around the font/pool, but if the font/pool is in a large open area, precise dimensions become irrelevant. In any event, a building committee will need to have a clear idea of how the baptismal font/pool will be used in the liturgy and then communicate that vision to the architect or designer, who, it is hoped, will make ample provision for spatial needs.

Another recent design trend is the incorporation of circulating water, a feature inspired by the *Didache's* reference to baptizing in "running water," that is, in a spring, river, or stream.[33] Continuously flowing water symbolizes baptism as a life-giving experience (cf. John 4:13-14), and, as a by-product, serves as a natural aural accompaniment to the liturgy. One requirement is an electric pump

---

[32] See Kuehn, *A Place for Baptism*, 112-13. See illustrations 120 and 121.

[33] The *Didache* 7.1 (late-first or early-second cent.).

preferably located out of earshot of the assembly, or in a place with adequate sound proofing. Many congregations find the costs of circulation equipment and electricity prohibitive, but some churches minimize costs by circulating the baptismal water only before, during, and after worship services. Also, circulating water will require regular cleaning of the font to avoid algae growth as well as maintenance to avoid leakage. Congregations located in coastal regions or islands (e.g., Singapore, Malaysia, and Indonesia) may find the symbolism of constantly circulating water particularly meaningful.

Just as a diversity of shapes and sizes has been used for baptismal fonts/pools, so various materials have been employed. Many of the larger fonts built in the post-Vatican 2 era use marble or granite. In some cases, a single piece of stone is hollowed out to form a tub or tomb-like structure (e.g., the black granite used at St. Mary of the Angels, Singapore). In other cases, slabs of granite or marble are fastened together and water-proofed in order to form the font. Stone fonts: (1) recall the biblical images of water from a rock (Num. 20:10-11) and/or Christ as the rock (1 Cor. 10:4); (2) suggest the gravity of the baptismal action; (3) hint of the permanent/eternal significance of baptism; and (4) make a strong visual impact. A variety of other heavy materials has been used, including poured concrete, brick, wood,[34] and metals such as copper and bronze. Lesser materials, especially plastic and glass, tend to be avoided except by churches facing severe budgetary constraints. To give a stronger, more permanent appearance, in-ground baptismal pools make use of ceramic tiles (e.g., Church of the True Light, Singapore)[35] or different types of stone (e.g., Church of the Covenant, Singapore) as inner linings.

Congregations that find the construction of a large stone font or pool financially difficult have resorted to more modest materials, e.g., glass, earthenware, or aggregate stone. Many such fonts do not necessarily *appear* cheap nor do they detract from the dignity of

[34] For a description of a font constructed out of wood (with a copper water container), see Kuehn, *A Place for Baptism*, 102-8.

[35] See Kuehn, *A Place for Baptism*, 44. See illustration 41.

baptism, especially if designed and constructed by competent and talented artists.[36] A metal washtub, whose appearance is enhanced by stones and potted plants, could even be used as a substitute for an immersion font/pool. Nevertheless, we might consider such fonts as only temporary measures until greater financial resources become available, keeping in mind the theological importance of baptism and the reality that our actions today will be our legacy to Christians of tomorrow.

Following the principle of "less is more," fonts/pools of recent decades have made minimal use of symbolic iconography. As noted above, the shape of the font/pool, whether cruciform, round, octagonal, or hexagonal is itself symbolic. Building committees and congregations have realized that there is little need to put symbols on a symbol.[37] Indeed, secondary symbols are counter-productive because they draw attention away from the font and its inherent symbolism. Nevertheless, common symbols incorporated into baptismal architecture include crosses, depictions of the baptism of Christ, and perhaps fish – although these are often quite minimal and understated.[38]

Other Baptismal Needs

Besides the font/pool, baptism has other physical needs. Some baptismal rites include "secondary" or "explanatory" ceremonies such as anointing the newly baptized (to depict the baptismal "anointing" of the Holy Spirit), clothing them in a new garment (cf. Gal. 3:27), and/or conferring a baptismal candle to symbolize the "illumination" of the newly baptized (cf. Heb. 6:4). For churches that celebrate these rites, supplies of oil, garments, and candles will need to be kept on hand or ordered in advance of the baptismal service. A special oil container (an oil *stock*) might also be needed for

[36] See Kuehn, *A Place for Baptism*, 129-32.

[37] The majority of the contemporary baptismal fonts illustrated in the books of Kuehn and Stauffer are unadorned.

[38] Examples include the cross designs in the fonts at Covenant Presbyterian Church and Church of the True Light, both in Little India, Singapore.

anointing. During the baptismal service, all of the above-mentioned items can be placed on a special table (a *credence table*) located near the font. A paschal candle placed close to the font might be lighted during the baptism, and then relocated near the altar for lighting during the Easter season. Practical needs for baptism involving an immersion pool include bath mats placed around the pool (to absorb displaced water), squeegees to push water into drain vents, and, if the font is sunk below floor level, a metal or nylon grating to prevent worshippers from falling into the font. When the candidates are fully immersed, changing rooms are also required, and these should be located as close as possible to the baptismal space on the same level.

Conclusion

The theological, pastoral, and liturgical importance of baptism invites Christian churches to consider baptismal architecture carefully. God's grace is not dependent on the type, size, or quality of the font, nor should we think that baptismal architecture is more important than God's baptismal grace or a person's baptismal faith. Rather, we attend thoughtfully to baptismal architecture so that we might express in visible form what we say about baptism in our confessional documents and liturgical books. Thus, baptismal architecture is one means of forming a community of Christ that seeks to live out the meaning of baptism.

For Further Reading

Christopherson, D. Foy. *A Place of Encounter: Renewing Worship Spaces.* Worship Matters. Minneapolis: Augsburg Fortress, 2004.

Keeran, Daniel. *Ancient and Medieval Baptismal Fonts.* N. p. Create Space Independent Publishing Platform, 2009.

Mauck, Marchita B. *Places for Worship: A Guide to Building and Renovating.* American Essays in Liturgy. Minneapolis: Augsburg Fortress, 1995.

CHAPTER 6

Baptism and its Participants

Baptism involves not only candidates but ministers, sponsors, parents, and a liturgical assembly. We might overlook these other participants because of a tendency to focus on the candidates, their "decision," and "salvation." But we need to consider all of those involved in order to gain a better understanding of the baptismal process. Furthermore, clarifying these roles can enrich the experience of baptism/Christian initiation for all participants and lead to a deepening of their sense of what it means to be a baptized Christian. This chapter seeks to define the roles of the various baptismal participants and describe the main actions of each. I will not enter into the fray over the proper age of baptismal candidates since: (1) arguments on both sides of the question have already been discussed in this book; and (2) churches have overcome much of the division over this question and moved toward mutual recognition of baptism due to the influence of the World Council of Churches' *Baptism, Eucharist and Ministry* (BEM) document.

Ministers of Baptism

Baptism is normally administered by ordained clergy. In their various confessional and disciplinary documents, Lutheran,[1] Anglican,[2] Methodist,[3] and Reformed[4] churches explicitly identify preaching and presiding at the sacraments as the chief work of ordained ministers (the office of ministry). BEM does likewise.[5] Because the means of grace are exercised in public services and require careful pastoral oversight, the sacraments are administered by those who are called and trained for the *public* ministry of the church. Yet, sacramental ministry is not unilateral since clergy are called to serve both God *and* the liturgical assembly. As BEM puts it: "…the ordained ministry has no existence apart from the community. Ordained ministers can fulfil their calling only in and for the community. They cannot dispense with the recognition, the support, and the encouragement of the community."[6] Thus, ordained clergy baptize in cooperation with the local Christian community and this relationship is best demonstrated when baptism is administered in a public service with laypersons serving in various liturgical roles.[7] Conversely, a normative practice of private baptisms, regardless of the location, obscures this mutual relationship and may suggest clericalism. Ordained ministers are therefore encouraged to plan *public* celebrations of baptism and

---

[1] See *The Augsburg Confession* (1530), BC, Art. V, 41.1.

[2] See *An Outline of the Faith, Commonly Called the Catechism*, in BCP 1979, 856, and *Articles of Religion*, Art. XXIII, BCP 1979, 872.

[3] *The Book of Discipline of The Methodist Church in Singapore* (Singapore: The Discipline Revision Commission of The Methodist Church in Singapore, 2009), 568.2.

[4] See *Westminster Confession* (1646), "Of the Church" (Art. XXV), Center for Reformed Theology and Apologetics, http://www.reformed.org/documents/wcf_with_proofs/index.html, and *The Directory for the Public Worship of God* (1645), "Of Baptism,"http://www.reformed.org/documents/index.html [accessed 4 March 2014].

[5] BEM, 6.22.

[6] BEM, 22.

[7] See UMG, 22.

involve lay members of the local congregation in the leadership of these services and in the entire baptismal process.

Denominational worship books provide for both ordained and lay ministerial roles in the baptismal liturgy. Ordained ministers: (1) introduce the service; (2) exhort the sponsors/parents and congregation; (3) offer the prayer of thanksgiving (over the water); (4) ask the questions involved in the renunciation and profession of faith; (5) baptize the candidates; and (6) administer the explanatory rites (handlaying, anointing, sign of the cross). Lay ministers might: (1) lead intercessory prayers;[8] (2) pour water into the font before or during the thanksgiving prayer; (3) hold a book or folder for the presiding minister so that the latter is free to raise his/her hands in the orans position during the prayer; and (4) perform other manual acts. An acolyte may lead a procession to the font (if the opening rites are performed elsewhere) while carrying a processional cross, and act as a server by passing napkins, an oil container, and other items to the presiding minister. Assembly singing after each baptism (e.g., an acclamation) and/or at the conclusion of the baptismal liturgy (e.g., a short acclamation, psalm or hymn as members of the baptismal party return to their places) will be led by a choir or cantor. At the Easter Vigil, a cantor or a lay assisting minister may lead a special sung litany as the ministers, candidate(s), sponsors, and parents make their way to the font/pool.[9]

Congregational Representatives

Because baptism is properly set within the local church's liturgy, it is only fitting that designated members act as a representatives of that church. In so doing, they symbolize the church's role in bringing persons to baptism and then welcoming them into the local fellowship. The tasks assigned to congregational representatives vary

[8] Some liturgical books allow for the placement of the prayers of intercession *within* rather than following the baptismal liturgy during the Sunday service since it is natural to intercede for the newly baptized. Such prayers are led by a lay liturgical minister. See "Holy Baptism," LBW, 309, and "Holy Baptism," CW, 360.

[9] "Resurrection of Our Lord: Vigil of Easter," ELW, 653.

from book to book; they might present the candidates for baptism,[10] give a lighted candle to the newly baptized (or parents of newly baptized children),[11] and lead the assembly's welcome of the newly baptized.[12]

Candidates for Baptism

Candidates for baptism are: (1) adults who have come to faith in Jesus Christ and desire to repent of sin and renounce former religious loyalties; and (2) young children whose parents are committed, active Christians who pledge themselves to the Christian nurture of their children. In both cases, baptism will involve a process of spiritual formation before and after baptism. Adult converts: (1) undergo prebaptismal formation (perhaps in the adult catechumenate), as well as postbaptismal formation in the form of mystagogy (explanation of the sacraments); (2) discern their vocation in the world; and (3) experience spiritual formation and growth through ongoing liturgical participation. In the case of infant candidates, parents and sponsors will receive prebaptismal instruction and preparation, and the baptized children will themselves undergo a process of formation leading to their confirmation or affirmation of baptism, at which time they profess the Christian faith and take personal responsibility for participation in the life and mission of the church. In some cases, confirmation will function as admission to Holy Communion and the attainment of full church membership. The recognition that baptism is a process involving life-long growth potentially bridges differences between churches that baptize only those who can speak for themselves, versus churches that baptize candidates of all ages.[13]

---

[10] "The Sacrament of Baptism," BCW, 405; "The Baptismal Covenant I," UMBW, 87; "Holy Baptism," CW, 352.

[11] "Holy Baptism," LBW, 311. It is also possible that the optional conferral of a baptismal garment and candle in the baptismal services of UMBW (91) and ELW (590-91) may be done by a congregational representative.

[12] "Holy Baptism," LBW, 312; "Holy Baptism," ELW, 591;"The Sacrament of Baptism," BCW, 414.

[13] Paul Fiddes, "The Baptism of Believers," BT, 79.

Although the church baptizes in order to make life-long disciples, it nevertheless may baptize those in danger of immanent death.[14] Baptism under such circumstances becomes a sign of God's faithfulness to believers as they venture into the "valley of the shadow of death." Liturgical resources are available for emergency baptism especially in Lutheran and Anglican worship books.[15] However, baptism should not be *delayed* to the point of death, as if the sacrament were merely a magical way of securing a place in the world to come and avoiding judgment, rather than a way of participating in Christ's mission to *this* world. Those who come to faith should be mindful that the forgiveness pronounced in baptism frees one for service to Christ in the present life and that baptism is properly sought as soon as it is practically possible and pastorally responsible.

There is nearly universal agreement that baptism is *never* administered to the dead.[16] Most Christians understand that a funeral is the appropriate way of commending a deceased person to God. Because the stillbirth of a child is often met with confusion and uncertainty, pastors will want to counsel the bereaved about the desirability of a funeral (rather than baptism), and use appropriate liturgical resources.[17]

Neither is baptism administered to those already baptized.[18] Because baptism is bound up with the forgiveness of sins, union with Christ in his death and resurrection, and the gift of the Holy Spirit, baptism has a "once for all" character that makes it unrepeatable. The

---

[14] UMG, 23. Not all Protestant churches are in agreement on this issue.

[15] For services of baptism in an emergency, see *Occasional Services: A Companion to Lutheran Book of Worship* (Minneapolis: Augsburg Publishing House; Philadelphia: Board of Publication, Lutheran Church in America, 1982), 16-22; BCP 1979, 313-14; *The Lutheran Service Book* (St. Louis: Concordia Publishing House, 2006), 858.

[16] See UMG, 23A. An exception is the Church of Jesus Christ of Latter-Day Saints, or the Mormon Church. See The Church of Jesus Christ of Latter-Day Saints, http://mormon.org/faq/topic/baptism/question/baptism-for-the-dead [accessed 11 March 2014].

[17] "A Service of Death and Resurrection for a Stillborn Child," UMBW, 170-71.

[18] UMG,16; "Services of the Baptismal Covenant (Introduction)," UMBW, 83.

action of rebaptizing a person calls into question the validity of God's promises and, in some cases, the validity of a baptism conferred in another church. While a person might question the authenticity of his/her prior baptism, e.g., due to a perceived lack of sincerity or maturity, rebaptism is entirely unnecessary. Baptized Christians who come to a profound sense of spiritual renewal can mark that experience in a public rite of affirmation of baptism.[19] When a person requests baptism because of *uncertainty* about whether he/she was baptized properly (using the trinitarian formula), or even baptized at all, a rite for *conditional baptism* may be used.[20]

Baptismal Sponsors

In the early church, converts from paganism needed an established, baptized Christian to vouch for their sincerity and help them in the baptismal formation process. Such persons were known as "godparents." Even after infants became the normal candidates for baptism, godparents still accompanied infant candidates to the baptismal service, held them during various ritual actions, and answered questions on their behalf (e.g., creedal interrogations). The role of godparent symbolized how baptism incorporated a person into the larger "family" of the Christian church.[21] There was a time in Protestant history when godparents had legal responsibilities within society, namely, to become foster parents of their orphaned godchildren and provide for the Christian nurture of these children.

---

[19] See "Affirmation of Baptism," ELW, 596-600; "The Baptismal Covenant III," UMBW, 106-10; "Baptism and Reaffirmation of the Baptismal Covenant," BCW, 435.

[20] See "Emergency Baptism," BCP 1979, 313. The whole rite is as follows:

If there is reasonable doubt that a person has been baptized with water, "In the Name of the Father, and of the Son, and of the Holy Spirit" (which are the essential parts of Baptism), the person is baptized in the usual manner, but this form of words is used: If you are not already baptized, *N.*, I baptize you in the Name of the Father, and of the Son, and of the Holy Spirit.

[21] Some Eastern Orthodox churches continue to require "godparents" who are not members of the candidate's biological family, in order to suggest that baptism is more than a private, family rite for blessing new infants.

More recently, in the twentieth century, the role of godparent or sponsor became largely honorary, at least in the popular mind, as any legal obligations have fallen away.

Most Protestant churches today continue to require godparents or sponsors who assume responsibility for the Christian nurture of a baptismal candidate. The mobility of populations today, however, necessitates that *parents* be the primary providers of Christian nurture for a young child.[22] Others may be designated as additional sponsors who assist parents in the Christian nurture of a baptized child and perhaps accompany parents through their prebaptismal preparation. Ideally, these persons are members of the baptizing congregation so that they can help foster a child's integration into that congregation.[23] Thus, the role of additional sponsors is more than ceremonial or honorary. In the case of an adult baptismal candidate, the sponsor "accompanies the candidate throughout the catechumenate, in prayer and in mutual learning, assisting the newly baptized to join in the ministry and mission of the community."[24] This person endorses the adult candidate by vouching for the sincerity of his/her conversion and intention to live the Christian life. The choice of baptismal sponsors for both adults and children needs to be made with care, for such persons should be capable of sharing their personal faith and modeling the Christian life.

Parents and other sponsors of an infant candidate do far more than celebrate the birth of a new child; they participate in a child's ongoing baptismal journey. They help the child grasp how baptism results in life-long learning and discipleship in the church. Parents and other sponsors provide for the instruction and formation that

[22] In some cultures, the role of godparent became largely honorific and ceremonial in nature. With a renewed understanding of baptismal sponsorship that emphasizes how additional sponsors assist parents with the Christian nurture of children, many official worship books prefer to speak of baptismal "sponsors" rather than "godparents."

[23] See UMG, 20, 20A, 20C. See also "Services of the Baptismal Covenant (Introduction),"UMBW, 82.

[24] UMG, 20C. See "Services of the Baptismal Covenant (Introduction)," UMBW, 83.

lead to the child's adoption of a Christian lifestyle. This means accompanying a child to worship and Christian education. Sponsors of a young child make promises to this effect in the baptismal liturgy and the church expects them to do this with sincerity.

Parents also serve as teachers of their baptized child. In societies dominated by a consumer mentality with its ideals of professionalism, parents/guardians might think that the Christian nurture of their child can be left to the church. But like any culture with its ideals, norms, and practices, the Christian faith is inculcated not only through instruction but also through hands-on participation[25] which will necessarily happen in the home. "Christianity is caught, not taught," and sixty minutes of Sunday School every week will accomplish little unless a child can participate in a family life imbued with the Christian ethos and Christian practices. Parents therefore model prayer, good works, and the love of neighbor. Additionally, if they are serious about Christian formation, they also model participation in the church's life of worship, learning, and service to the community. By doing so, they become credible examples for their child, moving beyond the role of moralists who lecture about the need to be Christian. In sum: parents/guardians are in partnership with the church, its pastors and Christian educators in the formation of their baptized children, as opposed to merely being "consumers" of the Christian formation that churches offer.

In the baptismal liturgy, parents and other sponsors of a child express and ritually enact their role through three actions. First, they present the child for baptism.[26] A precursor to this action is found in the *Apostolic Tradition* attributed to Hippolytus of Rome (ca. 217 CE), which speaks of Christians bringing baptismal candidates before the church (i.e., presenting them) for an examination to determine their

---

[25] For a discussion of how community is formed by both reflection and action, see Simon Chan, *Liturgical Theology: The Church as Worshipping Community* (Downer's Grove: IVP Academic, 2006), 66-67.

[26] See "Holy Baptism," ELW, 584; "Holy Baptism," BCP 1979, 301; and "Baptism," DSSB, 49. In some cases, a representative from the congregation will present the baptismal candidates; see "The Baptismal Covenant I," UMBW, 87.

fitness for participation in the catechumenate.[27] More than a mere formality, this act of presentation visibly symbolizes the personal responsibility parents take for their child. Second, as mentioned above, parents and sponsors of an infant candidate promise to model the Christian life for the child and provide nurture in the Christian faith.[28] While parental duties might be specified (e.g., bring a child to worship, teach the Lord's Prayer, creed, and Ten Commandments), sponsors (other than parents) promise a more general role in the nurturance of the newly baptized. Third, parents and sponsors (perhaps with the assembly) reject evil and either confess the faith by means of an interrogatory (question and answer) form of the Apostles' Creed (Lutheran, Anglican), or profess allegiance to Christ (Methodist). Protestants differ in their understanding of the renunciation and profession of faith by the parents of a small child; some hold that they answer both for themselves and "for" (or "on behalf of") their small child who is unable to speak for him/herself.[29] This understanding has been severely criticized by adherents of believer's baptism. By contrast, Lutherans and Methodists understand these actions as a reaffirmation of faith by parents as they prepare to fulfil their roles as baptismal sponsors. In other words, in renouncing evil and professing the faith of the church, parents and sponsors confirm their own faith and commitment which is lived out by imparting the Christian faith to a baptized child.

To a large extent, the question of what parents and additional sponsors actually do in renouncing evil and professing their allegiance to Christ or their trinitarian faith relates to the question of what is done in confirmation. If confirmation is something new over and against baptism – the young baptized person's mature confession of faith and declaration of allegiance to the church (and hence joining a church) – then the baptism of infants seems to be contingent on parental faith and a later profession of faith by the young person.

---

[27] *The Apostolic Tradition Ascribed to Hippolytus of Rome* 15 (ca. 217).

[28] "Holy Baptism," ELW, 584; "The Baptismal Covenant I," UMBW, 88; "Holy Baptism," BCP 1979, 302.

[29] See "Holy Baptism," BCP 1979, 302; "Baptism," DSSB, 49, 51.

By contrast, if confirmation is the baptized child's *affirmation* of a baptism – saying "yes" to God's baptismal promises and ongoing work in his/her life – then there is no need to assert a proxy faith or imply a provisional Christian initiation. The affirmation model of confirmation avoids any dichotomization that might pit baptism and confirmation against each other and raise questions as to whether baptism constitutes full and complete Christian initiation. Because of the diversity and complexity of views surrounding sponsorship, pastors and church staff providing prebaptismal counseling to parents need to be clear about what their denomination really intends when the liturgy requires parents and sponsors to reject evil and confess the trinitarian faith of the Church.

The mobility of populations today poses challenges for baptismal sponsorship. What happens if the family of a newly-baptized child moves to a new location? What if a sponsor chosen by the local church is required by work or family commitments to move? Similarly, what if a newly-baptized adult or that person's baptismal sponsor has to relocate on relatively short notice soon after the baptism? In all cases, congregations need to find sponsors or friends who can assist newly-baptized persons (and their families) with ongoing spiritual development. The communal nature of baptism requires that churches have plans for such contingencies.

The Congregation

Christians over the centuries have endeavored to maintain a vital connection between baptism and the Christian community's life and worship – with varying degrees of success. According to the late-first century *Didache*, members of the local church *may* fast with the baptismal candidates and ministers.[30] Later documents indicate that newly-baptized adults received their first communion with the rest of the church community at the time of their baptism.[31] But once infants became the primary candidates for baptism, the sacrament was administered in private soon after birth, with only the godparents in

[30] The *Didache* 7.1 (late-first or early-second cent.).

[31] Justin the Martyr, *First Apology* 65 (ca. 160); *Apostolic Tradition* 21.

attendance. As we noted in ch. 4, Reformed and Anglican Churches of the sixteenth century *mandated* the administration of baptism at the Sunday service so that the assembly might witness the reception of a new Christian into its fellowship and all present might be reminded of their baptism.[32] Nineteenth-century American revival camp meetings and the churches influenced by revival worship assumed the public celebration of baptism so that the event served as a new Christian's *public* testimony to their personal faith. In the twentieth century, private baptisms in Lutheran and Anglican churches remained common, in some cases for practical reasons such as the Sunday morning schedule of multiple services not allowing time for baptism. Nevertheless, the influence of liturgical renewal has made the Sunday liturgy a preferred baptismal time for many Protestants today, as indicated by various liturgical books.[33] Thus, in the last century there was a growing consensus that baptism is to be celebrated in a congregation's Sunday liturgy, and the Sunday liturgy of the local church is the rightful place of baptism.[34] As we will see in the following chapter, most modern baptismal rites are configured as acts of worship involving a liturgical assembly, whose role (often) is to confess the faith along with parents and sponsors, pray for the baptismal candidates, welcome the newly baptized into the community, and make various liturgical responses. The assembly is thus more than an audience who overhears the baptismal rite.

But the congregation's baptismal role is larger than even the liturgy. In a sense, the local congregation "provides" the pastors and teachers who give prebaptismal instruction, as well as the sponsors who (as noted above) assist in this process. Following baptism,

---

[32] "On Holy Baptism" (The Strasbourg Order of Baptism after 1537), CIRP, 38; "Of the Administration of Public Baptism to be Used in the Church," BCP 1549, CIRP, 89.

[33] "Notes on the Liturgy," LBW, 30; "Notes on the Services," ELW, 27; "The Sacrament of Baptism," BCW, 403; "Holy Baptism," CW, 346; "The Services of the Baptismal Covenant I," UMBW, 81. See also BEM 6.23.

[34] A notable exception was the baptism of Prince George of Cambridge on Wednesday, 23 October 2013, at the Royal Chapel of St. James Palace, London, UK.

the local community's worship/sacramental life nurtures newly-baptized Christians, and its service projects in the community give newly-baptized persons opportunities to live out their Christian calling. Furthermore, a church's mission work in the local community and overseas enables the newly baptized to participate in the making of new disciples. Lastly, the local church community's fellowship provides personal support which sustains the baptized in the Christian life, and this becomes especially crucial in times of personal crisis. In a sense, there is a reciprocal relationship between the church and baptism: baptism replenishes the church with new members and thereby gives vitality to its fellowship, while the church provides the very means and context for baptism and baptismal formation. The church and the sacrament of baptism cannot survive without each other!

Baptism Outside the Church's Liturgy

It is not unusual for baptism to be administered outside the liturgy of the Sunday assembly, and in some cases this is an exception to ordained presidency at baptism. Some Protestant churches (e.g., Anglican and Lutheran) permit lay persons to baptize in cases of imminent death and encourage their members to know the procedures for emergency baptism.[35] Others, such as Methodist[36] and Reformed[37] churches, discourage the practice. Much of the impetus for emergency baptism came from the teaching that baptism is necessary for salvation, which created the fear that those who died unbaptized are "damned." But those churches that allow the practice have transcended such a narrow view of baptism and affirm that baptism incorporates into the church and commissions a person for Christian discipleship. Churches also stipulate that if a person

---

[35] See "Holy Baptism," BCP 1979, 313-14, and UMG, 23.

[36] See "Services of the Baptismal Covenant (Introduction)," UMBW, 83. Note that John Wesley did *not* provide a rite for "private" (i.e. "emergency") baptism for American Methodists.

[37] See "Of Baptism," in *The Directory for Publick Worship*, http://www.reformed.org/documents/index.html [accessed 4 March 2014].

baptized under such circumstances survives,[38] the baptism should be recognized at a public worship service in order to encourage a relationship between the newly-baptized person and the church.

Conclusion

A few years ago the saying "it takes a village to raise a child" was used to highlight the communal nature of preparing children for life and citizenship in the modern world. In a similar way, Christians might say that "it takes a church to form a new Christian." Indeed, the church is in partnership with God in the making and sustaining of new Christians, just as it "partners" with God in caring for the creation and spreading the gospel. A candidate's attainment of full Christian maturity, of course, does not depend entirely on the local community, for ultimately the person's attainment of faith is a gift of the Holy Spirit, who works where and when he pleases. We can certainly take some comfort knowing that Christian initiation is not entirely in our hands! Yet, the recognition that God uses the local church to impart faith suggests that the local church take its role in Christian initiation very seriously. Indeed, we might wonder whether a baptismal practice that excludes the local church community entirely is not in some sense invalid.

[38] See UMG, 23B.

CHAPTER 7

The Baptismal Service

It might be tempting to reduce baptism to a pouring or sprinkling of water while saying the prescribed formula. In that case, we might suppose that baptism requires little thought, as long as we do the "right" things. But such thinking is short-sighted. Even in a service where the washing is the main action, it too must be performed with great care. When a service requires ceremonies and gestures in addition to the washing, these need to be administered thoughtfully because they unfold the meaning of baptism. Accordingly, this chapter seeks to provide practical guidance on the performance of all these ritual actions. This concern is not to be equated with ritualism or liturgical fussiness; a well-considered liturgical practice results in a consistency and competence that allows the focus to be on the meaning of the rite – rather than on the minister's awkwardness. The care that we take in celebrating a rite will serve both the assembly and God. At the same time, this chapter will provide historical and theological commentary so that worship leaders can relate baptism to larger theological and pastoral concerns and thereby avoid a merely ritualistic approach to baptism. The focus will be the rites used by churches in Singapore and elsewhere in Southeast Asia, namely, those in *Lutheran Book of Worship* (LBW), *Evangelical Lutheran Worship* (ELW), the *Diocese of Singapore Service Book* (DSSB, Anglican), the *United Methodist Book of Worship* (UMBW), the official baptismal rites of the Presbyterian Church in Singapore (PCS) and a rite used by some Singaporean Baptist Churches (BAP). For all of these, a profession of faith and a washing accompanied by the traditional baptismal formula ("I baptize you in the name of the Father," etc.) stand at the heart of baptism. Other shared elements (e.g., renunciation of the devil/evil, welcome into the congregation) vary in form and wording. Readers may find it helpful to refer to these baptismal services when working through this chapter.

The Shape of the Baptismal Liturgy

The baptismal rites of the "liturgical" or "traditional" Protestant churches (Lutherans, Anglicans, Methodists, and Presbyterians) explored in this chapter share a similar structure or shape, that might be outlined as follows:

Opening address (introduction to the service)
Presentation of the candidates
Admonitions/questions to parents, sponsors, assembly
Renunciation, adhesion (allegiance to Christ), profession of faith
Thanksgiving ("for water" or "at the font," or "for baptism")
Washing
Explanatory rites: clothing, laying on of hands, anointing, candle
Welcome into the congregation

Of course, there are some variations. LBW and ELW have no act of adhesion whereby candidates pledge personal loyalty to Christ, as in DSSB or UMBW. DSSB and UMBW place the renunciation and act of adhesion at the beginning of the service, rather than in juxtaposition with the profession of faith. The Presbyterian Church in Singapore adult rite (PCS-A) has no examination of (exhortation to) sponsors nor explanatory rites. The Baptist rite consists simply of questions to the candidate, the washing, and a charge to the newly baptized.The baptismal rites in LBW/ELW, DSSB, and UMBW are to be used for both adult and infant candidates (separately or together), and provide appropriate texts and responses both for those who can answer for themselves and for parents and sponsors of young children. Essentially, the composite (adult+infant) rites studied in this chapter are modeled on *adult baptism.* The point of using a composite rite is to symbolize one baptism administered to candidates of all ages. Admittedly, such rites can be somewhat complex and possibly confusing to members of the assembly who follow the service in a hymnal/worship book. Also, the UMBW rite (Baptismal Covenant I) can be used for those occasions related to baptism and church membership: confirmation or reaffirmation of faith, reception into the Methodist Church by those from other denominations, and reception into the local congregation for those coming from other Methodist congregations. Since church membership is conferred by baptism, it is fitting to ritualize membership rites within a baptismal context.[1]

Baptism in the Liturgy of the Sunday Assembly

As noted previously, most Protestants have long emphasized baptismal celebration within the Sunday liturgy, so that assembly members can witness the making of a new Christian and be reminded of their own baptism. An important liturgical rite such as baptism is appropriately included in the Sunday liturgy, since the latter is central to the church's life. In some liturgical books, such as DSSB,[2] the baptismal rite provided is a full service of Word and Sacrament that could "stand alone" as the liturgy for Sunday or another occasion.[3] The other services considered in this chapter are

---

1 "The Baptismal Covenant I," UMBW, 92-94; see "Holy Baptism," BCP 1979, 309-10.

2 "Baptism," DSSB, 48-53.

3 See "Baptism," BCP 1979, 299-310.

"detachable" rites meant to be inserted into the Sunday liturgy. Most liturgical books indicate that the baptismal rite proper (introduction of the rite through the assembly's welcome of the candidates) will take place after the biblical readings and sermon to symbolize how baptism is a response to God's Word.[4] When baptism follows the word portion of the liturgy, the sermon can offer encouragement to the candidates, sponsors and parents, remind all present about the meaning of baptism, set a tone of joy and expectation, and evoke a response of faith to God's baptismal promises. LBW and ELW suggest that when only infant candidates are involved, the baptism may take place during the gathering portion of the service.[5] According to the Lutheran document *Use of the Means of Grace* (UMG), this placement of the rite symbolizes how infants will later be instructed in the Word (during their years of maturation), and conveys the baptismal nature of the rite for confession and forgiveness that normally begins the Lutheran service.[6] Furthermore, when part of the gathering, the baptismal rite signifies how baptism itself serves as one's "entrance" into the church.

In recent years, two patterns of baptismal celebration have emerged in the services of the Easter Vigil. Some liturgical books place baptism immediately following the readings from the Old Testament, and before the eucharistic liturgy in order to juxtapose the biblical typologies of baptism with the actual celebration of baptism (e.g., Genesis 1:1–2:2, which suggests that baptism is a new creation).[7] Most books prescribe baptizing after the resurrection gospel and sermon in order to highlight one's baptismal participation in the resurrection of Christ.[8]

---

[4] See "Notes on the Liturgy," LBW, 30; "Notes on the Services," ELW, 28; "The Services of the Baptismal Covenant (Introduction)," UMBW, 81.

[5] "Notes," LBW, 30; "Notes," ELW, 28.

[6] UMG, 21B.

[7] "Vigil of Easter," LBW, 152; "Resurrection of Our Lord: Vigil of Easter," ELW, 652; "The Great Vigil of Easter," BCP 1979, 292.

[8] "Vigil of Easter," ELW, 653; "The Great Vigil of Easter," BCW, 309; "Vigil of Easter," BCP 1979, 295; "Easter Vigil or First Service of Easter," UMBW, 376. In

Service Introduction

Most baptismal services in Protestant worship books begin with an address that defines baptism, identifies its spiritual gifts (forgiveness, salvation, incorporation into Christ and his church), and points to the effects of baptism (holy living, participation in the life and mission of the local congregation). In some cases, the introduction includes a biblical quotation (e.g., Matt. 28:18-20) that serves as a warrant for baptism or a demonstration of the biblical foundation of baptism in the words and actions of Jesus Christ.[9] This introduction is addressed to the baptismal party (candidates, sponsors, parents) and to the assembly. Its didactic importance cannot be underestimated since it may be the only baptismal instruction that many church members receive following their own baptism or confirmation. Since most baptismal service introductions are brief, worship leaders are encouraged to use them, omitting them only when a shorter service is necessary (e.g., when baptizing a critically ill person or someone in danger of imminent death). By instructing the assembly about the meaning of baptism, the rite embodies Christ's own command to teach (Matt. 28).

ELW provides two options for the introduction. The option in the right column ("In baptism, our gracious heavenly Father..."), taken from LBW,[10] has a decidedly paschal tone, emphasizing baptism as salvation from sin and death and participation in Christ's death and resurrection, reflecting Luther's mainly paschal interpretation of baptism.[11] In line with the Lutheran doctrine of justification,[12] human salvation is seen to rest on the initiative of God in baptism, rather than on human feelings, decisions, and actions. But baptism

---

the case of ELW, the two options for the placement of the baptismal liturgy within the Easter Vigil (after the Old Testament readings or after the sermon and Hymn of the Day) parallel similar options for celebrating baptism within the Sunday liturgy.

[9] Presbyterian Church in Singapore, "Order for Adult Baptism" (Singapore: n.p. 1997), 1, henceforth PCS-A; BCW, 403-4.

[10] "Holy Baptism," LBW, 308.

[11] Martin Luther, *The Small Catechism* (1529), BC, 360.12.

[12] *Augsburg Confession* (1530), Art. IV, BC, 39.1.

is more than an individual matter, since it leads to living with the whole communion of saints – language that echoes the baptismal creed. Baptism is also associated with growth in Christian character and living, something that Luther emphasized.[13] The language of "growth" also reflects late-twentieth century ecumenical thinking whereby baptism initiates into a life-long spiritual formation process.[14] The paschal and soteriological emphases make this address especially appropriate for use at the Easter Vigil and during the 50-day long Easter season.

The material in the left column ("God who is rich in mercy…"), newly composed for ELW, begins with a reference to the correlative aspect of God's character, his mercy (Eph. 2:4), and speaks of baptism in terms of "new birth" (1 Peter 1:3), which is also a central biblical image for baptism. "Water and the Word" reflects the Augustinian/ Lutheran teaching that the Word is added to baptism not only in the sense of the sacrament having a divine command,[15] but also in the sense that the living Word, Christ himself, was "added" when his own baptism consecrated *all* water for baptism – an understanding expressed in the so-called "Flood Prayer" of Luther's baptismal rites (see ch. 2).[16] It is precisely by the Word that baptism *can* affect the new birth and deliver the baptized from sin and death. The language of "deliverance from sin and death"/ new life is found in Luther's

---

[13] See Martin Luther, *The Large Catechism* (1529), BC, 465.67, where the reformer writes: "Now, when we enter Christ's kingdom, this corruption [of the Old Adam] must daily decrease so that the longer we live the more gentle, patient, and meek we become, and the more we break away from greed, hatred, envy, and pride."

[14] See Jeffrey A. Truscott, *The Reform of Baptism and Confirmation in American Lutheranism*, Drew University Studies in Liturgy, No. 11 (Lanham, MD/Oxford: Scarecrow Press, 2003), 138, and BEM, 4.9.

[15] Luther, *Small Catechism*, BC, 359.1 and *Large Catechism*, BC, 458.14.

[16] For an excellent discussion of this point, see Dennis L. Bushkofsky and Craig A. Satterlee, *The Christian Life: Baptism and Life Passages*, Using Evangelical Lutheran Worship, Vol. 2 (Minneapolis: Augsburg Fortress, 2008), 63. Luther *explicitly* speaks of the baptism of Christ as an event that honors and glorifies baptism, with the presence of the Holy Spirit confirming the divine sanction of baptism (*Large Catechism*, BC, 459.21).

catechisms (cf. Rom. 6).[17] Union with the body of Christ (cf. Eph. 4:4-6), anointing with the Spirit (cf. 2 Cor. 1:21-22), and being joined with other Christians in mission, motifs given less emphasis by Luther himself, reflect more recent theological concerns. "Anointing by the Holy Spirit" perhaps reflects the fact that ELW's predecessor worship book (LBW) sought to highlight the pneumatic aspect of baptism by including a prayer for the seven-fold gifts of the Spirit and an anointing formula that uses spirit language.[18] The mission motif echoes ecumenical discussions about the relationship between baptism and participation in the church's mission,[19] as well as concerns that emerged in North American Lutheranism in the late-twentieth century.[20] The "new birth" image and Spirit language make this address appropriate for baptismal services celebrated on the Baptism of Our Lord and the Day of Pentecost.

The PCS-A rite, based on the North American *Book of Common Worship* (BCW),[21] begins with a quotation of the Great Commission (Matt. 28:18-20) to establish a biblical warrant for the baptismal act, in line with the *Westminster Directory for the Public Worship of God*, which states that before baptism "the minister is to use some words of instruction, touching the institution, nature, use, and ends of this sacrament, showing that it is instituted by our Lord Jesus Christ."[22] Reflecting the Calvinist doctrines of prevenient grace and predestination, baptism is conferred on those "whom God has chosen." In baptism one is sealed by God and thereby becomes the personal possession of God. The other benefits are freedom from sin and death and union with Christ in his death and resurrection. The language of "sealing" echoes John Calvin, who compared baptism

---

[17] Luther, *Small Catechism*, BC, 359.5-6, and *Large Catechism*, BC, 459.25.

[18] See the discussion below about the postbaptismal prayer for the seven-fold gifts of the Holy Spirit and the anointing using "seal of the Spirit" language.

[19] See BEM, 4.10.

[20] See UMG, 51, 51A.

[21] PCS-A, 1; see "The Sacrament of Baptism," BCW, 403-15.

[22] Center for Reformed Theology and Apologetics, http://www.reformed.org/documents/wcf_standards/index.html [accessed 22 March 2014].

to a seal on a document that confirms the authenticity of God's baptismal promises.[23] "Freedom from sin and death," which may have been borrowed from LBW,[24] is based on Rom. 8:2, while "uniting us with Jesus Christ in his death and resurrection" is derived from Rom. 6. The Presbyterian Church in Singapore rite for infants (PCS-I) begins with biblical passages appropriate for the baptism of children (Ps. 103; Mark 10:14-16).[25] The traditional Reformed language of covenant is used to provide a rationale for baptizing infants. The covenant is based on a three-fold pledge: the parents' renewal of their own faith, the promise to raise their children as Christians, and the liturgical assembly's promise to assist parents in providing Christian nurture for children. Hence, the covenant community surrounding baptized children is viewed as important.

Baptism in DSSB begins by summarizing the doctrine of salvation and affirming that baptism is the personal appropriation of the saving events in Christian history. The gifts of baptism are union with Christ in his death and resurrection (Rom. 6, cf. AR 27), forgiveness (Acts 2:38, cf. AR 27), and new life in the Spirit (Rom. 7:6). The language of "outward sign/inward grace" reflects classical Anglican sacramental theology, as well as Augustine's teaching.[26] The rubrical direction (6) suggests that this address is directed to the baptismal party only, although the entire assembly would benefit from hearing it.

UMBW's baptismal rite begins by identifying the principal benefits of baptism: initiation into the church, "incorporation" into salvation history, and new birth through water and the Holy Spirit. The initiatory aspect of baptism, of course, was emphasized by John

---

[23] John Calvin, *Institutes of the Christian Religion* IV.15.1 (1559), ed. John T. McNeill, tr. Ford Lewis Battles in LCC XXI (Philadelphia: Westminster Press, 1960), 1304.

[24] "Baptism," LBW, 308.

[25] Presbyterian Church in Singapore, "Order for Infant Baptism," 1.

[26] See AR 27, and *An Outline of the Faith Commonly Called the Catechism*, in BCP 1979, 857, 858, see Augustine of Hippo, *Questions on the Heptateuch* III.84 (ca. 410).

Wesley in the 1756 *Treatise*,[27] and is also a prominent idea in the two baptismal rites that he provided for Methodists in North America (derived from the BCP 1662).[28] The notion of being incorporated into the "mighty acts of God" echoes the Wesleyan idea of the saving benefits of Christ's works being *applied* to the individual, as seen in Charles Wesley's hymns "Come, Let us Use the Grace Divine,"[29] and "O Thou Who This Mysterious Bread."[30] New birth through water and the Spirit (John 3), also finds expression in Wesley's baptismal rites[31] and his baptismal writings.[32] "Without price" expresses the grace aspect of Wesleyan theology, which is also prominent in various Wesleyan hymns.[33]

Baptismal services among free churches usually do not begin with a formal theological address, but with either a quotation from or allusion to a biblical passage (e.g., Matt. 28:18-20), as in BAP, followed by a prayer. In the Pentecostal tradition, an extempore introduction by the minister provides an explanation of baptism.[34]

The Presentation of Candidates

Presenting the candidates for baptism is more than a formality. Since baptism is about incorporation into the fellowship of believers, it is important that the assembly form a relationship with those who are

---

[27] John Wesley, *Treatise on Baptism* II.3 (1756), in *The Works of John Wesley*, Vol. X (Grand Rapids: Zondervan, 1958), 188.

[28] John Wesley, "The Ministration of Baptism of Infants" and "The Ministration of Baptism to Such as are of Riper Years" (1784), JWPB, 142, 149.

[29] *United Methodist Hymnal* (Nashville: The United Methodist Publishing House, 1989), #606. Note especially the language in stanza 3: "…to each covenant the blood apply which takes our sins away." Henceforth UMH.

[30] UMH, #613. See stanza 2: "Unseal the volume of thy grace, apply the gospel word…").

[31] See Wesley, "Baptism of Infants" and "Baptism of Riper Years," JWPB, 139, 143,

[32] See John Wesley, "The New Birth" IV.2 (1760), WJW 2, 197.

[33] See UMH #606 and #613.

[34] See Daniel Albrecht, "Witness in the Water: Baptism and Pentecostal Spirituality," BT, 152.

about to be baptized and who will be the subject of the assembly's prayers in the baptismal service. For some members of the assembly, it may be their first introduction to the candidates. For the candidates, an introduction to the assembly is another reminder that baptism pertains to more than personal faith and salvation, but is also related to a life lived in community with other Christians. The omission of the presentation of candidates suggests both a lack of hospitality and theological understanding of baptism.

Candidates are introduced either by liturgical ministers, lay congregational leaders, or sponsors. If an ordained minister or lay church leader presents the candidates, the implication is that the church leadership (lay and clergy) has *approved* the candidates who have been duly prepared and examined by teachers and other leaders.[35] If a sponsor presents a candidate, the former vouches for the personal faith and commitment of the latter, somewhat like those mentioned in the *Apostolic Tradition* who attest to the ability of converts to hear the Word of God.[36] Those who introduce candidates necessarily take personal responsibility for their spiritual nurture.

When a candidate is introduced, it is appropriate (and traditional) to use the person's full name (John Smith, Lim Boon Hwa). When the person is addressed later in the service at the pronouncement of the baptismal formula ("*Name*, I baptize you in the name of the Father..." etc) and in the postbaptismal gestures (handlaying, anointing), only the given name (John, Boon Hwa) is used in order to underscore initiation into the family of God. This new relationship transcends biological ties.

Traditionally, adult baptismal candidates are asked if they *desire* baptism, as a way of establishing that they come to baptism freely and without any compulsion. The earliest documents describing baptism (The *Didache*, Justin's *First Apology*, and Tertullian's *De Baptismo*) however, give no indication of such a question, perhaps because

[35] In some Protestant denominations the local church leadership (board, consistory, church council) is required to officially approve all candidates for baptism. Such an action has a precedent in the ancient act of electing catechumens for baptism at the beginning of Lent (see ch. 3).

[36] *The Apostolic Tradition Ascribed to Hippolytus of Rome* 15 (ca. 217).

the full consent of baptismal candidates was established during the prebaptismal formation process. Precursors to the question "Do you desire baptism?" are the query "What do you seek?," which appears in the tenth-century *Abrosian Manual,*[37] and the question, "Dost thou wish to be baptized?," which is found in a number of later medieval liturgical manuals.[38] Following the Latin *Magdeburg Agenda*, Luther retained the question in both of his baptismal rites (1523, 1526), where it is directed to the *infant* who responded through the sponsors.[39] The 1523 rite for Zurich addresses the question to the child, but in Zwingli's revision of 1525, the *parents* are asked "Will ye that this child be baptized?"[40] In the baptism rite of the BCP 1549, the child is not only asked "What dost thou desire?" but also "Wilt thou be baptized?" – as in the Latin *Sarum Manual.*[41] The BCP 1552 retained only the second question.[42] Calvin's baptismal question in *The Form of Prayers and Ecclesiastical Chants* had no such question. The BCP 1662 and subsequently Wesley's rite ask adult candidates "Wilt thou be baptized in this faith?"[43]

Following the introduction of candidates, some current Protestant rites direct ministers to ask mature candidates (who can answer for themselves) whether they desire baptism.[44] Among the

---

[37] M. Magistretti, *Monumenta veteris liturgiae Ambrosianae*, Vol. 3 (Milan: 1904), in DBL, 197.

[38] See CIRP, 16, note 2.

[39] Martin Luther, *The Order of Baptism* (1523), LW 53, 100; *The Order of Baptism Newly Revised* (1526), LW 53, 109.

[40] Leo Jud, *A Short and Public Form for the Tender in Faith for the Baptism of Children* (1523), CIRP, 128; Ulrich Zwingli, *The Second Revision of the Zurich Order of Baptism* (1525), CIRP, 131.

[41] "Of the Administration of Public Baptism to be Used in the Church," BCP 1549, CIRP, 93-94.

[42] "The Ministration of Baptism to be Used in the Church," BCP 1552, CIRP, 109.

[43] "The Ministration of Baptism to Such as are of Riper Years and able to Answer for Themselves" (1662), BCP *Texts*, 423; Wesley, "Baptism of Riper Years," JWPB, 147.

[44] "Baptism," BCP 1979, 301; "Baptism," BCW, 405.

baptismal services studied in this chapter, only ELW has such a question, and the wording indicates that the desire for baptism is a response to the grace of God ("…trusting in the grace and love of God, do you desire…?").[45] When parents and other sponsors of young children are asked whether they desire to have their children baptized, the question is prefaced with a reminder that bringing children to baptism is a desire prompted by the Holy Spirit and an act of faith; social or familial pressure should play no role.

The validity of such an inquiry today may be open to discussion. On the one hand, only when adult candidates come voluntarily can they benefit spiritually from baptism.[46] In that case "Do you desire baptism?" is a reasonable question. On the other hand, it is not unreasonable to assume today that the candidates' very presence at the service of baptism signals a willing submission to baptism. Why ask what is obvious? Yet, there may still be social situations even today when persons are compelled to accept baptism. Worship leaders therefore need to be aware of their social context and of each candidate's situation when gauging whether to query about the desire for baptism.

The Promises of Sponsors and Assembly

Those who present others for baptism assume the role of nurturing the newly baptized in the Christian faith. Accordingly, Protestant liturgical books ask sponsors and parents to make promises along these lines.[47] Baptismal obligations should be discussed with the pastor well before the service so that parents and sponsors can reflect on these and answer sincerely when asked whether they will take an active part in the Christian nurture of their children. Since baptism should not proceed without the responsible participation of parents

[45] "Baptism," ELW, 584.

[46] Philip H. Pfatteicher, *Commentary on the Lutheran Book of Worship* (Minneapolis: Augsburg Fortress, 1990), 36.

[47] The same is true of the Roman Catholic Church's baptismal rite for children. See "Rite for the Baptism of Several Children," in *Rites of the Catholic Church*, Vol. 1 (New York: Pueblo, 1983), 198.

and sponsors, the examination of these persons appropriately appears at the *beginning* of the baptismal rite. Promises made by parents and sponsors, however, do not constitute the reason for baptism; the church baptizes in response to God's command, not because persons pledge themselves to a particular course of action.[48]

Liturgical examinations of or admonitions to godparents (sponsors) and parents appeared gradually during the Reformation era, as a response to the Anabaptist critique of infant baptism. Luther's rites included no formal exhortations to sponsors and parents, but he did expect that (1) sponsors (and parents) pay attention and pray sincerely during the baptismal service;[49] and (2) the "heads of households" teach the catechism to their children.[50] Neither of the rites used in Zurich during Zwingli's time contain any admonitions to or promises by parents or sponsors.[51] Just prior to the baptismal washing in Calvin's baptismal rite, the minister admonishes parents to teach the baptized child the basic tenets of the Christian faith (as summarized in the Apostles' Creed) as well as the contents of the Bible, and encourage the child to lead a Christian life.[52] Baptismal rites in the BCP 1549 and BCP 1552 *conclude* with an exhortation that stresses the duty of godparents to (1) help a newly baptized child to understand the gravity of the vow made in his/her stead by godparents; (2) encourage the child to attend worship; (3) provide for the child's instruction in the catechism; and (4) see that the child is raised to live a Christian life, keeping in mind that baptism, as

---

[48] Luther asserts that infants are not baptized because of the hopes and prayers of parents, sponsors, and the church, but because baptism has been commanded by God (*Large Catechism*, BC, 464.57).

[49] Luther, *Order of Baptism*, LW 53, 101-2.

[50] In his *Large Catechism*, Luther states that "heads of households" are to examine the catechetical knowledge of children and servants each week and encourage continued learning and revising if knowledge is deficient (BC, 383.4).

[51] See Jud, *Baptism of Children*, and Zwingli, *Revision of the Zurich Order of Baptism*, CIRP, 126-31.

[52] John Calvin, *The Form of Prayers and Ecclesiastical Chants with the Manner of Administering the Sacraments and Solemnizing Marriage According to the Custom of the Ancient Church* (1542), CIRP, 116.

rooted in Christ's death and resurrection, means the death of sin and a resurrection to righteous living.[53] John Wesley retained none of the postbaptismal examinations found in the BCP 1662 baptismal rites.[54]

The examination of/admonition to parents and sponsors in ELW is prefaced with a reminder that baptism is not so much a human work, but a reception of God's gifts.[55] The responsibilities enumerated are participation with children in the life and worship of the church, instructing children in the components of the catechism (a major Lutheran concern), providing the Scriptures to children, and nurturing them in the faith. The desired result is the children's development of a living faith and a commitment to Christian witness and service. The question "do you promise to help your children grow in the Christian faith and life?" underscores the ecumenical understanding that baptism initiates one into a process of life-long spiritual growth.

Following in ELW are the promises made by sponsors of adult candidates and the congregation. The former ritual form, a simplified version of LBW's question to sponsors of older candidates, asserts the Spirit's role in enabling sponsors to nurture others in the faith, suggesting that those who assume baptismal sponsorship need to be gifted for that role. The phrase "covenant of baptism" or similar language is found neither in the later works of Luther nor in the Lutheran confessional writings.[56] The promise made by the assembly –

---

[53] "Public Baptism," BCP 1549, CIRP, 94-95; "The Ministration of Baptism," BCP 1552, CIRP, 111.

[54] Wesley, "Baptism of Infants," "Baptism of Riper Years," JWPB, 143, 149.

[55] "Baptism," ELW, 584. Cf. LBW, 308.

[56] As far as I can tell, Luther only uses covenant language in a 1519 sermon on baptism and then ceases to do so in his baptismal writings after that. For him, God's command and promise – the latter to be received in faith – are central, and so the idea of our entering into a mutual covenant or agreement with God eventually drops out of his thinking. We might wonder whether covenant language in Lutheran initiatory rites does not blunt Luther's emphasis on the divine initiative in baptism and perhaps confuse Lutheran and Reformed baptismal theologies. See Jeffrey A. Truscott, "Luther's Pastoral Approach to Baptism," in *A Living Tradition: On*

not found in LBW – serves as a reminder that the whole congregation is involved in the spiritual formation of new Christians.

In PCS-A, no role for sponsors is envisioned, and hence there is no admonition to sponsors. Rather the assembly is asked to nurture the newly baptized such that they develop a personal faith and commitment to church life (section D). In PCS-I, the promises of parents forms a unit with the preceding explanation of the three-fold pledge. Using language reflecting Reformed covenant theology ("share with you in the grace of God," "...be enrolled in His church as God's children") the minister asks parents whether they (1) understand their obligations; (2) will teach the Christian faith to their children; (3) will be examples of Christian living for their children; and (4) will assist children in their confirmation instruction. The first three of these questions tie closely with the admonition to parents in Calvin's 1542 baptismal rite (see above). The fourth question reflects a common Protestant understanding of confirmation, although it might be pointed out that Calvin himself strongly asserted that *baptism* confers church membership, in which case the phrase "become truly members of the church" is perhaps questionable.[57] Presumably, parents will be instructed on the wording of their answers to these questions which are not specified in the order.

DSSB contains only a parenthetical remark about parents and godparents raising children to resist evil and follow Christ.[58] Given

---

the Intersection of Liturgical History and Pastoral Practice, eds. David Pitt, Stefanos Alexopoulos, and Christian McConnell (Collegeville: Liturgical Press, 2012), 136-53. Bryan Spinks, however, has argued that even when Luther used covenant language he did not mean a bi-lateral covenant in which a person cooperates in salvation. See Bryan D. Spinks, *Reformation and Modern Rituals and Theologies of Baptism: From Luther to Contemporary Practices* (Aldershot/Burlington: Ashgate, 2006), 6-7.

[57] Calvin states that by baptism, "we are received into the society of the Church" (*Institutes*, IV.15.1, LCC XXI, 1303). See also the baptismal rite in the 1542 *Form of Prayers*, which states that "we will receive this infant into his [Christ's] Church," CIRP, 115.

[58] "Baptism," DSSB, 49.

the importance of parents and sponsors in the life of those baptized in infancy, and given the example of the baptismal rites in the BCP 1549 and BCP 1552 with their exhortations to godparents, we might wonder whether a more fulsome enumeration of parental duties is needed. DSSB provides no form for the congregation to pledge support to the baptismal candidates or their sponsors.

Following what is essentially a renunciation and adhesion (addressed to the candidates), UMBW poses questions to parents and sponsors of young children, candidates who can answer for themselves, and the sponsors of the latter.[59] Parental nurturance of children is seen to have a two-fold dimension, taking place in the church but also (presumably) in the home through the teaching and example of parents. The goal is for children to personally accept the Christian faith, witness to that faith publicly, and develop a Christian way of life. Unfortunately, no reference is made to the Church's trinitarian faith or the catechetical components that are the basis of that faith. Although they previously pledged themselves to Christ and his church (section 4), mature candidates, somewhat redundantly, are queried about their commitment to faithful church membership and service to Christ in the world (section 6). Finally, sponsors are simply asked to support and encourage the mature candidates.

Except for the baptismal candidates themselves, there are usually no rites for examining and admonishing the various baptismal participants prior to the washing in the services of Baptist and other free churches. The assembly's welcome to the newly baptized, however, may be prefaced with words encouraging its members to support the newly baptized.[60] Although these churches might understand baptism as a qualification for church membership, any membership ritual is performed at a separate service for pastoral reasons.[61]

---

[59] "Baptismal Covenant I," UMBW, 88.

[60] See "The Baptism of Believers" (Baptist) in BT. The assembly is asked: "Do you welcome *Name* into the family of God in this local Church? (We do.). Do you promise to love, encourage, strengthen, guide, pray for, and care for *Name* as an equal partner in the Body of Christ? (We do.) (398).

[61] Paul Fiddes, "The Baptism of Believers," BT, 77.

Renunciation and Adhesion

Baptism is about union with Christ who offers humanity a way of being in right relationship with God through faith. Such union necessarily means turning away from all other paths to God, especially one's self-chosen works and efforts meant to appease God. Besides self-justification, sin also takes the form of trusting in those powers that are at odds with God: coercive military force, political domination, greed, racism, and addiction. These evil realities detract from the goodness of creation and from human life, and the gospels depict Jesus struggling against all that is opposed to God and to authentic human existence. Hence, to be united with Christ through baptism is to be joined with him in this battle against evil.

In the ancient church, baptism included a ritual for the renunciation of evil known as the *apotaxis* (Greek "stand apart from"), and sometimes a ritual for pledging personal allegiance to Christ, known as the *syntaxis* (Greek, "stand with"). Tertullian's treatise *De Corona* (*On the Crown*) mentions the renunciation of "the devil and his pomp and his angels" at baptism.[62] Later, in the fourth century, the *Mystagogical Catechesis* of Cyril of Jerusalem speaks of a *three-fold* act of renunciation while the candidates face west, the symbolic direction of darkness and evil, followed by a trinitarian confession of faith made while facing east, the direction of the rising sun or Christ.[63] The *Apostolic Constitutions* likewise refers to a three-fold renunciation, but this is followed by an explicit act of adhesion in which the candidates associate themselves with Christ (followed by a creedal confession).[64] John Chrysostom speaks of both a renunciation and pledge to Christ, without mentioning particular symbolic orientations, whether east or west.[65]

Some of the Protestant Reformers retained the renunciation, which in the medieval Western tradition did not include an act of adhesion. Three-fold renunciations addressed to the infant candidate

---

[62] Tertullian, *De Corona* 12.3 (ca. 213).

[63] Cyril of Jerusalem, *Mystagogical Catechesis* 1 (ca. 350).

[64] *The Apostolic Constitutions* VII.41 (ca. 381).

[65] John Chrysostom, *Baptismal Instructions* 18, 20-21 (ca. 390).

who answered *through the godparents* appeared in both of Luther's rites,[66] and in the first Zurich rite under Zwingli.[67] A more elaborate three-fold renunciation, also addressed to the infants (for whom godparents answered), is used in the BCP 1549,[68] while a single renunciation is explicitly directed to the godparents in the 1552 rite[69] – an alteration made in response to Bucer's strong objections to infants renouncing Satan through their godparents.[70] The baptismal rites of both Calvin and Wesley had no renunciations. Early Anabaptist and Pentecostal baptismal services eschewed such formalism.

In recognition that baptism is a journey from the realm of evil to that of Christ, contemporary Protestant rites include at least an act of renunciation. In LBW and ELW the renunciation is prefaced with "I ask you to profess your faith in Christ Jesus, reject sin, and confess the faith of the church." In this case, "profess your faith" refers not to reciting the words of the creed, but to professing the faith by

---

[66] Luther, *Order of Baptism* and *Baptism Newly Revised*, LW 53, 99, 108-109. For Luther, the power of the devil was quite real: "Remember, too, that it is very necessary to aid the poor child with all your heart and strong faith, earnestly to intercede for him that God . . . would not only free him from the power of the devil, but also strengthen him, that he may nobly resist the devil in life and death" (LW 53, 102).

[67] Jud, *Baptism of Children*, CIRP, 128.

[68] "Public Baptism," BCP 1549, CIRP, 93.

[69] "Ministration of Baptism," BCP 1552, CIRP, 108-9.

[70] See *The Judgment of Martin Bucer Upon the Book of Sacred Rites or of the Ordering of the Church and Ecclesiastical Ministration in The Kingdom of England Written at the Request of the Reverend Archbishop Thomas Cranmer*, CIRP, 102-3. Bucer basically argues that renunciations are inappropriate in the case of infants because (1) the rejection of evil is a matter of personal faith that should not be mediated by another; and (2) an infant cannot comprehend what is happening in a renunciation. He suggests that this aspect of infant baptism drives people to the Anabaptists, which might suggest that his critique is prejudiced by rivalry with Anabaptism. We might wonder whether Bucer would apply this same critique to the baptismal formula itself, which is also addressed to the infant ("*Name*, I baptize you, in the name..."etc).

submitting to baptism.[71] The rubrics indicate that this invitation to renounce Satan/evil is directed to "candidates for baptism as well as the parents and sponsors of young children," language that apparently includes infant candidates and implies that the parents and sponsors answer on their behalf, although this is not explicitly stated. Two forms of renunciation are provided in ELW: a three-fold interrogation in the left column (in the manner of the earliest Lutheran rites), or a single, composite interrogation in the right column, following the later Lutheran German Church Orders and LBW. The structure of the three-fold renunciation is meant to parallel the three-fold creedal interrogation that follows. Both forms identify a three-fold order of forces opposed to God: the *cosmic/spiritual* (devil), the *temporal* (world, etc), and the *personal* (sin). The profound evil embodied in such things as ethnic cleansing, the obsession with weapons and violence, and the ruthless displacement of populations for economic reasons forces contemporary Christians to boldly name evil and stand against it. Following the medieval liturgical tradition and Luther, LBW and ELW have no separate act of adhesion; the profession of the creed serves as the ritual pledge of allegiance to Christ. The assembly may also participate in the renunciation, either (1) at the Easter Vigil as a way for everyone to recall their baptismal passage from death to life; and/or (2) when only infants are baptized "as an expression of the whole church speaking on their behalf."[72]

While PCS-I has no act of renunciation and adhesion, these realities are at the heart of sections B ("Profession of Faith") and C ("Questions for the Person Being Baptized") of PCS-A.[73] In traditional Reformed language, section B affirms that faith leads to the establishment of a covenant with God, who preserves the faithful from Satan and nurtures them in the love of Christ. In response, the

[71] "Baptism," LBW, 310 (which adds, "..the faith in which we baptize."); "Baptism," ELW, 585. See Philip H. Pfatteicher, *Commentary on the Lutheran Book of Worship: Lutheran Liturgy in its Ecumenical Context* (Minneapolis: Augsburg Fortress, 1990), 47.

[72] See Bushkovsky and Satterlee, *Christian Life*, 61.The phrase "on their behalf" (i.e., of infants) seems meant to clarify the rubric in the ELW baptismal rite.

[73] PCS-A, 1.

faithful reject Satan and turn to Christ.[74] Of the five questions to the candidate (C), the first two are essentially a renunciation of evil and a pledge of loyalty to Christ, respectively. The third question, concerning fidelity to the Scriptures, is a logical appropriation of Calvin's language about teaching children the contents of the Bible.[75] The fourth pertains to faithful discipleship in daily life, a matter touched upon in Calvin's exhortation to parents. The fifth speaks about participation in the life of the church, which reflects the Reformed emphasis on baptism as ecclesial initiation as well as the twentieth-century concern that baptism leads to a *living* church membership. The whole series reinforces the understanding that baptism is related to a continuously unfolding process, rather than a momentary experience. PSC-I has no act of renunciation and/or adhesion.

In DSSB (section 7) the adhesion occurs *before* the renunciation, which is somewhat illogical if the baptismal journey is *from* sin and evil *to* the kingdom of Christ.[76] The precatory formula that follows (8) affirms the conventional ritual order. As in ELW all three orders of evil are renounced, but unlike ELW, DSSB explicitly states that parents and godparents answer for both themselves *and* their children.

As noted above, UMBW inserts a renunciation and adhesion (section 4) prior to a series of questions addressed to various members of the baptismal party. Traditionally, of course, the renunciation and adhesion took place prior to the washing/creedal profession of faith; pledging allegiance to Christ was seen to lead naturally to the confession of faith in the triune God. On the one hand, it is natural after presenting the candidates (as in UMBW) to examine them and then continue with other questions to them. On the other

---

[74] Calvin states that in baptism God assists us in the battle against sin and the devil by giving us the Holy Spirit (*Form of Prayers*, CIRP, 114).

[75] Calvin, *Form of Prayers*, CIRP, 116.

[76] Cf. CW, 353, where the traditional order is maintained. Note that neither BCP 1549 or BCP 1552 used a baptismal adhesion. The BCP 1662, however, did have a pledge of obedience to God's law (BCP *Texts*, 423).

hand, the apparent disassociation of personal faith in Christ from the confession of the triune nature of God is less than desirable. The first question, asked "on behalf of the whole church," seeks the rejection of the powers of evil that exist above and beyond the world, in the world, and in the self. By naming injustice and oppression as evils to be rejected, the second question reflects the Wesleyan concern for "social holiness." The third queries about the candidates' personal faith in Christ and intention to live out that faith as members of the church. The rubrics indicate that parents and sponsors speak only for themselves "while taking the responsibilities of sponsorship," implying that baptismal sponsorship is part of faithful discipleship.

The representative (model) Baptist service provided in BT gives two options for what is essentially renunciation and adhesion.[77] In the first option, the candidates affirm their trinitarian faith, repentance, and desire for baptism, and then pledge to serve God. In the second option, worded along classical lines but structured in the reverse manner of traditional renunciation-adhesion rites, candidates confess faith in Jesus Christ, affirm their renunciation of sin and evil, pledge to follow and serve Christ, and promise to live in fellowship with the church. The second option might be preferable for those communities that value ties with the ecumenical church.

The acts of renouncing Satan and pledging loyalty to Christ raise three questions:

1. *Can a baptismal rite contain a renunciation of Satan <u>without</u> an act of adhesion (pledge of loyalty) to Christ?* A number of ancient sources (*Apostolic Constitutions*, John Chrysostom) witness to both actions, while others (Tertullian, Cyril of Jerusalem, *Apostolic Tradition*) only indicate an act of renunciation. Modern Protestants inherited no baptismal act of adhesion, although the action is found almost universally today in Eastern and Oriental Orthodox baptismal rites.[78] It may be argued that in the Western tradition, the creedal profession and baptism themselves constitute the act of adhesion.

---

[77] "The Baptism of Believers (Baptist)," BT, 395.

[78] For the texts of these Eastern and Oriental Orthodox rites with acts of renunciation *and* adhesion, see BT, 272-73, 291, 310, and 427.

Yet, the ritual meaning of baptism suggests the importance and indispensability of the act of adhesion. If baptism is a change of allegiance from Satan to Christ, a spiritual passage from point A to point B, the act of adhesion is needed to express the full meaning of that journey. The profession of faith (Apostles' Creed) does in some sense express one's being joined to Christ, but it does so in a different manner than an act of adhesion. In the latter, the candidate expresses personal faith in Christ; in the creed/creedal interrogations that personal faith is joined to the faith of the church when all say the creed together. When adhesion and creed occur together, personal loyalty and shared, communal faith are appropriately juxtaposed, since the two things are interdependent realities. The personal journey of baptism especially is short-changed without an act of adhesion. Thus, what makes the most sense from a ritual point of view is an act of renunciation/adhesion by candidates/parents and sponsors of young children (alone) followed by a profession of the Apostles' (baptismal) Creed by *all* (baptismal party and assembly) so that the personal and communal aspects of the baptismal journey come to complete expression. Future compilers of baptismal rites may want to consider this question carefully.

2. *Should spatial orientation/re-orientation be part of the renunciation (and adhesion)?* Some ancient sources such as Cyril of Jerusalem[79] and the *Canons of Hippolytus* (ca. 330 CE),[80] as well as modern Eastern and Oriental Orthodox[81] rites, indicate that the renunciation of Satan is made while the candidates face west, the direction of the setting sun and darkness, while the act of adhesion to Christ is made facing east, or the direction of the rising sun. The change in physical orientation symbolizes the candidates' reorientation of life and redirecting of spiritual loyalty from Satan to Christ. The candidates participate *physically* in the reality expressed

[79] Cyril of Jerusalem, *Mystagogical Catechesis* 1.4-9.

[80] *Canons of Hippolytus* 19 (ca. 330).

[81] See "Rites of Christian Initiation" (Eastern Orthodox), BT, 272-73; "The Canon of the Sacrament of Holy Baptism" (Oriental Orthodox—Armenian), BT, 291; "Text of the Mystery of Holy Baptism" (Oriental Orthodox—Syrian, India), BT, 309-10.

in the very words they speak. Unfortunately, participation by means of movement and re-orientation is lacking not only in baptismal liturgies, but in Protestant public worship in general, the exception being those traditions where the presiding minister faces the assembly while speaking words directed to the assembly, and faces away from the assembly (toward the altar-table) when addressing God. Baptismal renunciation/adhesion might therefore be a time when Protestant Christians could participate through physical reorientation and thus experience the liturgy at a deeper level. Since many modern church buildings are not intentionally oriented on an east-west axis like ancient churches, the baptismal candidates might simply face in the direction of true west for the renunciation of Satan, and then turn to true east for the act of adhesion. A short pastoral explanation before the baptismal liturgy (or in the sermon) can help the assembly to understand the meaning of these actions.

3. *Is there a role for baptismal exorcism today?* Exorcism was commonly a part of the baptismal process since ancient times. The *Apostolic Tradition* indicates that those chosen to receive baptism underwent exorcism on a daily basis, including by the bishop, in the days leading up to baptism.[82] This emphasis reflects a concern that the candidates be morally and spiritually pure. Cyril of Jerusalem also mentions exorcism in a prebaptismal context.[83] In some cases, a prebaptismal anointing was understood in exorcistic terms, as in the *Apostolic Tradition*[84] and by John Chrysostom.[85] Exorcistic rites continued to be part of the baptismal rite in the Middle Ages, and were included in the rites prepared by Luther,[86] Jud,[87] and Cranmer.[88]

[82] *Apostolic Tradition* 20.

[83] Cyril of Jerusalem, *Procatechesis* 9 (ca. 350).

[84] *Apostolic Tradition* 21.

[85] John Chrysostom, *Baptismal Instructions* 3.27.

[86] Martin Luther, *Order of Baptism*, LW 53, 96; *Baptism Newly Revised*, LW 53, 107.

[87] Leo Jud, *A Short and Public form for the Tender in Faith for the Baptism of Children* (1523), CIRP, 126.

[88] "Public Baptism," BCP 1549, CIRP, 91.

It should be noted that in his 1526 revision of the baptismal rite, Luther removed the bulk of the exorcistic material, leaving only a generalized formula at the beginning and a longer formula prior to the gospel reading.[89] In his writings, Luther never emphasized the *literal* expulsion of demons from baptismal candidates, so he may have envisioned only a candidate's preservation from evil and the spiritual attacks of the devil, something that he himself was familiar with. Martin Bucer argued that any exorcism was inappropriate in baptism since the New Testament indicates that only certain persons were given the ability to cast out demons and exorcism was limited to those who were actually demonically possessed.[90] Accordingly, exorcism was removed from the baptismal rite of the BCP 1552. Rationalistic thinking since the Enlightenment has led to a discomfort with the idea of the devil or Satan in general, and consequently to a downplaying of the exorcistic aspect of baptism, perhaps to the impoverishment of the church and its baptismal candidates.

At the very least, worship leaders may want to consider whether intercessory prayer for the baptismal candidates could more adequately addresses the struggle against evil faced by all Christians. Some of the denominational catechumenates discussed earlier offer helpful resources in this regard. In *Welcome to Christ: Lutheran Rites for the Catechumenate*, a prayer for the candidates on the Fourth Sunday in Lent asks that the power of the devil be crushed and that God's people be protected from evil and preserved from sin.[91] This prayer reminds Christians of the presence of evil in the world and of the continuing need to struggle against it. In an age of genocide, ethnic cleansing, and the wanton abuse of children and women even by Christian *clergy*, such a prayer is not only relevant but necessary.

---

[89] Luther, *Baptism Newly Revised*, LW 53, 107-8. The two formulas are "Depart thou unclean spirit and make room for the Holy Spirit," and "I adjure thee, thou unclean spirit, by the name of the Father + and of the Son + and of the Holy Ghost + that thou come out of and depart from this servant of Jesus Christ, *Name*. Amen."

[90] Bucer, *Judgment*, xiii, CIRP, 101.

[91] *Welcome to Christ: Lutheran Rites for the Catechumenate* (Minneapolis: Augsburg Fortress, 1997), 28.

Not to be excluded or overlooked is more specific prayer or other types of ministry for those whose struggle against evil is profound. Wise and cautious pastoral discernment is needed to determine which baptismal candidates have such a need.

Profession of Faith

While the New Testament gives little evidence of an explicit act of confession on the part of baptismal candidates, such an act became an important component of baptism in the early church. Cyril of Jerusalem indicates that the renunciation of Satan was immediately followed by the candidates uttering a brief creedal statement while facing east: "I believe in the Father, the Son and the Holy Spirit, and in one baptism of repentance."[92] Then, after descending into the font, the candidates were submersed after each affirmative answer to three creedal questions.[93] The *Apostolic Tradition* also indicates a three-fold confession in conjunction with a triple immersion.[94] This trinitarian confession of faith is the origin of the Apostles' Creed, which is sometimes referred to as the "baptismal creed."

Reformation-era baptismal rites include a creedal profession of faith in one form or another. The baptismal orders of Luther,[95] the BCP 1549,[96] and the first rite used in Zwingli's Zurich[97] all employed a three-fold creedal questioning of the godparents. In keeping with a tendency to simplify, the BCP 1552 rite posed only one long creedal question to the godparents.[98] The creed was dropped entirely from Zwingli's revised rite, while Calvin's 1542 baptismal service

---

[92] Cyril of Jerusalem, *Mystagogical Catechesis* 1.9.

[93] See Cyril of Jerusalem, *Mystagogical Catechesis* 2.4. See Everett Ferguson, *Baptism in the Early Church: History, Theology, and Liturgy in the First Five Centuries* (Grand Rapids: Eerdmans, 2009), 478-79.

[94] *Apostolic Tradition* 21.

[95] Luther, *Order of Baptism*, LW 53, 99; *Baptism Newly Revised*, LW 53, 109.

[96] "Public Baptism," BCP 1549, CIRP, 93.

[97] Jud, *Baptism of Children*, CIRP, 128.

[98] "Ministration of Baptism," BCP 1552, CIRP, 109.

incorporated the creed into a long exhortation by the minister.[99] In a departure from the BCP 1662, John Wesley only included a creedal interrogation in the baptismal rite for older candidates.[100] Free Church baptismal rites have generally avoided creedal statements, preferring instead to inquire about the candidate's personal faith.

Nearly all modern baptismal rites include a form of the Apostles' Creed, which serves as a summary of the church's faith in the triune God. In making this confession, the candidates effectively join their faith to that of the universal church and commit themselves to proclaiming that faith in daily life. It is imperative that baptismal candidates learn the creed and its meaning, a task traditionally undertaken in prebaptismal instruction. It naturally follows the act of adhesion by the candidates who have just proclaimed their personal faith. In LBW, ELW, UMBW, and PCS-A, the articles of the Apostles' Creed are proclaimed by the candidates, parents and sponsors, and the whole assembly in response to three questions. In DSSB those who can answer for themselves, as well as parents and godparents, give a simple response ("I believe and trust in him") to creedal questions (11). Given its long history, association with baptism, and wide ecumenical acceptance, the Apostles' Creed commends itself for our use today more than any alternative.

From the introduction through the profession of faith, the baptismal group may stand before the assembly if gathering at the font would inhibit the assembly's participation in the baptismal rite. The baptismal group will move to the font/pool prior to the thanksgiving prayer which makes reference to water. The assembly should stand for the profession of faith and prayer of thanksgiving, because of the solemn, proclamatory nature of these actions. All profess the faith together, since the baptismal creed, a great symbol of the church's faith, is the common possession of the whole priesthood of Christ.

---

[99] Calvin, *Form of Prayers*, CIRP, 116.

[100] Wesley, "Baptism of Riper Years," JWPB, 146-47.

Prayer of Thanksgiving

The New Testament enjoins Christians to receive divine blessings through prayer, specifically *thanksgiving* that enumerates God's life-giving actions in history and petitions God to continue his saving work now and into the future (cf. Ps. 105). Jesus gave thanks over the bread and cup that he shared with his disciples on the night of his betrayal (Matt. 26:26-27), and 1 Tim. 4:4-5 speaks of receiving God's gifts through prayer which, with the Word of God, consecrates God's gifts to their particular use. It is little wonder that since ancient times baptismal rites have included prayers of thanksgiving made in connection with the baptismal font or baptismal water. The *Apostolic Tradition* briefly mentions that prayer was "made over" the baptismal water,[101] as does Cyprian who connects this action with the washing away of sins.[102] Tertullian states that the invocation of God's name sanctifies the water so that it may sanctify those washed in it.[103] Theodore of Mopsuestia emphasizes the action of the Holy Spirit in response to the prayer made over the water,[104] thus suggesting that the efficacy of baptism depends on the Holy Spirit.

Aware of numerous abuses surrounding baptismal water, the Protestant Reformers eschewed such prayers. Luther's celebrated Flood Prayer, however, was based on biblical images typically found in medieval prayers for the consecration of baptismal fonts at the Easter Vigil. It made no attempt to consecrate the water, but instead affirmed that *all* water had been consecrated by Christ's own baptism in the Jordan River. The prayer then focuses on the baptismal candidate, asking that the guilt of original sin be washed away and that the candidate receive God's help in the daily struggle against sin. Versions of Luther's prayer found their way into the baptismal rites used by Zwingli, the BCP 1549 and BCP 1552, and Wesley's baptismal rites for North American Methodists.

---

[101] *Apostolic Tradition* 21.

[102] Cyprian of Carthage, *Letter 70 to Januarius* 1 (ca. 256).

[103] Tertullian, *De Baptismo* 2.4.

[104] Theodore of Mopsuestia, *Baptismal Homily* III.8 (late-fourth or early-fifth cent.).

The position of the thanksgiving prayer in modern baptismal rites varies from book to book. In LBW, the thanksgiving is offered prior to the renunciation and profession of faith which precede the washing.[105] Similarly, in CW[106] and DSSB,[107] a thanksgiving prayer precedes the profession of faith, the renunciation of Satan having occurred earlier in both cases. However, in ELW[108] BCW,[109] and UMBW,[110] the thanksgiving is placed immediately prior to the baptismal washing. On the one hand, it could be argued that the placement of the renunciation/profession before the washing reminds us that a creedal interrogation constituted *the* form of baptism for many centuries and that baptism is connected to faith: one is baptized upon confessing faith in the triune God. On the other hand, if the essence of this prayer is to give thanks for God's use of water for redemptive purposes, especially in baptism, then the thanksgiving, with its multiple water images, is most logically offered immediately prior to the ritual action that involves water.

ELW has five options for the "thanksgiving at the font," but because of space limitations we will consider only the fourth ("Holy God, mighty Lord…"), which is taken from LBW. Like eucharistic prayers, this baptismal thanksgiving begins with the salutation and invitation to give thanks, but omits "Lift up your hearts" following the ancient custom of reserving this versicle and its response for the eucharistic liturgy.[111] Drawing on several familiar images from

---

[105] "Baptism," LBW, 309-10. The drafters desired to have a significant part of the rite placed before the renunciation and profession of faith in order to avoid the suggestion that everything depends on the candidate's acts of renouncing and professing, as if one is baptized *because* he/she has done these things. See Truscott, *The Reform of Baptism and Confirmation*, 112-13.

[106] "Holy Baptism," CW, 353-56.

[107] "Baptism," DSSB, 50-52. Note that the renunciation and profession of faith occur before two questions ("What dost thou desire?" "Wilt thou be baptized?") and the washing in the BCP 1549.

[108] "Baptism," ELW, 585-86.

[109] "Baptism," BCW, 410-12.

[110] "Baptismal Covenant I," UMBW, 90-91.

[111] Pfatteicher, *Commentary on the* LBW, 41.

Luther's Flood Prayer, the ELW thanksgiving alludes to six biblical passages where water is connected with God's creating/redeeming work: creation (Gen. 1), the great flood (Gen. 6), the rescue from Egypt (Ex. 14-15), the baptism of Jesus (Matt. 3:13-17), the "baptism" of Jesus' death and resurrection (Mark 10:38-39), and the new birth (John 3). Several of these passages are images of creation/re-creation, which suggests that baptism itself is a divine act of re-creation.[112]

This prayer has deep theological significance for Lutherans. The creation motif itself resonates with Luther's commentary on the First Article of the Apostles' Creed in his *Small Catechism*, which begins with the words "I believe that God has created me and all that exists."[113] The paschal (Easter-oriented) images of the great flood, Exodus, and Jesus' death and resurrection find a parallel in the *Small Catechism's* language about the drowning of the "Old Adam" through daily repentance and the raising up of a new righteous creature.[114] The language of being liberated from sin and death by Jesus' death and resurrection serves as a proclamation of good news for sinners, which for Luther was at the heart of liturgy and sacramental celebration. The allusions to Jesus' own baptism and his "making water a sign of the kingdom," suggest the connection between baptism and the living Word, Christ, which finds resonance with the *Small Catechism's* definition of baptism as water "enclosed in God's command and connected with God's Word."[115] The allusion to the Great Commission recalls Luther's teaching that baptism is conferred foremost in response to God's command, not because a person has faith or because parents, sponsors, and the church offer their fervent hopes and prayers for the recipient.[116]

From a historical perspective, the invocation of the Holy Spirit ("Pour out your Holy Spirit...") is striking. Prior to LBW, such

[112] Pfatteicher, *Commentary on the* LBW, 44.

[113] Luther, *Small Catechism*, BC, 354.2.

[114] Luther, *Small Catechism*, BC, 360.12.

[115] Luther, *Small Catechism*, BC, 359.1-2.

[116] See Luther, *Small Catechism*, BC, 463.53 and 464.57.

language was unfamiliar to Lutherans, who traditionally affirmed the presence and work of the Holy Spirit in the baptismal *washing* over and against the notion that the "sacrament" of confirmation constituted a separate conferral of the Holy Spirit.[117] But the language in the ELW prayer, which invokes the Spirit on neither the baptismal water nor the baptismal candidates, is ambiguous and hence can be understood as supportive of traditional Lutheran baptismal pneumatology. It merely affirms that the baptismal act is effective by the work of the Spirit, much in line with the teaching of John 3 and Luther's *Small Catechism*. The images of the washing away of sin, cleansing, and inheriting the kingdom of God all affirm the Lutheran understanding that baptism *saves*.

Like the eucharistic thanksgiving, the baptismal thanksgiving concludes with a doxology that serves as a trinitarian summary of the praise that is offered in the prayer. Indeed the entire prayer is trinitarian: the Father of creation is thanked, the saving words and deeds of his Son are recalled, and the Spirit is invoked to make this use of water a saving event.

A rubric suggests that water may be poured into the font before or during the thanksgiving. The action is not absolutely necessary, but by making the use of water obvious, it affirms the traditional Lutheran understanding that God uses the things of creation for redemptive purposes. In preparation, a pitcher or ewer filled with water might be placed on a table near the baptismal font/pool prior to the beginning of the service. An assisting minister will need to pour the water during the prayer so that the presiding minister's hands are free to be lifted in the *orans* ("prayer") position throughout the prayer. The minister's hands may be extended toward the assembly during the salutation.

PCS-A does not contain a baptismal thanksgiving that enumerates God's salvific acts involving water, but, like Calvin's

[117] Luther stated that this was precisely the meaning of Titus 3:5: "For [St Paul] teaches that the Holy Spirit is given in baptism, as Christ also teaches, indeed, in baptism we are reborn by the Holy Spirit" (*Kirchenpostille: Epistle in der Fruh-Christmas* ["Sermon for Early-Christmas Matin"] Titus 3:4-8 [1522], *D. Martin Luther's Werke* [Weimar, 1907], Band X, I.1.117, translation from CIRP, 172).

1542 rite,[118] provides a prayer that intercedes for the candidates ("Eternal and gracious God…").[119] God is asked to deliver "all who believe and are baptized" from death, bondage and sin, and to give them life, freedom, and righteousness. Furthermore, God is asked to bind the candidates to the church, guard them from evil, and strengthen them for service – all themes found in Reformation-era baptismal rites. Nothing in this prayer suggests the sacramental efficacy of baptism, nor are the sought-for benefits even tied explicitly to the baptismal act. A drastically revised version of the second thanksgiving prayer in BCW,[120] this PCS prayer omits much biblical material that actually seems quite amenable to Reformed-Calvinist piety, although the manner in which the original prayer relates the Holy Spirit to baptism might be problematic for some Reformed Christians. Given that elements of thanksgiving are absent from the PCS-A prayer, it is somewhat anomalous to end what is essentially an intercessory petition with a full trinitarian doxology.

Following the acts of renunciation and adhesion, DSSB provides a short thanksgiving prayer (10), which is introduced not with the traditional salutation and invitation to give thanks, but with an ascription of praise for God's faithfulness. Unlike the full Flood Prayer in the BCP 1549 and BCP 1552, the DSSB prayer alludes only to the Exodus event and Jesus' baptism. But like the BCP 1549 and BCP 1552, DSSB invokes the Holy Spirit upon the *candidates* for the sake of their new birth (John 3), inclusion in the church (1 Cor. 12:13), and attainment of everlasting life (cf. John 6:63; Rom. 8:11).[121] Somewhat like the prayer immediately prior to the baptism in the BCP 1662 ("Almighty and ever-living God…"), which asks God to "sanctify" the baptismal water, DSSB asks God to "bless" the water so that the baptized are delivered from sin –

[118] Calvin, *Form of Prayers*, CIRP, 115-16.

[119] PCS-A, 2.

[120] "Baptism," BCW, 411-12.

[121] "Public Baptism," BCP 1549, CIRP, 89-90; "Ministration of Baptism" BCP 1552, CIRP, 106-7.

although DSSB's connection between the Spirit and "new birth" is not present in the 1662 prayer.[122] The DSSB prayer's themes of the forgiveness of sins, new birth/regeneration, and joining the family of God are also expressed in the *Articles of Religion* (AR).[123] The section beginning "bless this water..." in DSSB, especially, makes clear the purpose of the prayer: to ask God to make baptism yet another of his saving works. Hence, the sacramentality of baptism as understood in classical Anglicanism, especially its emphasis on the role of the Holy Spirit, is maintained in this prayer.

Like ELW, UMBW places a "Thanksgiving over the Water" (10) prior to the washing. The salutation is followed by a simple invitation to pray, rather than an invitation to *give thanks* as would be expected. The first section of this trinitarian prayer recalls creation, the great flood, and the Exodus event – God's works involving water. Curiously, no mention is made of the condemnation of the wicked world in the great flood, nor of the destruction of Pharaoh's armies. But unlike similar baptismal thanksgiving prayers, allusion is made to Israel's Jordan crossing, thereby providing a link to the Christological section where Jesus' baptism is recalled. Besides the Lord's baptism, the second section of UMBW's thanksgiving remembers Jesus' time in Mary's womb, his call for the disciples to share in the baptism of his death and resurrection, and his command to make disciples of all nations (the latter two references also being in ELW's thanksgiving). Somewhat like Wesley's baptismal service where the Flood Prayer asks God to sanctify the recipients and a subsequent prayer (before the washing) seeks the sanctification of the baptismal water,[124] UMBW beseeches God for a pouring out of the Spirit upon the water to "bless" both water and recipients of baptism for the washing away of sin. Further benefits include life-long righteousness (a faint reference to Wesleyan perfection, perhaps), continual dying and rising with Christ (Rom. 6), and participation in Christ's final victory, an eschatological reference with parallels in the baptismal

[122] "Baptism," DSSB, 50-51; "Baptism of Riper Years," BCP *Texts*, 424.

[123] AR XXVII, BCP 1979, 873.

[124] Wesley, "Baptism of Infants," JWPB, 139, 141.

services in the BCP 1662 and Wesley's *Sunday Service* for Methodists (viz., the Flood Prayer and the prayer that immediately follows). In the epicletic (Spirit-focused) section of the thanksgiving, UMBW points more in the direction of baptismal regeneration than does Wesley. For UMBW the recipient of baptism is washed of sin *in the baptismal act*, while the prayers in Wesley's baptismal services are somewhat ambiguous on this point.

UMBW's thanksgiving may be punctuated with short (sung) responses after the first and second sections and with a concluding doxology.[125] Given that the doxology functions as a summary of the praise expressed in the whole prayer, it makes more sense for the minister to offer the doxology and for the assembly to respond with a simple sung "Amen."

During the prayer of thanksgiving, ministers using DSSB and UMBW may also raise the hands in the orans position (cf. Ps. 143:6; 1 Tim. 2:8), while an assistant holds the service book (or folder) for the minister. It is fitting for assemblies of all traditions to stand for the baptismal thanksgiving prayer, a solemn proclamation of God's mighty acts, and to be seated afterwards for the baptismal washing.

The Washing

The New Testament gives no clear indications about the actual administration of baptism.The narrative of Jesus' baptism may or may not indicate a full submersion into the water, since the phrase "came up out of the water"(Ιησοῦς εὐθύς ἀνέβη ἀπὸ τοῦ ὕδατος) could indicate Jesus' movement away *from* (ἀπὸ) the river to its bank, rather than the straightening of his body while still in the water. Other accounts of persons administering baptism in the New Testament, whether John the Baptizer, Jesus, or the Lord's disciples, mention only that baptism *was* administered and not *how* it was administered. Paul may or may not have had submersion in mind when he likened baptism to a death and burial (Rom. 6:4), although later authors would make such a connection.[126] Additionally, New Testament texts

[125] See "Baptismal Covenant Musical Responses," UMH, 53-55.

[126] See Cyril of Jerusalem, *Mystagogical Catechesis* 2.4.

do not provide the clearest picture of what words might have been used as the candidates were washed. The phrase "in the name of Jesus" (Acts 2:38, 8:16, 10:48, and 19:5), as well as the trinitarian language in Matt. 28:19, may be theological *interpretations* of the action, rather than an explicit baptismal formula.

Clearer evidence concerning the administration of baptism emerges in the late-first century and second centuries. The descriptions of baptism in the *Didache* and Justin's *First Apology* indicate the use of a trinitarian formula derived from Matt. 28:19. While the former document indicates a three-fold pouring of water, the latter says nothing about the exact manner of applying the water.[127] Tertullian indicates a three-fold immersion (or submersion) using some kind of trinitarian confession of faith.[128] The *Apostolic Tradition* likewise indicates a creedal interrogation with (most likely) a submersion of the candidate following each affirmative response.[129] Cyril of Jerusalem[130] and Ambrose of Milan[131] both speak of a triple submersion in conjunction with a creedal interrogation, while John Chrysostom[132] and Theodore of Mopsuestia[133] indicate the triple submersion of candidates accompanied by a trinitarian formula in the *passive*: "Name *is baptized* in the name of the Father," etc.[134] Thus, while submersion was a very common mode of baptism in the early church,[135] the baptismal formula consisted of either a creedal

---

[127] The *Didache* 7.3 (late-first or early-second cent.); Justin, *First Apology* 61 (ca. 155).

[128] Tertullian, *Against Praxeas* 26 (ca. 213).

[129] *Apostolic Tradition* 21. Insofar as the bishop or priest places his hand on the head of the candidate, *submersion* is the likely mode of baptism indicated here.

[130] See Cyril of Jerusalem, *Mystagogical Catechesis* 2.4.

[131] Ambrose, *On the Sacraments* 2.20 (ca. 390).

[132] John Chrysostom, *Baptismal Instructions* 26.

[133] Theodore of Mopsuestia, *Baptismal Homily* 3.18.

[134] It is quite clear from the literary context that Cyril, Ambrose, Chrysostom, and Theodore are all referring to a full submersion of the candidate's body into the baptismal font/pool.

[135] Everett Ferguson contends that nearly all fonts constructed during the church's first five centuries could accommodate immersion and that most ancient art

interrogation or the minister's pronouncement of a trinitarian formula based on Matt. 28:19. But eventually, a trinitarian formula, whether the Western, active version ("I baptize you in the name…") or the passive version associated with Eastern churches ("Name *is baptized* in the name…" etc.) would become standard. Since the majority of candidates from the seventh century on were infants, pouring or sprinkling would become the more common modes of administration in Western churches, while submersion remained the norm in Eastern churches.[136]

In Western churches, the inclusion of the candidate's name within the baptismal formula only emerged gradually. Interrogatory formulas (as in *Apostolic Tradition*) never made use of the name, and no extant sources from the first several centuries indicate a declarative formula that did so.[137] The earliest instance of the practice only appears in the *Missale Gothicum*, a liturgical document from around 700 CE. Once the majority of baptismal candidates became infants, the prebaptismal catechumenal rites that formerly involved adults and made use of the candidates' names (as at the election at the beginning of Lent) were compressed into the baptismal rite itself, since there was no longer any point in staging out the baptismal process. Thus, the name of the (child) candidate was given prior to

---

works depicting a baptismal candidate standing in water (e.g., Jesus) also show the baptizer's hand on the head of the candidate which is a likely indication of baptismal immersion (*Baptism in the Early Church*, 849, 851). Some artistic depictions of baptism, however, show a figure who is standing in water that is only ankle-deep, which rules out baptismal immersion. See Robin M. Jenson, *Baptismal Imagery in Early Christianity: Ritual, Visual, and Theological Dimensions* (Grand Rapids: Baker Academic, 2012), 14.

[136] The three most common modes of baptism today are *affusion*, pouring water over the candidate's head, *immersion*, pouring water over the candidate who stands in water, and *submersion*, plunging the candidate's entire body beneath the surface of the water. See Philip H. Pfatteicher, *A Dictionary of Liturgical Terms* (Harrisburg, PA: Trinity Press International, 1991), s.v. "Affusion," "Immersion," and "Submersion."

[137] Lizette Larson-Miller, "'That You May Be a Christian': Baptism, Identity and Naming," in *A Living Tradition,* 173-74.

the baptismal washing and then incorporated into the formula.[138] The insertion of the candidate's name became a normal part of the baptismal act in the baptismal rites of the Protestant Reformers.[139]

The Reformers were satisfied with the declarative (active) trinitarian formula (name included) and the various ways of baptizing that they had inherited, whether submersion, pouring, or infusion (dipping only the head into the font).[140] The rites of Luther and Cranmer indicated that the child is to be *dipped* into the font.[141] The first Zurich rite indicated dipping, but no mode is suggested in Zwingli's revision of that rite.[142] Calvin's baptismal rite was likewise silent on the mode of baptism. Wesley was willing to accept "washing, dipping, or sprinkling."[143]

Generally, flexibility as to the mode of baptism prevails among Protestants. LBW prescribes pouring or immersion.[144] ELW recommends a "generous" use of water, whether that means pouring or immersing (submersing).[145] While recognizing that the divine action in baptism does not depend on the amount of water used, Lutherans believe that an ample pouring better signifies the biblical images of washing and cleansing and that submersion aptly portrays death and burial with Christ.[146] PCS-A indicates sprinkling which is the likely presumption for infants as well.[147] DSSB directs the minister to dip candidates into water or pour water over them.[148] UMBW states that

---

[138] Larson-Miller, "'That You May Be a Christian,'" 182.

[139] Larson-Miller, "'That You May Be a Christian,'" 180.

[140] Luther, *Order of Baptism*, editor's note 2, LW 53, 100.

[141] Luther, *Order of Baptism*, LW 53, 100; *Baptism, Newly Revised*, LW 53, 109; "Public Baptism," BCP 1549, CIRP, 94; "Ministration of Baptism," BCP 1552, CIRP, 110.

[142] Jud, *Baptism of Children*, CIRP, 129.

[143] Wesley, *Treatise on Baptism* (1756) I.2, *Works of Wesley* X, 188.

[144] "Notes on the Liturgy," LBW, 31.

[145] "Notes," ELW, 28; UMG, 26.

[146] Bushkovsky and Satterlee, *Christian Life*, 69.

[147] PCS-A, 2. BCW mentions pouring, sprinkling, or immersion (413).

[148] "Baptism," DSSB, 52.

candidates and parents can *choose* from among sprinkling, pouring, or immersion (submersion), and then expounds the symbolic meaning of each of these modes.[149] All of these rites employ the traditional Western trinitarian formula, but only LBW and ELW explicitly indicate a three-fold application of water and permit the use of the passive formula.[150] The latter formula emphasizes the divine work in and through baptism and so underscores the Lutheran belief that *God* is the one who actually baptizes.[151] Baptists and Pentecostals baptize by a single submersion with an accompanying trinitarian formula.[152]

Each baptismal mode has symbolic meaning. Submersion is an image of drowning and therefore suggests one's baptismal death and resurrection with Christ (Rom. 6). Immersing/pouring images a washing from sin and renewal (Titus 3), while sprinkling is associated with cleansing from dirt (Ezek. 36:25). Consistency in the mode of baptism avoids the appearance of catering to different consumeristic tastes and gives clearer witness to *one* baptism for the forgiveness of sins.

Some Christians question the necessity of a *three-fold* use of water. Certainly the New Testament does not explicitly command such a practice, and some churches have argued that their single pouring or immersion points to the unity of the Godhead. However, the antiquity of a three-fold washing, its long ecumenical usage (in both East and West), and its symbolic witness to the triune identity of God strongly commend the practice to contemporary Christians. Avoiding a three-fold pouring or submersing merely for reasons of expediency or convenience detracts from the symbolism of baptism and undermines the trinitarian faith of the church at precisely the time when it needs to be proclaimed with clarity.

---

[149] "Baptismal Covenant I (Introduction)," UMBW, 81.

[150] "Baptism," LBW, 311; "Baptism," ELW, 590.

[151] "Notes," ELW, 28. Cf. Luther, *Large Catechism*, BC, 457.10.

[152] See Fiddes, "The Baptism of Believers," BT, 75, 77; Daniel Albrecht, "Witness in the Waters: Baptism and Pentecostal Spirituality," BT, 152.

Must the traditional trinitarian formula be used when baptizing? In some cases, Christians have sought alternatives to the language of "Father, Son, and Holy Spirit" for the sake of gender-inclusivity. Some proposals, e.g., "I baptize you in the name of the Creator, Redeemer, and Sanctifier," however, do not really constitute a name but a list of the works of God and hint of modalism, the unorthodox belief that God has made self-revelation in three forms, i.e., that God acted in different *modes* at different times, as opposed to existing as three distinct trinitarian persons all at the same time. Furthermore, the New Testament names God only as Father, Son, and Holy Spirit, and only by invoking that name can it be clear that the person being baptized is now incorporated into the new reality brought about by the death and resurrection of Jesus, who as the divine Son, accomplished his Father's will and is witnessed to by the Spirit. If the church does not call on the triune God when initiating a new convert, that person is left uncertain whether the gospel promises have anything to do with him or her. As UMG puts it: "The [triune] name is a summary of the power and presence of the triune God and of that teaching which must accompany every baptism."[153]

Some practical matters related to the baptismal washing:

1. In preparation for baptism a heavy cover may in some cases need to be removed from the font – a task that cannot be left to the last moment.
2. The baptismal font is filled with water before the beginning of the Service. A pitcher or ewer filled with water is placed near the font if the latter is filled during the thanksgiving.
3. Candidates who are to be immersed are requested to wear simple, loose-fitting attire. Infants need not be dressed in elaborate baptismal gowns.
4. Prior to the washing, the minister may need to ask the name of the baptismal candidate or perhaps have it written in some convenient place, in order to avoid mistakes when speaking the baptismal formula.

[153] UMG, 24B.

5. When a pedestal-type font is used, the adult candidate will bend so as to have the head over the font, while a parent or sponsor holds an infant so that his/her head is over the font. The minister scoops water from the font and then pours it over the candidate's head using his/her hand or a clamshell, a traditional symbol of baptism.
6. Immersion may take place in one of three ways. In the first method, the candidate stands or kneels in a pool of medium depth. The minister, standing outside the pool beside the candidate, pours water over the candidate's head, with the excess water running back into the font. According to a second method, the minister (standing in or out of the water) helps the kneeling candidate to hold clasped hands over his/her mouth and nose, and then gently plunges the candidate forward into the water and pulls the person out again. A third form requires both candidate and minister to be standing in the pool. The minister stands somewhat behind the person and helps the candidate to hold clasped hands over mouth and nose. With the other forearm wrapped around the candidate's back, the minister gently pushes the candidate backwards into the water and pulls him/her out again.[154]
7. The actions and the words accompanying baptism should be deliberate and unhurried. As much as possible, the assembly should be able to see and hear the baptismal act.
8. Small towels may be provided for the candidates. Immersion requires the provision of rooms for the candidates to change into dry clothing.
9. If candidates are immersed in the main liturgical space, provision is made for drying the floor around the pool following the baptisms, whether with mops or squeegees.
10. The congregation may say "Amen" following each baptism and/or sing a short acclamation of thanksgiving for the newly baptized.

[154] Bushkovsky and Satterlee, *Christian Life*, 69.

11. Following baptism, all return to their places, and this action may be accompanied by assembly song in the form of an acclamation, psalm, or hymn.[155]

Postbaptismal Rites

Over the centuries, Christians have elaborated baptism with a number of biblical rites and gestures. Both the laying on of hands (cf. Acts 8:17, 19:6) and anointing (cf. 2 Cor. 1:21-22) have been used to ritualize the baptismal gift of the Holy Spirit (Acts 2:38). Somewhat less common have been the conferral of a new garment to symbolize being clothed with Christ in baptism (Gal. 3:26-27) and the giving of a candle as a symbol of spiritual enlightenment (cf. Matt. 5:16; Heb. 6:4, 10:32).

Only in the late-second and early-third centuries does sure evidence of such rites emerge. Tertullian speaks of a postbaptismal anointing, likely involving the sign of the cross, that he likens to priestly anointing, followed by a handlaying that "invited" and "welcomed" the Holy Spirit.[156] Cyprian of Carthage also mentions these postbaptismal rites, speaking of the handlaying as a conferral of the Holy Spirit and a perfection with the "Lord's seal."[157] Cyril of Jerusalem describes both a prebaptismal anointing of the entire body that gives a share in Christ and a postbaptismal anointing of the forehead and various body parts that is associated with the Holy Spirit.[158] The *Apostolic Tradition* attributed to Hippolytus of Rome likewise describes anointings before and after baptism by the priest, the first being associated with exorcism, while the second

[155] For baptismal acclamations, see #200-215, *Evangelical Lutheran Worship* (Pew Edition) (Minneapolis: Augsburg Fortress, 2006). For hymns see #157-195, *Lutheran Book of Worship* (Pew Edition) (Minneapolis: Augsburg Publishing, 1978); #442-459, ELW Pew Edition; and UMBW, 84-85 for a list of hymns in *United Methodist Hymnal* that are appropriate for baptism.

[156] Tertullian, *De Baptismo* 7-8; *Concerning the Resurrection of the Flesh* 8 (ca. 195 or later).

[157] Cyprian, *Letter* 73 to Jubaianus 6, 9 (ca. 256).

[158] Cyril of Jerusalem, *Mystagogical Catechesis* 2.3, 3.1, and 3.4.

used the "oil of thanksgiving." In addition, *Apostolic Tradition* mentions two postbaptismal actions by the bishop: (1) a handlaying whose accompanying prayer asks God to grant the newly baptized worthiness of receiving the forgiveness of sins and to give divine grace; and (2) an anointing of the head with the "oil of thanksgiving" that was accompanied by a trinitarian formula and possibly involved marking with the sign of the cross.[159] The text gives no indication of the meaning of these two postbaptismal anointings, but most likely the episcopal anointing, along with the handlaying, are meant to affirm or ratify the baptism that took place out of the assembly's view. Theodore of Mopsuestia speaks of the newly baptized being clothed in a white garment and receiving an anointing on the forehead; the latter is associated with Jesus' reception of the Holy Spirit at his baptism, implying a conferral of the Spirit to the newly baptized.[160] The postbaptismal conferral of a candle to the newly baptized only emerges in the Middle Ages with its appearance in Roman liturgical books and the *Sarum Manual* in England.[161]

In his first baptismal service, Luther retained three traditional postbaptismal ceremonies administered by the priest:

1. marking the sign of the cross on the forehead of the newly baptized with *chrism* (holy oil), accompanied by an ancient formula that speaks of regeneration by water and the Holy Spirit, the forgiveness of sins, and being anointed to eternal life;[162]
2. placing of a band of linen over the head of the newly baptized in order to cover the chrism, along with a formula about

[159] *Apostolic Tradition* 21.

[160] Theodore of Mopsuestia, *Baptismal Homily* III.27.

[161] See CIRP, 16, note 7 and the *Sarum Rite* (1543), DBL, 301-2.

[162] The formula in question is at least as old as the *Gelasian Sacramentary*, whose earliest editions date to the seventh-century. See *The Gelasian Sacramentary* XLIV, ed. H. A. Wilson (Oxford: 1894).

receiving a robe that is to be brought unstained to the final judgment;[163] and

3. giving the newly baptized a lighted candle with accompanying words about "guarding" one's baptism so that one might meet the Lord when he comes to the marriage (i.e., the eschaton; cf. Matt. 25:1-13)

Of these, only the linen band ("robe") ceremony remained in Luther's 1526 revised rite – albeit with a slightly revised version of the anointing formula.[164]

The first baptismal rite for Zurich also retained the anointing and robe ceremonies with formulas similar to those known by Luther. Zwingli's revision, however, only kept the robe with a slightly revised accompanying formula.[165] The revised rite is prefaced with a statement about the removal of additional ceremonies that lacked biblical foundations.[166] In a similar but more radical move, Calvin included none of the traditional postbaptismal ceremonies in his 1542 baptismal service, arguing that these were merely human inventions that promote superstition and distract from the central actions and meaning of baptism. For him only ceremonies that edify were to be retained, while those that detracted from true devotion were to be avoided.[167]

In the baptismal rite of BCP 1549, Cranmer retained the conferral of a white robe ("crisom") and its long formula about receiving the garment as a token of innocence and preserving that quality in order to obtain eternal life. Likewise retained was the postbaptismal anointing of the head along with the traditional formula about regeneration through water and the Holy Spirit,

[163] Note: the linen band ceremony is a vestige of an earlier conferral of a robe that covered the entire body.

[164] Luther, *Order of Baptism,* LW 53, 100-101; *Baptism Newly Revised* (1526), LW 53, 109.

[165] Jud, *Baptism of Children,* CIRP, 129; Zwingli, *Revision of the Zurich Order of Baptism*, CIRP, 131.

[166] Zwingli, *Revision of the Zurich Order of Baptism*, CIRP, 130.

[167] Calvin, *Form of Prayers,* CIRP, 116-17.

etc.[168] Following the recommendations of Bucer's *Censura*, Cranmer omitted these ceremonies from the 1552 rite, but a marking with the sign of the cross on the child's forehead, a preliminary ceremony in the 1549 rite, is placed immediately after the baptismal washing in the 1552 baptismal service. The slightly modified formula speaks militaristically of receiving the cross as a symbol of confessing the faith of Christ crucified, battling the powers arrayed against God, and being Christ's faithful soldier to the end.[169] The postbaptismal structure of the 1552 baptismal rite (sign of the cross, Lord's Prayer, prayer for the newly baptized, and exhortation to godparents) was retained in both of the BCP 1662 rites (infant and adult), except that the adult rite contained an exhortation to the newly baptized themselves.[170] John Wesley kept the postbaptismal signing ceremony only in the rite for infants,[171] perhaps in order to avoid the impression that adults were regenerated in baptism.

Contemporary Lutheran baptismal services provide several postbaptismal ceremonies: clothing in a white garment, handlaying with prayer using Spirit-language, anointing on the forehead with a "seal of the Holy Spirit" formula, and the conferral of a lighted candle. While the handlaying and anointing are obligatory in both LBW and ELW, the garment and candle rites are optional.[172]

In keeping with a Lutheran tradition that has ancient roots, the first postbaptismal gesture in ELW is the (optional) conferral of a baptismal garment.[173] The action may be accompanied by the words

---

[168] "Public Baptism," BCP 1549, CIRP, 94.

[169] "Ministration of Baptism," BCP 1552, CIRP, 110.

[170] "Baptism of Riper Years" (1662), BCP *Texts*, 425.

[171] Wesley, "Baptism of Infants," and "Baptism of Riper Years," JWPB, 142, 148.

[172] "Baptism," LBW, 311 (concerning the baptismal garment, see "Notes," LBW, 31); "Baptism," ELW, 590-91.

[173] In LBW, the garment is not conferred until *after* the anointing, which is unfortunate, since if the candidates were immersed, they would need to dry themselves and change into dry clothing before receiving the garment and proceeding with the handlaying and anointing rites. If the latter two rites take place in front of the altar, LBW would conceivably have the newly baptized walking to the altar while soaking wet! Fortunately, ELW solves this problem.

"All who are clothed in Christ have put on Christ",[174] although "All who are *baptized* have put on Christ" (cf. Gal. 3:27) would have been more biblical. Alternatively, the assembly may sing "You have put on Christ" (ELW #211) during the presentation of the garment.[175] If candidates have been immersed they may need time to change into dry clothing before putting on the special baptismal garment.[176] In that case, the assembly either continues singing the acclamation or sings a baptismal hymn. If the location of the font/pool does not afford the assembly an adequate view of the actions that follow the washing (garment, handlaying, anointing, candle, and welcome), the ministers, sponsors, parents, and newly baptized may reassemble in a more convenient location (e.g., before the table). An assembly song may also need to take place while this movement occurs, and such singing may be a continuation of songs begun during the garment presentation.

The handlaying prayer in LBW and ELW is derived from the seventh-century *Gelasian Sacramentary*.[177] Previously used only in Lutheran confirmation rites, this prayer for the seven-fold gifts of the Spirit was introduced into the *baptismal* rite of North American Lutherans by LBW as a way of heightening the importance of baptism by suggesting that the form and matter of confirmation (i.e., ritualizing the gift of the Holy Spirit) belong to baptism.[178] ELW, however, softens LBW's rather strong "pour out" to "sustain *Name* with the gift of your Holy Spirit," in order to avoid the appearance of a separate conferral of the Spirit apart from the baptismal washing. The ELW rubrics state that the handlaying and prayer do not constitute a distinct action, but rather serve as a ritual expression

---

[174] Bushkovsky and Satterlee, *Christian Life*, 71.

[175] Bushkovsky and Satterlee, *Christian Life*, 71.

[176] For suggestions about the design of a baptismal garment, see Bushkovsky and Satterlee, *The Christian Life*, 71-72.

[177] *The Gelasian Sacramentary* XLIV.

[178] For the history surrounding this prayer's incorporation into LBW and the theological questions it raised for Lutherans, see my *Reform of Baptism and Confirmation*, chs. 2-4.

of the Spirit's bestowal in the baptism itself.[179] Indeed, Lutherans have insisted that the Spirit is conferred in the baptismal washing.[180] The first two lines of the handlaying prayer are spoken only once. Each of the newly baptized then receives the laying on of hands (to the head) accompanied by the remaining lines ("Sustain *name* with the gift..."). Laying different hands on two different people at once, or laying both hands on multiple persons in quick succession while praying, gives the impression of haste and suggests a partial, piecemeal giving of the Spirit's gifts.

The marking with the sign of the cross, found in Luther's baptismal orders and other early Protestant baptismal services, uses the same Eastern Orthodox-inspired formula as in LBW, which was gleaned from Protestant sources.[181] A sign of belonging to Christ the crucified one, the action recalls other times when the cross is made: at the invocation, the announcement of forgiveness, and the benediction of the Lord's Supper liturgy. Every time that one makes the cross – an action commended by Luther in the *Small Catechism*[182] – baptism is recalled. Although optional, the use of oil for this gesture would strengthen its biblical associations; oil signifies both a relationship to Christ who is the "anointed One" (Acts 10:38), and membership in his royal priesthood (cf. 1 Peter 2:9).[183] The words and formula are said for each newly-baptized person.

Following Luther's 1523 baptismal rite, LBW and ELW suggest giving a lighted candle to each of the newly baptized as a reminder of their baptismal enlightenment (renewal) by Christ. The first option in

---

[179] "Notes," ELW, 29.

[180] See note 117 above.

[181] See Truscott, *Reform of Baptism and Confirmation*, 67-69. For examples of Eastern baptismal services whose postbaptismal anointing formulas use "seal of the Spirit" language, see "Rite of Christian Initiation (Eastern Orthodox)", BT, 281, and "Text of the Mystery of Holy Baptism (Oriental Orthodox – Syrian, India)", BT, 316. The "Confirmation" portion of the Roman Catholic Church's *Rite of Christian Initiation of Adults* uses the following anointing formula: "Be sealed with the gift of the Holy Spirit" (BT, 337).

[182] Luther, *Small Catechism*, BC, 363.1, 4.

[183] "Notes," ELW, 29.

ELW ("Jesus said…"), based on John 9:5 and 8:12, links discipleship with the light of Christ; to follow him is to truly see and reflect his goodness and glory into the world. The second, based on Matt. 5:16, links illumination with a life that glorifies God. The newly baptized may light the candle on their baptismal anniversary each year not only as a memento of their baptism, but also as a reminder of the baptismal life lived as a consequence of baptism.

The congregational welcome that concludes the ELW baptismal rite, derived from LBW, focuses on inclusion into the body of Christ and participation in the mission of the church, the latter emphasis reflecting UMG's statement that "baptism and baptismal catechesis join the baptized to the mission of Christ."[184] In baptism, one does not merely become a Christian, but a member of the church and joins it in worship and in service to the world. The welcome is therefore more than a means of involving the assembly; it is an expression of the ecclesial dimension of baptism. The welcome is always spoken by the congregation, not just a minister or congregational representative, and is never omitted. The ELW welcome is based on language in LBW, but unlike the LBW words of welcome it does not require modification when only a single candidate is baptized.

Neither PCA-A nor PCS-I utilize any postbaptismal ceremonies.[185] However, in PCS-A, the minister offers a brief statement that connects baptism to membership in Christ's priesthood ("God has made them…") and then invites the assembly to welcome the newly baptized, presumably through an informal gesture such as applause. The minister then presents the newly baptized with baptismal certificates and gifts, and congregational leaders offer the "right hand of fellowship" (Gal. 2:9) to the newly

---

[184] See UMG, 51A.

[185] See "Baptism," BCW, 413-14, which includes a postbaptismal handlaying with two possible formulas, and an optional marking of the sign of the cross on the forehead of the newly baptized (use of oil optional). All of the accompanying formulas affirm the conferral of the Holy Spirit in the washing, rather than in the postbaptismal ceremonies themselves.

baptized as a gesture of welcome.[186] PCS-I provides no acts or gestures of welcome, somewhat surprising given the traditional Reformed emphasis on baptism as incorporation into the covenant community.

The DSSB baptismal service concludes with three postbaptismal rites.[187] First, following a tradition going back to the BCP 1549 and BCP 1552, DSSB prescribes a marking with the sign of the cross on the forehead(s) of the newly baptized.[188] The minister then leads the assembly in a version of the traditional Anglican cross-marking formula, although it is not apparent why the assembly should speak words traditionally reserved for the minister. If congregational participation is desired at this point, a sung or spoken acclamation is preferable. In any event, the baptismal group will need to be visible to the assembly for the cross ceremony as well as for the (optional) candle ceremony and congregational welcome that follow, which may dictate movement to a more convenient location. Second, following the medieval *Sarum Manual*, as well as the BCP 1979 and ELW, a lighted candle may be given to newly baptized adults/older children or to the parents/sponsors of small children.[189] The formula is based on Matt. 5:14 and 16 and combines a gospel *declaration* ("you are the light of the world") with a gospel *imperative* ("let your light shine"), a fitting summary of what baptism means. Finally, DSSB concludes with the *Alternative Services Book's* welcome to the newly baptized, which draws on phraseology from LBW.[190] The assembly's welcome might better have concluded with the acclamation "Thanks be to God," rather than the repetitive "we welcome you."

---

[186] PCS-A, 2.The original context of the gesture in Galatians is the acceptance of Paul's apostolic ministry by the Jerusalem leadership, rather than baptism.

[187] "Baptism," DSSB, 52-53.

[188] "Baptism," DSSB, 52.

[189] "Baptism," BCP 1979, 313; "Baptism," ELW, 591.

[190] *The Alternative Services Book: Services Authorized for Use in the Church of England in Conjunction with the Book of Common Prayer* (Cambridge: University Press, 1980), 234; "Baptism," LBW, 312.

The baptismal washing in UMBW is followed by a handlaying and *possibly* other (optional) gestures. Baptized family members may join the minister in the handlaying, although there is no ancient precedent for a baptismal handlaying conferred by laypersons. The accompanying formula affirms the Spirit's presence in the baptismal washing and reflects the ecumenical concern that baptism leads to discipleship. Ceremonies that *may* follow include (1) marking the sign of the cross on the newly baptized using a formula similar to ELW (use of oil optional); (2) conferring a baptismal garment with a formula that stresses new life; and (3) presenting a lighted candle with accompanying words based on Matt. 5:16. When small children are baptized, the candle may be given to the parents or sponsors, in which case the formula is re-worded to address the latter – although we might question the wisdom of focusing on parents and sponsors when the ceremony is really meant to express the meaning of *baptism*, not the role of those involved in the Christian nurture of baptized children.The cross-marking has the strongest grounding in historic Methodist liturgical practice, while the candle ceremony and its accompanying words seem to express traditional Methodist pastoral concerns about public witness. In any event, UMBW warns that the optional ceremonies should not overshadow the washing itself in importance.[191] Following these, a baptismal certificate may be presented to the newly baptized. Finally, the congregation welcomes the newly baptized with words that speak of baptism as incorporation into God's new creation (a faint echo perhaps of Wesley's new birth theology) and Christ's royal priesthood. Acting as a representative of the world-wide church, the local church welcomes the newly baptized into the universal body of Christ.

UMBW users should note that if baptism is administered by immersion, the candidates will need the opportunity to change into dry clothing (perhaps including a special baptismal garment) before the service proceeds with these secondary ceremonies. Furthermore, if the font/pool is not in view of the assembly, the ministers, sponsors, newly baptized, and parents of newly-baptized children may need to

[191] "Baptismal Covenant I," UMBW, 91.

reassemble in a more visible location for the explanatory rites and congregational welcome.

Conclusion

Baptism is so rich in meaning that one action alone cannot express all of its biblical associations and interpretations, e.g., new birth, reception of the Holy Spirit, cleansing from sin, being clothed in Christ. Through sight and sound, word and action, the church ritualizes the candidate's rejection of evil, attainment of faith in Jesus Christ, and commitment to discipleship. Worship leaders responsible for planning the celebration of baptism are wise to make full use of the rites and gestures offered by their denominational liturgical books so that the meaning of baptism is conveyed to all present at the baptismal service. They are especially encouraged to use the gift of water in a way that adequately expresses our baptismal death and resurrection with Christ, for this paschal reality is at the heart of what it means to become a Christian.

For Further Reading

Cross, Anthony R. *Baptist Sacramentalism.* Eugene, OR: Wipf & Stock Publishers, 2007.

Green, Michael. *Baptism: Its Purpose, Practice and Power.* London: Hodder and Stoughton, 1987.

Stookey, Laurence H. *Baptism: Christ's Act in the Church.* Nashville: Abingdon, 1982.

Vander Zee, Leonard J. *Christ, Baptism and the Lord's Supper: Recovering the Sacraments For Evangelical Worship.* Downer's Grove: IVP, 2004.

Willimon, William H. *Preaching and Leading Worship.* Revised Edition. Louisville: Westminster John Knox Press, 2008.

CHAPTER 8

Baptism and its Renewal

Many Christians think of baptism as the beginning of their Christian life, but as little more than that; it is done once and then forgotten. But as we will see, baptism keeps returning in one way or another! Put differently, baptism is both recapitulated and renewed through various aspects of Christian life. This chapter highlights how this recapitulation/renewal takes place in and through the church's (Sunday) liturgy, penitential and occasional rites, confirmation/affirmation of baptism, and through various practices in daily life. Readers are encouraged to reflect on how their own churches might better draw out the baptismal implications of these things in order to keep baptism "alive" for each Christian.

Liturgical Participation

Most fundamentally, baptism is renewed through participation in the church's liturgy. When the sign of the cross is made (during the trinitarian invocation), all present are reminded that they were marked with the cross in baptism as a symbol of obedience and service to Christ. When the creed is recited, Christians re-articulate the very faith that they professed in baptism. The reception of the communion elements – a participation in the Lord's body and blood (1 Cor. 10:16-17) – is a re-union with Christ since baptism is personal union with him in his death and resurrection (Rom. 6:5). Communion is also a way to experience again the forgiveness promised and granted in baptism. Finally, the trinitarian benediction at the conclusion of the service reminds assembly members of their baptism by and into the triune God.

The Daily Office, especially Morning Prayer or Matins, also serves as a renewal of baptism. Both LBW and ELW conclude the morning service with a "Paschal Blessing" consisting of the resurrection narrative plus the *Te Deum* canticle.[1] The purpose of this rite is to proclaim that every morning the people of God rise to new life with Christ in and through baptism.[2] ELW Morning Prayer may also conclude with a "Thanksgiving for Baptism" that is even more baptismally-focused.[3] In the morning service of DSSB, an opening rite of confession and absolution serves as a return to baptismal repentance, and the baptismal (Apostles') Creed is a reminder that baptism unites one with all those who confess the triune God.[4]

The liturgical calendar affords opportunities to recall baptism.[5] The Second and Third Sundays in Advent, with their narratives concerning John the Baptizer, as well as the Baptism of our Lord (First Sunday after Epiphany), bring to mind Christian baptism. The entire season of Lent, as we noted earlier, was originally a time of baptismal preparation, and continues to serve that purpose especially in churches that use the adult catechumenate. All Christians renew

---

1 "Morning Prayer (Matins)," LBW, 53-54; "Morning Prayer (Matins)," ELW, 704-5.

2 "Notes on the Services," ELW, 49.

3 "Morning Prayer," ELW, 702-3.

4 "Morning Prayer," DSSB, 1-2, 10.

5 See ch. 4 for a more complete discussion about baptism and the liturgical calendar.

their baptism during Lent through intensified spiritual practices, especially prayer, fasting, and works of charity.[6] When the final baptismal preparation of adult catechumens takes place during Lent and baptism is conferred at the Easter Vigil, Christians naturally recall their baptismal death and resurrection with Christ. Alternatively, baptism may take place on Pentecost in order to underscore the baptismal gift of the Holy Spirit. Finally, baptism on the feast of All Saints highlights the sacrament's role in conferring membership in the body of Christ's holy ones. When baptism is not celebrated on these feast days, a rite of affirmation of baptism ("renewal of the baptismal covenant") for the entire assembly is an appropriate way of renewing baptism.

Confession and Forgiveness

Confession and forgiveness in all its forms is the renewal of baptism *par excellence*, since baptism is about repentance from sin and reconciliation with God. For that reason, confession and forgiveness deserves special attention here.

The confession of sin has been a vital aspect of the divine-human relationship. God could not dwell among a sinful, guilty people, and so commanded the observance of one day in the Israelite liturgical calendar for confessing sin, namely, the Day of Atonement or *Yom Kippur* (Lev. 16). The meaning of the sacrifices and the scapegoat rite is that something (sin) must be put to death and/or that sin and guilt must be driven far from the people, so as not to contaminate the people's relationship with a holy and righteous God. In the New Testament, John the Baptizer administers a baptism of repentance for the forgiveness of sins, that is, as a sign of entrance into the new era ushered in by Jesus (Mark 1). People cannot have a part in Jesus

[6] Recently the Anglican Primate of Canada offered a series of liturgical proposals for renewing baptismal identity. Among these is a gathering rite for the Sundays in Lent whose purpose is to foster reflection on the questions of commitment in the church's baptismal service. Also included is a special Ash Wednesday liturgy for persons renewing their baptismal commitment during Lent. See Anglican Church of Canada, Office of the Primate, "Becoming the Story We Tell," http://www.anglican.ca/primate/becoming/ [accessed 14 April 2014].

or the kingdom of God unless they are aware of their sinfulness and need for the forgiveness and reconciliation that Jesus offers. Early writers counseled Christians to "confess their sins" as a way of finding healing (James 5:16) and as a way of maintaining a holy life (1 John 1:9). It is unclear whether biblical authors had in mind a liturgical rite of confession or merely informal encounters with others.

The early church developed procedures for dealing with especially serious and scandalous sins (murder, adultery, apostasy). Those judged guilty were excommunicated (barred from receiving communion) and put under a strict regimen of prayer and fasting; in a sense, they were treated as catechumens, or people who had to relearn the Christian way of life all over again. Eventually, persons who underwent this *canonical penance* were reconciled to the church just before the Lord's Supper liturgy on Maundy Thursday so that they could rejoin the church for the the sacrament. Thus, serious sin was not merely an individual matter in early Christianity, but something with implications for the integrity of the church and its meal fellowship in Jesus Christ. Although a once-in-a-life experience, canonical penance was only applied rarely, and usually as a last resort. Eventually it fell into disuse.

In the Middle Ages, penance came to be applied to all Christians. The Irish church developed a system of *tariffed penance* which was administered to individuals, and could be repeated as often as needed. The practice was so named because different penitential procedures and actions were exacted for different sins. Special manuals specified the length of the penitential period, the relative severity of different sins, what kinds of penalties were applied to particular sins (e.g., fasting), and how penitents of different stations in life were to be treated (e.g., laypersons versus priests). Peter Lombard identified penance as the fourth sacrament, viewing it as a way of regaining the purity that was received in baptism. Its three steps were inward contrition, oral confession (to a priest), and deeds of satisfaction.[7] The Fourth Lateran Council (1215) made confession to a priest a prerequisite for receiving communion.

---

[7] Peter Lombard, *The Sentences* 4.14.1, 4.16.1 (ca. 1152).

Protestants mostly rejected the traditional teaching and practice of penance. Calvin argues that penance could not be considered a sacrament because it had neither a command nor a promise from God.[8] Having dispensed with individual confession and absolution, Protestants came to rely on public rites of confession and absolution to deal with sin. The BCP 1549 provided a special penitential service for Ash Wednesday which was later revised for use at other times as well.[9] In something of a revival of canonical penance, early Anabaptists excommunicated errant sinners who had previously been rebuked both privately and publicly by church leaders. The point was to ensure congregational unity of heart and mind before eucharistic sharing at the Lord's Table.[10]

Lutherans were unique in their approach to penance. Early in the *Babylonian Captivity of the Church*, Luther lists penance as one of the sacraments, but changed his mind by the time he finished that treatise, arguing that penance had no outward sign like the water of baptism or the bread and wine of the Lord's Supper.[11] In that same work, he enumerates many abuses of penance such as compelling people to go to confession and insisting that all sins be confessed. Yet, Luther states that individual confession and absolution should be retained because the word of absolution comforts persons troubled by their sins.[12] Elsewhere, he stresses the importance and need for (private) confession over and against those Protestants who believed that confession was no longer necessary now that they were free from the Pope. For Luther, confession is actually a *return* to or reappropriation of baptism, since the latter signifies repentance

---

8 John Calvin, *Institutes of the Christian Religion* (1559) IV.19.17, ed. John T. McNeill, tr. Ford Lewis Battles, in LCC XXI (Philadelphia: Westminster Press, 1960), 1464-65.

9 "The First Day of Lent, Commonly Called Ash Wednesday" (Commination) (1549), BCP *Texts*, 92-98, 176-81.

10 *The Schleitheim Confession* (1527), in *Anabaptism in Outline* (Scottdale, PA: Herald Press, 1981), 215.

11 Martin Luther, *The Babylonian Captivity of the Church* (1520), LW 36, 81, 124.

12 Luther, *Babylonian Captivity*, LW 36, 86.

and conversion of life. If private confession and absolution were to continue, Luther insists that (1) it be strictly voluntary; (2) the requirement of confessing all known sins be dropped; and (3) the focus be placed on the absolution and the comforting of consciences with a gospel word.[13]

Contemporary Protestantism knows three forms of confession and forgiveness: (1) brief orders celebrated within the Sunday liturgy;[14] (2) corporate penitential services celebrated occasionally;[15] and (3) services for individual "penitents" celebrated privately and as needed.[16] Practically all Protestants are familiar with (1), while (2) and (3) are less widely known and used.

When celebrated at the very beginning of the liturgy, a brief order for confession and forgiveness makes human sin and brokenness the context for worship. The assembly acknowledges that it comes before God as broken sinners who need the forgiveness of God which is announced in the absolution (words of pardon) and later in the biblical readings. The whole service then becomes a response to God's forgiving mercy. The absolution may take one of three forms: *declaratory*, which announces God's forgiveness (e.g., "...I therefore declare to you the entire forgiveness of all your sins..."), *precatory*, which prays for that forgiveness (e.g., "[May] almighty God...forgive

---

[13] Martin Luther, *The Large Catechism*, BC, 476-80.

[14] "Brief Order for Confession and Forgiveness," LBW, 195; "Confession and Forgiveness," ELW, 166-68; "Confession and Pardon," BCW, 52-57; "A Penitential Order: Rite Two," BCP 1979, 351-53; "Prayers of Penitence," DSSB, 27-30; "Prayers of Penitence," CW, 168-70; "A Service of Word and Table I (Confession and Pardon)" UMBW, 35. For a discussion about confession and forgiveness see Jeffrey A. Truscott, *Worship: A Practical Guide* (Singapore: Genesis, 2011), 131-33.

[15] "Corporate Confession and Forgiveness," LBW, 318-21; "Corporate Confession and Forgiveness," ELW, 601-6; "A Penitential Order: Rite Two," BCP 1979, 351-53 (note that in addition to serving as preparation for the eucharistic service, this rite in BCP 1979 can also serve as a separate ["stand alone"] penitential service with the inclusion of suitable prayers, etc).

[16] "Individual Confession and Forgiveness," LBW, 322-23; "Individual Confession and Forgiveness," ELW, 607-8; "Reconciliation of a Penitent," BCP 1979, 446-52; "A Service of Repentance and Forgiveness for Use with a Penitent Individual," BCW, 1023-24.

you all your sins"), or *indicative* (e.g., "your sins are forgiven," or "I forgive you all your sins").[17] The assembly may make the sign of the cross at the words of absolution (pardon), as a reminder that Christ gained humanity's forgiveness on the Cross. In order to connect the act of confession with baptism, it is appropriate to lead a brief order from the baptismal font. The rite may also be celebrated at the conclusion of the service of the Word just before the communion liturgy, where it serves as a response to the Word or as a means of self-examination in preparation for communion. Some liturgical books allow for either placement of the brief order within the service.[18] Factors such as the liturgical calendar and the emphasis of the biblical readings determine the placement of the rite.[19]

Some books permit the omission of the brief order altogether at certain times, recognizing that such orders are a later addition to the liturgy and ultimately cannot bear the full weight of the church's penitential needs.[20] Specifically, it might be omitted on festive occasions when the service will be lengthy. In ELW, the brief order

---

[17] Lutherans use both declaratory ("Brief Order for Confession and Forgiveness," LBW, 195; "Holy Communion," ELW, 168) and indicative ("Holy Communion," ELW, 168) forms, while Anglicans prefer the precatory form (cf. "Holy Eucharist: Rite Two," BCP 1979, 360; "Holy Communion," DSSB, 30). UMBW uses either the indicative (35) or precatory (45) form. BCW uses declaratory and precatory forms, along with a kind of indicative form (56-57).

[18] "The Holy Eucharist: Rite Two," BCP 1979, 359; "Service of Word and Table I," UMBW, 21, "Notes," CW, 331.

[19] For example, on Maundy Thursday it is especially appropriate to place the order prior to the Lord's Supper liturgy, as a response to the New Testament reading from 1 Cor. 11:17-34 where Paul speaks of self-examination prior to participation in the Lord's Supper. Similarly, if a gospel reading speaks of repentance/confession (e.g., Luke 18:9-14, Lectionary 30 C), the confession is likewise appropriately placed at the conclusion of the service of the Word as a response.

[20] Philip H. Pfatteicher and Carlos Messerli, *Manual on the Liturgy: Lutheran Book of Worship* (Minneapolis: Augsburg Publishing House, 1979), 195-96; cf. Lorraine S. Brugh and Gordon Lathrop, *The Sunday Assembly: Using Evangelical Lutheran Worship*, Vol. 1 (Minneapolis: Augsburg Fortress, 2008), 111.

may be replaced on occasion by a thanksgiving for baptism, which is another way of recalling baptism.[21]

Since baptism is continually lived out through repentance and confession as a Christian *community*, some churches (mainly Lutheran[22] and Anglican[23]) celebrate services of corporate confession and forgiveness as follows: (1) on penitential days (e.g., the final days of Lent); (2) as regularly-scheduled services (e.g., a fifth Sunday of the month, or the last Friday of every month); (3) on occasions such as conflict between parties within the church; and (4) at times of lament for the congregation, community, nation or world that may involve the "confession of corporate wrongs." This service could also be used during a small-group retreat whose content naturally leads to confession and forgiveness. The stand-alone character of the service, with its appointed lessons and a sermon, enables specific homiletical attention to confession, something that might not otherwise happen in a congregation's liturgical life. When the service is a regular part of congregational worship, the assembly comes to appreciate how baptismal repentance is concretized through a ritual act of confession. When used as a response to occasions of lament, the church's role as intercessor for the community and world comes to the fore, as does corporate responsibility for social ills. In sum, this service takes confession beyond the pale of the individual and makes confession the work of the whole church, who confesses *its* sins and the sins of the community, nation, or world. While confession on behalf of others or the world is overlooked by Protestants, globalization and an increasing awareness of social interdependence makes this type of confession a relevant liturgical form.

The structure of the corporate confession rite in ELW is (1) *gathering* with greeting/invocation and a preparatory prayer; (2) *service of the Word* (biblical readings and sermon); (3) *response* consisting of an extended prayer of confession (as in the traditional

---

[21] "Holy Communion (Thanksgiving for Baptism)," ELW, 169.

[22] "Corporate Confession and Forgiveness," LBW, 318-21; "Corporate Confession and Forgiveness," ELW, 601-6.

[23] See note 15 above.

Ash Wednesday liturgy), absolution, peace, and prayers; and (4) *sending* (blessing and dismissal).[24] Since informal conversation is also a means of sharing the gospel, the word section could include "mutual conversation and consolation" (i.e., words of encouragement and reconciliation) shared among assembly members with guidance by the ministers. This conversation might be an opportunity for a quarreling family to settle a dispute over money, or for a congregation to think through a common response to a social problem, such as racial inequality.[25] The sermon proclaims the grace and mercy of God so that people are free to confess. Additionally, it encourages the assembly to receive the absolution as a true Word from God. Following a general absolution addressed to all, participants may come forward and kneel at the altar rail for an individualized laying on of hands, which will be accompanied by an indicative absolution formula. The purpose of the handlaying is to embody and personalize the absolution, which is appropriate if the participants are experiencing deep personal pain.

An extended service of confession and forgiveness is led by an ordained minister who wears the usual vestments (e.g., alb, stole). Normally, he or she will preach the sermon and guide any conversation among members of the assembly. Since confession is closely associated with the sacrament of baptism, an ordained minister will also lead the prayer of confession, pronounce the absolution, and lay hands on individual penitents if that action is included. In churches that tie ordination to sacramental ministry, it would be inappropriate for non-ordained persons to lay hands on penitents and pronounce an absolution formula. In cases where informal conversation among assembly members occurs, an ordained minister may need to be available after the service for further conversation and counseling.

[24] The structure of the corporate confession rite in LBW is similar, except that Psalm 51 precedes the lessons and there is no exchange of the peace.

[25] Some very fine suggestions about how to use "mutual conversation and consolation" in the corporate confession service are given in Pfatteicher and Messerli, *Manual on the Liturgy*, 190.

While brief penitential orders in the Sunday service prepare worshippers for receiving God's Word and the Sacrament, and corporate orders express communal guilt/lament and foster reconciliation, individual confession focuses primarily on restoring relationships. In confessing before another person, the penitent (individual who desires to confess) takes responsibility for a sinful action, recognizing that it has damaged relationships with God and other people. The absolution offers forgiveness that restores the penitent's relationship with God by overcoming guilt. Pastoral conversation gives guidance to the penitent concerning how to restore relationships with those who have been hurt by the penitent's sins. Since individual confession seeks to overcome the effects of sin, it is really the working out of what baptism signifies – dying to sin and rising to new life. Therefore, individual confession does not constitute a true and unique sacrament in its own right. Yet, because of its integral relationship with baptism and biblical basis, especially in the command and promise expressed in John 20:23 ("If you forgive the sins of any…"), individual confession possesses a sacramental character.[26]

Rites for individual confession are found in LBW, ELW, and BCP 1979.[27] In the latter two books, a brief invocation or greeting by the minister is followed by a prayer of confession that allows the penitent to (1) name the specific sins that burden his/her conscience; (2) express sorrow and the desire for forgiveness; and (3) state the intention to amend his/her life. After the confession, the minister may then engage the penitent in spiritual conversation

---

[26] It is precisely for the latter reason that Luther's associate in Wittenberg, Philip Melanchthon, was willing to consider confession a sacrament. See *Apology to the Augsburg Confession* (1530), Art. XIII, BC, 219.4.

[27] "Individual Confession and Forgiveness," LBW, 322-23; "Individual Confession and Forgiveness," ELW, 607-8; "A Service of Repentance for Use with a Penitent Individual," BCW, 1023-24; "The Reconciliation of a Penitent," BCP 1979, 447-52. It should be noted that the BCW rite is for use at the conclusion of a pastoral counseling session at which the penitent has confessed one or more sins that are burdensome to the conscience.

and counseling, including words of admonition and comfort. ELW provides two indicative forms for the absolution:

> *Name*, in obedience to the command of our Lord Jesus Christ, I forgive you all your sins in the name of the Father, and of the + Son, and of the Holy Spirit.
>
> *Name*, by water and the Holy Spirit God gives you a new birth, and through the death and resurrection of Jesus Christ, God forgives you all your sins. Almighty God strengthen you in all goodness and keep you in eternal life.[28]

BCP 1979 provides indicative and precatory forms of absolution:

> Our Lord Jesus Christ, who has left power to his Church to absolve all sinners who truly repent and believe in him, of his great mercy forgive you all your offenses; and by his authority committed to me, I absolve you from all your sins: In the Name of the Father, and of the Son, and of the Holy Spirit.
>
> Our Lord Jesus Christ, who offered himself to be sacrificed for us to the Father, and who conferred power on his Church to forgive sins, absolve you through my ministry by the grace of the Holy Spirit, and restore you in the perfect peace of the Church.[29]

The rites for individual confession in LBW, ELW, and Reconciliation Form Two in BCP 1979 all provide for the reading of psalms and other Scripture verses. Because private confession involves the exercise of the church's power to forgive or retain sins, and is thus a means of grace, LBW and ELW assume that private confession is *always* made before an ordained minister. BCP 1979 permits the reconciliation

---

[28] "Individual Confession," ELW, 608. The form of absolution in LBW is similar to that in ELW, but the former stresses the minister's role as an ordained minister.

[29] "Reconciliation of a Penitent," BCP 1979, 448.

of a penitent before a deacon or lay person, but in those cases a declaration of forgiveness replaces the absolution.[30]

Although private confession can be made anywhere at any time, intentionality and preparation are necessary if the practice is being introduced to a congregation. Stated times are established so that church members become accustomed to the practice. For example, one Friday afternoon per month could be designated for private confession as a way of recalling the crucifixion and the need for each Christian to "crucify" sin. More times for private confession could be set aside during the last week of Lent and during Holy Week so that the rite serves as a preparation for the Paschal Triduum (Maundy Thursday, Good Friday, and the Vigil of Easter). To stress its relationship with the means of grace, private confession takes place in the worship hall or liturgical space of the church building near the altar rail during these stated times. In order to maintain privacy and confidentiality, no other activities should be taking place in the liturgical space. If confession grows out of a counseling session in the pastor's office, the minister and penitent move to the liturgical space or worship hall. What occurs there is not merely a continuation of the counseling session, but an unequivocal confession by the penitent and absolution from the minister. The use of a set form (as described above) can help ensure that this actually happens. Besides offering a clear and honest absolution, the pastor may also want to encourage the penitent to believe what the absolution says, e.g., by saying, "Cling to this promise: the word of forgiveness I speak to you comes from God."[31]

Occasional Services

In addition to the Sunday liturgy, the Daily Office, and rites of confession, baptism is renewed when the church's occasional rites are celebrated. Although not overtly baptismal, Wesley's Covenant

---

[30] "Reconciliation of a Penitent," BCP 1979, 446.

[31] "Individual Confession," ELW, 608; cf. Martin Luther, *The Small Catechism* (1529), BC 361.27 ("Do you also believe that my forgiveness is God's forgiveness?").

Renewal Service, could nevertheless be understood as a renewal of baptism.[32] Church membership rites (transfer, renewal) also have baptismal implications because changing or renewing church membership really involves a decision about how to live out the implications of one's baptism. Accordingly, some liturgical books merge membership rites into the baptismal service,[33] while others ritualize membership transfer/renewal in a separate service of affirmation of baptism.[34] Because other life transitions, such as a change in vocation or retirement, require reflection on how God desires one to live as a baptized Christian, these too can be marked by a rite of affirmation of baptism in which the participants pledge faithfulness to God's calling in light of their baptism. Insofar as marriage constitutes the union of a man and a woman, every Christian marriage service is a reminder of personal union with Christ in baptism (Rom. 6). This connection is made explicit in the nuptial "Declaration of Intention" in UMBW: "I ask you now, in the presence of God and these people, to declare your intention to enter into union with each other, through the grace of Jesus Christ, who calls you into union with himself as acknowledged in your baptism."[35]

Even death is an occasion when baptism can be recalled, since it is the completion of the journey begun in baptism.[36] Accordingly, ELW's funeral service includes a "Thanksgiving for Baptism," that begins with optional quotations from either Rom. 6 or Gal. 3. The baptismal creed is professed following the sermon, and baptismal language is woven into the first two intercessory petitions ("Almighty God, in Holy Baptism you have knit your chosen people together into one communion…" and "Grant that all who have been baptized into

[32] "Covenant Renewal Service," UMBW, 288-94.

[33] "Baptism and Reaffirmation of the Baptismal Covenant," BCW, 431-45; "Holy Baptism," BCP 1979, 299-310; "Services of the Baptismal Covenant," UMBW, 86-94.

[34] "Affirmation of Baptism," LBW 324-27; "Affirmation of Baptism," ELW, 596-99.

[35] "A Service of Christian Marriage I," UMBW, 117.

[36] Martin Luther, *The Holy and Blessed Sacrament of Baptism*, LW 35, 30.

Christ's death and resurrection may die to sin and rise to share the new life in Christ"). Similarly, UMBW employs baptismal language in the words that accompany the placing of a pall[37] on the coffin ("As in baptism *Name* put on Christ, so in Christ may *Name* be clothed in glory").[38] The thanksgiving prayer in the Commendation praises God "for our baptism and place in your Church with all who have faithfully died."[39] Hence, baptism is linked to participation in the communion of saints.

Confirmation

Even if they do not recognize the full baptismal implications of all churchly rites and services, most modern Protestants likely see a connection between baptism and confirmation (aka affirmation of baptism). Some may see it as the occasion for children baptized in infancy to take ownership of the vows made in their stead at baptism by confessing the Christian faith for themselves. Still others view it as a time to acknowledge God's baptismal promises and respond to them by pledging a life of service and discipleship in and with the church. All Protestants recognize that confirmation/affirmation of baptism is inherently dependent on and takes its meaning from baptism.

Confirmation began its life as a component of baptism, but eventually took on a life of its own. Its origins lay in the uniquely Roman and North African tradition of postbaptismal anointing and handlaying conferred by bishops. Tertullian understands the first of these actions as priestly in character, akin to Aaron's anointing by Moses (Lev. 8:12), while the handlaying, which "invites and welcomes" the Holy Spirit, is likened to Jacob's blessing of his grandsons Ephraim and Manasseh (Gen. 48:15-20).[40] Cyprian speaks of the anointing as

[37] A pall is a large liturgical cloth placed over a coffin for the funeral service. Usually white and decorated with a cross pattern, it recalls the garment given to the newly baptized.

[38] "A Service of Death and Resurrection," UMBW, 141.

[39] "A Service of Death and Resurrection," UMBW, 150.

[40] Tertullian, *De Baptismo* 7, 8 (ca. 200); cf. *De Resurrectione Carnis* 8 (after 195).

granting the "grace of Christ," while the handlaying (presumably by a bishop) confers the Holy Spirit, becoming a means of "perfecting" with the Lord's seal.[41] Augustine similarly alludes to the conferral of the Holy Spirit in connection with these postbaptismal rites.[42] As time goes on, it becomes clear that any rite for the conferral of the Holy Spirit is to be performed by a bishop, but there was some fluidity, or perhaps confusion, as to which episcopal action – whether handlaying or anointing – conferred the Holy Spirit. Innocent I (pope 401-17 CE) stipulates that only bishops may sign the forehead with consecrated oil (chrism), an action that he says grants the Holy Spirit,[43] while Gregory I (pope 590-604 CE) permitted presbyters (priests) to perform this action in the absence of a bishop.[44] The *Gelasian Sacramentary*, a seventh-century Roman liturgical book, directs the bishop to "seal" the newly baptized by laying hands on them while praying for the seven-fold gifts of the Holy Spirit.[45] He then signs them with chrism (consecrated oil) on the forehead. Both the *Gelasian Sacramentary* and the eighth-century *Ordo Romanus XI*, a set of rubrical instructions, indicate that these actions were performed even on infants.[46] The latter document uses the language of "confirming" with respect to both of the actions. A homily for Pentecost from the seventh century (or perhaps the fifth) only refers to the bishop's imposition of hands as a "confirmation." This same document, perhaps the first attempt at a theology of confirmation, speaks of baptism in terms of washing and new birth, while confirmation is referred to as an "increase in grace" that

[41] Cyprian, *Letter* 70 to Januarius (ca. 256); *Letter* 73.9 to Jubaianus (ca. 256).

[42] Augustine, *Sermon* 324, *Miscellanea Agostiniana*, Vol. 1, 490.

[43] Innocent I, *Letter to Decentius* 3 (416). As Johnson notes, it is somewhat strange for Innocent to emphasize the role of this anointing in conferring the Holy Spirit, when he alludes to accounts in Acts in which apostolic *handlaying* confers the Holy Spirit! It appears that Innocent was unsure as to which postbaptismal action conferred the Holy Spirit.

[44] Gregory I, *Letter* 26 to Januarius (594).

[45] *The Gelasian Sacramentary*, ed. H. A. Wilson (Oxford: 1894), XLIV (see DBL, 235).

[46] *Ordo Romanus* XI, 100, 101 (ca. 700) (see DBL, 251).

strengthens one for spiritual battle.[47] Eventually, the postbaptismal *anointing* for the Holy Spirit comes to be understood as the *sacrament* of confirmation. Thomas Aquinas states that the chrism is the proper matter of the sacrament and the formula "I sign you with the sign of the cross and I confirm you with the chrism of salvation, in the name of the Father…" is the proper sacramental form.[48]

The development of the theology of confirmation is intimately related to the practicalities of administering Christian initiation in its fullness. In the late-patristic era, areas outside of Rome knew of a Christian initiation practice that was complete *without* any postbaptismal rites administered by bishops.[49] Holy Roman Emperor Charlemagne (ca. 742-814 CE), however, sought to spread Roman liturgical practice throughout his empire. Consequently, bishops, who administered vast dioceses, found it impossible to be present at all baptisms and administer the required anointing and handlaying that were to be part of the baptismal rite. If they were present at baptisms, bishops were to confirm the newly baptized who then received their first communion, otherwise, the newly baptized could receive their first communion from the priest, confirmation being deferred to another time. This pattern of baptism, first communion, and a later confirmation became the norm in churches outside of Rome. We need to emphasize that it is not really the separation of confirmation from baptism, but its *addition* to baptism in the non-Roman west, that resulted in this widespread delay between baptism and confirmation – something that was not the case in the earlier Roman-North African liturgical tradition.[50] The pastoral and practical difficulties surrounding confirmation meant that it had to be explained and theologically justified, and some of the

---

[47] Eusebius Gallicanus (seventh century), or Faustus of Riez (fifth century), *Homily 29 on Pentecost* 1-2 (see DBL, 257-58).

[48] Thomas Aquinas, *Summa Theologiae*, Question 72.

[49] For example, Hildephonse of Toledo, *De Cognitione Baptismi* (see DBL, 164).

[50] Maxwell E. Johnson, *Rites of Christian Initiation: Their Evolution and Interpretation*, rev. exp. ed. (Collegeville: Liturgical Press, 2007), 251.

attempts by medieval theologians along these lines included the assertions that confirmation strengthened one for public witness, conferred a "fuller" gift of the Holy Spirit, or gave Christian virtues.[51] Aquinas viewed confirmation as a strengthening for the spiritual battle that one encounters as one matured, thereby forming a basis for Christians to associate confirmation with adolescence and maturity.[52] Because confirmation was not easily accepted throughout the non-Roman west, authorities attempted to impose a minimum age by which baptized children were to be confirmed, with certain penalties imposed on parents who failed to bring their children to confirmation (e.g., denial of entrance to the church). Eventually, age seven became the fixed maximum age by which children were to be confirmed – most likely because many parents waited until their children reached that age before bringing them to the church to receive that sacrament. In the late-thirteenth century, the Council of Lambeth made confirmation a requirement for receiving Holy Communion, believing that the spiritual benefits of confirmation were crucial to the development of a good Christian character.[53]

The Protestant Reformers reacted negatively to the theology and practice of confirmation that they had inherited. Luther could see no biblical basis for according confirmation the status of a sacrament, since Christ gave no promises about it that might be received in faith.[54] Furthermore, Luther interprets Titus 3:5 to mean that the Holy Spirit is given in the baptismal washing and there *only*:

> You hear: *the water*, that is the bath: you hear: *to be born again*, that is, the regeneration and the renewal, and the Spirit whom here St. Paul interprets as the Holy Spirit. And here it is to be noticed that the apostle knows nothing of the sacrament of confirmation. For he teaches that the Holy

[51] Johnson, *Rites of Christian Initiation*, 253.

[52] Johnson, *Rites of Christian Initiation*, 254-55.

[53] Johnson, *Rites of Christian Initiation*, 256.

[54] Martin Luther, *Babylonian Captivity*, LW 36, 91-92.

> Spirit is given in baptism, as Christ also teaches, indeed, in baptism we are reborn by the Holy Spirit.[55]

However, Luther suggests that pastors could examine the faith of children and then lay hands on and "confirm" those whose knowledge appeared adequate and whose faith seemed sincere.[56] In fact, instruction in the basic tenets of the faith was in his view a prerequisite for admission to the Lord's Supper.[57] Thus, Luther helped to revitalize postbaptismal catechesis, but he provided no rite of confirmation.[58] Later Lutheranism developed a number of forms of confirmation, which may or may not have involved a liturgical rite. Nearly all forms of Lutheran confirmation included catechetical instruction in preparation for receiving Holy Communion and a public profession of faith.[59] Somewhat unique was confirmation in the Brandenburg Church Order, which stipulated that when baptized children had received catechetical instruction, they were to be examined and confirmed either by a bishop or a pastor, and if the latter, only in the presence of an episcopal representative. Handlaying with prayer was required, but anointing with chrism (holy oil) was reserved for baptism only.[60]

In response to the Anabaptist criticism that infants were unsuitable for baptism because they were incapable of faith, understanding, and mature commitment, the Strasbourg Reformer Martin Bucer pioneered an instruction-based confirmation

---

[55] Martin Luther, *Kirchenpostille: Epistle in der Fruh-Christmas* ("Sermon for Early-Christmas Matin") Titus 3:4-8 (1522), *D. Martin Luther's Werke* (Weimar, 1907), Band X, I.1.117, translation from CIRP, 172.

[56] Martin Luther, *Predigt am Sonntag Lätare Nachmittages* ("Sermon for Laetare Afternoon"), March 15, 1523, WA 11, 66.

[57] Martin Luther, *Small Catechism*, BC, 348.11.

[58] Arthur Repp, *Confirmation in the Lutheran Church* (St. Louis: Concordia, 1964), 20.

[59] Jeffrey A. Truscott, *The Reform of Baptism and Confirmation in American Lutheranism*, Drew University Studies in Liturgy, No. 11 (Lanham/Oxford: Scarecrow, 2003), 128-29.

[60] "The Brandenburg Church Order" (1540), CIRP, 182-84.

that was first used in Ziegenhain, Germany.[61] Children with sufficient knowledge to participate in the Lord's Supper were to be presented by their parents and (baptismal) sponsors for a public examination conducted by the church leadership on Christmas, Easter, or Pentecost. After the children had answered the questions satisfactorily and "surrendered" themselves to Christ and the church, the assembly then prayed for their perseverance in the faith and for an "increase of the Holy Spirit." The rite concluded with a handlaying administered by the pastor – understood as *the* act of confirmation – followed by a formal admission to the Lord's Supper and an admonition to submit to the discipline of the church. These regulations for Ziegenhain were incorporated into a church order for Cassel, which also contained a series of questions and answers that dealt with the creed, baptism, and the Lord's Supper. These were followed by a long prayer and then the actual handlaying with an accompanying formula that emphasized the *reception* of the Holy Spirit (!), protection from evil, and help in doing good. It is doubtful whether Bucer had in mind a sacramental conferral of the Holy Spirit; more likely he viewed the handlaying as a blessing.[62]

The BCP 1549 provided a reformed rite of confirmation that began with a series of explanatory rubrics. The proper candidates were those who could recite the Apostles' Creed, Lord's Prayer, and Ten Commandments, and the purpose of the rite was for the confirmands to openly confess the faith, receive strength against temptation by the laying on of hands, and vow obedience to the will of God. The final rubric stated that children who die before confirmation – having been baptized – are saved. Then followed the catechism, i.e., articles of the faith in a question and answer form. The rite of confirmation proper began with versicles and responses, followed by the traditional prayer for the seven-fold gifts of the Spirit, as found in the *Gelasian Sacramentary*. Then came a prayer which asked God to mark the candidates as his own, and to "confirm and strengthen" them with the inward anointing of the Holy Spirit

[61] "Order of Church Discipline," CIRP, 179-81.

[62] "Church Order of Cassel," CIRP, 180-81.

– language that echoes the traditional medieval understanding of confirmation. Next was the signing with the cross and a handlaying for each candidate with the formula: "I sign thee with the sign of the cross, and lay my hand upon thee in the name of the Father," etc. No mention was made of anointing. A final prayer that connects the handlaying to the apostolic actions mentioned in Acts 8 asked God to lead the newly confirmed to knowledge of His Word and to obedience, that they may attain eternal life. The rite concluded with a trinitarian blessing. Following that were ordinances pertaining to (1) the priest's provision of catechetical instruction; (2) the parental duty to send their unconfirmed children and servants to this instruction; and (3) the notification of bishops when there are candidates for confirmation. A final rubric stated that only the confirmed may be admitted to the Lord's Supper.[63]

A number of significant changes were made in the confirmation rite of the BCP 1552.[64] In the prayer following the versicles, God was petitioned to "strengthen" the candidates with the Holy Ghost, rather than *send* it down upon them – a shift away from strong, sacramental language. Then followed the handlaying accompanied by a prayer asking for grace and an "increase" in the Holy Spirit. The signing and its accompanying material having been omitted, the rite proceeded with the 1549 prayer for God's continued guidance and strengthening of the newly confirmed and concluded with the benediction. Thus, the 1552 confirmation rite strove to avoid the impression of an objective conferral of the Spirit in confirmation. Due to criticism from Bucer about the inadequacy of offering catechetical instruction only once in six weeks, it was now to take place *every* Sunday and holy day 30 minutes before Evening Prayer.[65] The concluding rubric stipulated that those admitted to the Lord's Supper must not only

---

[63] "Confirmation," BCP 1549, CIRP, 236-43.

[64] "Confirmation," BCP 1552, CIRP, 251-53.

[65] Martin Bucer, *The Judgment of Martin Bucer Upon the Book of Sacred Rites or of the Ordering of the Church and Ecclesiastical Ministration in the Kingdom of England Written at the Request of the Reverend Archbishop Thomas Cranmer*, XVIII, in Bucer, *Scripta Anglicana* (Basel, 1577), 477-81, CIRP, 248-49.

be confirmed, but also be able to "say the catechism" – a revision that reflected Bucer's catechetical emphasis.[66] The ritual core of confirmation remained unchanged in the BCP 1559 and BCP 1662, although the latter added a prayer for the spiritual preservation of the entire assembly, and changed the final rubric to "and there shall none be admitted to the Holy Communion, until such time as he be confirmed, *or be ready and desirous to be confirmed*" (emphasis added) – suggesting a more flexible attitude toward admission to the Lord's Supper.[67]

Like Luther, Calvin could see no biblical basis for considering confirmation a sacrament.[68] Furthermore, he believed that the power that has been imputed to confirmation (e.g., "strengthening for battle") robbed baptism of its power and importance.[69] Also, like Luther, Calvin would have preferred that confirmation involve an examination of faith with a laying on of hands as a "solemn benediction."[70] Neither Calvin nor Zwingli, who also rejected the sacramental status of confirmation,[71] prepared rites of confirmation for their churches. But, as noted above, Martin Bucer prepared a confirmation rite, albeit one that was used in a Lutheran Church Order. Rites of confirmation were virtually nonexistent in Reformed churches of the sixteenth century, with the exception of Strasbourg.[72]

Similarly, John Wesley saw no need for confirmation, and so did not include any rite in his *Sunday Service* for American Methodists.

---

[66] Bucer, *Judgment Upon the Book*, CIRP, 249.

[67] "The Order of Confirmation, or Laying on of Hands upon Those that are Baptized and Come to Years of Discretion" (1662), BCP *Texts*, 433.

[68] Calvin, *Institutes* IV.19.5, 7, LCC XXI, 1452-53, 1455.

[69] Calvin, *Institutes* IV.19.8, LCC XXI, 1456.

[70] Calvin, *Institutes* IV.19.4, LCC XXI, 1452.

[71] Ulrich Zwingli, *Commentary on True and False Religion* (1525), in *The Works of Huldreich Zwingli*, ed. Clarence H. Heller, tr. Samuel M. Jackson (Philadelphia: Heidelberg Press, 1929), 184

[72] "On the Confirmation of Children," CIRP, 174-78.

Confirmation is of course irrelevant for believer-baptizing churches such as Anabaptists and Pentecostals.

In the twentieth century, mainline Protestants began to reconsider confirmation and its meaning, largely because of confusion, uncertainty, and a concern that confirmation had come to overshadow baptism in significance. The rediscovery of the importance of baptism by the liturgical movement and the recovery of the adult catechumenate also led to a rethinking of the role of confirmation.[73] Eventually, Christian initiation in mainline Protestantism experienced four major shifts in the late-twentieth century:

1. *A re-emphasis on the fullness of baptism.* In order to ritually enhance baptism, especially with regard to the role of the Holy Spirit, many late-twentieth century baptismal rites incorporated actions traditionally associated with confirmation, namely, handlaying with prayer for the Holy Spirit and anointing with the sign of the cross. However, these ceremonies were not understood as conferring something new, but as expressing more fully what was given in the baptismal washing, namely, the gift of the Holy Spirit.

2. *A greater emphasis on the connection between baptism and confirmation.* In some cases this was accomplished by re-titling the confirmation rite "affirmation of baptism" or "affirmation of the baptismal covenant," in order to suggest that confirmation is, in fact, a way of recalling baptism and publically declaring one's intention to live out its ethical implications.

3. *The provision of multiuse rites for occasions of baptismal significance.* Since decisions regarding church membership have baptismal implications, liturgical books combined confirmation and various church membership rites into

[73] North American Lutherans, for example, undertook a major study of confirmation in the late 1960s and early 1970s. See Truscott, *The Reform of Baptism and Confirmation*, 127-46.

multiuse affirmation of baptism rites, or simply appended these rites to the baptismal service.

4. *The separation of confirmation and first communion.* Due to the perceptions that first communion was a "reward" for undergoing confirmation instruction and that confirmation cum admission to first communion granted full membership status – leading some young people to cease participation in church life – a number of Protestant churches officially removed the requirement that communicants be confirmed and allowed younger children to receive communion following catechetical and practical instruction on the Lord's Supper.[74]

All of these shifts are discernible in official rites used for confirmation, as we see below.

Rather than a rite of confirmation, LBW provides a service of affirmation of baptism for those persons baptized in infancy who desire to acknowledge (affirm) their earlier baptism, profess their faith, and commit themselves to participation in church life.[75] The connection between baptism and confirmation is expressed in an explanatory rubric which underscores (1) the role of baptism (rather than confirmation) in conferring church membership; and (2) the divine action in baptism, which is essentially what one affirms in this rite.[76] This same affirmation rite can be used on other pastoral occasions, namely, when persons (1) begin their participation in a local church; and (2) renew their church membership. After persons affirming their baptism are introduced, the minister reminds the candidates of their baptism and of the spiritual nourishment they

[74] In 2011, the Lutheran Church in Singapore adopted a policy whereby children could begin receiving communion prior to their confirmation. See *A Promised Feast for Children: First Communion for Children* (Singapore: Lutheran Church in Singapore, 2011).

[75] "Affirmation of Baptism," LBW, 324-27.

[76] "Affirmation of Baptism," LBW, 324.

have received in the church.[77] This short address contains language that can be varied if the candidates have already begun receiving communion on a regular basis. Then follows the renunciation of evil (a single question) and an interrogatory profession of faith (three-fold). After the intercessory prayers, the candidates are questioned as to their intentions about participating in church life. Similar to the BCP 1979, the minister offers a prayer that asks for a strengthening with the Holy Spirit and an increase in the seven-fold gifts of grace. Afterwards, the minister lays hands on each candidate while praying for the gift of the Spirit to be stirred up, for the candidate's faith to be confirmed, and for God to grant the candidate empowerment for service and patience in suffering.[78]

LBW's successor, ELW, provides an affirmation rite with a similar structure, but with several significant changes.[79] This rite can be used when the entire assembly affirms its baptism (with suitable alternative formulas and prayer) and when persons affirm their baptism in conjunction with a significant life passage (e.g., retirement, change of vocation). An opening address to all candidates speaks of giving thanks for the gift of baptism, and is followed by a prayer for the candidates to be upheld in the "gifts and promises" of baptism. The renunciation is now a three-fold interrogation which is followed by the three-fold profession of faith. Following a long question to the candidates (as in LBW), the assembly is questioned as to its intention to support the candidates. The "blessing" prayer for the seven-fold gifts has been recast such that the lines about rebirth through water and the spirit are prayed over all the candidates, while the lines alluding to the seven-fold gifts, now using the language of "stir up" rather than "strengthen," is one of two optional handlaying formulas. The other formula, taken from LBW, is to be used only at confirmation.[80] Somewhat redundant and clumsy is the retention

[77] "Affirmation of Baptism," ELW, 597.

[78] "Affirmation of Baptism," LBW, 327.

[79] "Affirmation of Baptism," ELW, 596-99. For a history of the development of this rite, see Truscott, *The Reform of Baptism and Confirmation*, ch. 5-7.

[80] "Notes," ELW, 32.

of the words addressing God in this option ("Father in heaven") after the minister has already addressed God directly in the opening portion of the prayer ("We give you thanks, O God...").

These two Lutheran affirmation/confirmation rites represent a certain amount of ongoing ambiguity – if not confusion – in Lutheran thinking. Despite attempts to renew the meaning of confirmation, these rites have not completely dispelled the impressions of mature confession-making and responsibility-taking. Such perceptions will always tend to undermine the importance of baptism by making it seem contingent on a later confirmation or affirmation of baptism. Yet, the frequent references to baptism plus the avoidance of strong Spirit language do seem to strike a balance that gives baptism its due theologically. The grouping of confirmation with various other occasions for affirming baptism serves to underscore that all of these are related to baptism. Additionally, the limited use of the term "confirmation" mitigates the sense of a separate, distinct sacramental rite that might compete in importance with baptism.

The PCS "Order for Confirmation"[81] begins by reminding candidates of the earlier baptism to which their parents brought them, and then sets forth the purpose of confirmation as the candidates' expression of the personal (mature) desire to follow Christ and participate in the Lord's Supper. The candidates are asked to "acknowledge" their earlier baptism, and are then examined as to their intentions regarding discipleship – using the same set of questions found in the PCS baptismal rite for adults (PCS-A). The act of confirmation is essentially a declarative formula whereby the minister receives the candidates as members of the church and admits them to the fellowship of the Lord's Supper. Thus, confirmation is here associated with discipleship and admission to the Lord's Supper.

The confirmation rite in DSSB[82] begins with a reading of Acts 8:4, 12, 14-17, which is viewed as a model/warrant for

[81] Presbyterian Church of Singapore, "Order for Act of Confirmation," *The Presbyterian Church of Singapore Book of Worship* (Singapore, n. p., 1984), 39-43.

[82] "Confirmation," DSSB, 54-58.

confirmation, whose purpose is to strengthen candidates with the gift of the Holy Spirit. The opening address invites the candidates to declare their intentions to live a Christian life and fulfil the duties and obligations of their baptism. Then follows the renewal of the baptismal vows, which consists of material drawn from the baptism rite: adhesion, renunciation (3), and trinitarian interrogation (4). The confirmation proper (6) is a version of the seventh-century *Gelasian Sacramentary's* prayer for the seven-fold gifts of the Spirit, which acknowledges the *baptismal* gift of the Holy Spirit, but also prays for the Spirit to "rest" on the candidates. This is followed by the laying on of hands for each candidate with an accompanying formula that asks for an "increase" of the Holy Spirit. Like the Presbyterian rite, confirmation in DSSB is seen as a consequence of and corollary to infant baptism. But the pneumatic emphasis of the service creates a certain amount of tension and ambiguity with respect to the relationship of confirmation to the earlier baptism. Is confirmation a *second* outpouring of the Holy Spirit apart from and in addition to that in baptism? Does confirmation confer something not given in baptism or complete baptism? Unfortunately, resolving such questions is beyond the scope of this study.

Although retaining the term "confirmation," UMBW also highlights the baptismal significance of confirmation, but in a manner different from LBW/ELW. Along with rites for reception into the Methodist Church and reception into a local congregation, confirmation is essentially appended to the Baptismal Covenant service and can be celebrated on the same occasion as baptism, much like the baptismal service in BCP 1979.[83] UMBW's confirmation/ re-affirmation of faith rite begins with the words "Remember your baptism and be thankful," and water may be used in various tactile ways to recall the earlier baptism of the candidates. Then follows a handlaying accompanied by a formula asking for the Spirit's continued work in those who have been "born through water and

[83] "The Baptismal Covenant I," UMBW, 92-93, Cf. "Holy Baptism," BCP 1979, 309-10.

the Spirit."[84] This formula avoids the sense of a quasi-sacramental conferral of the Holy Spirit that competes with the baptismal gift of the Spirit. The pastoral introduction to the UMBW baptismal services makes clear that confirmation is only for those baptized in infancy, and not for those who are baptized as adults.[85] Thus, like LBW and ELW, UMBW tries to protect the integrity of baptism by suggesting that confirmation is a consequence of baptism, rather than a distinct maturity rite altogether.

The Renewal of Baptism in Daily Life

The church's liturgy sustains each Christian in a life of ongoing service, witness, and prayer, and it is in personal prayer and other devotional acts that Christians return to baptism. Martin Luther recommended a form of daily prayer that contained several echoes of baptism. Brief rites for morning and evening began with a trinitarian invocation accompanied by making the sign of the cross over one's self. Supplicants then recited the Apostles' Creed and the Lord's Prayer, two symbols of the Christian faith ritually conferred on baptismal candidates since ancient times. An optional prayer included the request that the "wicked foe have no power over me," – a hint of the baptismal renunciation.[86]

Additional ways for individuals (and families) to renew baptism in daily life include the following:

1. *Observing the anniversary of baptism.* It is human nature to remember days of personal significance, e.g., birthdays, anniversary of marriage, etc. For Christians of all denominations and liturgical traditions, baptism is such an occasion. The celebration of a baptismal anniversary is enhanced by lighting the candle that was given at baptism (or another baptismal candle) both as a reminder of the

[84] "The Baptismal Covenant I," UMBW, 92.

[85] "The Baptismal Covenant I," UMBW, 83.

[86] Luther, *Small Catechism*, BC, 363.1-364.5.

event and as an encouragement to shine with the light of Christ before the world.

2. *Displaying baptismal certificates.* Most churches give newly baptized persons a certificate of baptism as an official testimony to and personal memento of the event. Rather than storing this document, recipients might consider framing it and then placing it prominently in the home, e.g., the wall of one's bedroom, so that each day begins and ends with baptism. Churches might present framed certificates as a way of encouraging their display in the home.

3. *Making the sign of the cross upon entering a worship space.* For many Christians, the Sunday liturgy takes place in the same space where they were baptized. For others, it is the space where they have witnessed numerous baptisms. Thus, every time one enters the liturgical space, one is reminded of baptism, and making the sign of the cross on one's self at that time recalls one's baptism and manifests the baptismal nature of the space and the liturgy. The cross is also a sign of one's spiritual neediness, which will be addressed in the liturgy of Word and Sacrament.

4. *Developing a discipline of private confession.* Despite Protestant misgivings about private confession, people today still need to share their spiritual burdens and receive forgiveness from God. The rise of the secular counseling industry witnesses to this need. In affording individuals the opportunity to disburden their hearts of troubling thoughts and memories (i.e., sins), and to receive pardon or absolution, private confession actualizes the ongoing meaning of baptism as the death of the sinner and the rising up of a new creature. In confessing and naming a sin, one starts to assert mastery over it and suppress it. The forgiveness spoken by a fellow Christian – whether lay or ordained – removes the guilt (burden) and enables one to

"move on." Forgiveness (absolution) is especially crucial: an objective word of forgiveness coming from another person has a level of credibility and concreteness that one might not experience in confessing alone before God. Additionally, this objective absolution rules out the possibility of merely "forgiving" one's self. Insofar as the church offers forgiveness by the command of Christ and with the promise of his very presence in the forgiving action (Matt. 18:18; cf. John 20:21-23), private confession is an encounter with Christ and a renewal of baptismal union with him. Those who practice private confession are advised to avoid legalistic practices, e.g., straining to find as many sins as possible to confess, or worrying about confessing completely, as though the grace of God depended on the quality of one's confession. Rather than on the confession itself, the emphasis is best placed on the absolution (pardon, forgiveness), and receiving it in faith. A worthy confession is not one in which sins are *confessed* whole-heartedly and completely (an impossibility), but one in which the words "I forgive you" are *believed* whole-heartedly.

5. *Fasting.* Christians have long known the practice of fasting in order to suppress the desires of the flesh and to focus more on God through prayer and good works (cf. Matt. 6:16-18). Controlling the appetite for food, which could easily rule a person's life if left unchecked, is really an act of penitence and therefore a way of living out the meaning of baptismal repentance. Because it is an *embodied* form of penitence, fasting reminds us of our creaturely dependence on God, and the need to offer our *bodies* sacrificially to God (Rom. 12:1). Traditionally, Christians have fasted one or more days per week, especially on Friday, the day of Jesus' crucifixion. Fasting could take the form of abstaining from one or more meals altogether, and/or abstaining from certain foods for certain periods, as with Orthodox Christians who avoid dairy products and eggs during Great Lent.

Conclusion

In the church's Sunday liturgy and occasional rites, the Christian worship assembly repeatedly returns to baptism. Confession and the Lord's Supper help Christians to live out their baptismal death and resurrection with Christ, as well as their personal union with him and his people, the church. In confirmation, Christians affirm God's baptismal gifts and pledge to joyfully respond to those gifts with lives of service to God. A personal spirituality centered on baptism might be cultivated through a number of practices that allow the Christian to reappropriate or live out the meaning of baptism. In liturgy and daily life, baptism is a continual source of life, like an ever-flowing stream.

For Further Reading

Fisher, J. D. C. *Christian Initiation: Confirmation Then and Now*. Chicago/Mundelein, IL: Hillenbrand Books, 2005.

Johnson, Maxwell E., ed. *Living Water, Sealing Spirit: Readings on Christian Initiation*. Collegeville: Liturgical Press, 1995.

Montefiore, Hugh. *Confirmation Notebook*. London: SPCK, 1984.

Osmer, Richard R. *Confirmation: Presbyterian Practices in Ecumenical Perspective*. Louisville: Geneva Press, 1996.

Stevick, Daniel B. *Baptismal Moments, Baptismal Meanings*. New York: Church Hymnal Corporation, 1987.

Wingeier, Douglas E. *Confirmation: Ten Affirmations*. Nashville: Discipleship Resources, 1982.

CHAPTER 9

Baptismal Issues

While the author of Ephesians asserts that the unity of the church is based on "one Lord, one faith, one baptism" (4:5), Christianity continues to experience division, and some of the discord focuses on baptism. Yet, in recent years, Christians have made great strides in overcoming this division, thanks in large part to the *Baptism, Eucharist and Ministry* (BEM) document of the World Council of Churches. The insights of BEM have enabled churches to move beyond the old polemical battles over baptism and toward the mutual recognition of baptism, despite differences in theology and practice.

This chapter will highlight some of the problematic issues surrounding baptism, describe positive developments concerning these, and (it is hoped) offer further constructive suggestions. Additionally, a brief section will be devoted to the contextualization of baptism, an issue that has not received the attention that it deserves.

Infant Baptism

During the church's earliest centuries, there was almost no opposition to the baptism of infants. Since the Reformation, however, questions over infant baptism have divided the church. This divisiveness is attested to by the very fact that BEM needed to address the question. Efforts to bridge the gap continue today in the form of interchurch dialogs, and although progress – if we might call it that – has been slow, churches are finding common ground as they realize that the differences are not as wide as previously thought.

In the New Testament, nothing enjoins infant baptism, nor do any narratives explicitly suggest that the practice was known in the primitive church. The baptism of households in Acts (16:15, 33, 18:8), taken by some as indirect evidence for infant baptism, really supports nothing more than an argument from silence. Narratives in the gospels and Acts depict only adults receiving baptism, usually as a response to apostolic preaching. Yet, the New Testament does not specifically *prohibit* the practice, which may be one reason why the early church apparently found no reason to withhold baptism from infants.[1]

The baptism of infants can only be documented with certainty from the late-second or early-third century. Tertullian, whose opposition to the practice actually proves its existence, essentially argued that baptism was unnecessary for innocent infants.[2] Although mentioning the baptism of infants in the context of a vigil service, the *Apostolic Tradition* is no longer regarded as a reliable witness to Roman liturgical practices of the early-third century. Origen of Alexandria (ca. 184-254 CE), argued that infants needed baptism in order to be cleansed from sin.[3] As Everett Ferguson notes, Origen was not thinking of original sin as understood in the later Western

[1] For a discussion of the history of infant baptism, see Frank C. Senn, *Introduction to Christian Liturgy* (Minneapolis: Fortress, 2012), 158-60.

[2] Tertullian, *De Baptismo* 18 (ca. 200).

[3] Origen, *Commentary on Romans* 5.9.11 (ca. 246), as cited in Everett Ferguson, *Baptism in the Early Church: History, Theology, and Liturgy in the First Five Centuries* (Grand Rapids: Eerdmans, 2009), 368.

theological tradition, but more in the sense of *ritual defilement* as understood in the Hebrew Scriptures, in which case the forgiveness granted in baptism is extended to include this ceremonial impurity.[4] The manner in which Origen develops his argument, according to Ferguson, indicates that the practice of infant baptism had preceded his theological justification of it. This is actually one of many instances in the early church in which theology followed actual practice.

Cyprian of Carthage witnesses to the practice of infant baptism in the context of a discussion about the appropriate time for baptizing infants. One of Cyprian's fellow bishops, Fidus, argued for baptizing on the eighth day in order to follow Old Testament ceremonial law pertaining to circumcision, and because kissing the feet of a newborn infant is "repulsive." In response to Fidus, Cyprian advances three counter arguments. First, a bishop should not be disgusted with kissing a newborn, but should consider that it had just come from the hand of God who made it. Second, there is no need to wait until the eighth day since physical circumcision had been abrogated by the resurrection which conferred on all believers a spiritual circumcision.[5] Third, if baptism can affect the forgiveness of sins for hardened sinners, it ought not to be withheld from a recently born infant who has not sinned in actuality. Yet, Cyprian acknowledges that infants are subject to death because of being born physical creatures like Adam, and this sin is forgiven in baptism. But while Cyprian links infant baptism and infant sin, he does not connect the latter with childbirth as Augustine does in his doctrine of original sin.[6] We have already noted that Augustine was aware of the practice of infant baptism, and on that basis developed a doctrine of original sin and the need for grace, over and against the Pelagian notion that a person had the "free will" to choose between good and evil and thus could attain salvation by one's own efforts.[7] We must note that

[4] Ferguson, *Baptism in the Early Church*, 369.

[5] Cyprian, *Letters* 64.3-4 (ca. 252), as cited in Ferguson, *Baptism in the Early Church*, 370.

[6] Ferguson, *Baptism in the Early Church*, 371.

[7] See ch. 4, "Baptism and Time."

it is *later* Christians who will argue in the opposite direction, namely, that because of original sin, infants *must* be baptized. By the early Middle Ages, the question was settled, and the belief and practice of infant baptism was received by the magisterial Reformers (Lutheran, Anglican, Reformed). By contrast, the Eastern churches have baptized infants even without resorting to a doctrine of original sin.

On the basis of these theological discussions about infant baptism, we cannot ascertain the exact reason *why* infants were baptized. Ferguson, however, has developed an interesting theory based on his examination of funerary inscriptions dating from the late-second/early-third century, many of which indicate that children were baptized immediately prior to their death, suggesting that they were gravely ill at the time of their baptism. Since early Christians associated baptism with entrance into heaven (based on their reading of John 3:5), there would have been a natural desire to seek baptism for a seriously ill child, to ensure his/her place in heaven, and ministers of the church would have found such a request difficult to refuse. Due to the high infant mortality rate in the ancient world, the baptizing of infants developed into the pastoral norm. "Acquiescence" to this development is the reason why there never was any debate about the appropriate age of baptismal candidates.[8]

But beyond avoiding debate, the early church strove to speak positively and constructively about infant baptism. Augustine even developed a theory of its efficacy, i.e., an understanding of what it did and meant for the recipient. Ferguson draws attention to a letter from Augustine to Bishop Boniface in which he speaks of *infant faith*:

> ...even if that faith that is found in the will of believers does not make a little one a believer, the sacrament of faith itself, nonetheless, now does so. For, just as the response is given that the little one believes [i.e., the response of the parent at the child's baptism], he is also in that sense called a believer, not because he assents to the reality with his mind [the

[8] Ferguson, *Baptism in the Early Church*, 378-79.

> infant cannot assent] but because he receives the sacrament of that reality. [9]

(Infant faith will later be one of Martin Luther's arguments against the Anabaptist position in infant baptism.) For John Chrysostom, infant baptism is about bestowing the benefits that make children brothers and sisters of Christ and vessels of the Holy Spirit; for him it has nothing to do with the remission of sin, which is unnecessary in the case of infants whom he views as sinless.[10]

Finally, Senn suggests that infant baptism may have been more widely practiced than was originally thought. He notes that Augustine was officially enrolled as a catechumen eight days after his birth. Later, when he became ill as a young boy, his mother arranged for an "emergency" baptism which was called off when he recovered. Only at age thirty, and with the influence of Ambrose, did he finally receive baptism. Between this enrollment and baptism, i.e., his time as a catechumen, Augustine considered himself a Christian. His view was based on his receiving the sign of the cross at his enrollment. On the basis of Augustine's initiatory experience, Senn argues that baptism in the early church was a process that could last an entire lifetime. The baptismal process that began with one's enrollment as a catechumen in infancy was eventually completed with election, baptism, and postbaptismal instruction in the sacred mysteries (*mystagogia*) as an adult. Senn concludes:

> If baptism is understood as including everything in the process, and infants were enrolled as catechumens, "infant baptism" was being practiced far more regularly than we have assumed if we think of baptism only as the water bath.[11]

[9] Augustine, *Letter* 98.10 (ca. 408, or 413/414), as cited in Ferguson, *Baptism in the Early Church*, 807.

[10] Cited in André Hamman, O.F.M., *Baptism: Ancient Liturgies and Patristic Texts* (New York: Alba House, 1967), 166.

[11] Senn, *Introduction to Christian Worship*, 160.

Thus, the practice of infant baptism might represent the telescoping of the baptismal process – an emergency *completion* of baptism, rather than emergency *baptism* per se. Even if some children had not been baptized in water, they were nevertheless participants in a baptismal process.

As for the Reformation era, we have noted previously the Anabaptist argument that infants are unsuitable candidates for baptism because baptism requires explicit faith and conscious commitment to Christian discipleship. We have also noted how Reformed and Lutheran Churches at the time of the Reformation attempted to meet the objections of Anabaptism by developing forms of confirmation that emphasized catechetical instruction, a personal profession of faith, and a vow of obedience to the church and/or an act of commitment to church life. The aim of this form of confirmation (in contrast to the sacramental form that focused on the conferral of the Holy Spirit) is to ensure that those baptized in infancy develop into Christians with personal faith and commitment.

The ongoing effort to overcome differences concerning infant baptism has more recently focused precisely on the point made by Senn, namely, that baptism involves a *process*. In their dialog with Anglicans, Baptists in the United Kingdom have proposed attending to the entire "journey" of Christian life with "initiation" as the first part of the journey, followed by "the rest of the journey of discipleship." Initiation is understood as a process wherein baptism may take place at different points, either at the beginning (infant baptism) or at the end (baptism of confessing adults). In the case of the former, a public profession of faith will take place at the conclusion of initiation, i.e., at one's confirmation, while for the latter the public profession of faith and baptism will be concurrent.[12] The Anglican response to the proposal was favorable, saying that the mutual recognition of a common initiation "journey" is possible, provided that (1) the baptism of an infant is regarded as true and

[12] Faith and Unity Executive Committee of the Baptist Union of Great Britain, The Council for Unity of the Church of England, *Pushing at the Boundaries of Unity: Anglicans and Baptists in Conversation* (London: Church House Publishing, 2005), 45.

complete baptism in and of itself; and (2) the rebaptism of any person baptized in infancy is ruled out. We should note that for many Anglicans initiation is essentially completed at confirmation and first reception of Holy Communion, although some Anglicans (e.g., the Episcopal Church in the United States) permit children to receive communion prior to confirmation. While BEM, to some extent, recognizes a baptismal process,[13] this more recent discussion between Baptists and Anglicans in the UK puts the issue in sharper focus and has found resonance in similar understandings expressed by scholars like Paul Fiddes (Baptist)[14] and Frank Senn (Lutheran). It seems that thinking in terms of an initiatory process, and thus the fullness of Christian initiation, holds great potential for overcoming divisions over infant baptism.

There is at the same time another set of questions regarding infants and Christian initiation, namely, those that might be posed to churches that baptize only persons who can answer for themselves. What is the ecclesiastical status of infants whose families attend believer-baptizing churches? Do such children have a place in the covenant community? Many committed Christians find it difficult to think of their children as "pagans" who are beyond the pale of the new covenant. Does not the fact that a child was born into a Christian household suggest that the unmerited grace of God is operative for him or her? Naturally, Christian parents might desire to celebrate this "prevenient" grace, even if their own church does not baptize infants. In response to this pastoral situation, many believer-baptizing churches provide dedication rites in which (1) parents offer (dedicate) their infant children to God; (2) ministers exhort the parents to raise their children in the Christian faith; and (3) the assembly prays for the children and parents.[15] (Such infant dedication rites may or may not adequately address the question of

[13] BEM, 4.9; 4.12; 5 (Commentary 12).

[14] Paul Fiddes, "The Baptism of Believers," BT, 73-80.

[15] See Daniel Albrecht, "Witness in the Water: Baptism and Pentecostal Spirituality," BT, 161-62.

where children born of Christian parents figure in God's covenant of grace in Jesus Christ.)

To some extent practices like confirmation and infant dedication fulfill the recommendations of BEM that (1) infant-baptizing churches avoid "indiscriminate" baptism and work to ensure that children baptized in infancy become committed Christians; and (2) believer-baptizing churches find ways to express the belief that children of Christian parents are under God's protection.[16] Although far from perfect, these practices at least recognize the critique of the other tradition and attempt to address the questions raised. But more work is needed in this area.

Mode of Baptism

The New Testament contains neither an explicit command to baptize in a particular manner, nor any detailed descriptions of how baptism was carried out in primitive communities.The Greek word βαπτίζω certainly has the sense of dipping, immersing, or plunging a person or thing into water, but the amount of water used in biblical accounts of baptism is not always discernible. Some ancient depictions of Jesus' baptism in the Jordan River show the Lord Jesus standing in water up to his waist, which suggests the submersion of a person who bends forward from the knees and/or waist, or possibly is pushed backwards into the water.[17] Yet other depictions show what is perhaps a composite figure representing both Christ and a typical baptismal candidate standing in ankle-deep water, making submersion impossible.[18] As for ancient baptismal fonts, many permitted a full dunking of the candidate (submersion),[19] while others would have only allowed the pouring of large amounts of

[16] BEM, 6.16.

[17] For example, see the mosaic in the dome of the baptistery of the Arians in Ravenna, Italy, which appears on the front cover of Johnson's *Rites of Christian Initiation* and the jacket of Ferguson's *Baptism in the Early Church*.

[18] Robin M. Jenson, *Baptismal Imagery in Early Christianity: Ritual, Visual, and Theological Dimensions* (Grand Rapids: Baker Academic, 2012), 15-16. See figure 1.7.

[19] Ferguson, *Baptism in the Early Church*, 849.

water over the candidate who stood in a (shallow) pool (immersion). The earliest instructions about baptism, found in the late-first/early-second century *Didache*, direct that baptism take place in "running water," which may have referred to a natural body of water such as a river or stream where submersion would have been possible. If running water is unavailable, then other water ("cold" or "hot") could be used; at the very least, water was to be poured over the candidate three times "in the name of the Father and of the Son and of the Holy Spirit."[20] Previously, we noted how submersion was mentioned by a number of early Christian writers.[21] Thus, there seems to be strong evidence that baptismal submersion was widely practiced in the ancient church, and, short of that, churches would have poured water on candidates already positioned in a font or natural body of water.

During the Reformation, Protestant churches generally considered pouring, dipping, and sprinkling to be acceptable ways of baptizing.The baptismal rites of Luther, Jud, and the first two Anglican Prayer Books directed the minister to "dip" the child into the font. For Luther, it was a matter of portraying the meaning of the word "baptize" (German "Taufe"), rather than an insistence that immersion is the only true (biblical) mode of baptizing.[22] The latter position only begins to be advanced by English Baptists in the seventeenth century. Some modern Baptists continue to insist on baptizing by submersion and will accept previously baptized persons into their fellowship only on the condition that their baptism was by submersion. Obviously, there are ecumenical ramifications involved here: the insistence on a particular mode potentially calls into question the legitimacy of baptism in churches that do not stipulate that particular mode. The resolution to this tension is by no means easy.

On the one hand, all churches must recognize that much of the biblical language surrounding baptism *demands* submersion. The

[20] The *Didache* 7.1 (late-first or early-second cent.).

[21] See ch. 7.

[22] Martin Luther, *The Holy and Blessed Sacrament of Baptism* (1519), LW 35, 29.

New Testament images of death and resurrection, (re-)birth by water and the Spirit, and washing are most aptly portrayed when the candidate is plunged under the water. It is difficult for both the candidate and assembly to perceive a correspondence between baptism and these biblical images if the act consists of no more than a moist hand placed on the candidate's head. The Lutheran theologian Edmund Schlink points to another dimension of baptismal symbolism when he asserts that submersion is one way of depicting how "the life of the baptized is taken hold of in a way that involves the whole person."[23] In the late-twentieth century, churches that never accorded much importance to baptismal submersion (e.g., Anglican, Roman Catholic) began to construct large fonts/pools for immersion due to a renewed appreciation for liturgical symbolism (see ch. 5). Those churches who take symbolism and the corresponding liturgical praxis seriously have a certain amount of sympathy with churches that baptize solely by submersion. In that sense, there has been some convergence on the question of the mode of baptism.

But, on the other hand, an *insistence* on baptism by submersion (or any one particular mode) is theologically problematic. Precisely because the New Testament prescribes no particular mode of baptism and attaches no salvific meaning to the water itself, the validity of baptism cannot be made to depend on the mode of administration.[24] Far more meaning is attached to the action as a whole, whether that meaning is expressed by the images of death and resurrection, rebirth through water and the Spirit, being clothed with Christ, washing and renewal in the Spirit, or adoption as children of God. For those Christians who understand baptism as a means of grace, insisting on a particular mode of baptism seems to make the grace of God dependent on human action – a form of works righteousness. Other churches might find the insistence on a particular baptismal mode troubling because, for them, the inward working of the Spirit

---

[23] Edmund Schlink, *The Doctrine of Baptism*, tr. Herbert J. A. Bouman (St. Louis: Concordia Publishing House, 1972), 186.

[24] Schlink, *Doctrine of Baptism*, 186.

signified by baptism, rather than the outward act itself, is more theologically and pastorally decisive. These two theological camps would accordingly argue that the mode of baptism should be a matter of Christian freedom – although they might not mean to imply that the mode of baptism is unimportant.

Besides having negative ecumenical implications, the insistence on a particular mode is also problematic pastorally. Potentially, a focus on the "proper" baptismal mode takes attention away from the proper baptismal *life*. It also creates a certain amount of confusion in the church because those not baptized by the "proper" mode question the validity of their previous baptism and, in some cases, request re-baptism, which many churches will refuse to do on theological and ecumenical grounds.

While it is not necessary for any church to give up its normal mode of baptizing, churches are nevertheless challenged to a theology and practice that takes into consideration the broader ecumenical implications. Those churches that require baptism by submersion may consider welcoming into membership those previously baptized by other modes when these individuals publically profess their faith and vow loyalty to their new church. Such an action is not so much a compromise of the norm, but rather a service to the unity of the whole church. At the same time, churches that accept a variety of baptismal modes might acknowledge the aptness of submersion (from a biblical perspective) and encourage its practice. The enactment of these measures would, I believe, relieve some of the tension surrounding a traditionally troublesome question.

Rebaptism

Some churches will administer baptism in cases where it is believed that an earlier baptism is invalid, e.g., when a person was baptized as an infant, or because the earlier baptism was administered with a mode considered invalid. Yet, such rebaptism is theologically and ecumenically problematic. This second baptism tends to deny the "once-for-all" character of baptism as a participation in Christ's death and resurrection and a conferral of the Holy Spirit (Acts

2:38). Baptism is no more repeatable than Christ's resurrection itself! Furthermore, to question the legitimacy of another church's baptism by rebaptizing one of its member is to question the legitimacy of the church itself, since "church" is dogmatically defined as a community within which the Word is proclaimed and the sacraments are celebrated.[25] Any church that rebaptizes seems to suggest that its fellowship *alone* constitutes the true church. Ultimately, theologies and practices that delegitimize the baptism of other churches discredit the whole church in the eyes of the world by suggesting division on a very basic matter.

Yet, recently there have been positive developments on this issue. Without requiring any rebaptism, Baptist churches in Great Britain and elsewhere have accepted into their fellowship persons who were baptized as infants and then later confirmed. The Baptist Union of Great Britain states that "many Baptists will want to welcome and affirm those who have a different story to tell of how they have been baptized and come to faith, while still declaring our conviction that believers' baptism is the pattern that is set out for us in Scripture."[26] How might Baptist and other churches receive the already-baptized into their fellowship? While I do not know of any liturgical form for this purpose, the following is a proposed ritual outline:

1. The candidates profess their faith through either personal testimony, a formal confession of faith, or both. A testimony might mention the person's earlier baptism and confirmation.
2. The candidates pledge loyalty to the local church.
3. The ministers pray that the newly-received members be sustained by God in their new ecclesial commitment and receive spiritual support from the assembly.

As noted previously, some persons question the validity of their earlier baptism because of a perceived lack of sincerity on their

[25] See *Augsburg Confession* (1530), Art. VII, BC, 42.1 and AR XIX.

[26] Baptists Together, http://www.baptist.org.uk/Groups/220594/Believers_Baptism.aspx [accessed 18 April 2014].

part and consequently request a second baptism. In such cases, the most responsible action is to give these persons the opportunity to reaffirm their faith in a service that includes intercessory prayer and a handlaying accompanied by a formula that uses the language of renewal or strengthening. When there is uncertainty about whether baptism has occurred at all, there may be a "conditional" baptism.[27] Rebaptism is thus not the only option in pastorally difficult situations.

Essentially, all churches today are challenged to practice a *dual-track* Christian initiation which necessarily involves a certain degree of ambiguity. On the one hand, believer-baptizing churches will baptize confessing adults by submersion (usually) while admitting to membership those baptized in infancy and later confirmed in other churches, regardless of the mode of baptism used. On the other hand, churches that have traditionally upheld infant baptism will evangelize and baptize adults, possibly using the adult catechumenate as their model. Any theological inconsistency in this proposal is really the lesser of two "evils," when compared with the possible fracturing of the church's unity (in the case of believer-baptizing churches), or the failure to seek out and baptize adults (in the case of traditionally infant-baptizing churches). The acceptance of the lesser evil is done in service to the greater good of the church and its mission in the world, and thus in service to Christ who is the head of the church. Furthermore, these inconsistencies might also be considered acceptable pastoral concessions made in the recognition that Christian initiation is not a "one-size-fits all" proposition, and that faithfulness to the church's apostolic calling means ministering to people who come to the church with a variety of needs and backgrounds.

Personal and Family Difficulties

There are some pastoral and missional contexts in which potential converts find themselves hesitant to receive baptism, usually for cultural-political reasons or because of the implications of baptism for family relationships. When a convert's family adheres to another

[27] See "Holy Baptism," BCP 1979, 313.

faith, he or she may delay baptism or decline it altogether out of fear that his/her family may react negatively. In some cases, this resistance to a family member's conversion to Christianity has to do with the fact that Christians cannot perform rites meant to pacify "ancestral spirits" who might otherwise (it is believed) bring retribution on the family for succeeding generations. Because of the importance placed on ancestral pacification, a person may be disowned by the family if he/she receives baptism. When family influence is strong, persons drawn to Christianity may spend years participating in church life while remaining unbaptized. Thus, this category of persons poses a significant pastoral challenge for churches.

On the one hand, the church universal can tolerate the unbaptized in its midst. Since its earliest centuries, the church has recognized an entire category of unbaptized persons in the catechumens, or those preparing for baptism. As noted above, Augustine was technically a catechumen for thirty years.[28] From a pastoral standpoint, baptism cannot be forced on potential adult candidates who are neither ready nor willing to receive it. Baptism leads to a lifelong Christian commitment, and those not prepared to make such a commitment will likely not persevere in the faith. Forcing baptism on such persons for the sake of pragmatic agendas can only do them harm.

On the other hand, the church cannot compromise on the baptismal command which is at the heart of its apostolic calling. Such a compromise occurs when churches:

1. Create a category of "saved" persons in distinction from the baptized
2. Justify the undue delay or omission of baptism on the basis of God's freedom over and against the sacraments to save
3. Fail to encourage baptism.

Regarding 1 above, while a person's initial confession of faith ("salvation") might be distinct in time from their baptism (which

[28] Admittedly, many ancient Christians had a prolonged catechumenate and delayed baptism until nearly the hour of their death, fearing that any postbaptismal sin would result in a harsh penitential process.

might be delayed for personal reasons), the New Testament does not know of a class of "saved" persons in distinction from the baptized. Rather, it asserts that one cannot be saved without baptism (cf. Mark 16:16; 1 Peter 3:21). A formal category of the "saved, but not baptized" seems to legitimize baptismal deferment or omission and, worse, gives the impression that baptism is unimportant or only an optional part of the conversion process. Consequently, converts might experience no desire to request baptism, and the church might not perceive the need to encourage them to receive baptism. While Christian initiation might not be a one-size-fits-all proposition, and churches need to minister sensitively to each and every individual, they nevertheless need to communicate the expectation that those who come to faith will receive baptism (cf. Acts 2:38), both as an act of obedience and an act of faith in expectation of receiving the Holy Spirit. There may indeed be situations where persons will delay their baptism or perhaps never receive baptism; but building an entire ecclesiastical culture around that pastoral situation ultimately does the church and its mission a disservice. Perhaps those persons who have made an initial expression of faith, but have not received baptism, could be classified as "catechumens," a term that suggests and anticipates a future baptism.

With respect to 2 above, it is sometimes argued that since baptism is not absolutely necessary (faith being what really matters), there is no pastoral need to press the matter of baptism with those who seem hesitant to request it. It is certainly true that God is free to bring people to salvation in ways other than through baptism. John Calvin held that in cases where a person could not receive baptism, the grace of God was not so bound to the sacrament that grace would be withheld from a believing person.[29] Yet, the church cannot take control of the freedom of God over and against the sacraments in order to use it for the church's own purposes – since it is *God's* freedom and not the church's. Additionally, the "freedom of God" argument seems

[29] John Calvin, *Institutes of the Christian Religion* (1559) IV.15.1, ed. John T. McNeill, tr. Ford Lewis Battles, in LCC XXI (Philadelphia: Westminster Press, 1960), 1323.

to play baptism off against faith, which is not biblically justified, since those who in faith accepted the apostolic message obediently received baptism (cf. Acts 2:41). Furthermore, we should note that Calvin and other theologians who acknowledged that baptism is not absolutely necessary were thinking of exceptional situations in which persons were *unable* to be baptized. Turning the exception into the rule would have the disastrous pastoral consequence of creating a church of unbaptized believers, which is as biblically unfaithful as a church of unbelieving baptized persons! It is one thing if a person *cannot* be baptized, but quite another if he/she *will* not be baptized – or if the church will not offer baptism. Here a famous dictum of St. Augustine is instructive: "it is not the lack of baptism but contempt for it that damns." Arguably, any attempt to set aside the baptismal command suggests such "contempt," and thus subjects the church to God's judgment.

Finally, with regard to 3 above, it is undoubtedly difficult in some cases for pastors and church workers to encourage the baptism of unbaptized but faithful participants in church life when it is known that their families will object to baptism. In some cases, although rare, the decision to receive baptism may place one in physical danger. Yet, rather than avoiding a discussion about baptism, pastors and church workers might find ways for the church to better support individuals who hesitate to receive baptism, e.g., through cell groups, baptismal sponsors, one-on-one meetings with church staff. In reality, the church will become a new family to baptized converts, in which case Christian communities need to give serious thought about how they might fulfill that role.

The Contextualization of Baptism

The word "contextualization" refers to the use of elements from the local cultural to express the meaning and purpose of Christian worship.[30] Cultural elements include music, architecture, customs,

[30] Lutheran World Federation, *Nairobi Statement on Worship and Culture: Contemporary Challenges and Opportunities*, http://www.worr.org/images/File/Nairobi%20Statement.pdf [accessed 19 April 2014]. This document also appears as

ways of speaking, and thought patterns. The theological basis for contextualization is the doctrine of the Incarnation. As a Jew of first-century Palestine, Jesus, the incarnate Son of God, identified with a particular culture, its people and customs, thus enabling him to communicate the gospel in a manner relevant to his milieu. By extension, the church adapts its liturgy to the local culture by means of those cultural elements that are consonant with the gospel. Specific methods include (1) *dynamic equivalence*, whereby a Christian idea or term is expressed using the local culture's equivalent term; (2) *creative assimilation*, which involves adding cultural actions and gestures to sacramental services in order to adapt the liturgy to culture and enhance the meaning of the services, e.g., the presentation of flowers to the newly baptized in Japanese Christian worship assemblies; and (3) *organic progression*, which means supplementing and completing the church's liturgy by developing rites and observances for situations in which there are no available resources from the tradition that are appropriate, e.g., when Christians in Singapore and Hong Kong hold special services marking the Lunar New Year (aka "Chinese New Year").[31] But because the essence of both Christian worship and the local culture are to be respected, contextualization should *not* result in:

1. Changing the meaning of a Christian concept, action, or sacrament
2. Replacing a required liturgical action that has strong biblical resonance (e.g., making the sign of the cross, anointing)
3. Using a cultural element in a way that cheapens or demeans it.

Below are suggestions for contextualizing Christian initiation using the second and third of the methods described above.

Appendix A in Jeffrey A. Truscott, *Worship: A Practical Guide* (Singapore: Genesis, 2011), 219-25. For analysis and commentary on the Nairobi statement, see ch. 6 of that book.

[31] Truscott, *Worship: A Practical Guide*, 63-67.

1. According to the method of creative assimilation:
   a. Asian architectural styles might be used for baptismal architecture. For instance, the chapel of the Tao Fong Shan Christian Center in Hong Kong, an octagonal-shaped building using a traditional Chinese style, contains a baptismal font shaped like a small pagoda. This particular font design suggests the sacred importance of baptism insofar as pagodas are used for housing sacred relics and writings. Artistic creative assimilation is used at the cathedral of the East Kowloon Diocese (Anglican) in Hong Kong, where a lotus design is inscribed on the floor near the baptismal font, perhaps suggesting the purification and spiritual awakening granted in the sacrament of baptism.
   b. Newly-baptized Christians might receive a small oil lamp instead of a candle to symbolize baptismal enlightenment. The oil lamp is more appropriate in the Asian context, especially in churches whose members are primarily of Indian ancestry.
   c. The welcome of the newly baptized into the congregation – usually expressed only in words – might be expressed ritually by giving the newly baptized a hot beverage (e.g., tea), much like hosts in Japan and China serve tea to their visitors. Following their first reception of communion the newly baptized might briefly imbibe tea, much in the manner of the neophytes receiving a mixture of milk and honey, as described in the *Apostolic Tradition*. Or perhaps immediately after the newly baptized are welcomed into the congregation, they could share a beverage with church leaders as a gesture of welcome and fellowship.
   d. Also as a welcoming gesture, the newly baptized might be given a red packet (*hong bau*) with a scripture verse.

2. Following the method of *organic progression*, the Lunar (Chinese) New Year could be used as a time for baptism

in addition to or in place of other baptismal times/seasons. Since the Lunar New Year (LNY) is traditionally a time for family gatherings in China and Singapore, the celebration of baptism might highlight the role of baptism in initiating candidates into the family of the church. Alternatively, in years when the LNY occurs close to Ash Wednesday (e.g., 2015, 2018), baptismal preparation could take place throughout Lent (following the ancient practice) since the family theme would still be fresh in people's minds. In the Asian context where new Christians often experience family opposition to baptism, stressing a person's incorporation into a new family might prove pastorally beneficial.

Baptism and the Use of Water

Some Christian communities do not baptize with water at all, but instead practice a "baptism of the Spirit" ritualized through handlaying.[32] A water-less baptism, however, raises the question of the action's sacramental validity, since a constituent part of baptism, the matter (water), is missing. The New Testament assumes the application of water (cf. Acts 8:36, 10:47), as does the very meaning of the word "baptize." Passages in Acts that speak of the conferral of the Holy Spirit through an apostolic handlaying (Acts 8:14-17, 19:6) must not be read in isolation from the rest of the Acts of the Apostles, where water baptism is the norm. Other New Testament passages clearly connect water and the Spirit (John 3:5; Titus 3:5), thus making water-less baptism exegetically problematic if not impossible.

The manner in which churches regularize emergency baptism also attests to the normativity of baptism *in water*. In some churches, when those baptized in haste due to impending death survive, an ordained minister will certify that the baptism was conducted properly by asking several questions, including whether water was

[32] BEM, 7.21c.

used.[33] In other churches, those previously baptized in emergency circumstances are introduced to the assembly as follows: "I present to this community of faith *Name*, who on *Date*, was *baptized with water* in the name of the Father, and of the Son, and of the Holy Spirit."[34] Thus, the use of water is viewed as indispensable for the administration of baptism.

Admittedly, there are situations and places where water is in short supply or not readily available, e.g., deserts or remote areas with little infrastructure. But even in these cases, small amounts of water can still be found in plants or perhaps in water puddles. If water were absolutely unavailable, then human life could not exist at all in a particular place. It is difficult to think of water being utterly unavailable in anything other than *very* exceptional circumstances. Although the church is bound to baptize with water and consider any initiatory action without water an invalid baptism, it still believes that the lack of a proper baptism does not condemn a person so long as faith is present. In that case, the question of the nonavailability of water does not create an insurmountable pastoral problem for the church.

Conclusion

Significant differences over baptism remain, and churches need to continue in dialog with the goal of achieving mutual recognition of baptism. Additionally, the matter of contextualizing the baptismal liturgy needs further attention for the sake of the church's mission in the world. Contextualization is especially urgent since there are implications for the celebration of the Lord's Supper, another mark of the church's unity. It is to this meal and its liturgy that we now turn our attention.

---

[33] "Order for Lay Baptism," *The Occasional Services from the Service Book and Hymnal* (Minneapolis: Augsburg Publishing House [et al], 1962), 10-11.

[34] *Lutheran Book of Worship: Occasional Services* (Minneapolis: Augsburg Publishing House; Philadelphia: Board of Publication, Lutheran Church in America, 1982), 18. Emphasis added.

For Further Reading

Infant Baptism

Beasley-Murray, George R. *Baptism in the New Testament.* Milton Keynes, UK: Paternoster Press, 1962.

Bromiley, Geoffrey W. *Children of Promise: The Case for Baptizing Infants.* Eugene, OR: Wipf & Stock, 1998.

Cullman, Oscar. *Baptism in the New Testament.* London: SCM Press, 1964.

Wright, David F. *Infant Baptism in Historical Perspective: Collected Studies.* Milton Keynes, UK: Paternoster, 2007.

Contextualization

Chicago Statement on Worship and Culture: Baptism and Rites of Life Passage. Geneva: Lutheran World Federation, 1998.

Chupungco, Anscar J. *Liturgical Inculturation: Sacramentals, Religiosity, and Catechesis.* Collegeville: The Liturgical Press, 1992.

Baptism and Christian Unity

Saarinen, Risto, and Michael Root. *Baptism and the Unity of the Church.* Grand Rapids: Eerdmans, 1998.

CHAPTER 10

The Lord's Supper among the Protestant Reformers

While Christians refer to their rite of initiation using only two terms – baptism or christening – their sacred meal has many names. "Lord's Supper" is perhaps the most biblical, based on the terminology Paul uses when denouncing the practices of the Corinthian church: "So, then, when you come together, it is not the *Lord's Supper* you eat, for when you are eating, some of you go ahead with your own private suppers" (1 Cor. 11:19-20). The term suggests a connection with the meals that Jesus had with his disciples and others, as well as his own presence in the meals celebrated by Christians. The word "Eucharist" derives from the accounts of the Last Supper where Jesus "gave thanks"(εύχαριστήσας) over the bread and cup (Luke 22:17, 19; 1 Cor. 11:24), and stresses the action of *prayer*, specifically, prayer that remembers God's saving acts in history and petitions God to make known his saving power in this meal event. The most common term among Protestants, "Holy Communion," reflects Paul's understanding that the meal offers "participation" or "communion" (κοινωνία) in the body and blood of the risen Christ (1 Cor. 10:16). "Mass" derives from the traditional closing formula of the liturgy "*Ite, misse est*" or "Go, you are sent," and therefore suggests a link to the church's mission in the world. We are nourished at the meal for carrying out the *missio Dei* in the world.

All of these terms have been used by Protestants. "Mass" was used by early Lutherans, but other Protestants generally rejected the term because of its connection with the Roman Catholic sacrificial understanding of the sacrament. "Lord's Supper" (German: *Herrnmahl*) is frequently used in the Lutheran confessional writings of the latter half of the sixteenth century. "Eucharist," the favored term of modern Roman Catholicism, is often used by "high church" Anglicans and "evangelical-catholic" Lutherans, although it is not unknown within the Reformed-Presbyterian tradition.[1] "Holy Communion" is probably the most utilized term in Protestantism today, even if official worship books use words like "Eucharist," or "Service of Word and Table." Although the variety of terminology might be cause for confusion, it also reminds us of the near impossibility of reducing the meaning of the meal to just one thing. Indeed, all Protestants would affirm that forgiveness, fellowship, healing, strengthening, and a foretaste of heaven are signified and enacted when they gather for a meal in memory of the risen Lord Jesus Christ. A Greek term for the meal, μυστήριον or mystery, which hints of incomprehensibility, suggests a meaning that cannot be exhausted by any one word. In that case, we can be grateful for the many names the Supper has, even if our own tradition favors one over others.

The purpose of this chapter is to explore how the Lord's Supper was understood and celebrated by the founders of the major Protestant traditions, with special attention given to the relationship between theology and liturgy. It is hoped that readers will gain a deeper

[1] See "The Holy Eucharist," BCP 1979, 315; "The Service for the Lord's Day," BCW, 67.

appreciation of their own tradition's eucharistic faith and practice after it is viewed in relationship to other Protestant understandings.

Martin Luther

Generally considered the first great polemical blow against the medieval sacramental system, Martin Luther's *Babylonian Captivity of the Church* (1520) identifies three distortions or ways in which the Mass had been taken captive to the tyranny of the papacy: (1) the withholding of the cup from the laity; (2) the doctrine of transubstantiation; and (3) the understanding that the Mass is a good work and sacrifice.[2] Regarding the first captivity, Luther argues that the church is bound to administer the Supper in its entirety because the sacrament was instituted with the sharing of both bread and cup. Against the doctrine of transubstantiation, according to which the "substance" of bread and wine are changed into the substance of Christ's body and blood while maintaining the outward appearance ("accidents") of bread and wine, Luther argues that the elements can remain what they are even while conveying the substance of Christ's body and blood. Ultimately, transubstantiation is unnecessary, since Christ's presence in the elements is assured by his own words ("this is my body…this cup is the new covenant in my blood"). Contrary to the widespread view that the Mass is a good work and sacrifice offered by the Church to God in order to obtain the merits of Christ's saving death, the Mass is a *testament* or act of bequeathing by which Christ promises to give his body and blood for the forgiveness of sins.[3] As an act of promise, the Mass elicits the faith of the participants, and any view of the Mass as a good work overthrows the role of faith and robs the Mass of its saving power, since salvation is by faith

[2] Martin Luther, *The Babylonian Captivity of the Church* (1520), LW 36, 27-57.

[3] Here Luther interprets the Greek word *diatheke* ("covenant") in the Last Supper accounts in light of Hebrews 9:16-17, where *diatheke* is rendered in Latin as *testamentum* ("will").

alone.[4] Furthermore, this works-righteous view of the Mass turns its meaning upside-down:

> What godless audacity is it, therefore, when we who are to receive the testament of God come as those who would perform a good work for him! ...When we ought to be grateful for the benefits received, we come arrogantly to give that which we ought to take. With unheard-of perversity we mock the mercy of the giver by giving as a work the thing we receive as a gift, so that the testator, instead of being a dispenser of his own goods, becomes the recipient of ours.[5]

Related to this criticism, but distinct from it, is Luther's objection that the Mass had been transformed into a sacrifice of Christ, whereby the consecrated elements, the body and blood of Christ, are offered by the priest to God as a propitiation for human sin. To the contrary, it is impossible for the Mass to be both a testament whereby we receive promises from God, and to be the offering of a sacrifice, since one cannot give and receive something at the same time![6] In objecting to the Mass as a "sacrifice and good work," Luther was criticizing two qualitatively different things: on the one hand, a *piety* that would presume to come before God with human efforts rather than humbly receive his gifts, and, on the other hand, a *theology* about what actually happens in the Mass with the elements. Luther's critique of the medieval Mass is significant because it will determine the shape of the reformed Mass liturgies that he prepared for German Christians.

Luther takes a more pastoral approach in his two catechisms.[7] The "sacrament of the altar" (i.e., the Lord's Supper) is the "true body and blood" of the Lord Jesus Christ given "under" the sacramental elements of bread and wine. Because the Lord's Supper is "set within"

---

[4] Luther, *Babylonian Captivity*, LW 36, 38-39.

[5] Luther, *Babylonian Captivity*, LW 36, 48.

[6] Luther, *Babylonian Captivity*, LW 36, 52.

[7] Luther, *Small Catechism*, BC, 362.1—363.10; *Large Catechism*, BC, 467.1—476.87.

and "bound" to God's Word, we can be assured that the true body and blood of Christ are present in the elements. The chief benefit of the sacrament is the forgiveness of sins, which is obtained when the eating and drinking is accompanied by a believing trust in the words "given for you" and "shed for you for the forgiveness of sins." It is these two things – the divine Word of promise and the faith of the recipient – that together constitute the heart of the sacrament, such that worthy reception is a matter of whether one believes Christ's words "given...shed...*for you.*" The unworthy recipient is one who does not believe them. Yet, even the unworthy person will receive the true body and blood of Christ, since Christ's presence is bound to his Word, rather than to the faith of the recipient. Although no Christian should be compelled to receive the sacrament, all should receive it "frequently" and those who fail to receive it over a long period cannot even be considered Christian.

Luther's doctrine of the real or bodily presence of Christ in the Supper led to a bitter dispute with other Protestant Reformers, particularly with Ulrich Zwingli who had written against this teaching in 1525 (see below). To address the objections of Zwingli and others, Luther had to explain, first of all, how Christ could be present on many altars simultaneously. He does so by way of analogy: just as the preaching of one person imparts the presence of Christ wholly and completely to many human hearts, such that Christ is not divided up, so Christ gives himself wholly and completely to many Christians in the eucharistic bread. Christ who is omnipresent, who can be in the human heart *and* at the right hand of God simultaneously, can also be in the eucharistic elements while remaining at God's right hand. Sounding much like Augustine, Luther explains how this is accomplished: "For as soon as Christ says: 'This is my body,' his body is present *through the Word and the power of the Holy Spirit.* If the Word is not there, it is mere bread; but as soon as the words are added they bring with them that of which they speak."[8] For Luther, the bread can rightly be called Christ's *body* because, as the divine

[8] Martin Luther, *The Sacrament of the Body and Blood of Christ – Against the Fanatics* (1526), LW 36, 340-41. Emphasis added.

Son of God, he created it, and because his words now designate the bread as that which is to be used as his body.[9] Yet, for Luther, the bread remains substantially bread.

But Luther's essentially literal interpretation of the Words of Institution raises the question of how one substance can "be" another substance. How can "bread" be "body"? To assert this seems to violate the law of *identical predication*, i.e., the rule that two substances cannot be one substance, or that one thing cannot be another thing. Neither faith nor scripture, his opponents contended, allow for such a violation. But to the contrary, Luther argues, faith knows of a union of persons in Christ so that we can ultimately say "God is man and man is God." Scripture itself knows of the union of two kinds of beings such that we can refer to one thing using the name of another, e.g., when Psalm 104:4 states that "He makes his angels winds and his ministers flames of fire." For Luther, this means that "he who sees this wind or flame sees an angel." Likewise, the biblical account of Jesus' baptism would allow one to point to the dove and say "This is the Holy Spirit."[10] Luther then concludes:

> Why then should we not much more say in the Supper, "This is my body," even though bread and body are two distinct substances, and the word "this" indicates the bread? Here, too, out of two kinds of objects a union has taken place, which I shall call a "sacramental union," because Christ's body and the bread are given to us as a sacrament. This is not a natural or personal union, as is the case with God and Christ. It is also perhaps a different union from that which the dove has with the Holy Spirit, and the flame with the angel, but is also assuredly a *sacramental union*.[11]

---

[9] Martin Luther, *That These Words of Christ, "This is My Body," etc. Still Stand Firm Against the Fanatics* (1527), LW 37, 43.

[10] Martin Luther, *Confession Concerning Christ's Supper* (1528), LW 37, 297-99.

[11] Luther, *Confession Concerning Christ's Supper,* LW 37, 300. Emphasis added.

Luther's notion of "sacramental union" is definitive for his understanding of the real presence, and is distinct from the theory of consubstantiation, which has incorrectly been attributed to Luther and classical Lutheranism. In reality, Lutherans have rejected consubstantiation because it posits a localized and circumscribed presence of Christ.[12]

Another issue for Luther involved the ascension: if Christ ascended to heaven or the "right hand of God" (Acts 2:33; Heb. 10:12), how can he be present bodily on earth and also present in the Lord's Supper? Noting that Christ ascended in order to fill all things (Eph. 4:10), Luther argues that there is no localization of Christ in heaven, but rather "he is above all creatures and in all and beyond all creatures."[13] Even though Christ is in all things, he does not desire to be sought in all things, but only when and where he commands us to seek him through his Word. In the sacrament, Christ "binds his body and blood so that they are received corporeally in the bread and wine."[14] In that case, there is no "de-scension" of Christ into the eucharistic elements, and neither is Christ drawn into them by the liturgical words and actions.

Luther defines the "right hand of God" not as a specific place where an object might be located, but rather as the *almighty power of God* which can be both nowhere and everywhere at the same time.[15] Since the right hand of God is everywhere (*dextera Dei ubique est*), including in the sacramental elements, and since Christ's body is at the right hand of God, the Lord's body is necessarily present in the bread of the Supper.[16] But this is not a localized presence; when Luther used the phraseology "in the bread," he (like the ancient church Fathers) does not mean to imply a circumscribed presence.

---

[12] *Formula of Concord* (1580), *Epitome*, Art. VIII, BC, 508.42.

[13] Luther, *Sacrament of the Body and Blood*, LW 36, 342. Zwingli's writings give the impression, at least, that the Ascension brings about the localization of Christ in Heaven.

[14] Luther, *Sacrament of the Body and Blood*, LW 36, 343.

[15] Luther, *That These Words of Christ*, LW 37, 57.

[16] Luther, *That These Words of Christ*, LW 37, 64.

Rather, his point was to confess that Christ's body is present in the Supper such that the communicants do not eat mere bread but the very body of Christ.[17] Luther later elaborated on this point, making a distinction between (1) Christ present everywhere; and (2) Christ present in a salvific way for Christian believers. Again, he makes the point by way of an analogy:

> See, the bright rays of the sun are so near you that they pierce into your eyes or your skin so that you feel it, you are unable to grasp them and put them into a box, even if you should try forever. Prevent them from shining in through a window – this you can do, but catch and grasp them you cannot. So too with Christ: although he is everywhere, he does not permit himself to be so caught and grasped; he can easily shell himself, so that you get the shell but not the kernel. Why? *Because it is one thing if God is present, and another if he is present for you.* He is there for you when he adds his Word and binds himself saying, "Here you are to find me." Now when you have the Word, you can grasp and have him with certainty....
>
> ...you will not catch him by groping about, even though he is in your bread, unless he binds himself to you and summons you to a particular table by his Word, and he himself gives meaning to the bread for you, by his Word, bidding you to eat him. This he does in the Supper, saying, "This is my body."[18]

So what good does eating the body of Christ do for a person? Here Luther acknowledges that the physical eating of Christ does no good unless it is accompanied by faith. He distinguishes between physical and spiritual eating, and asserts that the physical eating of Christ's body in the Supper is beneficial when it is accompanied by a spiritual eating, that is, when one believes that the body one eats was

[17] Luther, *That These Words of Christ*, LW 37, 65.

[18] Luther, *That These Words of Christ*, LW 37, 68-69. Emphasis added.

given for the forgiveness of sins according to the words "This is my body which is given for you," etc. Indeed, unless the physical eating is accompanied by the spiritual eating (i.e., faith), one eats in an unworthy manner and thus brings judgment upon oneself (cf. 1 Cor. 11:27). It is precisely because Christ is present in the sacrament that the physical eating can be harmful to a communicant.[19]

Naturally, the benefits of the Supper extend beyond merely providing the church with a venue for the public proclamation of Christ and its own self-identification. Contrary to Zwingli, Luther maintains that "Take, eat; this is my body given for you" means more than to proclaim and preach Christ's death, and the Lord's Supper is not to be confused with a sermon. While the latter publicly proclaims Christ's death such that "whoever grasps it, grasps it," the former distributes the body and blood of Christ to each individual so that he/she may have the forgiveness that is the benefit of Christ's death, which has just been proclaimed in the sermon. Those who then receive the sacrament "preach" Christ to their neighbors, even to those who are not Christians. For Luther, to think of the sacrament only in terms of "commemoration" is to render it useless. Indeed, the sacrament has a two-fold purpose: (1) to strengthen the troubled and tempted conscience; and (2) to increase love for the neighbor, such that the entire Christian way is encapsulated in the Lord's Supper. [20]

The importance and distinctiveness of Luther's theology of the Lord's Supper cannot be overemphasized. His was the first systematic critique of the Mass among sixteenth-century Reformers, and he essentially laid the groundwork for those Reformers who followed him. But we dare not lump Luther together with all of these, especially with the Swiss Reformers; Luther was unique in asserting that the very body and blood of Christ are (1) eaten *orally* by all recipients thereof; and (2) eaten even by the *unworthy*. It is no exaggeration to suggest that many Protestants then and now (perhaps even some who belong to Lutheran churches!) would find these two

---

[19] Luther, *That These Words of Christ*, LW 37, 85-87.

[20] Luther, *Sacrament of the Body and Blood*, LW 36, 348-53.

affirmations unacceptable despite Luther's strenuous and sincere attempts to understand the Lord's Supper based on biblical texts.

Beside eucharistic theology, Luther's other significant contribution was his reform of eucharistic liturgy. Luther prepared two revised versions of the Mass, albeit somewhat hesitantly out of fear of creating a new legalism. The first of Luther's two reformed Masses, the *Formula Missae* (1523), is actually a commentary on how to revise the Latin Mass in an evangelical manner.[21] Luther did not envision it as an unchangeable prototype for all times and places. It reveals an overall conservative approach, especially in the service of the Word, which shows little difference from the traditional Latin Mass as we can see in the following table.

MEDIEVAL LATIN MASS	LUTHER'S FORMULA MISSAE (1523)
Introit	Introit
Kyrie	Kyrie
Gloria in Excelsis	Gloria in Excelsis
Collect	Collect
Epistle	Epistle
Gradual and Alleluia	Gradual and Alleluia
Gospel	Gospel
Sermon	Creed
Creed	Sermon

In line with his conservatism, Luther was willing to keep the lectionary, but advocated a sermon in the vernacular.

Much more radical was Luther's revision of the canon of the Mass (liturgy of the Lord's Supper), where he omitted those elements that seemed to make the Mass into a sacrifice offered to God, e.g., the offertory prayer, the four petitions following the Sanctus, and the traditional *Unde et memores* petition that followed the Words of

[21] Martin Luther, *An Order of Mass and Communion for the Church at Wittenberg* (1523), LW 53, 19-40.

Institution.[22] The following comparative table reveals the extent to which Luther omitted material from the traditional Latin Mass.

MEDIEVAL LATIN MASS	LUTHER'S FORMULA MISSAE (1523)
Offertory Prayer	Preparation of the elements
Preface	Preface
Sanctus	
4 Prayers	
Consecration petition	
Institution Narrative	Institution Narrative
Anamnesis/Oblation	Sanctus
4 Prayers	
Doxology	
Lord's Prayer	Lord's Prayer
Peace	Peace
Agnus Dei	Agnus Dei
Distribution of elements	Distribution of elements
Post-communion prayer	Post-communion prayer
Dismissal	Benediction (The Lord bless you)

Essentially, Luther created a new eucharistic prayer consisting of everything from the preface through the Lord's Prayer, with the emphasis falling on what he believed was at the heart of the Lord's Supper, namely, the Institution Narrative with its words of promise.[23]

[22] The text of the *Unde et memores* prayer is: "Therefore also, Lord, we your servants, and also your holy people, having in remembrance the blessed passion of your Son Christ our Lord, likewise his resurrection from the dead, and also his glorious ascension into heaven, do offer to your excellent majesty from your gifts and bounty a pure victim, a holy victim, an unspotted victim, the holy bread of eternal life and the cup of everlasting salvation" (translation from PEER, 165).

[23] Luther, *Order of Mass*, LW 53, 31.

Although radical, Luther's revision of the canon was subtle in its actual performance. Since the priest traditionally recited the four prayers while the choir chanted the Sanctus, few if any worshippers would have noticed the removal of these prayers, since they were said in a low voice. Moreover, because Luther directs the priest to elevate the bread and cup during the Benedictus ("Blessed is he..." etc.) of the now relocated Sanctus, which was the moment for the elevation in the medieval Mass, his actions would not have appeared any different to worshippers. Luther viewed the elevation as a concession to the "weak in faith," who might have been offended by its obvious omission.[24] Nevertheless, ceremonial elaborations such as the making of multiple signs of the cross over the elements, and the placing of part of the host into the chalice were to be omitted.[25] Luther suggests a split distribution whereby the bread is blessed and then distributed and likewise the cup as a way of following the Institution Narrative literally. But he admits that this order is novel and raises the question of what to do with the Sanctus and Lord's Prayer. Liturgical vestments were permitted, as long as "ostentation" was avoided. Luther says nothing about reserving the sacrament, although previously he had allowed it only for purposes of taking communion to the sick.[26]

Luther also provided a number of other pastoral and liturgical instructions. The Mass was only to be celebrated if there were people present to receive communion, i.e., private Masses were to be discontinued. Those desirous of communing were to submit their names to the presiding minister (bishop) and be examined every year as to their understanding of the Lord's Supper and its spiritual benefits. Communicants were to gather in the chancel so that they might be seen by all and have their lives scrutinized. Preparations such as private confession and fasting were deemed appropriate,

---

[24] Luther, *Order of Mass*, LW 53, 28.

[25] Luther preferred not to mix water into the wine at the preparation.

[26] Martin Luther, *Receiving Both Kinds in the Sacrament* (1522), LW 36, 257. The Lutheran confessions will emphatically reject the reservation of the sacrament; see *Formula of Concord* (1580), *Solid Declaration*, Art. VII, BC, 588.

but were not to be demanded. In accordance with the institution of Christ, both bread and wine were to be distributed. Luther envisioned congregational singing in the vernacular during the Mass, e.g., after the Sanctus and Agnus Dei. In general, the *Formula Missae* evidences Luther's understanding that the liturgy is a matter of evangelical freedom whereby leaders are at liberty to act according to what they believe is appropriate for their local circumstances – although this did not mean scandalizing the assembly or dispensing with the preaching of the Word or the Lord's Supper entirely.

Luther's *Deutsche Messe* or *German Mass* (1526)[27] was meant for assemblies comprised of uneducated laypeople. The order was:

Introit psalm or German hymn
Kyrie eleison (sung three times)
Collect prayer
Epistle
German Hymn
Gospel
Creed (hymn version) and preparation of the elements on the altar
Sermon
Paraphrase of the Lord's Prayer
Exhortation to communicants
Words of Institution (bread)
Distribution of Bread (while German Sanctus is sung)
Words of Institution (cup)
Distribution of the cup (while German Agnus Dei is sung)
Post-communion prayer
Benediction

There were few changes prior to the sermon, except for the omission of the Gloria in Excelsis.[28] Following the sermon, the minister read

[27] Martin Luther, *The German Mass and Order of Service* (1526), LW 53, 61-90.

[28] Eventually a hymn version of the Gloria was composed by Nikolaus Decius (c. 1485-c. 1550). See *Lutheran Book of Worship* (Pew Edition) "All Glory Be to God on High" (Minneapolis: Augsburg, 1978), #166. Henceforth LBW/PE.

a paraphrase of the Lord's Prayer and admonished the assembly to receive the Supper in faith. An even simpler consecration followed, but each element was now to be distributed after the relevant words of the Institution Narrative. Following the consecration of the bread, the German Sanctus ("Isaiah Twas the Prophet Who Did See"[29]) or other hymns were to be sung while the priest elevated the elements. Luther believed that this action visually portrayed the words of the Sanctus ("High on a lofty throne in splendor bright") and expressed the assembly's "adoration" of Christ in the sacrament. The cup was then blessed and administered during the German Agnus Dei[30] or remaining hymns. The Mass concluded with Luther's own post-communion collect ("We give thanks to thee, Almighty God, that thou hast refreshed us with this thy salutary gift...") and the Aaronic benediction. Luther hoped that the *Deutsche Messe* would be used with Christian liberty and not become a source of abuse.

Lutheran eucharistic liturgies in Germany tended to follow the outline of either the *Formula Missae* (the "Brandenburg-Nürnberg family") or the *Deutsche Messe* (the "Bugenhagen family"). Yet many of the proposed changes in the *Deutsche Messe* were not incorporated into liturgies of the latter group. Only the placement of the Lord's Prayer and exhortation before the Institution Narrative, along with Luther's post-communion prayer, gained any popularity. [31]

Luther's writings on the Lord's Supper are mostly polemical, and therefore not so agreeable to modern ecumenical sensibilities. But at least two aspects of his work are commendable to the church of our time. First is his grounding sacramental theology in the Word of God; the Supper is what it is because Christ says so! This is not naïve biblicism, but an attempt to take God at his Word. Modern Christians who live in a world uncertain and confused about God's presence can experience both challenge and renewal as they ponder

---

Cf. *Evangelical Lutheran Worship* (Minneapolis: Augsburg Fortress, 2006), #410. Henceforth ELW/PE.

[29] For the text of this hymn, see LW 53, 82-83 or PEER 198-99.

[30] See "Lamb of God, Pure and Sinless," LBW/PE, #111, ELW/PE, #357.

[31] Editor's note, PEER, 190.

Luther's affirmation that God in Jesus Christ is to be found at the table. Second, Luther's insistence on the gift character of the Supper is applicable to any age since human nature is to focus on the self, its efforts, decisions, and responses, and less on being thankful for God's blessings.

Yet, we must not take Luther uncritically, especially when it comes to his liturgical revisions. While Luther's sensitivity to the assembly's needs for consistency and familiarity should surely be emulated, the sparseness of his eucharistic services may seem unsuitable in an ecumenical age that offers a great variety of eucharistic prayers with rich biblical imagery. Luther's polemicism and conservatism must be balanced with the modern worship assembly's need to thank God for the gifts of the Supper in a way that does justice to God's goodness and mercy.

Ulrich Zwingli

Unlike Martin Luther and John Calvin, Ulrich Zwingli did not provide a comprehensive work that catalogued and systematically attacked all the perceived erroneous doctrines and practices of the Lord's Supper. Instead, his writings on the Supper were chiefly devoted to denying any doctrine of the real or bodily presence of Christ, whether that of the Roman Catholic Church, Luther, or others.

Zwingli takes his understanding of the Lord's Supper from the name "Eucharist," declaring that the Supper is "the thanksgiving and common rejoicing of those who declare the death of Christ, that is, trumpet, praise, confess, and exalt His name above all others."[32] The eating and drinking in the Lord's Supper ("sacramental eating") does not have anything to do with salvation, for only Christ's death alone is saving, in which case salvation is possible only through faith, rather than sacramental eating.[33] This assertion relies on his understanding that Christ offers salvation by virtue of his divine nature, rather

[32] Ulrich Zwingli, *On True and False Religion* (1525), in *The Latin Works of Ulrich Zwingli*, Vol. 3, tr. Samuel Macauley Jackson, ed. Clarence N. Heller (Philadelphia: The Heidelberg Press, 1929), 200.

[33] Zwingli, *True and False Religion*, *Works of Zwingli*, 205-206.

than his human nature. Thus, eating the flesh of Christ (if that were possible) would profit us nothing (cf. John 6:63). To say that we partake of the flesh and blood of Christ really means that we are partaking of sensible things, which is contrary to reason and to the concept of belief, which is all about grasping insensible, unseen things. If we perceive that the eucharistic bread is the flesh of Christ, it would be so by the senses and not by faith.[34] Although the Words of Institution suggest the identity of the eucharistic bread and the body of Christ ("This is my body"), Zwingli argues that the word "is" means "signifies" or represents, just like when Christ himself, explaining the parable of the sower, states that "the seed *is* the Word of God." In both cases, the phraseology is to be taken figuratively, rather than literally.[35] Essentially, no sensible object could be a matter of faith for Zwingli.[36] In contrast to Luther who held that the body and blood of Christ are distributed and received (orally eaten) in the Lord's Supper, Zwingli holds that Christ's actual human body cannot be present in the Supper. By virtue of the ascension (Mark 16:19; cf. Luke 24:50-51; Acts 1:9-11), the human nature of Christ is in heaven, making it impossible for it to be on altars during the eucharistic liturgy. [37]

The Lord's Supper for Zwingli is primarily a commemorative act rendered by the worship assembly:

> The Eucharist…is nothing but the commemoration by which those who firmly believe that by Christ's death and blood they have become reconciled with the Father proclaim this life-bringing death, that is, preach it with praise and thanksgiving.[38]

---

[34] Zwingli, *True and False Religion, Works of Zwingli*, 213-14.

[35] Zwingli, *True and False Religion, Works of Zwingli*, 224-27.

[36] Zwingli, *True and False Religion, Works of Zwingli*, 227.

[37] Ulrich Zwingli, *On the Lord's Supper* (1526), in *Zwingli and Bullinger*, LCC XXIV, tr. G. W. Bromiley (Philadelphia: The Westminster Press, 1953), 214-15.

[38] Zwingli, *True and False Religion, Works of Zwingli*, 237.

What is symbolized by the bread and the mutual eating of it is the body of the *fellowship*, which is the church.[39]

Like Luther, Zwingli was responsible for two reformed eucharistic services. The first, *An Attack on the Canon of the Mass* (1523),[40] was a very conservative revision, as revealed in the following outline:

Introit
Kyries
Gloria in Excelsis
Collect
Epistle
Gradual
Gospel
Nicene Creed (and preparation of the elements)
Preface dialog
Preface
Sanctus and Benedictus
Four prayers
Words of Institution
Invitation (Matthew 11:28)
Distribution of elements
Thanksgiving
Nunc Dimittis
Benediction

There were few changes in the service of the Word, except that it provided no collect, gradual, or readings for days that commemorated saints. The eucharistic liturgy began in the usual manner with the Sursum Corda (dialog), preface, and Sanctus, which was followed by four prayers that essentially replaced the old canon of the Mass. The first of these was a recital of salvation history from creation to Christ that led into the Lord's Prayer (prayed by all). A reflection of Zwingli's eucharistic theology, the second prayer asked that our souls, which are inherently spiritual, be fed with the spiritual food of God's

[39] Zwingli, *True and False Religion*, *Works of Zwingli*, 232.

[40] Ulrich Zwingli, *An Attack on the Canon of the Mass* (1523), PEER, 183-86.

Word, which is the true bread. The prayer then acknowledged that eating Christ's flesh and drinking his blood would be in vain without faith in Jesus' atoning sacrifice for the sins of the world. A quotation of John 6:63 ("The Spirit gives life, the flesh counts for nothing") – a key verse for Zwingli's interpretation of the eucharistic presence of Christ – segued to an invocation of the Spirit (or epiclesis) that asked for the Spirit to "quicken" the worshippers and never deprive them of the Word. The third prayer, with language reminiscent of the traditional eucharistic anamnesis, returned to the theme of reconciliation in Christ, and asked God to strengthen the faith of worshippers that they might overcome worldly hardships. Perhaps as a concession to conservatives, the prayer referred to Christ who "offered himself to be the food of our souls under the forms of bread and wine; so that the memory of his generous deed may never be abolished."[41] Acknowledging that the remembrance of Christ cannot be made by words alone, God was asked to empower Christians for authentic Christian living that reveals Christ, as well as for the unity that makes this authenticity possible. The fourth prayer incorporated the Agnus Dei ("Lamb of God, you take away the sins of the world; have mercy on us") and becomes a petition for worthy communion leading to the Institution Narrative from 1 Cor. 11, including 1 Cor. 11:26. Matthew 11:28 ("Come to me, all you who labor…") was appended as an invitation to communion. The elements were to be distributed with the traditional formulas suggestive of the real presence ("The body/blood of our Lord Jesus Christ preserve you to everlasting life"). The rite concluded with a brief prayer of thanksgiving, followed by the Nunc Dimittis ("Lord, now let your servant depart…") and a blessing. Although the didacticism of the prayers took an evangelical slant, with an emphasis on faith, the work of Christ, and human sinfulness, the overall shape and continuing identification of the elements with Christ's body and blood suggests a Reformer who is restraining himself from too freely expressing his own eucharistic theology.

[41] Zwingli, *Attack on the Canon of the Mass,* PEER, 185.

But prompted by pressure exerted from radicals, Zwingli produced his *Action or Use of the Lord's Supper* (1525),[42] which was a more drastic revision. The order was:

Preparation of the elements
Collect
Epistle: 1 Corinthians 11:20-29
Gloria in Excelsis (spoken antiphonally between men and women)
Gospel: John 6:47-63
Apostles' Creed (spoken antiphonally between men and women)
Exhortation
Lord's Prayer (no doxology)
Prayer of Humble Access
Words of Institution
Breaking of bread
Distribution of elements
Post-communion (Ps.113)
Thanksgiving prayer
Dismissal

To be used only on Easter, Pentecost, the autumn time, and Christmas, the service provided two fixed readings: 1 Cor. 11:20-29 and John 6:47-63. The preface dialog, Sanctus, and four prayers were excluded; only an exhortation to communion and the Institution Narrative remained. The elements were served to the communicants who remained seated at a table, undoubtedly in imitation of the Last Supper, as well as to convey the fellowship aspect of the meal which Zwingli emphasized in his doctrinal writings. The post-communion consisted of an antiphonal recitation of Ps.113:1-9 (women and men alternating), a brief prayer of thanksgiving, and the dismissal. Thus, the focus in this much briefer service is the communal sharing of the elements, as opposed to thanksgiving for the benefits received.

When pondering the significance of Zwingli's teaching on the Lord's Supper, it is no doubt striking that he expended most of his literary effort saying what is *not* offered in the Lord's Supper,

[42] Ulrich Zwingli, *Action or Use of the Lord's Supper* (1525), PEER, 187-88.

namely, the bodily presence of Christ. Of course, had Zwingli lived longer, he might have had more opportunities to express what it does give to the communicant. It also unfortunate that his second and final eucharistic liturgy (not unlike Luther's *German Mass*) was minimalistic, although it might not have been his intention to encourage liturgical reductionism. Perhaps also a longer life would have allowed him to develop the Lord's Supper service in other ways that emphasized the fellowship aspect of the meal, something that seems to be lacking in our own day.

John Calvin

Much more systematic and constructive than Zwingli on the Lord's Supper was John Calvin, whose ideas influenced the liturgical work of other reformers, especially the great reformer of the Scottish church, John Knox (c. 1514-72). Calvin's most important work on the Lord's Supper is in Book IV of his *Institutes* (1559).

For Calvin, the Lord's Supper is the means by which God sustains his children in the new life that they have obtained through the Word of God. The elements of bread and wine signify the invisible, spiritual food that Christians receive from the flesh and blood of Christ. Visible signs adapted to human capacity, the eucharistic elements serve as "guarantees" or "tokens" that just as bread and wine nourish the body, so the human soul is fed by Christ himself.[43] When Christians receive the bread, they can be assured that Christ's sacrificial death will be efficacious in them; when they receive the cup, they are assured that the covenant made in Christ's blood is renewed or continued in them. The Supper also confirms participation in the body of Christ such that, by way of an "exchange," everything that belongs to Christ, viz., eternal life, the Kingdom of heaven, now belongs to each Christian.[44] Indeed, the sacrament is a witness to the spiritual blessings of Christ as if Christ himself were present; the

---

[43] John Calvin, *Institutes of the Christian Religion* (1559), IV.17.1, in LCC XXI, ed. John T. McNeill, tr. Ford Lewis Battles (Philadelphia: Westminster Press, 1960), 1361.

[44] Calvin, *Institutes* IV.17.2, LCC XXI, 1362.

words of Christ, "Take, eat, drink" indicate that his body and blood are now the possession of communicants. The words "which is given for you," "which is shed for you," make clear that Christ's body and blood are given for the benefit of the recipients.

The chief purpose of the sacrament is not to impart the body of Christ, but rather to "seal and confirm that promise by which he testifies that his flesh is food indeed and his blood is drink [John 6:55], which feed us to eternal life [John 6:54]."[45] The Supper necessarily directs us to the Cross where Christ's promises were fulfilled, and only by grasping the saving significance of his death do Christians "eat" Christ rightly. Christ is only the bread of life insofar as he took on our mortality, made himself a sacrifice, and subjected himself to death in order that we might share in his immortality, receive the benefits of his sacrifice, and partake of his resurrection. The body of Christ is given to us through the gospel, and it is received in faith.

Calvin notes that two dangers are to be avoided in eucharistic theology. The first is divorcing the sacramental sign from that which it signifies by having too little regard for the sign and thereby separating it from the mystery it represents. The second is having too high of a regard for the sacramental sign and thereby obscuring the mystery to which it points. For Calvin, eating Christ's flesh and drinking his blood means more than simply believing in Christ, since a true partaking has the effect of enlivening the soul. In that case, one does not receive new life from Christ simply by knowledge. By eating the bread, the soul is led (by faith) to become a partaker in Christ and the spiritual life that he gives. Unlike Zwingli, Calvin holds that "eating" and "believing" are not synonymous, but emphasizes that eating follows from faith – that is, we eat because we believe.[46] A further distinction is that communion with Christ is not merely communion with his spirit but communion with his flesh and blood, as suggested by the language of John 6:55 and 6:53. Calvin's concern is to avoid stripping Christ of his flesh and blood and turning him into a "phantasm."

---

[45] Calvin, *Institutes* IV.17.4, LCC XXI, 1363.

[46] Calvin, *Institutes* IV.17.2, LCC XXI, 1365.

Calvin's understanding of the eucharistic presence of Christ is somewhere between Zwingli and Luther. He holds that the bread is a symbol of the body of Christ, but, like Zwingli, he does not understand it to be the body itself; this does not contradict Christ's words ("This is my body") since a symbol is often referred to using the name of the thing signified. But the symbol (bread) truly shows the thing itself (the body of Christ). "Therefore, if the Lord truly represents the participation in his body through the breaking of bread, there ought not to be the least doubt that he truly presents and shows his body."[47] Thus, when we see the symbol we are to believe that the thing signified is present, for God would have no other purpose to give us the symbol except to assure us that the reality is present. But the presence of Christ is not localized such that it can be touched with the hands, chewed by the teeth, and swallowed by the mouth. Like Zwingli, Calvin holds that Christ's body is contained in heaven where it was received after the ascension, and thus, as a true human body, cannot be given in the eucharistic elements nor be ubiquitous as Luther held. In fact, Calvin says, there is no need for a localized presence since participation in Christ is given through the Spirit.[48] Christ can still be present in the Supper even though it is not a bodily presence.[49] Ultimately, communion with Christ in his body and blood (in heaven) is a mystery, which Calvin says that he *experiences* rather than *understands*.[50]

How then did Calvin interpret the Words of Institution, which Luther and others took as evidence of a bodily presence of Christ? Like Zwingli, Calvin maintains that "this is my body/blood" are to be interpreted figuratively rather than literally. In the Bible, the name of the thing signified is sometimes transferred to the signifier, e.g., "the lamb is the Passover," (Ex.12:11) or vice versa, as when the Ark of the Covenant is called God's face (Ps. 84:8) or the dove is referred to as the Holy Spirit (Matt. 3:16). Because an earthly thing

[47] Calvin, *Institutes* IV.17.10, LCC XXI, 1371.

[48] Calvin, *Institutes* IV.17.12, LCC XXI, 1372-73.

[49] Calvin, *Institutes* IV.17.31, LCC XXI, 1403.

[50] Calvin, *Institutes* IV.17.32, LCC XXI, 1403.

is consecrated to represent a heavenly reality, and truly represents it as more than a "bare and empty token," the name of the signified is rightly given/transferred to the signifier. Accordingly, "...the body of Christ today is called bread, inasmuch as it is the symbol by which the Lord offers us the true eating of his body."[51] Christ's body can be called bread, since it is the symbolic means by which there is a true eating of his body.

Calvin therefore also rejects transubstantiation. To begin with, ancient authors clearly distinguished the earthly and heavenly parts in the sacrament, the former being bread and wine, rather than items that only appeared to be bread and wine. Furthermore, this doctrine overthrows the nature and meaning of a sacrament, because if the signifier is only the empty appearance of bread, it does not offer an analogy that leads us from the visible to the invisible (heavenly). As a consequence of his understanding that Christ is not physically present in the eucharistic bread, Calvin rejects devotion to the consecrated bread, as when it is carried in procession or otherwise displayed for purposes of adoration.[52] The sacrament was given so that it might be received, rather than adored. Accordingly, "we ought rather to have adored him spiritually in heavenly glory than to have devised some dangerous kind of adoration, replete with a carnal and crass conception of God."[53]

For Calvin, communion with the body and blood of Christ does not come through the agency of the elements, but through the Holy Spirit who lifts hearts and minds to heaven, where this communion takes place. From heaven, Christ reigns in glory and exerts his power and presence on his people, feeding them with his body and blood by the power of the Holy Spirit. The elements symbolize this communion and direct us to heaven.[54] Calvin believes that with this pneumatological understanding he avoids both (1) detracting from Christ's heavenly glory (which is the case when he is

[51] Calvin, *Institutes* IV.17.21, LCC XXI, 1386.

[52] Calvin, *Institutes* IV.17.36-37, LCC XXI, 1412-14.

[53] Calvin, *Institutes* IV.17.36, LCC XXI, 1413.

[54] Calvin, *Institutes* IV.17.18, LCC XXI, 1381.

enclosed in earthly, corruptible elements); and (2) distorting Christ's human nature, as when it is claimed that his body is in many places at once.[55]

Calvin's pneumatological emphasis had implications for the question of whether wicked persons or unbelievers receive the body and blood of Christ. Because the manner of eating is "spiritual," Calvin argues that those devoid of Christ's spirit (and hence without faith) cannot eat the flesh of Christ. For him, Christ simply cannot be received without some benefit being conferred on the recipient, for Christ is always present with his benefits. Thus, in the Lord's Supper, the body and blood of Christ are *given* to but not *received* by the wicked since they do not have the Spirit.[56] Here Calvin's understanding contrasts with the Lutheran view that the body and blood of Christ are *both distributed to and received by* the wicked and unbelievers, although such persons do not receive them to their benefit.[57]

Unlike Zwingli, Calvin draws out more of the pastoral implications of his teaching. Besides communion with Christ for the spiritual nourishment of Christians, the purpose of the Supper is to (1) be a public, outward remembrance of Christ's death;[58] and (2) inspire holy living and mutual love within the church.[59] Thus the Lord's Supper must take place in conjunction with preaching that will confirm faith and arouse Christians to right living, and that when distributed to the sick there should be words that express the promises and declare the meaning of the sacrament.[60] Because the wicked and unbelieving eat to their condemnation, all would-be communicants should examine themselves as to their belief in Christ

[55] Calvin, *Institutes* IV.17.19, LCC XXI, 1382.

[56] Calvin, *Institutes* IV.17.33, LCC XXI, 1405-06.

[57] Luther, *Confession Concerning Christ's Supper*, LW 37, 367. Cf. *Formula of Concord, Solid Declaration*, Art. VII, BC, 598.32.

[58] Calvin, *Institutes* IV.17.37, LCC XXI, 1414.

[59] Calvin, *Institutes* IV.17.37, LCC XXI, 1414-15.

[60] Calvin, *Institutes* IV.17.39, LCC XXI, 1416-17.

as Savior and their desire to imitate Christ and live in harmony with fellow Christians.[61]

For Calvin, worthy reception has to do with recognizing one's *unworthiness* and relying on the mercy of God – that is, coming to the sacrament in faith and in love (imperfect though these might be).[62] Calvin is critical of spiritualities that require a perfection that cannot be obtained, since these only drive people away from the sacrament. Instead, he argues, the sacrament was "ordained not for the perfect, but for the weak and feeble, to awaken, arouse, stimulate, and exercise the feeling of faith and love, indeed, to correct the defect of both."[63]

As for liturgical matters, the manner of reception and the form of the bread (whether leavened or unleavened) and wine (whether red or white) are matters that can be decided locally. Following ancient custom, all should take the elements into their hands. The Supper should be celebrated at least once a week, with public (intercessory) prayer and preaching.[64] After the table is prepared with the elements, the minister should recite the Words of Institution, discourage the participation of the unworthy, and then offer prayer for worthy reception in faith. Psalms should be sung as the people receive the elements, with ministers breaking the bread and distributing the cup. After this, there should be an exhortation focusing on faith and mutual love.[65] Frequent reception is urged for the sake of remembering Christ's Passion in order that faith might be strengthened.[66] The cup is to be given to all, since withholding it contradicts the biblical institution of the Supper. The doctrine of concomitance, which was traditionally used to support the withdrawal of the cup by positing that the whole Christ is given even under one element, is rejected by

---

[61] Calvin, *Institutes* IV.17.40, LCC XXI, 1418.

[62] Calvin, *Institutes* IV.17.42, LCC XXI, 1419-20.

[63] Calvin, *Institutes* IV.17.42, LCC XXI, 1420.

[64] Calvin, *Institutes* IV.17.43, LCC XXI, 1421.

[65] Calvin, *Institutes* IV.17.43, LCC XXI, 1421-22

[66] Calvin, *Institutes* IV.17.44, LCC XXI, 1422.

Calvin because it essentially makes the bread into the blood of Christ and the wine into his body.[67]

In 1542, Calvin provided a eucharistic rite for the church in Geneva, where he had been recalled following an exile in Strasbourg.[68] This service, contained in *The Form of Church Prayers and Manner of Celebrating the Supper,* evidenced the theology expressed in the *Institutes*. His main purpose was to provide a full service of Word and Sacrament that imitated the simplicity of the early church's liturgy. Unfortunately, he was never able to achieve a weekly celebration of the Lord's Supper in Geneva.[69] Although the influences of Bucer and Guillaume Farel (1489-1565) are apparent, it was largely Calvin's own work. In general, it bore little resemblance to the medieval Mass in either the service of the Word or the eucharistic liturgy ("The Manner of Celebrating the Supper"). We can outline the entire service as follows:

Sentence of Scripture (Ps. 124:8)
Confession
Prayer for pardon
Metrical psalm
Prayer for Illumination
Bible Reading
Sermon
Intercessions
Paraphrase of the Lord's Prayer
Apostles' Creed
Preparation of the elements
Words of Institution
Exhortation
Breaking of bread
Distribution of elements

---

[67] Calvin, *Institutes* IV.17.47, LCC XXI, 1425-26.

[68] John Calvin, *The Form of Prayers and Manner of Ministering the Sacraments according to the Usage of the Ancient Church* (1542), PEER, 215-18.

[69] "John Calvin *The Form of Church Prayers* 1542 (editor's introduction)," PEER, 213.

Prayer of thanksgiving
Benediction

The Lord's Supper portion began with a reading of 1 Cor. 11:23-29 ("For I received from the Lord..."), which led into the "excommunication" or formal banning from communion of all unworthy recipients: idolaters, blasphemers, despisers of God, heretics, sectarians, perjurers, etc. What then followed was not a eucharistic prayer, but rather an exhortation to the communicants, who were first of all encouraged to be in a state of true repentance, to trust in the mercy of God in Jesus Christ, and to seek to live in right relationship with neighbors. Those who do so are promised that they are truly God's elect to whom the promises of the Supper apply. Additionally, they are assured that even though they continue to struggle against sin, Christ will still receive them at his table and make them worthy recipients at the table. The "medicine" of the Lord's Supper is precisely for those who know their need of it, and the only preparation is the personal recognition of that need.

Then came three exhortations. First, the communicants are to trust Christ's promise that they will be partakers of Christ's body and blood "in order that we may possess him entirely and in such manner that he may live in us, and we in him."[70] Then all were encouraged to believe that even though simple bread and wine were visible, spiritual benefits would be conferred – another way of expressing Calvin's idea that the sacramental sign points to what will truly be accomplished spiritually, namely, the nourishment of Christian souls. Second, worshippers were to receive the sacrament believing that Christ's passion and death avail for their justification. Finally, reflecting the idea that communion with the body and blood of Christ takes place in heaven, worshippers were exhorted to "raise hearts and minds on high, where Jesus Christ is, in the glory of the Father" and hence where worshippers will be nourished by "his substance." The communicants were then reminded (again) that bread and wine are but signs, and that they should spiritually seek the "reality" where the

[70] Calvin, *Form of Church Prayers*, PEER, 217.

Word of God says it is located. This final portion of the exhortation, strangely, makes no mention of the Holy Spirit, who Calvin says is instrumental in this heavenly communion with Christ's body and blood. For that matter, no mention is made of the Spirit anywhere in this exhortation.

Then followed the distribution of the elements, with communicants going forward, *unlike* the practice of many Reformed churches today. Although no distribution formulas were given in the 1542 edition of the rite, formulas provided in later editions invited the communicants to "eat the body" and "drink the blood of Christ."[71] Communion was to be accompanied by the singing of appropriate psalms or the reading of relevant scripture verses. The service concluded with a post-communion thanksgiving prayer and benediction.

Positively, the centrality of the Words of Institution (as in Luther's *Formula Missae*), the medicinal allusion, and reference to the passion (in the exhortation) enabled Calvin's eucharistic liturgy to underscore the grace-filled character of communion and make clear that worshippers receive God's gifts. Yet, the emphasis on introspection perhaps undermined Calvin's gracious encouragement to avoid the pursuit of spiritual perfection as a preparation for communion. Inexplicably missing was an invocation of the Holy Spirit, who otherwise figured prominently in Calvin's eucharistic theology. Also missing was eucharistic praying, and because he replaced that element with exhortation, there is no sense of offering thanks to God for the gifts to be received in the Supper. Consequently, we are left with a rather wordy and joyless rite. It is odd that a theologian who emphasized the sovereignty of God did not provide a communion liturgy with prayer at its center, as did Zwingli and Bucer. The only prayer with eucharistic content was that for worthy communion included in the intercessions,[72] a feature that, in a small way, drew

[71] "Calvin: *Form of Church Prayers* 1542 (editor's introduction)," PEER, 214.

[72] "Finally, O God and Father, grant also to those who are gathered here in the name of thy Son Jesus, to hear his Word (and to keep His holy Supper), that we may acknowledge truly, without hypocrisy, what perdition is ours by nature, what

together Word and Sacrament and injected an element of prayer into the celebration of the Supper. Ultimately, many Reformed churches recovered the more ancient practice of surrounding the Supper with prayer.

Thomas Cranmer and the *Book of Common Prayer*

Thomas Cranmer penned a number of works on the Lord's Supper, the last and most important being *A Defense of the True and Catholic Doctrine of the Sacrament of the Body and Blood of our Savior Christ* (1550).[73] He devoted the first five of its "books" (chapters) mainly to offering a clear and correct understanding of Lord's Supper. In the remaining books, Cranmer presents arguments against transubstantiation, the bodily presence of Christ in the sacrament, the eating of Christ's body and the drinking of his blood by the unworthy, and the sacrifice of the Mass.

The core of the First Book[74] consists of the following affirmations:

1. Those persons who are aware of their sin and hunger for forgiveness will be fed by God, while those who lack this awareness will not be fed. In this case, the feeding involves a spiritual eating which the physical eating in the sacrament signifies.
2. This food is nothing other than Christ himself (cf. Matt. 11:28; John 6:35), who spiritually nourishes all good Christians with his body and blood so that they become more spiritually perfect.
3. Although Christ compares his flesh and blood to food ("meat") and drink, he is certainly more than earthly,

condemnation we deserve and heap upon ourselves from day to day by our unhappy and disordered life..." (translation from LWC, 201).

[73] Thomas Cranmer, *A Defense of the True and Catholic Doctrine of the Sacrament of the Body and Blood of our Savior Christ* (1550), ed. Charles H. H. Wright (London: Charles J. Thynne, 1907; repr., Eugene, OR: Wipf and Stock, 2004).

[74] Cranmer, *Defense*, 12-33.

physical food because he nourishes both body and soul and does so forever.

4. The physical experience of the sacrament serves to confirm the spiritual: just as the sensible elements of bread and wine nourish our bodies, we ought to believe that Christ himself nourishes our souls.
5. Bread and wine were designated as the sacramental elements by Christ because they represent the spiritual union of Christians: just as many grains are ground and made into one loaf and many grapes pressed into a single container, so many Christians are joined spiritually to Christ and each other.
6. The bread and wine also offer other analogies: (1) just as they become one with the human body that eats and digests them to become a composite whole, so all Christians are formed into one body with each other and with Christ; (2) just as one loaf and one cup are given to all communicants, so Christ gives himself to each believing Christian to feed on them spiritually; and (3) just as an arm or leg that is cut off from the body receives no nourishment from the body, so the wicked who are cut off from the body of Christ do not feed on Christ's body and blood spiritually.
7. The purpose of the sacrament is to move Christians to live in harmony with each other, because they recognize that they are joined together in Christ.
8. True eating and drinking occurs when people believe they are forgiven in Christ and united with him, and this faith is worked by the Holy Spirit, and confirmed by the outward elements.

All of these truths should lead believers to desire the sacrament. Because the Supper offers forgiveness and peace, and confirms God's saving promises, those who eat and drink in faith have everlasting life.

Following is a summary of Cranmer's arguments against those doctrines that he believed obscured a true eating of the sacrament (Books 2-5).

Transubstantiation. New Testament texts effectively rule out a doctrine of transubstantiation. The first cup that Christ gave to his disciples in Luke 22 (v. 17) could only be wine since it was given before Christ "consecrated" it through a blessing. The blood of Christ was spiritually present throughout the whole Supper. Furthermore, because Christ refers to the "fruit of the vine" (Matt. 26:29; Mark 14:25), rather than his "blood," when the meal was ended, he could not have been thinking of a material change in the wine. In 1 Cor. 10:16b ("And is not the bread that we break a participation in the body of Christ?"), Paul refers only to "bread," rather than the body of Christ, even though the reference is clearly to something that has been consecrated. Also, when he speaks (10:17) of our being "partakers of one bread and one cup" (*sic*), the language likewise would not indicate transubstantiation.[75]

Transubstantiation goes against natural reason and the senses. It is manifest that leftover wine will go sour and bread will mold, which only happens to true bread and wine, not to things that only appear to be bread and wine. Additionally, because leftover elements are sometimes burned, defenders of transubstantiation would have to admit that Christ is being burned, or that only the accidents of bread and wine are being burned without their substance, which defies reason.[76] Transubstantiation is contrary to the senses, since we can clearly see bread and wine on the table. Although faith means believing in unseen things, faith does not ask us to disbelieve what we see in everyday life. Neither is faith contrary to the senses, but rather the senses can confirm faith, as when Thomas put his hand into the side of Christ and confirmed the resurrection. The suggestion that there is only the appearance of bread and wine in the Supper is an affirmation of *docetism*, the heretical position that Christ only *appeared* to suffer. For that matter, if the senses are not to be trusted,

[75] Cranmer, *Defense*, 35-40.

[76] Cranmer, *Defense*, 41.

then the Supper itself could well be an illusion.[77] Cranmer concludes that patristic authors as a whole teach that the bread remains bread even after consecration. In that case, proponents of transubstantiation either have to abandon that doctrine, or otherwise be considered christological Nestorians, since Nestorius held that the nature of God did not remain in Christ after the Incarnation.

Cranmer then proceeds to counter three arguments advanced by proponents of transubstantiation. First, regarding the assertion that Christ's words "This is my body" implies a change in the substance of the bread and wine, Cranmer argues that if such were truly the case, every celebration of the Lord's Supper creates a new Christ who is essentially made out of bread. This would then lead to various contradictions, e.g., that if the crucified body of Christ was not made of bread, but the body eaten in the Supper is made of bread, then the body eaten in the Supper is different from the one that was crucified.[78] Second, while proponents argue that the substance of bread cannot remain, otherwise Christ is *inpanated* (made into bread), Cranmer holds that since there is nothing more than a sacramental joining of Christ to the bread, he is no more turned into bread than the Holy Spirit is turned into water in the sacrament of baptism. If Christ really does make the bread his body, transubstantiation implies that Christ is united to the bread in both nature and person, which is a greater unity than the union of his humanity with the Godhead, which is in person only![79] Third, as for the argument that Christ cannot be giving material bread, since John 6:51 speaks of Christ giving his flesh for the life of the world, and hence the substance of bread cannot be present, Cranmer counters that Christ is not even speaking of sacramental bread or eating in this passage, since he often speaks of spiritual bread (e.g., "I am the bread of life," etc. John 6:35).[80]

---

[77] Cranmer, *Defense*, 42-45.

[78] Cranmer, *Defense*, 67.

[79] Cranmer, *Defense*, 71-72.

[80] Cranmer, *Defense*, 72-73.

Despite his rejection of transubstantiation, Cranmer does recognize a kind of transformation of the bread:

> And yet the bread is changed, not in shape, nor substance, but in nature, as Cyprian truly saith, not meaning that the natural substance of bread is clean gone, but that by God's Word there is added thereto another higher property, nature, and condition, far passing the nature and condition of common bread, that is to say, that the bread doth show unto us, as the same Cyprian saith, that we be partakers of the Spirit of God, and most purely joined unto Christ, and spiritually fed with his flesh and blood; so that now the said mystical bread is both a corporal food for the body, and a spiritual food for the soul.[81]

Cranmer finds support for this spiritual change in *De iis qui initiantur Mysteriis*, attributed to Ambrose of Milan, which speaks about a change not in the substance but in the nature of bread and wine. Specifically, the sacramental elements obtain a higher nature and should be received as holy food and drink. Through the working of the Holy Spirit, they can provide a spiritual feeding with the body and blood of Christ from heaven.[82] This change does not involve the annihilation of the substance of the elements. By maintaining that bread and wine undergo no substantial change, we avoid the difficulties and absurdities engendered by the doctrine of transubstantiation, e.g., that only the accidents or appearances of bread and wine are consumed in the Supper (contrary to reason), or that the substance of Christ's body is present without any accidents.

The presence of Christ in the sacrament. The creedal affirmation of Christ's ascension into heaven and session at the Father's right hand, as well as biblical passages referring to the ascension (e.g., Mark 16:19) and his session (e.g., Heb. 10:12), demonstrate that the human nature of Christ remains in heaven.[83] While Christ is present

[81] Cranmer, *Defense*, 75.

[82] Cranmer, *Defense*, 88-89.

[83] Cranmer, *Defense*, 103-4.

everywhere according to his divinity, his humanity (post-ascension) remains in one place and thus Christ cannot be bodily present in the Supper. The very nature of a body is to be in one place at a time, rather than to be omnipresent (ubiquitous). Even though Christ's body became immortal after the resurrection and ascension, its basic nature did not change, otherwise it would not be a body.[84] Those who teach the bodily presence of Christ in the Lord's Supper are thus guilty of two errors: of confounding (i.e., confusing) the two natures of Christ (divinity and humanity), and of dividing or separating the human nature or body of Christ into a visible and natural man who is in heaven, and another who is present simultaneously in all eucharistic elements.[85]

While his opponents held that the bodily presence of Christ is assured by Jesus' words "This is my body…" etc., Cranmer maintains that these words are a figure of speech, because in ordinary speech we would not say that bread is "Christ's body" nor is wine his "blood." Neither would we say that we eat the body of Christ or drink his blood because that would be repugnant to Christians. In this case, (as Zwingli and Calvin argue), we refer to a signifier using the name of the thing signified, something that is well attested in Scriptures. When Christ spoke of eating his flesh and drinking his blood in John 6, he must have been referring to something spiritual rather than literal since (as with Zwingli) eating Christ's flesh would be to no avail (6:63). Furthermore, since Christ's words are "spirit and life," the whole discourse of John 6 cannot be referring to carnal eating, but rather to a spiritual one.[86]

Because the presence of Christ is tied to consecration, Cranmer then takes up this topic briefly. He defines consecration as "the separation of anything from a profane and worldly use unto a spiritual and godly use."[87] The eucharistic consecration is effected by God, through the Words of Institution, such that those with

---

[84] Cranmer, *Defense*, 104-9.

[85] Cranmer, *Defense*, 118-19.

[86] Cranmer, *Defense*, 129-130.

[87] Cranmer, *Defense*, 181.

faith spiritually feed upon Christ, for God's operation is not in the elements themselves, but in the hearts of those who receive them in faith by the operation of the Holy Spirit.[88]

Eating by the unworthy. On the basis of John 6:47-51, Cranmer argues that there is no carnal eating of the flesh of Christ, but rather a spiritual eating that takes place through faith. While both the good and the bad ate the manna in the wilderness, the eating of Christ's flesh is different precisely because (1) eating his flesh means believing him; and (2) believing him leads to eternal life. In that case, it is impossible for unbelievers and the wicked to truly eat the flesh/drink the blood of Christ.[89] The spiritual eating by true believers does not involve the mouth or digestive system, but the soul. Like Calvin, Cranmer maintains that while both believers and unbelievers eat the sensible sacrament of Christ's body and blood, only true believers engage in the spiritual eating of Christ's body and blood that leads to eternal life.[90] If someone could receive the body and blood of the Lord, and yet not have the Spirit of Christ, then the implication is that Christ's body is divided from his Spirit, and (by extension) his humanity is divided from his divinity. Any suggestion that the wicked have the Spirit of Christ is contrary to Scripture (cf. Rom. 8:9).[91] 1 Cor. 11:27 does not support the idea that the unworthy eat the body and blood of the Lord, since Paul is only referring to the sacramental bread and cup, rather than the true body and blood.[92] In those places where ancient authors apparently did speak of the "body and blood" being received by the unworthy (e.g., Judas), they were speaking of the "sacrament" rather than the literal body and blood, i.e., they were speaking figuratively.[93]

In this same Book (4) Cranmer also takes up the question of sacramental adoration, which he argues is the worship of a visible

[88] Cranmer, *Defense*, 185-87.

[89] Cranmer, *Defense*, 200.

[90] Cranmer, *Defense*, 213.

[91] Cranmer, *Defense*, 216.

[92] Cranmer, *Defense*, 217-18.

[93] Cranmer, *Defense*, 221.

creature. He discounts the idea that it is the worship of the unseen object of faith, since (in reality) worshippers go from place to place to venerate the reserved sacrament, rather than sitting in one place to worship quietly. It is really the worship of nothing at all, if the bread and wine are only the appearance of bread and wine. Even the true body and blood of Christ cannot be worshipped, since "the flesh availeth nothing (John 6:63)." Adoration of the sacramental elements is inappropriate since they only represent Christ's body and blood. Sounding much like Calvin, Cranmer states that the true worship of Christ happens when we lift our hearts and minds to heaven.[94]

The Mass as a sacrifice. Cranmer condemns the notion that the Mass is a propitiatory (atoning) sacrifice for the living and the dead because this view essentially nullifies the one and only sacrifice of Christ (Heb. 9:23-28). Rather than offering the blood of animals, Christ offered his own blood, and rather than going into the holy of holies of the Temple, Christ ascended into heaven where he perpetually makes intercession for a sinful humanity, displaying his body. Thus, unlike the sacrifices of the Old Testament, Christ's own sacrifice does not need to be repeated, because it is sufficient for all times and for all people. Cranmer distinguishes between Christ's *propitiatory sacrifice,* by which he offers himself to the Father as an atonement for sin, versus a *thanksgiving sacrifice* by which Christians offer themselves and all that they have to Christ and to the Father.[95] So perfect and sufficient was Christ's own propitiatory sacrifice that

> we may look for none other priest, nor sacrifice, to take away our sins, but only him and his sacrifice. And as he, dying once, was offered for all, so, as much as pertained to him, he took all men's sin unto himself. So that now there remaineth no [more] sacrifices for sin, but extreme judgment at the last day....[96]

---

[94] Cranmer, *Defense*, 224-31.

[95] Cranmer, *Defense*, 235.

[96] Cranmer, *Defense*, 237.

In that case, there can be no more offering of Christ now in the life of the church.

Although the Old Testament sacrifices might have been called "sin offerings" and the like, in truth they could not atone for human sin (cf. Heb. 10:4). Rather, they were figures meant to foreshadow the more perfect sacrifice of Christ which was to come later. These actions were called "sacrifices for sin" according to the practice whereby a sign takes on the name of the thing signified. While some Old Testament sacrifices allowed sinners who were cast out from the worship assembly to return to it, and the church has similar "sacraments," in neither case do the actions bring reconciliation with God.[97]

Thus, nothing done in the Mass can merit the forgiveness of sins for the priest, the living, or for the dead, and any doctrine that suggests that this is possible contradicts the gospel. Since Christ himself is the only true sacrifice, the priest cannot be doing the same thing as Christ himself, and it is blasphemous to suggest that he can, or that the church needs such a ministry, since Christ's sacrifice is sufficient for the remission of our sins. Christ's own sacrifice cannot be dependent on the action of the priest,[98] and the priestly office of the church is not a continuation of Christ's priesthood (cf. Heb. 7:23-28). Rejected is the argument that priests are only making the same sacrifice that Christ made, since the implication is that Christ is crucified every day, which makes priests worse than the original killers of Christ.[99]

Since the Mass involves no sacrificing by which one person does something for another, votive Masses for special intentions, especially those involving only a priest, are ruled out. The merits of Christ's sacrifice cannot be transferred to others, but must be received by each individual who receives communion for him/herself. Furthermore, there is no divinely-instituted distinction between priests and laypeople whereby priests can offer the Mass

---

[97] Cranmer, *Defense*, 238-39.

[98] Cranmer, *Defense*, 240.

[99] Cranmer, *Defense*, 241.

for the sake of others nor eat the elements for them. The role of the priest is to preside over the liturgy and distribute the elements to the people for their benefit.[100] Private Masses, as well as multiple Masses each day, were unknown in the ancient church, but were a later development that arose due to superstition and greed. Neither did ancient authors understand the Mass in a sacrificial sense; when they called it a "sacrifice," they were referring principally to the sacrifice of praise and thanksgiving, and not to any sacrifice for sin. Similarly unknown in the ancient church was the view that the Mass liberates souls from purgatory or offers remedies for various earthly ills (e.g., bad weather, sickness); these were later "inventions" of a church that had departed from the norms of the primitive church.[101]

Cranmer's eucharistic theology was obviously influenced by Zwingli and Calvin. Zwingli's insistence on the unprofitability of eating Christ's flesh (John 6:63), the impossibility of a bodily presence due to the ascension, and the metaphoric interpretation of the Words of Institution, all find their way into the *Defense*. However, Cranmer was not a pure Zwinglian, for the Lord's Supper is more to him than an act of commemoration. Indeed, along Calvinistic lines, Cranmer believed that God uses the Supper to sanctify Christians, and so we find the motifs of spiritual food and spiritual eating, the analogical relationship between physical and spiritual eating, the role of the Holy Spirit in facilitating this spiritual eating, and an emphasis on the benefits received in the Supper. For Cranmer, like Calvin, the action of the Lord's Supper is primarily directed from God to the assembly, rather than from the assembly to God, as in Zwingli.

Of course, this is not to suggest that Cranmer brought no original thought to the *Defense*. The themes of Christ's one perfect sacrifice and his spiritually feeding believers go beyond the continental Reformers and will have a lasting influence on Anglican liturgy.

The first *Book of Common Prayer* was compiled under Cranmer's leadership in late 1548 and came into use on Pentecost Day 1549. In broad outline the "Service for the Lord's Supper, and the Holy

[100] Cranmer, *Defense*, 246.

[101] Cranmer, *Defense*, 253-56.

Communion (commonly called the Mass)"[102] consisted of the following:

Introit (Choir)
Lord's Prayer (priest)
Collect for Purity (priest)
Introit psalm (priest)
Nine-fold kyrie
Gloria in Excelsis
Greeting and collect of the day
Collect for the king
Epistle
Gospel
Nicene Creed
Sermon
Exhortations (optional)
Offertory sentences
Procession with offerings
Preparation of elements
Preface dialog
Preface (five proper)
Sanctus and Benedictus
Eucharistic Prayer (including intercessions)
Lord's Prayer
Peace
Exhortation to communion and invitation to confession
Confession and absolution
Comfortable Words
Prayer of Humble Access
Distribution of elements (accompanied by Agnus Dei)
Post-communion sentences
Prayer of thanksgiving
Benediction

[102] "The Supper of the Lord, and Holy Communion, Commonly Called the Mass," BCP 1549, PEER, 234-43.

The service of the Word differed little from that of the Latin rite used during Cranmer's time, except that the sermon was now to follow the creed, as in the Lutheran liturgy. The two optional exhortations, which concerned participation in Holy Communion, were taken from the Order for Communion that appeared in 1548. The first focused on repenting from sin and coming to the Table with faith in the gospel promises connected to the Supper. The second reminded communicants of the need to be reconciled with neighbors before receiving communion, and invited those with troubled consciences to seek out their priests for confession and absolution.[103] The Offertory was completely changed in meaning and action: the people now come forward to deposit their offerings in a "poor box" rather than at the altar (for "Mass intentions"), and those who were to commune remained in the choir area while non-communicants departed. The choir sang one or more of the Offertory sentences which dealt with charity and good works. The minister prepared the elements on the altar, but gone were the accompanying offertory prayers that expressed a sacrificial theology.

The communion liturgy began in the usual fashion, with the preface dialog, followed by introductory words and then one of the proper prefaces (Christmas, Easter, Ascension, Pentecost, and Trinity). No preface was provided for non-festive Sundays or weekdays (after Epiphany and Pentecost), which meant that the liturgy effectively offered no christological reason for giving thanks and praise during Ordinary Time. The Sanctus and Benedictus were followed by the eucharistic prayer, which began with intercessions "for the whole state of Christ's Church," including saints and the faithful departed. The consecration prayer proper opened by affirming the one and all-sufficient sacrifice of Christ on the Cross. Making the sign of the cross over the elements, the priest invoked the Word and Holy Spirit to "bless and sanctify" the elements so that "they may be unto us the body and blood of thy most dearly beloved Son Jesus Christ…." The Institution Narrative conflated the various New Testament accounts, but with none of the non-scriptural embellishing phraseology. The

[103] "The Supper of the Lord," BCP 1549, LWC, 249-52.

priest was required to take the bread and cup into his hands at the appropriate words (= the "manual acts"), but was to remain facing the altar without showing the elements to the people. The anamnesis-oblation recalled the passion, resurrection and, most appropriately, in light of its theological importance for Cranmer, the ascension. Thanks was offered for the benefits obtained by these events, and God was asked to accept the sacrifice of *praise and thanksgiving*, rather than the elements themselves. In a further move away from medieval sacrificial theology, the oblation (offering) was identified as the self-sacrifice of the worship assembly. This naturally led to a request for participants to worthily receive "the most precious body and blood" of Christ, be filled with "grace and heavenly benediction," and be made one body in Christ. In language echoing the *Supplices te* petition of the Roman Canon, request was made that the angels take the prayers of the assembly to the Tabernacle of heaven – rather than the elements to the heavenly altar. Perhaps reflective of Eastern liturgies, this final portion was infused with penitential language ("And although we be unworthy through our manifold sins... pardoning our offenses"), thereby underscoring the grace character of the sacrament. Essentially, the consecration prayer memorialized the sacrifice of Christ on the Cross and ruled out the interpretation that the eucharistic action itself is a sacrifice offered to God for the living and the dead.

Following in the usual order was the Lord's Prayer and peace. On the basis of the self-offering of Christ, who is the Lamb of God, the assembly was invited to "keep a joyful and holy feast with the Lord." At this point the priest turned to the assembly and invited it to make confession while kneeling. The prayer of confession, beautifully and memorably worded, would become a classic piece of liturgical literature; its craftsmanship evident in rhythmic cadences and balanced phraseology as in the following: "We do earnestly repent, and be heartily sorry for these our misdoings; *the remembrance of them is grievous unto us; the burden of them is intolerable*." Cast in the precatory form, the absolution likewise contained elegant language: "Almighty God...have mercy upon you, pardon and deliver you from all your sins; confirm and strengthen you in all goodness, and bring you to everlasting life; through Jesus Christ our Lord." Then followed the Comfortable Words, scripture verses that promise salvation to believers and forgiveness to the repentant. The Prayer of Humble Access ("We do not presume to come…") was read by the priest who knelt while facing the altar. Both bread and wine were distributed, beginning with the priest who communes himself, then the ministers who assist with the distribution, and finally the people, who were to receive the bread directly into their mouths in order to avoid superstitious practices. The traditional distribution formulas were retained ("The body/blood of our Lord Jesus Christ, which was given/shed for thee, preserve thy body and soul unto everlasting life"). During the distribution, the choir sang the Agnus Dei ("Lamb of God, you take away the sins of the world," etc.), and then, after communion, it sang one or more biblical sentences pertaining to discipleship, holy living, or faithfulness.The prayer of thanksgiving echoed the themes of "spiritual food" and holy living found in the *Defense*. A blessing concluded the service.

The 1549 service represents a compromise between traditional Catholicism and emerging Protestantism. Many of the outward, visible aspects of the traditional Mass remained, e.g., vestments, choral singing, the use of unleavened bread (albeit of a "thicker" variety than previously), and kneeling. Also retained was the overall liturgical shape of Word-Sacrament, texts such as the Kyrie, Gloria in Excelsis, the creed and the Agnus Dei, prayer for the dead, the liturgical calendar, and lectionary. Yet, the service was in English, communion was received in both kinds, and adoration of the sacrament and private Masses were abolished. While the "Word and Spirit" consecration formula and the distribution formulas might have hinted of the real presence, the removal of both the elevation and reservation of the elements pointed in a different direction theologically. Practically everything suggestive of a sacrificial Mass was eliminated and the one and all-sufficient sacrifice of Christ was extolled. Additionally, sacrifice was expressed in terms of praise and thanksgiving and self-offering. Worthy reception by the communicants was also stressed.

Thus, the influence of the author of the *Defense* is readily discernible in this service.

Yet, the BCP 1549 did not please all factions in the Church of England, and may have been intended only as an interim measure toward a more thorough-going reform. Martin Bucer prepared a critique of the Prayer Book that had a significant impact.[104] Already in early 1551 Cranmer and other bishops discussed and agreed upon a number of changes. A more thoroughly-reformed (i.e., Protestant) Prayer Book with none of the conservative gestures was authorized for use beginning on All Saints Day 1552.

The revised service of Holy Communion,[105] no longer called the "Mass," did away with many of the traditional outward trappings: instead of the alb and stole, the surplice was to be worn by the priest, a change probably due to Bucer's influence;[106] stone altars were removed and replaced by wooden tables; and only the Gloria in Exclesis was to be sung.[107] The order of service was:

Lord's Prayer
Collect for Purity
Ten Commandments (with response, "Lord have mercy upon us, and incline our hearts to keep this law.")
Collect for the day
Collect for the king
Epistle
Gospel
Nicene Creed (spoken)
Sermon
Notices
Almsgiving with sentences

---

[104] Arthur Roberts, *A Review of the Book of Common Prayer, Drawn Up by Martin Bucer, Briefly Analyzed and Abridged* (London: James Nisbet and Co., 1853; repr., Nabu Public Domain Reprints, 2014).

[105] "The Order for the Administration of the Lord's Supper or Holy Communion," BCP 1552, PEER, 246-49.

[106] Roberts, *A Review by Bucer*, 6-7.

[107] "*The Book of Common Prayer* 1552 (editor's introduction)," PEER, 244.

Intercessions
Exhortation to communion and invitation to confession
Confession and absolution
Comfortable Words
Preface dialog
Preface (five proper)
Sanctus (without the Benedictus)
Prayer of Humble Access
Eucharistic prayer
Words of Institution
Distribution of the elements
Lord's Prayer
Prayer of oblation or thanksgiving
Gloria in Exclesis
Benediction

The Introit was omitted and the Ten Commandments were inserted after the Collect for Purity, suggesting that worshippers prepare by reflecting on the Law.[108] The sermon was followed by notices about upcoming feast and fast days and an exhortation to remember the poor. The term "offertory" was dropped, but the scriptural sentences were retained and *spoken* by the priest as the wardens gathered the offerings of the people. Gone was the movement of the people into the choir to deposit their offerings prior to communion, and thus the association between charity and the Supper. Also deleted was the instruction pertaining to the placement of the elements on the table, perhaps to dispel the impression of an offertory with sacrificial overtones.[109] The intercessory prayers were placed after the offering ("almsgiving") and were made only for the "church militant" (i.e., the living), the petitions for saints and the faithful departed having been deleted to avoid suggesting a sacrifice for the dead.[110] A new

[108] This change may have been inspired by Calvin's Strasbourg liturgy. See John Calvin, "The Form of Church Prayers," LWC, 198.

[109] "The First and Second Prayer Books of Edward VI (editor's introduction)," LWC, 241.

[110] "*The Book of Common Prayer* 1552 (editor's introduction)," PEER, 244.

exhortation focused on encouraging people to receive communion, which suggests a lack of popular enthusiasm for the sacrament. A second exhortation, focused on worthy communion, encouraged reconciliation with the neighbor, while a third called for repentance and amendment of life. These were followed by the penitential material from the 1549 rite (invitation to confession, prayer of confession, absolution, and Comfortable Words). When there were no communicants on "holy days," everything up through the intercessory prayers was to be said, and the confession and eucharistic liturgy were to be omitted.

The eucharistic liturgy began with the dialog and proper preface as before. The Benedictus was removed so that a real or bodily presence of Christ was not implied. Previously situated just before the communion, the Prayer of Humble Access was placed after the Sanctus and was shorn of the phrase "in these holy mysteries." Both of these changes were meant to avoid any hint of eucharistic adoration.[111] The prayer is made at "God's board" (table) rather than the "altar" so as not to connote a sacrifice. Like its predecessor, the 1552 eucharistic prayer began with a long preamble memorializing the one and sufficient sacrifice of Christ. But instead of the consecration formula with its "Word and Spirit" language, there followed this petition:

> Hear us, O merciful Father, we beseech thee; and grant that we, receiving thy creatures of bread and wine, according to thy Son our saviour Jesus Christ's holy institution, in remembrance of his death and passion, may be partakers of his most blessed body and blood....

This change owed to Bucer's objection to the "bless and sanctify" language in the 1549 rite.[112] The new prayer also reflected Cranmer's distinction between receiving the elements versus receiving the body and blood of the Lord, since the former is true for all recipients and the latter only for the godly; hence the need to petition a partaking of

[111] "*The Book of Common Prayer* 1552 (editor's introduction)," PEER, 244.

[112] Roberts, *A Review by Bucer*, 13-16.

the Lord's body and blood. Thus, the new prayer was more supportive of a *receptionist* view whereby faithful communicants receive the body and blood of Christ without there being any change in the elements. A slightly revised version of the Words of Institution followed, but the anamnesis-oblation of the 1549 service ("Wherefore, O Lord heavenly Father, according to the institution...") was omitted and the oblation ("...entirely desiring thy fatherly goodness mercifully to accept this our sacrifice...") appeared as the first of two optional post-communion prayers (see below). As in the services of Zwingli, Luther, and Bucer, the elements were distributed immediately after the Words of Institution so that the action followed its biblical warrant.[113] Insofar as there was no "Amen" following the Words of Institution, the eating and drinking occurred within the context of prayer. This suggests that the elements are consecrated in order to be received by the people – as opposed to being adored.

Communion took place according to the manner stipulated in the BCP 1549. To further dispel suggestions of transubstantiation or a bodily presence, a more normal kind of bread was to be used, and any "leftovers" were for the priest's own use. Additionally, new distribution formulas that reflected Cranmer's notion of spiritual eating and that ruled out a bodily presence were provided:

> Take and eat this, in remembrance that Christ died for thee, and feed on him in thy heart by faith with thanksgiving.
>
> Drink this in remembrance that Christ's blood was shed for thee, and be thankful.

Communion was only to be celebrated when a "good number" of persons were present to commune with the priest. In small parishes with no more than twenty members, there had to be at least three or four communicants. Due to Bucer's concerns about the pastoral advisability of communing only once per year,[114] the minimum was raised to three times a year, Easter being one of these. Although the

---

[113] "*The Book of Common Prayer* 1552 (editor's introduction)," PEER, 245.

[114] Roberts, *A Review by Bucer*, 7.

communicants still knelt to receive communion, a concluding rubric – the infamous "Black Rubric" – declared that this posture was meant to convey humility and reverence, and should not be taken to imply the adoration of the sacrament, since the true body and blood of Christ are in heaven. This rather extraordinary apologetic rubric was occasioned by a significant public controversy on the matter of kneeling to receive the elements.[115]

Following communion, the Lord's Prayer was said with the people repeating each petition after the priest. The new post-communion prayer, based on the old oblation, with its references to the sacrifice of praise and thanksgiving and the self-offering of the communicants, had a certain logic: having received communion, the assembly responded by requesting the benefits of communion and by offering their very lives to God. Omitted was the reference to receiving "the most precious body and blood of thy Son Jesus Christ." The old reference to the assembly's prayers being taken to heaven by the angels was deleted, undoubtedly because Bucer had questioned the scriptural basis of such language.[116] The previous thanksgiving prayer was provided for optional use as well. The service concluded with the Gloria in Excelsis (said or sung) and the blessing.

With the 1552 service, Cranmer achieved a liturgy more in line with the continental Reformers and with his own *Defense*. It was now nearly impossible to extrapolate a real, bodily presence or a sacrifice, the two doctrines that Cranmer attacked in the *Defense*. Here was a rite that embodied the Protestant *lex credendi*. Twenty-first century Christians influenced by the liturgical movement might lament the loss of the 1549 rite's classical eucharistic prayer structure with its sense of thanksgiving and offering. Essentially, the 1552 eucharistic prayer is a prayer for worthy communion. The relocation of the Gloria in Excelsis to the post-communion unfortunately robs the service of the Word of an element of praise and thanksgiving. Finally,

---

115 "The First and Second Prayer Books of Edward VI (editor's introduction)," LWC, 242-43, 283-84.

116 Roberts, *A Review by Bucer*, 16. The amended language that Bucer proposed was not adopted.

the lack of sung elements (with the exception of the Gloria), made for a less aesthetically pleasing and interesting rite, especially when we consider that the sixteenth-century Anglican church did not sing congregational hymns.

Yet, the new location of the intercessions resonated with ancient documents such as Justin's *First Apology* and the Liturgy of Addai and Mari; coming after the preface in the 1549 rite, the intercessions separated the praise of the eucharistic prayer from the warrant for that praise contained in the proper preface. Additionally, the 1552 eucharistic prayer, not unlike the prayer in Luther's 1523 *Formula Missae* placed the focus on Christ and those words of his that express the central meaning of the Supper, viz., "this is my body." Undoubtedly, in a time of ignorance and confusion, such a refocusing on the christological center of the Supper was needed and welcomed.

Although banned during the rule of Queen Mary (1553-58), the BCP 1552 was restored in 1559 under Elizabeth with minor changes, and remained practically unchanged until 1662. In the previous year, the Convocation (the church's constitutional body) met and made numerous changes to the Prayer Book, although most of these were not significant. In May 1662, the king approved a bill authorizing the new Prayer Book, which began its official life in August of that same year.

The eucharistic service of the BCP 1662[117] contained essentially the same words as the 1552 service, but there were a number of small changes that impacted the *manner* in which the service was celebrated. These were made both for the benefit of the "catholic" or "Laudian" party as well as for Presbyterians. The word "Offertory" was restored and the communion elements along with the monetary offering were to be placed on the table. During the eucharistic prayer, now called "The Prayer of Consecration," the minister was to take the paten (plate) and cup into his hands at the appropriate words of the Institution Narrative, as well as *break* the bread. The

[117] "The Order for the Administration of the Lord's Supper or Holy Communion," BCP 1662, PEER, 279-82.

latter actions were also favoured by Presbyterians, who advocated these in their *Exceptions to the Prayer Book*. Consecration of the elements was now clearly distinguished from their consumption because of the placement of the word "Amen" following the Words of Institution. Further underscoring eucharistic consecration was the rubric to consecrate any new bread and wine needed for the distribution. Unused elements were to be placed back on the table and covered with a linen cloth; they were not for the priest's personal use. After the service these were consumed and not carried out of the church. These rubrics concerning additional and unused elements were both influenced by the Scottish *Book of Common Prayer* of 1637. The so-called "Black Rubric" on kneeling, which had been omitted from the Elizabethan Prayer Book, was restored, but was reworded so as to deny a corporeal presence rather than a real and essential presence. Thus, was ruled out *a particular understanding* of Christ's presence, not that presence entirely.[118] The 1662 eucharistic service represented a compromise between two positions, and favors neither. It continues in use among Anglicans throughout the world and became the basis of the Lord's Supper liturgy prepared by John Wesley for the Methodists in North America.

Menno Simons and Balthasar Hübmaier

Menno Simons set forth his eucharistic theology in a section of his *Foundation of Christian Doctrine* (1539).[119] He describes the Supper in terms of (1) a memorial of Christ's death where bread and wine signify the body and blood of Christ; (2) an admonishment to Christian unity and love; (3) an incitement to true Christian living; and (4) a communion in the body and blood of Christ. The latter is not something mysteriously effected by Christ through the partaking of the elements, but occurs when the communicants come to the table as partakers of Christ who truly live a Christian life and display Christian virtues. For Simons, the emphasis is on how the *communicants*, rather than the *elements*, embody Christ. Like Zwingli,

---

118 "*The Book of Common Prayer* 1662 (editor's introduction)," PEER, 278.

119 Simons, *Foundation*, CWMS, 142-58.

Simons holds that the elements do not contain the flesh and blood of Christ since the true body of Christ is in heaven on account of the ascension.[120] He also rejects the teachings of propitiatory sacrifice and transubstantiation. In arguing against the latter, Simons adopts the Zwinglian interpretation of John 6 whereby "eating Christ's flesh" is understood spiritually. Because only the Word of Christ and his saving death can forgive sins, communion does not remit the sins of participants. Hence, Simons is far from Luther's understanding of the Lord's Supper.

The only Anabaptist eucharistic rite committed to writing appeared in an essay by Balthasar Hübmaier (ca. 1480-1528) entitled *A Form of the Supper of Christ.*[121] Preparation began a week prior with a confession of sins, and the service proper consisted of:

Reading and exposition of Scripture
Congregational response (the hymn "Stay with us, O Christ")
Further teaching on the scripture text "from one to whom something is revealed"
Self-examination according to 1 Corinthians 11
Silence
Lord's Prayer
Pledge of love
Prayer of thanksgiving
Breaking and distribution of bread as the Words of Institution are spoken
Exclamation of thanks
Passing of the cup as the Words of Institution are spoken
Call to live the baptismal covenant
Benediction[122]

---

[120] Simons, *Foundation*, CWMS, 143

[121] *Balthasar Hübmaier, Theologian of Anabaptism,* tr. and ed. H. W. Pipkin and John H. Yoder (Scottdale, PA: Herald Press, 1989).

[122] Frank C. Senn, *Introduction to Christian Liturgy* (Minneapolis: Fortress Press, 2012), 52-53.

Hübmaier refers to the Supper as a "sacrament," but understands it primarily as a memorial of Christ's suffering and death to be celebrated regularly. The elements are nothing more than bread and wine, and do not convey the bodily presence of Christ. He does, however, speak of a spiritual eating that takes place through faith and thus he hints of a "kind of sacramental presence of Christ."[123] Stressing worthy participation, Hübmaier's rite provided for a time of self-examination in which worshippers reflected on their willingness to suffer with Christ. Exhortations that stressed mutual love and upright living were also included.

By and large, the Lord's Supper in sixteenth-century Anabaptism usually did not involve set service orders and tended to be informal. Leaders chosen from among local congregation members presided and preached at communion services held once every quarter. Normal service components were hymn singing, Bible readings, prayer, preaching, and the breaking of the bread done in connection with the reading of the Institution Narrative.[124] The eucharistic theology and practice of sixteenth-century Anabaptists would influence Baptist and Brethren churches in the seventeenth and eighteenth centuries respectively.

John and Charles Wesley

John Wesley (1703-91) was an Anglican priest who led a revival aimed at evangelizing those neglected by the established church in England during a time of rapid industrialization and population shifts. Wesley especially desired that Christians receive the sacrament on a regular basis, and he himself took communion on average of twice weekly.[125] Following the sixteenth-century Reformers, Wesley rejects transubstantiation, withholding the cup from the laity, the

[123] Roger E. Olson, "The Baptist View," in *The Lord's Supper: Five Views,* ed. Gordon T. Smith (Downers Grove, IL: IVP Academic, 2008), 97.

[124] James F. White, *Protestant Worship: Traditions in Transition* (Louisville: Westminster John Knox Press, 1989), 87.

[125] John C. Bowmer, *The Sacrament of the Lord's Supper in Early Methodism* (London: Dacre Press, 1951), 55.

Mass as a propitiatory sacrifice of Christ, and the adoration of the elements.[126] Like Calvin and Cranmer, he denies a bodily presence in the Supper since (1) the words "this is my body" are figurative; and (2) Christ's body resides in heaven as a consequence of the ascension. Also, like the aforementioned theologians, Wesley speaks of the Supper as a memorial of Christ's death, the eating and drinking serving as an outward sign of an invisible grace. More along Lutheran lines, however, Wesley refers to the Supper as a means of grace whose effect is brought about by God alone through the power of the Holy Spirit.[127] It grants the forgiveness of sins, strength, and refreshment, and leads to perfection.[128] The eucharistic hymns composed by John's brother, Charles, and edited by John, epitomize Wesleyan eucharistic theology. How the elements become a divine means of grace is a mystery (Hymn 57) and a localized presence is denied (Hymn 63). The all-sufficiency of Christ's sacrifice on Calvary is stressed (Hymns 116-127), while the church's sacrifice of praise and thanksgiving and its self-offering is joined to the self-offering of Christ who takes us into the Father's presence.[129]

Representative of Charles Wesley's eucharistic hymns is *Victim Divine*:

> Victim divine, Thy grace we claim,
> While thus Thy precious death we show:
> Once offered up a spotless Lamb,
> In Thy great temple here below,
> Thou didst for all mankind atone,
> And standest now before the throne.

---

[126] *Roman Catechism, Faithfully Drawn out of the Allowed Writings of the Church of Rome, with a Reply Thereto* (1749), in *The Works of John Wesley*, Vol. X (Grand Rapids: Zondervan Publishing House, 1958), 117-22.

[127] John Wesley, *The Means of Grace* II.3, WJW 1, 382.

[128] John Wesley, *The Duty of Constant Communion* II.2 (1732), WJW 3, 429.

[129] *Hymns of the Lord's Supper by John Wesley and Charles Wesley* (Bristol: Felix Farley, 1745; repr., Madison, NJ: The Charles Wesley Society, 1995), vii.

Thou standest in the holy place,
As now for guilty sinners slain;
The blood of sprinkling speaks, and prays,
All prevalent for helpless man;
Thy blood is still our ransom found,
And speaks salvation all around.

The smoke of Thy atonement here
Darkened the sun, and rent the veil,
Made the new way to Heaven appear,
And showed the great Invisible;
Well pleased in Thee, our God looked down,
And calls His rebels to a crown.

He still respects Thy sacrifice;
Its savor sweet doth always please:
The offering smokes through earth and skies,
Diffusing life, and joy, and peace;
To these, Thy lower courts, it comes,
And fills them with divine perfumes.

We need not now go up to Heaven,
To bring the long sought Savior down;
Thou art to all already given,
Thou dost e'en now Thy banquet crown:
To every faithful soul appear,
And show Thy real presence here![130]

Remarkable is the manner in which this hymn describes the sacrifice of Christ using images and motifs of the Old Testament sacrificial cult, much like the New Testament Letter to the Hebrews. But even more important is the theology of Christ's sacrifice. On the one hand, it is present in heaven (stanzas 3 and 4) before the throne of the Father, who finds it pleasing. On the other hand, Christ's sacrifice is made present to the church through the Lord's Supper, which becomes

[130] LBW/PE, #202.

the very anamnesis (representation) of that sacrifice. Thus, there is no need to seek Christ in heaven. The sacrificial theology combined with the language of "real presence" makes the hymn appealing to Christians who understand the Supper as an epiphany of the Lord and a means of grace.

As for eucharistic practice, Wesley holds that a Christian should receive communion "as often as he/she can" because it is commanded by Christ. Self-examination and prayer are recommended forms of preparation, but are not absolutely necessary. More important is the "habitual preparation" of keeping God's commands and desiring to receive God's promises. Wesley believed that struggles and doubts should not prevent Christians from receiving communion, since the Supper is a means of grace that strengthens the weak in faith.[131] In that sense he viewed Holy Communion as a "converting sacrament," although he never advocated giving communion to non-Christians or using the sacrament as an evangelistic tool.

The political and ecclesiastical situation in America following the Revolution prompted John Wesley to appoint ecclesiastical leadership and to prepare a service book for American Methodists. The various liturgies in the *Sunday Service* were based on those in the BCP 1662, which Wesley admired for its theological and scriptural soundness. Whereas the normal Anglican Sunday Service consisted of Morning Prayer, Litany, and the first part of the Holy Communion Service (or ante-communion), Wesley envisioned a shortened Morning Prayer, no Litany (which he relegated to weekdays), and a full service of Holy Communion *every Sunday*.[132] The order of Wesley's Sunday eucharistic service was:

Lord's Prayer (elder)
Collect for Purity
Ten Commandments (with the assembly's response of
  "Lord, have mercy upon us," etc.)
Collect for the "Supreme Rulers of these United States"
Collect for the day

[131] John Wesley, *Journal* (June 27, 1740), WJW 19, 158.

[132] John Wesley, *Letter to Dr. Coke and Mr. Asbury* (1784), JWPB, ii (34).

Epistle
Gospel
Sermon
Offertory sentences
Collection of offerings
Intercessions
Exhortation to communion and invitation to confession
Prayer of confession (elder)
Absolution
Comfortable Words
Preface dialog
Preface (five proper)
Prayer of humble access (elder)
Prayer of consecration
Distribution of elements
Lord's Prayer (elder and assembly)
Prayer of oblation
Gloria in Excelsis
Extempore prayer (optional)
Benediction[133]

Wesley essentially left the Prayer Book's service of the Word intact, with the provision of traditional lectionary readings and most of the old collects. However, the collect for the king became a prayer for the "Supreme Rulers of these United States." The Nicene Creed was omitted most likely because the Apostles' Creed had already been used during Morning Prayer. Gone were the long exhortations to worthy communion, which Wesley probably thought were unnecessary for American Methodists. Due to his rejection of priestly absolution, Wesley transformed the BCP 1662's precatory absolution formula ("Almighty God… have mercy upon you…") into a prayer addressed to God, and changed "you" to "us" to include the liturgical minister (elder). Apparently to minimize the distinction between elder and

[133] John Wesley, "The Order for the Administration of the Lord's Supper" (1784), JWPB, 125-39.

assembly members, Wesley altered the BCP 1662 rubrics so that both elder and assembly stood from the Comfortable Words through the Sanctus and knelt together for the Prayer of Humble Access and consecration prayer. Wesley omitted the rubric about the minister arranging the elements on the table, since that action would have been difficult for the elder who (apparently) was to remain kneeling with the assembly. The manual actions during the consecration were retained.[134] The consecration of additional elements, now governed by a permissive "may" rubric, was performed by repeating the entire prayer consecration, not just the Words of Institution. Apparently, Wesley rejected the traditional belief that the consecration was effected by the Words of Institution.[135] Unused elements were returned to the table, but nothing is said about consuming them immediately after the service. Only the first of the BCP 1662's post-communion prayers was retained. The Gloria in Exclesis was spoken, and the elder was at liberty to offer extempore prayer prior to the Benediction. Because most of them were irrelevant to the American context, the concluding rubrics concerning various communion-related matters were dropped, including the Black Rubric about kneeling. Nothing was said about vestments nor singing liturgical texts, although Wesley assumed the use of eucharistic hymns during the service.

Overall, Wesley's Lord's Supper liturgy witnesses to the conservatism of someone who deeply appreciated the BCP 1662. Although there were a number of omissions, these were likely made in the interest of minimizing the time needed, now that the Lord's Supper was to be celebrated every week. The streamlining of rubrics represented an adaptation to the American context where a simpler rite was necessary. Thus, the *Sunday Service* was not so much an abbreviation, but a revision of the BCP 1662.[136] If we could fault

[134] Not all versions of the Lord's Supper service contain the rubrics for the manual actions, although White argues that Wesley intended that the manual acts be retained. See JWPB (Introduction), 4.

[135] JWPB (Introductory Notes), 21.

[136] Editor's introduction, JWPB, 8.

Wesley for anything, it would be for the very minor decision to leave the minister on his knees for the consecration, thereby making the manual acts awkward to perform. But even greater censure is due Wesley's early American adherents who, following his death in 1791, mostly ignored the *Sunday Service*, except for the second half of the eucharistic service and the occasional rites.[137]

Free Church Traditions

It is generally agreed that the Englishmen John Smyth (1570-1612) and Thomas Helwys (1575-1616) founded the Baptist movement in Holland in 1610. Contacts with Anabaptists led early Baptists to adopt a Zwinglian understanding of the Supper, which rejects the ideas of a bodily presence contained in the elements and a physical eating and drinking of the Lord's body and blood. Smyth and Helwys basically viewed the Supper as a memorial of the passion and death of Christ who is present spiritually to the participants.[138] Roger Olson observes that while Baptist confessional documents from the sixteenth through the twentieth centuries do not refer to a bodily presence of Christ even in a mystical sense, some do "include language that one can interpret as sacramental in the sense that memorializing Christ's death [in the Lord's Supper] has the effect of spiritually nourishing believing participants."[139] However, this presence is not different from the Lord's presence in any other act of worship or devotion. Some early Baptists did refer to the Lord's Supper as a sacrament, but eventually the term "ordinance" came to be preferred. Practices were also shaped by Anabaptist patterns, with quarterly or even less frequent celebrations of the Lord's Supper.

Most Pentecostal churches have traditionally held a "low" or non-sacramental view of the Lord's Supper, which they normally refer to as an "ordinance" rather than a "sacrament." Zwinglian memorialism has predominated and most Pentecostals deny any bodily presence of Christ. The frequency of celebration can vary from weekly to a few

[137] James F. White, *Protestant Worship*, 158.

[138] Olson, "The Baptist View," *Five Views,* 97.

[139] Olson, "The Baptists View," *Five Views*, 101.

times a year.[140] Prescribed service orders are generally eschewed in favor of an informal, free-flowing celebration that is relatively brief. An ordained minister usually presides and only those who have come to a conscious faith (not necessarily having been baptized) receive the elements. The use of unfermented grape juice is the norm among Pentecostals.

Some voices have called for a more "sacramental" approach within Pentecostalism. Church of God theologian and bishop Daniel Tomberlin seems cautiously open to the idea of Christ's presence in the elements, based on a theology of the Incarnation.[141] Less reserved is his affirmation that, through the operation of the Spirit, Jesus comes in bread and cup and thus allows participants to "become partakers of the divine nature." He draws an analogy with the Pentecostal beliefs that (1) the "energies of God" are transferrable to material objects (e.g., handkerchiefs); and (2) God's anointing is always experienced in a tangible manner. This sacramentalism is actually not new in Pentecostalism, for he writes:

> ...early Pentecostal leaders intuitively knew that there is a "presence" inherent in the holy meal. Baptism in the Holy Spirit brought into their lives a "real presence" that anointed the sacred acts of worship. This understanding of "real presence" became associated with the Lord's Supper. It is evident that Pentecostals understood that at the table, through the power of the Holy Spirit, Christ is present.[142]

Drawing on Gregory of Palamas, Tomberlin states that worshippers partake of the "energies" of both Son and Spirit, who work interdependently in the Supper, such that we encounter one through the activity of the other. Specifically, "the Spirit makes Christ really present in the bread and cup," and this presence is "Christo-Pneumatic." The dual emphasis on Son and Spirit means that Zwinglian and

---

[140] White, *Protestant Worship*, 201.

[141] Daniel Tomberlin, *Pentecostal Sacraments: Encountering God at the Altar* (Cleveland, TN: Center for Pentecostal Leadership and Care, 2010), 162-63.

[142] Tomberlin, *Pentecostal Sacraments*, 171.

Anabaptist theologies of eucharistic presence are inadequate for Pentecostals.[143]

The presence of Christ and Spirit make the Supper healing and prophetic. More than a "mere ritual," the Supper is a means of grace that both forgives sins and heals the body. Here, Tomberlin notes parallels between early Pentecostal writers and ancient theologians such as Ignatius of Antioch who refers to the Eucharist as the "medicine of immortality." At the same time, the presence of the Spirit in the Supper brings about a prophetic call for the renewal of holiness and the use of spiritual gifts. Those who come to the Table experience a greater awareness of sin and repentance as they stand in the presence of God. As a prophetic act, the Lord's Supper brings about greater discipline and accountability, as well as unity of the fellowship and personal holiness. Finally, the Supper is prophetic by anticipating the marriage supper of the Lamb and by enabling worshippers to participate in the eschaton.[144]

Tomberlin states that Pentecostals are challenged to make the Lord's Supper a more regular component of their public worship. Since movement is an important part of Pentecostal worship (e.g., in altar calls), the worshippers should come to the altar rather than be served the elements at their seats, the former method being preferred in early Pentecostalism. Tomberlin suggests the inclusion of the following elements in the communion service:

Scripture reading
Homily
Intercessory prayer (based on the Lord's Prayer)
Eucharistic liturgy
  a. Short eucharistic prayer
  b. Words of Institution
  c. Distribution

The Supper could be integrated either during the praise and worship or during the closing altar call. A single loaf and a single

[143] Tomberlin, *Pentecostal Sacraments*, 175.

[144] Tomberlin, *Pentecostal Sacraments*, 175-83.

cup are recommended in order to portray the reception of spiritual nourishment from *one* Lord (Eph. 4:5).[145]

Tomberlin's suggestions above are indeed welcome. But why not insert the above four-fold order *after* the opening praise and worship, so that the latter becomes like a gathering rite for the service of Word and Sacrament? Might not these four elements be swallowed up by what is sometimes a long and boisterous time of praise and worship? We might wonder also whether placing the four-fold eucharistic rite within the altar call might give the impression that the Lord's Supper is a mere afterthought to the service, rather than its vital center.

Conclusion

The Protestant theological and liturgical heritage is one to be celebrated and studied. Yet, we need not limit ourselves to using the more drastically revised eucharistic rites of the sixteenth century. For one thing, the Reformers themselves would not want us to do that! They appreciated how different contexts called for different rites, and so warned against the idolization of even their own services. Furthermore, the twentieth-century liturgical movement and greater contact with Eastern Orthodox and Oriental churches have made Protestant Christians aware of the great variety of eucharistic prayers that have been used throughout the centuries. These, too, can inspire our eucharistic praying today. Indeed, since the Reformation many Protestants have not been slavish in their use of sixteenth-century services. We can certainly learn from our Protestant forebears; but let us keep learning!

For Further Reading

Borgen, Ole E. *John Wesley on the Sacraments: A Theological Study*. Nashville: Abingdon Press, 1972.

Cuming, Geoffrey. *A History of Anglican Liturgy*. 2nd ed. London: Macmillan Co., 1982.

Gerrish, Brian A. *Grace and Gratitude: The Eucharistic Theology of John Calvin*. Eugene, OR: Wipf & Stock Publishers, 2002.

---

145 Tomberlin, *Pentecostal Sacraments*, 183-90.

Sasse, Hermann. *This is My Body: Luther's Contention for the Real Presence in the Sacrament of the Altar*. Minneapolis: Augsburg Publishing House, 1959.

Vajta, Vilmos. *Luther on Worship: An Interpretation*. Philadelphia: Muhlenberg Press, 1958.

Walker, Michael J. *The Theology of the Lord's Supper amongst English Baptists in the Nineteenth Century*. Didcot, Oxford: Baptist Historical Society, 1992.

Wallace, Ronald S. *Calvin's Doctrine of the Word and Sacrament*. Edinburgh: Oliver & Boyd, 1953.

CHAPTER 11

The Lord's Supper and Time

One aspect of the Reformation that Protestants continue to cherish and claim is the restoration of God's Word to a central place in public worship. Most Protestant worship services today focus on the reading of the Scriptures and preaching based on those readings. A "traditional" or "evangelical" service order for most Sundays would consist of a call to worship, hymn/song, confession and pardon (or absolution), readings, sermon, song of response, offering, prayers of intercession (or pastoral prayer), final hymn, and benediction. In some services, these elements might be rearranged so that the sermon becomes the climax to the service, thereby sending the assembly back into the world with God's Word and its application still fresh in people's minds. Drawing on a tradition that goes back to the Reformation, "liturgical" Protestant churches (e.g., Lutherans and Anglicans) might use the first part of the Holy Communion Service (i.e., the "Service of the Word" or *synaxis*) on Sundays without communion. Besides the singing of ancient liturgical texts such as the Kyrie and Gloria in Excelsis, this service order includes the reading of Scriptures, sermon, prayers, and offering. On communion Sundays, Protestants will then celebrate a full service of "Word and Sacrament" in which the preaching service or *synaxis* precedes the liturgy of Lord's Supper. A minority of Protestants have a full service of Word and Sacrament each week, with the percentages of those congregations that do higher among Anglicans and Lutherans. It also seems that increasing numbers of Protestant congregations are adopting a weekly service of Word and Sacrament. If anything, one never hears of a congregation adopting a *less*-frequent celebration of the Lord's Supper! Thus, Protestants are recovering the ancient *fullness* of worship, whereby the Sunday assembly hears the Scriptures read and expounded and then celebrates the Lord's Supper, giving thanks for bread and wine in the name of Christ, believing that he himself is present to the assembly in both of these actions. This chapter seeks to invite congregations that have not done so to adopt the tradition of a weekly celebration of the Lord's Supper at the Sunday worship gathering. History, theology, and pastoral need suggest our adopting the ancient sense that *the Lord's Day is for the Lord's Supper*. Hence, this is a chapter about the sacrament and *time*.

Worship in Word and Sacrament through the Ages

Is it possible to connect the Lord's Supper with Sunday – the "Lord's Day," first day, or "eighth day"? Christians believe that the Lord's Supper is rooted in the various meals at which Jesus himself was present, some of which had definite time associations. The synoptic gospel accounts of the mass feedings (Mark 6:30-44, 8:1-10) make no specific time references, while the feeding of the five thousand in John (6:1-15) occurred just before the Passover. Narratives about the meals Jesus ate with particular individuals such as Matthew (Matt. 9:9-13) or Zacchaeus (Luke 19:1-10) do not say when those events occurred. However, the synoptic gospels do record that Jesus ate a *Passover* meal with his disciples on the night of his betrayal (Matt. 26:26-29; Mark 14:22-25; Luke 22:15-20), and John's chronology situates that meal before Passover, on the Day of Preparation (cf. John 19:31). The question of which tradition is correct is entirely moot; the point is to suggest that Jesus himself is a new Passover Lamb (cf. John 1:29, 36), whose sacrificial death is a means of salvation for God's people. Thus, even though the once-yearly pattern of celebration was not determinative for the celebration of the Christian sacred meal, the association with Passover (a particular time designation) still infused the Lord's Supper with important theological meaning.

But even in the apostolic age, the Supper was being associated with Sunday. Luke narrates a meal that occurred on the very evening after Jesus' resurrection on the first day (24:13-35), in which the risen Lord was manifested to two disciples "in the breaking of the bread." It has been suggested that this particular story expresses the meaning of Christian worship with its dual focus: the Scriptures are interpreted concerning Jesus' death and Christians break bread knowing that the risen Lord is present.[1] Luke mentions that the Christian community in Jerusalem gathered for "the study of the apostles' teaching, fellowship, the breaking of bread, and prayer" (Acts 2:42), but says nothing about specific days. Yet, he does record a Christian gathering on the "first day" in which Paul preached and broke bread with Christians in Troas (Acts 20:7-12), which may well be a reference to the celebration of the Lord's Supper on a Sunday. Other New Testament passages that speak of the first day or the "Lord's Day" (1 Cor. 16:2; Rev. 1:10), may hint of Christian worship gatherings – possibly with the Supper – on Sunday. Similarly, the first-century *Didache*, which directs Christians to come together on the "Lord's Day" to break bread and give thanks (ch. 14),[2] may also be referring to the first day of the week (Sunday).

References to Sunday worship gatherings in Word and Sacrament become more common in the second century. Justin the Martyr (d. 165 CE), states that Christians come together on Sunday for a service involving Scripture reading, preaching, intercessory prayer, and the Lord's Supper (ch. 67). He explains that the liturgy occurred on that day both because it was the first day of creation and because it was

---

[1] Gordon W. Lathrop, *Holy Things: A Liturgical Theology* (Minneapolis: Fortress Press, 1993), 48.

[2] The *Didache* 14 (late-first or early-second cent.), PEER, 24.

the day of Jesus' resurrection.[3] The late-first/early-second century *Epistle of Barnabas,* speaks of Christians observing the eighth day (Sunday) as a celebration of Jesus' resurrection; presumably this included a celebration of the Lord's Supper.[4] It would therefore appear that beginning in the late-first and early-second centuries – certainly in the third century CE – Christians were assembling on Sunday to celebrate a "Eucharist." Once Christians started meeting on Sunday *morning* for communal worship, the "Supper" would have consisted only of the bread and cup, rather than a full meal because (1) providing meals for large groups was difficult; and (2) the authorities were prohibiting evening meal gatherings.[5] By the third century, Sunday had been established universally as *the* day of Christian worship with the Lord's Supper at the heart of the observance. But it did not become a *day of rest* in the Roman Empire until Emperor Constantine's official declaration in 321 CE.

During the Middle Ages, the week became crowded with commemorations for various saints, all of which were observed with the celebration of special Masses conducted by priests who were required to say Mass at least once per day. Additionally, persons of financial means paid money to have Masses "said" for the repose of deceased relatives. The proliferation of Masses for saints, the dead, and other special "intentions" (concerns) competed with – although perhaps did not eclipse – the Sunday Mass, which was usually well-attended and, in some places, celebrated with great splendor and pageantry.

The Protestant Reformers inherited the pattern whereby the Sunday Mass of the Lord's Supper was the focal point of Christian liturgical life. Although they took issue with the theology and piety of the medieval Mass, they never questioned the normativity of

---

[3] Justin the Martyr, *First Apology* 67.1 (ca. 155), PEER, 29-30.

[4] The *Epistle of Barnabas* XV.8-9 (late-first or early-second cent.), SW, 372.

[5] On this second point, see the discussion about Pliny the Younger's Letter to Emperor Trajan (ca. 112 CE) in Paul F. Bradshaw and Maxwell E. Johnson, *The Origins of Feasts, Fasts, and Seasons in Early Christianity* (Collegeville: Liturgical Press, 2011), 6-7.

a weekly celebration of the Lord's Supper on Sunday. Indeed, by abolishing the weekday Masses[6] and the various private Masses for the dead and other special intentions, they restored the Sunday Eucharist to its original primacy. In providing two reformed Masses, Luther assumed a full service Word and Sacrament on Sunday as the normal pattern. Furthermore, he encouraged Christians to receive communion frequently, even stating that those who went for long periods without communion could not be considered Christians.[7] To counter the accusation that Lutherans had "abolished" the Mass, the *Apology of the Augsburg Confession*, prepared by Luther's colleague, Philip Melanchthon, states that Lutheran churches celebrated the Mass "every Sunday," when communion is offered to all who want it, after they had been "examined and absolved."[8] In 1524, Martin Bucer proposed a Sunday service (*Grund und Ursach*) consisting of both Word and Sacrament.[9] From 1525 to 1539, he continuously edited the evangelical Mass used in Strasbourg, and this work culminated in the *Psalter with Complete Church Practice* (1539).[10] The service of the Lord's Supper contained therein was to be celebrated *every Sunday* in cathedral churches and once a month in other places.[11] John Calvin states that the Lord's Supper should be celebrated at least once a week at a public service that includes prayer and preaching.[12] Unfortunately, he failed to institute a weekly Eucharist at the church in Geneva. In England, the BCP 1549 assumed a *daily* celebration in

[6] Martin Luther, *An Order of Mass and Communion for the Church at Wittenberg* (1523), LW 53, 37-38. Luther will later speak of the sacrament as being given as "daily food" and being administered and celebrated "daily." See Martin Luther, *Large Catechism* (1529), BC, 469.24, 470.39.

[7] Luther, *Large Catechism*, BC, 471.40.

[8] *Apology of the Augsburg Confession* (1531), Art. XXIV, BC, 258.1.

[9] Martin Bucer, *Grund and Ursach* (1524), as cited in LWC, 161-62.

[10] Martin Bucer, *Psalter with Complete Church Practice* (1539), PEER, 206-12.

[11] "Martin Bucer: The Psalter with Complete Church Practice, 1539 (editor's introduction)," PEER, 204.

[12] John Calvin, *Institutes of the Christian Religion* IV.17.43 (1559), in LCC XXI, ed. John T. McNeill, tr. Ford Lewis Battles (Philadelphia: Westminster Press, 1960), 1421.

cathedral and collegiate churches and a weekly celebration in parish churches, with members of the latter expected to commune at least once a year.[13] Daily celebration of the Lord's Supper in cathedrals was assumed in the BCP 1552, and if that could not happen, the eucharistic *synaxis* was still to be used. Due to Bucer's influence, the BCP 1552 raised the minimum number of yearly communions for each Christian from one to three.[14] John Wesley, who received communion at least twice weekly, directed Methodist leaders in the United States to celebrate the Lord's Supper *every Sunday*.[15]

Thus, with the exception of Zwingli and his quarterly communions, the Reformers of the sixteenth century, and later John Wesley, desired a weekly celebration of the Lord's Supper with many, if not all, of those present receiving the sacrament. Early Protestant leaders were not against the Lord's Supper, only the abuse of it. They did not seek to abolish the Mass, but rather to reform it theologically and liturgically. Furthermore, they were at pains to encourage Christians to receive the sacrament frequently or, in Wesley's case, "constantly." This commitment was not a misplaced traditionalism or a romanticism for earlier times. Luther and his followers understood the Supper as constitutive of Christian identity and as a "mark" of the church.[16] Both Luther and Calvin believed that there was great spiritual benefit in receiving the eucharistic elements, namely, the assurance of forgiveness and continued fellowship with the Lord Jesus Christ. It is for reasons such as these that the Reformers sought to make the Supper a central part of church life and Christian spirituality. Thus, if the Lord's Supper seems peripheral to Protestant worship life today, it is not because of the Reformers.

---

[13] "The Supper of the Lord, Commonly Called the Mass," BCP 1549, LWC, 250 and 267.

[14] "The Order for the Administration of the Lord's Supper or Holy Communion," BCP 1552, LWC, 283; see Arthur Roberts, *A Review of the Book of Common Prayer, Drawn Up by Martin Bucer Briefly Analyzed and Abridged* (London: James Nisbet and Co., 1853; repr. Nabu Press, 2014), 7.

[15] John Wesley, *Letter to Dr. Coke and Mr. Asbury* (1784), JWPB, ii (34).

[16] Martin Luther, *On the Councils and the Church* (1539), LW 41, 152-53.

The divorce between the Lord's Day and the Lord's Supper among Protestants is attributable to several factors. First, the role of the sacraments in church life was diminished due to Enlightenment-era theology which denied that sacraments conveyed supernatural grace and held that they could do no more than induce Christians to good behavior.[17] Second, the rise of the "autonomous individual," or the tendency to separate one's identity from relationships with other persons and communities (also an Enlightenment tendency), combined with a distrust of institutions, led people to perceive little need for the Supper. Being a Christian became a very private matter and the church and its sacraments were viewed as something of an intrusion into the individual's spiritual life. Third, social conditions in North America in the eighteenth and nineteenth centuries contributed to the infrequent celebration of the Lord's Supper in Protestant churches. Early America had few institutions for the education of clergy, and pastors, who needed to be trained in Europe, were often in short supply. Those available usually served several churches spread over a vast territory. Consequently, congregations often had to wait months for the arrival of a circuit-riding pastor who could preside at the Lord's Supper. Although more stable and settled social conditions later allowed for regular pastoral leadership, the older pattern of infrequent communion services was neither challenged nor changed in many instances. Missionaries took this pattern of eucharistic celebration to Africa, Asia, and elsewhere, and, being mostly focused on "saving souls for Christ," they saw little need to change it in their mission context.

Due in large part to the liturgical renewal movement's recovery of earlier patterns of worship, the late-twentieth century church witnessed a revival of eucharistic faith and practice, which is reflected in the worship books and official statements of various Protestant churches. Below is a survey of what these sources say in regard to the frequency of the Lord's Supper and its place in the life and faith of the church.

[17] See ch. 1.

1. Lutheran

A. *Lutheran Book of Worship* (1978). The service provided for the Sunday worship assembly, "Holy Communion," is said to be composed of two "principal parts": the service of Scripture reading and preaching and the service of the Lord's Supper, which together form a unified whole. Attention is drawn to *Augsburg Confession* Art. XXIV which "regards Holy Communion as the chief act of worship on Sundays and other festivals."[18]

B. *Use of the Means of Grace* (1997). The Evangelical Lutheran Church in America's statement on the practice of Word and Sacrament declares that Holy Communion is celebrated weekly. It speaks of the sacrament's role in constituting the church's fellowship and in empowering the church for its mission in the world. Members are encouraged to receive the sacrament "frequently."[19]

C. *Evangelical Lutheran Worship* (2006). The "principal" service of worship centers on the Word of God and the sacraments. The basic pattern of the Sunday service is "gathering, word, meal (i.e., the Lord's Supper), and sending."[20]

2. Reformed-Presbyterian

A. *Book of Common Worship* (1993). Introductory materials describe the worship of the Sunday assembly in the following terms: "Gathered on the Lord's Day, Christians celebrate the age to come, which was revealed in the risen Christ, by remembering the words and deeds of Jesus and celebrating the presence of the risen Christ among them in the Word proclaimed and in the bread and cup of the Eucharist."[21] The Lord's Supper is understood as one of the historical "norms" of Christian worship, and consequently the basic outline of

---

[18] "Notes on the Liturgy," LBW, 25.

[19] UMG, 35, 35A, 35C.

[20] "Holy Communion," ELW, 163.

[21] "The Service for the Lord's Day: A Description of its Movement and Elements," BCW, 34.

the Lord's Day service is "Gathering, The Word, The Eucharist, and Sending."[22]

B. *The Worship Sourcebook* (2004). Although not explicitly endorsing a weekly celebration of the Lord's Supper, the basic pattern of worship includes the Lord's Supper, which can be celebrated in any liturgical season or in any service with any biblical theme.[23]

C. *Book of Order* (Presbyterian Church U.S.A.). The "Directory for Worship" states that "it is appropriate to celebrate the Lord's Supper as often as each Lord's Day. It is to be celebrated regularly and frequently enough to be recognized as integral to the Service for the Lord's Day" (W-2.4009).[24]

3. Anglican

Church of England. Official canons state that Holy Communion is to be celebrated on all Sundays, feasts, and on Ash Wednesday in all cathedrals (B.13.1) and parish churches (B.14.1), as well as on Maundy Thursday in the latter. All confirmed persons are to receive Holy Communion "regularly," especially at Christmas, Easter, and Pentecost.[25]

4. Methodist

A. *United Methodist Book of Worship* (1993). The "basic pattern" of Sunday worship is four-fold: entrance, proclamation and response, thanksgiving and communion, and sending forth. "A Service of Word and Table" is provided for regular use on Sundays.[26]

---

[22] "An Outline of the Service for the Lord's Day," BCW, 46.

[23] *The Worship Sourcebook* (Grand Rapids: Baker Books, 2004), 25, 306.

[24] *The Constitution of the Presbyterian Church (U.S.A.) Part II: The Book of Order* (Louisville: Office of the General Assembly, 2013), 97.

[25] *The Canons of the Church of England* (London: Church House Publishing, 2000), 29-30, 33.

[26] "General Services: The Basic Pattern of Worship," UMBW, 13-15; "A Service of Word and Table I," UMBW, 33-39.

B. *This Holy Mystery: A United Methodist Understanding of Holy Communion* (2004). "The complete pattern of Christian worship for the Lord's Day is Word and Table – the gospel is proclaimed in both Word and Sacrament. Word and Table are not in competition; rather they complement each other so as to constitute a whole service of worship. Their separation diminishes the fullness of life in the Spirit offered to us through faith in Jesus Christ."[27] Accordingly, congregations are "encouraged" to adopt a weekly celebration of the Lord's Supper.

5. Other Protestants

Disciples of Christ (website): "The Lord's Supper or Communion is celebrated in weekly worship. It is open to all who are followers of Jesus Christ. The practice of Holy Communion has become the central element of worship within the Disciples tradition."[28]

6. Ecumenical

World Council of Churches, *Baptism, Eucharist and Ministry* Document (1982). Because it "deepens" Christian faith, the Lord's Supper should be celebrated "frequently" and Christians should be encouraged to commune frequently. The connection with the Lord's resurrection suggests that the Supper be celebrated "at least every Sunday."[29]

The Nature of the Sunday Assembly's Worship

A weekly celebration of the Lord's Supper on Sunday suggests itself for several theological reasons. The first has to do with the very nature of worship itself. Perhaps as a result of Enlightenment rationalism combined with twentieth-century consumerism, we might reduce

---

[27] *This Holy Mystery: A United Methodist Understanding of Holy Communion* (Nashville: The General Board of Discipleship of the United Methodist Church, 2004), 18-19.

[28] The Disciples of Christ, "Baptism and Communion," http://disciples.org/our-identity/communion-and-baptism/[accessed 15 March 2015].

[29] BEM, 16.30-31.

worship to personal experience and therefore evaluate a particular service according to how it "makes me feel," or "what I get out of it." Worship leaders are assessed on their ability to provide certain kinds of experiences to worshippers, especially ones that appeal to the emotions. Completely overlooked is the question of what *God* is doing in our worship. In fact, God is active in the assembly's liturgy, encountering us through the appointed means of grace, the Word and the sacraments. Since the Scriptures are the written Word of God (2 Tim. 3:16), preaching that faithfully expounds the biblical readings becomes a means for Christ to speak to his people, for "whoever listens to you, listens to me" (Luke 10:16). Besides the audible, spoken Word, God also comes to us through the *sacramental* Word (the Supper, baptism). In his famous definition, Augustine says the following: "The Word is added to the element, and there results the sacrament, as if itself also a kind of *visible word*."[30] The sacrament of the Lord's Supper is thus the visible, embodied means of God's self-giving whereby God establishes and sustains a relationship with his people. We can easily relate this understanding to the doctrine of the Incarnation: just as Jesus Christ is the "Word made flesh" (John 1:14) or the very communication or deed of God in embodied, human form, so the sacrament of the Lord's Supper is the visible, embodied form of Christ's self-giving love to his people. Worship that is a true witness to the God of the Incarnation expresses the gospel in tangible, visible means. Without the sacramental sign commanded by Christ – the Lord's Supper – the Sunday worship of Christians fails to make use of the Word in the fullest possible way and therefore does an injustice to the church's faith in the Incarnation and its incarnational faith. To say that the sacrament is a visible form of the Word is not to suggest that it is merely an object lesson in the gospel that may or may not be used at the church's discretion. To the contrary, says theologian Simon Chan, the sacramental form of the Word is indispensable to Christian worship, for "we come to know what the proclaimed Word is by actually entering into communion with the Real Presence effected by the Spirit in the

[30] Augustine, *Tractate* 80 on John 15:3. Emphasis added.

Lord's Supper. Word without Sacrament remains incomplete...."[31] Neither am I suggesting that a public worship service without the Lord's Supper is wrong or defective; non-eucharistic worship in the form of daily Morning and Evening Prayer has long been a part of the Christian experience. But when the church gathers on the day of the resurrection, the eschatological eighth day (Sunday), it gathers principally to proclaim and witness to Christ and to experience his living presence. That witness is incomplete without the Lord's Supper, one of the chief means by which Christ is present to his people.

Worship in Word and Sacrament each Sunday is also necessary as a reflection of the proclamation-fulfillment dynamic that operates in worship.[32] When God proclaims that something will happen, it happens – whether that is the inflicting of a punishment or the conferring of a blessing. God's Word (communication) precedes, leads to, and even causes its concrete fulfillment in the lives of God's people. When the Word is proclaimed in worship through the reading of Scriptures and preaching, God's curses and blessings, judgment and mercy are announced. When the Lord's Supper (and/or baptism) is celebrated, that proclamation/announcement comes to fulfillment in the embodied action of the sacrament. On the one hand, God's judgment is concretely fulfilled in that those who eat and drink without being in right relationship with their neighbors (Matt. 5:23-24; 1 Cor. 11:27-34) bring judgment on themselves by the very act of partaking. On the other hand, God's mercy is fulfilled tangibly when repentant sinners eat and drink for their forgiveness and salvation: they eat and drink God's forgiveness! Just as all of God's biblical promises would have been empty without their eventual fulfillment, so the proclamation of the Word in worship is empty and unfulfilled without the Supper.

---

[31] Simon Chan, *Liturgical Theology: The Church as Worshipping Community* (Downers Grove, IL: IVP Academic, 2006), 66.

[32] Cf. Chan, *Liturgical Theology*, 68. Chan speaks of the Word as "preparing" for the Supper by creating the faith that enables the sacrament to be received "effectually," a point with which I agree.

For pastoral reasons as well, Word and Sacrament must be kept together in the same service. As Chan explains, these two dimensions of the liturgy correspond to how a faith community is formed: by instruction and participation. By participating in community life, we learn the community's habits and ways such that they become ingrained and habitual. At the same time, critical reflection helps us to understand the community's rules and ideas so that we can apply and defend them when challenged. The Word in worship is the verbal dimension that corresponds to (and embodies) this critical reflection, while the sacrament forms spiritual habits that allow us to "assimilate a primary theology" (i.e., the church's deepest beliefs about God and its encounter with God in worship). The ancient baptismal catechumenate brought both aspects together by explaining the church's practices and sacraments as candidates prepared for their baptismal initiation through increasing levels of participation in the church's liturgical life.[33] Evangelical spirituality has "failed," Chan says, because it has tried to build a Christian life based more on critical reflection than on habits. He concludes: "evangelicalism has created a largely hearing community rather than an aural-tactile community, a Word community rather than a Word-and-Sacrament community. But the whole of worship must include hearing, singing, and praying (Word) *and* seeing, touching, eating, and drinking (Sacrament)."[34]

More basically, we could say that we need the *embodied* means of grace as flesh and blood human beings. It may seem counter-intuitive to make an assertion like this in an age when human relationships are conducted through various electronic means such as email and mobile phone conversations. Yet, at the same time, coffee shops are full of people engaging in one to one conversations and sports arenas are crowded with people interacting with each other in response to their teams' exploits. Direct contact with other humans in proximity to their bodies – embodied interaction – is still meaningful and useful, even if people do not explicitly say so, or still use other means of

[33] In some cases in the ancient church, an explanation of the sacraments was only given *after* baptism had taken place.

[34] Chan, *Liturgical Theology*, 67. Emphasis original.

interaction. Embodied gestures also remain important for expressing our words and commitments to one another. A husband or wife still needs a kiss or embrace from the spouse to give concrete meaning to the words "I love you." A child needs a birthday present or Christmas gift – however small – as a sign of parental love. Similarly, we need something tangible to confirm God's love in Christ for us, and the Lord's Supper offers precisely that in a sip of wine and a piece of bread.

This need for tangible confirmations of God's love is neither romanticism nor idolatrous religiosity. The more sacramentally-minded of the Reformers affirmed the earthly and tangible character of the sacraments. Against his opponents who disparaged the sacraments because of their outward, external nature, Luther asserts that "faith must have something to believe – something to which it may cling and upon which it may stand. Thus, faith clings to the water and believes it to be baptism."[35] Luther's associate, Philip Melanchthon, suggests that the sacraments make an appeal to the heart through the senses,[36] and John Calvin speaks of the sacraments as means by which God condescends to our human capacities in order to guarantee the promised spiritual blessings.[37]As far as these Reformers were concerned, the sacraments are not gratuitous and unnecessary, but necessary components of the *missio Dei*.

Finally, a weekly celebration of the Lord's Supper is needed because of the spiritual gifts it offers us! First of all, as sinners we need God's forgiveness. While baptism makes us God's children and endows us with the Holy Spirit, we still continue to struggle against sin – or in Luther's words, we carry the "old Adam" around our necks. Baptism does not make us pure or perfect, but rather initiates us into an ongoing struggle for greater sanctification that will only be completed in the life to come. Thus, we need the Supper because it offers the tangible assurance that we have a forgiving God who receives us back into his household if and when we fall, lapse,

[35] Luther, *Large Catechism*, 460.29.

[36] *Apology of the Augsburg Confession*, Art. XIII, BC, 219.5.

[37] Calvin, *Institutes of the Christian Religion* IV.17.1, LCC XXI, 1361.

or backslide. Second, we need the *holistic* healing that the Supper offers to body, mind, and spirit. To know one's self as a forgiven sinner who is welcome at the Lord's Supper is to be "healed" of guilt, anxiety, and the dread of God's judgment – all of which can "cripple" a person. Insofar as body, mind, and spirit are interconnected, the spiritual healing offered by the Supper has a role in a person's physical healing as well – however the Spirit sees fit to make that happen. Finally, we need the hope offered by the Supper, beset as we are by personal conflict, political instability, and concerns about the destruction of the earth itself. Such concerns can leave us wanting for purpose, meaning, and joy – in a word, *hopeless*. To eat the Supper in the presence of Jesus who promises to "come again in beauty and power to share with us the great and promised feast,"[38] is to find purpose, meaning, and joy. It is to know that sin, death, and evil will not have the final word, and that all of our hopes and longings will be fulfilled in God's coming Kingdom. Although our spiritual needs are deep and unending, the gifts of the Supper are profound and limitless. Thus, just as intermittent eating or exercise could never meet our bodily needs, so intermittent celebrations of the Supper are inadequate for meeting our spiritual needs.

Arguments about a need for *infrequent* communion must therefore be rejected. While it is true that preparation for the Supper is useful, this need is hardly a reason for ruling out a weekly celebration. Luther holds that adequate preparation consists in simply believing the words "given and shed for you," while Calvin states that it is enough to recognize one's unworthiness for the Sacrament. Surely, examining one's heart to ponder along these lines does not take an entire month – or longer! Also problematic is the argument that a weekly celebration of the Lord's Supper leads to its disparagement by the faithful. No reasonable person would argue for an infrequent proclamation of the Word on the grounds that a frequent reading of the Scriptures and preaching would lead to contempt for the Word! If there is a need for one of the means of grace to be administered regularly, then the same is surely true of the other.

---

[38] "Holy Communion," LBW, 223.

The Lord's Supper and Sacred Time

In a previous chapter we suggested that certain days in the church's calendar are especially appropriate for baptizing because of their baptismal content, e.g., the Baptism of Our Lord, Easter, or Pentecost. Similarly, certain days are appropriate for the celebration of the Lord's Supper and certain days are less appropriate, if not altogether inappropriate. This determination rests on the distinction between liturgical *feasts*, days of joy and celebration, versus *fasts*, days that are solemn, meditative, and penitential in character.[39] As a meal that celebrates the Lord's resurrection and his promise to come again, the Lord's Supper is properly part of services on Christmas, Epiphany, Easter, and Pentecost. Sunday has always been understood as a commemoration of the resurrection, and has never been a fast day. Thus, Sunday has been the premier time for celebrating the Lord's Supper – even during the penitential seasons of Advent and Lent.

So as to underscore the connection between "feasting" and the Lord's Supper, a number of Protestant worship books provide eucharistic prayers specifically for the various feasts of the liturgical calendar.[40] Recognizing the more solemn, contemplative character of Good Friday, most books provide a non-eucharistic "proper liturgy" for that day. Indeed, as a traditional fast day, the character of Good Friday hardly suits for the Lord's Supper. Some Anglican churches, however, will administer Holy Communion on Good Friday by distributing elements consecrated at the previous day's Maundy Thursday service, i.e., giving the "reserved" sacrament.[41] A similar practice is common among Orthodox Christian Churches, which never celebrate the Lord's Supper on a fast day. Although an Ash Wednesday Holy Communion service is traditional in many mainline Protestant churches, we might question the logic of celebrating the Supper on what has traditionally been a *fast day*.

[39] For a fine discussion about feasts and fasts, see Frank C. Senn, *Introduction to Christian Liturgy* (Minneapolis: Fortress Press, 2012), 104-6.

[40] "Great Thanksgivings," UMBW, 54-71; "Resources for the Liturgical Year," BCW, 165-400.

[41] "Good Friday," BCP 1979, 282.

Many Protestants would find encouragement to engage in their own ascetical fasting during Lent, if their churches began that season with a liturgical fast on Ash Wednesday. Thus, the preferred pattern is to celebrate the Lord's Supper on all Sundays, major feasts of the church calendar, and Maundy Thursday (which commemorates the Supper's institution), while abstaining from it on Ash Wednesday and Good Friday.

The Lord's Supper and Rites of the Life Cycle

In lieu of the pagan *refrigerium* or graveside meals, early Christians celebrated the Lord's Supper in conjunction with a believer's funeral. Augustine mentions that the "sacrifice for our redemption" (i.e., the Eucharist) took place at his mother Monica's graveside funeral.[42] This practice owes to the early Christian understanding that a funeral is a joyous event that celebrates the deceased person's entry into eternity. The customs of wearing white clothing and singing psalms during the procession to the burial site (e.g., Pss. 22, 23, 116) further underscores this attitude. As James White observes concerning early Christian funerals: "The dominant theme ... was the sense of hope for those who had died in the Lord. The focus was not on human sin, but on God's victory in Jesus Christ."[43] The death anniversary was subsequently commemorated with another celebration of the Lord's Supper. Eventually, special Masses came to be held for the commemoration of both local and universal saints. Protestants abolished all special Masses for the dead, because these were understood as sacrifices that liberated the dead from purgatory and assured their place in heaven. Luther argues that funerals should proclaim the resurrection, rather than try to effect the eternal disposition of the dead.[44]

With the influence of the liturgical movement and its emphasis on early Christian worship patterns, some Protestants have recovered

---

[42] Augustine, *Confessions* IX (ca. 400), LCC VII, 197.

[43] James F. White, *A Brief History of Christian Worship* (Nashville: Abingdon Press, 1993), 67.

[44] Martin Luther, *Preface to the Burial Hymns* (1542), LW 53, 326.

the funeral Eucharist. A number of current worship books provide for the celebration of Holy Communion at funerals, usually following the prayers of intercession and peace.[45] If the Christian funeral serves to proclaim the resurrection, it is only fitting to share the meal of the resurrected Lord, who is made known in the breaking of the bread (Luke 24:35). Because it is a heightening of fellowship with the risen Lord and with fellow communicants, the Lord's Supper is comforting to mourners, who might otherwise feel alone in their grief. To celebrate communion within the funeral liturgy is to assert our belief that the church on earth maintains fellowship with the church in heaven, an idea affirmed by John and Charles Wesley.[46]

The service of Christian marriage has also been a traditional time for the Lord's Supper. Admittedly, we know little about marriage in the early church, other than there being some official encouragement for believers to marry other believers. At first, Christian marriage ceremonies were private affairs conducted in the home. But during the Middle Ages, marriage came increasingly to be regarded as a legal "contract" (rather than a covenant) between two individuals. This resulted in the service being conducted at the church door, where all other legal agreements were made in order to be public events. By the late Middle Ages, the service had moved into the church and included a special "nuptial Mass," in which the bride and groom were blessed just before communion.[47] The Reformers rejected the idea that marriage is a sacrament that confers a special character on the recipients. Luther holds that marriage is a universal that does not particularly pertain to the gospel. Nevertheless, he believes that it has been instituted by God for the good of humanity. Accordingly, he retained a simple service consisting of the mutual consent at the church door, the exchange of rings, the joining of hands and the

---

[45] "Burial of the Dead," LBW, 336; "Funeral," ELW, 671; "The Funeral: A Service of Witness to the Resurrection," BCW, 928-38; "The Burial of the Dead: Rite Two," BCP 1979, 498; "A Service of Death and Resurrection," UMBW, 150, 152-54.

[46] See Charles Wesley's hymn "Let Saints on Earth in Concert Sing," http://www.hymntime.com/tch/htm/l/s/o/lsonicsi.htm [accessed 28 June 2014].

[47] White, *Brief History*, 95-96.

recitation of Matt. 19:6, Bible reading, exhortation, and a prayer of blessing.[48] He says nothing about a nuptial mass. By contrast, Martin Bucer favors the inclusion of weddings during the Sunday *Holy Communion* service in order that the bride and groom can receive the sacrament. The Anglican Prayer Books of the sixteen and seventeenth centuries only specify that the married couple receive communion on the day of their marriage service.[49] Otherwise, Holy Communion was largely disassociated with marriage in Protestant practice until the twentieth century, when its celebration was encouraged, albeit with the proviso that the entire assembly (not just the bride and groom) be invited to receive the elements.[50]

The Lord's Supper has also played a role in the church's ministry to the sick, although initially the emphasis was on anointing. The New Testament mentions the laying on of hands and anointing (Mark 5:23; James 5:14), but says nothing about communion for the sick. In the early church, healing ministry primarily involved an anointing administered by lay persons. However, in the Middle Ages, the church's healing ministry became both clericalized and connected entirely with dying. The anointing or *extreme unction* as it came to be called, was often followed with the final administration of Holy Communion, a practice known as *viaticum*. Luther and Calvin reject the anointing of the dying, but approve of giving communion to the sick. While Luther somewhat reluctantly retained the *reservation* of the communion elements for the sick,[51] Calvin rejects this practice and insists on a whole new celebration of the Supper in the presence of the sick person. The BCP 1549 provided for the communion

---

[48] Martin Luther, *The Order of Marriage for Common Pastors* (1529), LW 53, 111-14.

[49] "The Form of Solemnization of Matrimony (1549/1662)," BCP *Texts*, 71, 441.

[50] "Marriage," LBW, 330; "Marriage," ELW, 684; "Christian Marriage: Rite II," BCW, 853-76; "An Order for Marriage," BCP 1979, 436; "A Service of Christian Marriage II," UMBW, 137.

[51] Martin Luther, *Receiving the Sacrament in Both Kinds* (1522), LW 36, 257.

of the sick from the reserved sacrament,[52] but the BCP 1552 deleted any reference to eucharistic reservation for the sick, due to theological objections raised to the practice.[53] All Protestant traditions retained some form of visitation to the sick with the giving of Holy Communion, a special emphasis in early Methodism.[54] Currently, mainline Protestantism knows two practices of communing the sick: (1) taking "reserved" elements directly from the Sunday eucharistic service to sick persons; and (2) celebrating a new communion service in the "sick room." The former practice is understood as an extension of the assembly's communion, and so symbolizes the sick person's unity with the Sunday assembly. Communing the sick from a reserved sacrament might include a short explanatory address, a confession, Scripture readings, and prayer.[55]

The Lord's Supper is also part of the healing services that emerged in mainline Protestantism in the late-twentieth century, perhaps due to the influence of (or as a reaction against) the miraculous healings associated with appearances of Mary and/or those healings associated with Pentecostalism.[56] Lutheran, Anglican, and Methodist healing services usually include anointing and the laying on of hands for healing, but are not viewed as curative or as replacements for professional medical treatment. The celebration of Holy Communion serves as another enacted gesture of healing, assuring participants that the risen Lord comes with his gifts of healing and wholeness.

---

[52] "The Order for the Visitation of the Sick and the Communion of the Same" (1549), BCP *Texts*, 79-81.

[53] White, *Brief History*, 272.

[54] White, *Brief History*, 272.

[55] "Distribution of Communion to Those in Special Circumstances," *Lutheran Book of Worship: Occasional Services* (Minneapolis: Augsburg Publishing; Philadelphia: Board of Publication, Lutheran Church in America, 1982), 76-79; "A Service of Word and Table V (with Persons who are Sick and Homebound)," UMBW, 51-53.

[56] "Healing," ELW, 660-665; "A Service of Wholeness for Use with a Congregation," BCW, 1005-15.

Conclusion

A number of factors suggest the appropriateness and need for a weekly celebration of the Lord's Supper. Of course, the move to weekly communion will require a major shift in theology and practice for many Protestant congregations. Those leading such an effort will need to guide the assembly to deeper understandings of the nature of worship, the Lord's Supper, and the assembly's own spiritual needs. This teaching may take years to complete, and undoubtedly some church members will need a thorough convincing. Additionally, many of the practicalities need to be thought through carefully with the lay leadership of a congregation, e.g., issues of timing, especially when multiple services take place on Sunday morning. There is merit in the suggestion that interim steps be taken, such a celebrating the Supper every Sunday during an entire season (e.g., Easter) before moving to a weekly celebration throughout the year. Although the process may prove difficult, those who undertake it can do so knowing that they are striving to fulfill the Lord's command to "do this," and that they will experience the joy of his presence at the table each Sunday.

CHAPTER 12

The Lord's Supper and its Physical Requirements

The Lord's Supper is a ritual meal and, like any meal, it has certain physical requirements: food and drink, serving vessels, and a table. Certainly, the church's eucharistic Supper is unlike other meals because of the kind and amount of food, the place where it is celebrated, and its religious meaning. Even though the Supper is deeply spiritual, it is necessary to attend carefully to the material side for the sake of the spiritual. This chapter will discuss the various physical requirements for the Lord's Supper toward the goal of shaping sound liturgical practice.

Although there are certain commonalities, each Protestant tradition has its own unique understanding of the Supper and way of celebrating it. But even within a tradition there might be a great variety of acceptable practices. Thus, any attempt to deal with the physical requirements of the Supper needs to consider and be respectful of the great diversity in Protestant practice. At the same time, if we take seriously the slogan "the church of the Reformation always needs to be reformed" (*ecclesia reforma semper reformanda est*), it is also necessary to challenge Christians to think critically about communion practices. Consequently, this chapter will be somewhat prescriptive, but only for the sake of inviting reflection, not in order to impose rigid uniformity. If the sights, sounds, and smells of worship form the assembly as much as the spoken words, then thoughtful and judicious attention to the physical/material side of the Lord's Supper is necessary.

The Table and its Space

The physical structure (or "liturgical center") used for the Lord's Supper has traditionally been known by two names. "Altar" suggests a place for ritual sacrifice in a temple, while a "table" is the setting of a domestic meal. In the Old Testament, the Temple contained both an altar for sacrifice (Ex. 29:36), and a table for the Bread of the Presence (Ex. 40:23; 1 Kings 7:48), the latter being a perpetual thank-offering set before the Lord. In the New Testament, Paul speaks of the "table of the Lord" in the context of a discussion about the Lord's Supper (1 Cor. 10:21). The Book of Revelation contains images of the heavenly altar (e.g., 6:9, 8:3), but does not specifically mention the Lord's Supper. It can safely be assumed that apostolic-era Christians used tables for their celebrations of the Lord's Supper, but there are no prescriptions for eucharistic tables in the New Testament. Both terms were used in the patristic era. Ignatius of Antioch states that "there is one flesh of our Lord Jesus Christ and one cup of his blood that makes us one, and *one altar*...."[1] Augustine speaks of both the "table of the Lord" and the "sacrament of the altar."[2] The medieval church preferred "altar," which may have had a role in the rise of excessively realistic theologies of eucharistic sacrifice.

The Reformation brought changes in architecture and terminology. Luther speaks of both the "Lord's table" and the "altar," but he envisioned the altar being pulled out from the wall so that the

[1] Ignatius of Antioch, *Letter to the Philadelphians* 4 (ca. 115 CE).

[2] Augustine of Hippo, *Sermon* 272 (ca. 415); *City of God* X.6 (ca. 420).

priest could face the people – essentially transforming it into a table.[3] The more radical Zwingli abolished the altar altogether and had people receive the elements while seated around a regular wooden table at the front of the nave.[4] Bucer states that the "altar-table" (*altartisch*) is to be brought closer to the people and that the minister is to stand behind it and face the assembly during the communion service.[5] Calvin preferred the word "table." The BCP 1549 referred to the "altar," which the priest was to face, except when speaking directly to the people.[6] With the BCP 1552, the traditional stone altar was replaced by a wooden table located in the chancel or in the nave (main body of the church), running from the liturgical east to west, with the priest standing on the north side.[7] When the table was placed in a divided chancel with choir seating on either side of a central aisle, communicants sat in the south side. John Wesley's communion service for American Methodists had the elder presiding at a wooden table, which he faced when praying, otherwise he faced the people when speaking to them.[8] With the exception of Zwingli, sixteenth-century Reformers all envisioned communicants coming to the front of the church and then either kneeling or standing near the table when receiving the elements. Wesley gave minimal instructions concerning the communion of the people, since there were few church buildings for early American Methodists, and those that were available had the simplest of appointments. Pentecostal Christians

---

[3] Martin Luther, *The German Mass and Order of Service* (1526), LW 53, 69. See also *The Order of Mass and Communion for the Church at Wittenberg* (1523), LW 53, 29.

[4] Ulrich Zwingli, *Action or Use of the Lord's Supper* (1525), LWC, 150.

[5] Martin Bucer, *Psalter with Complete Church Practice* (1539), LWC, 168, 172.

[6] "The Supper of the Lord, and the Holy Communion, Commonly Called the Mass," BCP 1549, PEER, 235.

[7] "The Book of Common Prayer 1552 (editor's introduction)," PEER, 244.

[8] John Wesley, "Order for the Administration of the Lord's Supper" (1784), JWPB, 135.

refer to the area around the pulpit and other liturgical centers as the "altar,"[9] while the place of the Supper is called a "table."

Today, Protestants generally speak of the "table" or "Lord's Table" as the place of the Lord's Supper or "Meal."[10] This preference reflects not only the traditional rejection of sacrificial theology (i.e., the idea that the sacrament is a repetition of Calvary), but also the understanding that the Supper is the action of the whole people of God (not just the minister) who gather around pulpit and table to receive the means of grace.[11] "Table" thus underscores the communal nature of the Supper, in contrast to theologies that might reduce the sacrament to individual "doses" of grace.

As a liturgical center with a particular purpose, the table needs to be designed with functionality in mind. Ideally, it would be about .91 m high or approximately the height of a kitchen counter top. Anything lower will make reaching for the communion vessels difficult. A rectangular top or *mensa* measuring 2 m long by 1 m wide is adequate. A table of significantly smaller dimensions will fail to convey the Supper's importance, while a table of monumental proportions will visually overwhelm the liturgical space. To be in harmony with the whole liturgical space, the table is scaled to the room, neither dominating it nor becoming lost in it. To be in harmony with the liturgy, it is scaled to fit the human body. An oval-shaped *mensa* is not so desirable, but is better than a circular one which might make it difficult for the minister to find a center point for positioning him/herself during the liturgy.

---

[9] See Daniel Tomberlin, *Pentecostal Sacraments: Encountering God at the Altar* (Cleveland, TN: Center for Pentecostal Leadership and Care, 2010).

[10] "Notes on the Liturgy," LBW, 28; "Notes on the Services," ELW, 22; UMG, 36; "The Service for the Lord's Day: A Description of Its Movement and Elements," BCW, 33, 41; "The Holy Eucharist: Rite II," BCP 1979, 354; "Holy Communion," DSSB, 36, 44; "The Order for the Celebration of Holy Communion also called The Eucharist and The Lord's Supper," CW, 175; "A Service of Word and Table I," UMBW, 35-39. BCP 1979 refers to both the "table" and the "altar."

[11] See for example UMG, 39, which states that "the gathered people of God celebrate the sacrament."

"Table" and "meal" suggest the use of wood. Preferable is a hardwood without knots, heavy grain marks, or natural imperfections that draw attention to themselves. A natural rather than varnished finish helps to bring out the wood's inherent beauty. Less commonly used are metals such as brass and iron. A table of stone, suggestive of an altar, can be visually striking and convey the importance of the sacrament. Materials not recommended include clear Lucite, plastic, and imitation wood, all of which appear cheap and disposable, and seem to denigrate the sacrament. Since the table is already a symbol of the Supper and of Christ himself, there is no need to adorn it with more symbols (e.g., crosses, words, depictions of the Trinity); these are only distractions.

Altar-tables were traditionally set against the east wall since Christians (like people of other religions) faced eastward to pray. Also, long decisive for Christians was the belief that the risen Christ will return from the direction of the rising sun, the Mass being viewed as the anticipation of Christ's Second Coming. Today it is impractical for many church buildings to be designed so that the assembly faces true east during the liturgy. Hence, it is impossible to exploit the old symbolism.[12] More meaningful and practical for contemporary churches is a placement of the table that expresses the assembly's theology of the Lord's Supper itself, and in many cases this means the arrangement advocated by Luther and Bucer: a free-standing table that allows the minister to face the assembly.

A free-standing table has certain architectural requirements that must be considered carefully. The people-gathered-around-the-table effect is enhanced if some of the assembly seating – or perhaps only that of the choir – is positioned at a perpendicular angle to the table. It is unnecessary for assembly seating to "wrap" a full 360-degrees around the table in order to convey this understanding; the presider may even have difficulty maintaining eye contact with those seated behind him or her. An area approximately 1.5 m wide should be

[12] Lorraine S. Brugh and Gordon W. Lathrop, *The Sunday Assembly*, Using Evangelical Lutheran Worship, Vol. 1 (Minneapolis: Augsburg Fortress, 2008), 179.

left between the table and the wall or panel behind the table for ease of movement. It is best to avoid placing decorative paintings, sculptures, or stained glass immediately behind the table so that the minister's silhouette can be seen against a neutral background.The table should be elevated above the main worship space by two or three small steps in order to make the eucharistic actions visible to the assembly. Inadequate height makes it especially difficult for those seated at the opposite end of the room to see and participate in the eucharistic actions.

A free-standing table is possible even when there is an existing altar against a back wall. The latter may simply be moved out from the wall, so that the minister is able to stand behind it. Bedok Lutheran Church in Singapore repositioned its existing altar in precisely this way. Alternatively, if space is available, a new table may be placed in front of the existing table, and the old table is then used for holding communion vessels or other items (e.g., flowers, offering bags, or basins).

The question of where to locate the table within the overall plan of the liturgical space is often overlooked. Usually, it is assumed that the table will sit on the central axis of the space. However, there is no theological reason for a centralized location; an off-center location may actually draw the eye toward the table. Furthermore, the liturgical and theological equality of Word and Sacrament is aptly portrayed when the table and pulpit are placed beside one another across the front of the chancel.[13] These two liturgical centers may even be placed at opposite ends of the liturgical space in order to suggest their uniqueness and to highlight the transition made from the liturgy of the Word to the liturgy of the Meal. Examples of this arrangement include St. Patrick's Cathedral, Parramatta, New South Wales, Australia, and St. Meinrad's Archabbey, St. Meinrad, Indiana, USA. In some cases, the entire assembly moves from the Word area to the Meal area when the eucharistic liturgy begins.

---

[13] James F. White and Susan J. White, *Church Architecture: Building and Renovating for Christian Worship* (Akron, OH: OSL Publications, 1998), 46.

In many churches where worshippers come forward to receive communion, an altar rail is placed along the front of the liturgical space just before the table, or possibly around the table area on three or more sides. To avoid the appearance of a barrier, the rail should have an open design and be no more than .6 m tall. Since the communicants kneel on a step in front of the rail (as a sign of humility and submission) and place their arms on the rail, a relatively low height is necessary. Ideally, the material matches that of the other liturgical centers, whether wood, stone, or metal. The communicants should be kneeling on the same level as the area where the ministers move when distributing communion. Although not an absolute necessity, an altar rail can also be used for other actions involving kneeling: private prayer, the reception of ashes on Ash Wednesday, or anointing for healing.

Bread and Wine

Traditionally, Christians have used either leavened or unleavened bread for communion. In the Old Testament, unleavened bread was mainly associated with religious activities, such as the seven-day feast following the Passover (Ex. 12) and with various sacrifices (Lev. 2:5ff). It was also eaten at normal meals (e.g. Gen. 19:3). If the so-called "Last Supper" was a Passover meal, then the bread that Jesus and his disciples ate was *unleavened.* However, the New Testament does not command the use of unleavened bread for the Lord's Supper. Neither does evidence from the early church indicate the widespread use of unleavened bread. In the Middle Ages, the use of unleavened bread coincides with the rise of a sacrificial theology whereby the eucharistic actions amounted to the offering of Christ's body and blood to God as a kind of repetition of Calvary. Since Old Testament sacrifices used unleavened bread (cf. Lev. 2:4), it was natural for Christian priests to use unleavened bread in their "sacrifice." Although he rejects the idea that the Mass is a repetition of Calvary, Luther, with his typical conservatism, was content to use the traditional communion wafers, as was Zwingli. However, the BCP 1549 called for something "thicker" than the traditional communion wafers, while the BCP

1552 specified that the bread should be the same as that eaten at a normal meal.[14] John Calvin was flexible, stating that the bread could be either unleavened or leavened. Most worship books today permit either type of bread.[15]

Traditional wafer bread has both advantages and disadvantages. It calls to mind the sacrifices of the Old Testament involving unleavened bread, the Passover, and the Last Supper. From a practical standpoint, wafers can be stored for longer periods than normal bread. A presider's host (large wafer) is easily broken at the *fraction* (ceremonial breaking of the bread), and, with individual wafers, there is no need to break off pieces for each communicant. Yet, individual wafers obscure Paul's image of partaking of one loaf (1 Cor. 10:17). By supporting an individualistic understanding of Christianity and the Supper, wafers undermine the sense of a community sharing a common faith and a common meal. Any analogy with the Old Testament feast of Unleavened Bread is less than apt, since that observance occurs once annually and lasts for eight days, while the Lord's Supper is celebrated weekly.

Preferable is a leavened loaf of tasty, well-made bread that offers an association with common meals and proclaims that God comes to us through everyday things. Furthermore, a loaf of freshly baked bread connects better with biblical images of feasting (e.g., Is. 25:6; Rev. 19:9) and most aptly expresses Paul's idea of the church being a single body because of sharing a single loaf (1 Cor. 10:17). Besides appealing to the imagination, fresh bread appeals to the senses of taste and smell and so serves as a reminder that God seeks to redeem the whole person, soul, mind, and body. Yet the sense/taste factor should not be overplayed by selecting a bread with frostings, nuts, raisins, or other additional ingredients, items that only draw attention to themselves and detract from the spiritual meaning of the

[14] "The Supper of the Lord," BCP 1549, LWC, 266; "The Order for the Administration of the Lord's Supper," BCP 1552, LWC, 283.

[15] "Notes on the Liturgy," LBW, 28; Philip H. Pfatteicher and Carlos R. Messerli, *Lutheran Book of Worship: Manual on the Liturgy* (Minneapolis: Augsburg Publishing House, 1979), 232; UMG, 44; Brugh and Lathrop, *Sunday Assembly*, 187-89; "Service for the Lord's Day: Description," BCW, 43.

Supper. A loaf made from pure wheat flour (cf. Ex. 29:2; Ps. 81:16) is sufficient. A cross design cut into the top of the loaf is appropriate, but not absolutely necessary; bread becomes a means of communion with the Lord Jesus because of his promise, not because of how we adorn it.

A loaf does have a few minor drawbacks. First, crumbs will inevitably fall on the table and floor when the loaf is broken and pieces distributed to communicants. However, there can be no shame or scandal about the "mess" of a few crumbs when the Lord himself had a "messy" birth like the rest of humanity, and was not ashamed to give himself over to a "messy" execution. Second, some loaves are difficult to tear apart. Yet, ministers who experience such a problem may opt to use a pita-type bread that is easily torn apart for distribution. Alternatively, certain kinds of home-made communion breads are readily broken into smaller pieces.[16] Finally, people with allergies to wheat and/or gluten may be unable to eat traditional types of bread. But this problem is easily surmounted with the provision of a few wheat-free or gluten-free wafers. Thus, despite these slight difficulties, a loaf of common bread is recommended over wafers.

Like bread, wine has deep biblical resonance. Always consumed at banquets and at common meals in Old Testament times, wine was also a component of a sacrificial offering that included a lamb, flour, oil, or any combination of these items. It was also used for treating wounds. Beginning in the Hellenistic period of Judaism (from the third century BCE), it was used in the Passover liturgy.[17] There can be little doubt that Jesus shared a cup of wine with his disciples during the meal in the upper room. "Fruit of the vine" (Mark 14:25; Matt. 26:29; Luke: 22:18) can only refer to wine, since neither the Hebrew nor Christian scriptures know of any unfermented grape beverage. While the overuse of wine leading to drunkenness is disparaged in the Bible, (cf. Is. 28:7; Prov. 20:1), wine is also an image of God's abundant blessing (Gen. 27:28;

---

[16] For the recipe go to http://recipes.sparkpeople.com/recipe-detail.asp?recipe=467108 [access 9 July 2014].

[17] S.v. "Wine," *Interpreters Dictionary of the Bible.*

Joel 2:24), Jesus' own teaching (Matt. 9:17), and the eschatological day of salvation (cf. Is. 25:6; Mark 14:25). In its own right, wine (or juice) symbolizes the unity of the church: as the juice from many grapes forms one drink, so many individuals form the one church. Additionally, the crushing of the grapes and the resulting red-colored juice symbolize suffering.

Following the biblical example and the historical tradition of the church since its earliest times, Lutherans, Anglicans, Presbyterians, and other Protestant churches use fermented grape wine in the Lord's Supper. The type of wine (shiraz, merlot) is not as important as following the example of the Lord in using wine, and believing the promises that Christ makes concerning the cup. The color of wine does not assure a communion in Christ's blood; that reality is assured by the Lord's own words of promise. Any thought that the Lord's blood is received because we use wine that looks like blood is magicalism. Even white wine could be used, and may even be preferable because any stains left on communion linens are easier to launder. Varieties of wine that might strike worshippers as novel and thus distracting (e.g., sparkling, rosé, and others fruit wines) are discouraged. Port wine has long been used by many Anglicans (who add water to the chalice) and can be stored for longer periods because of its higher alcohol content.

The use of grape juice in communion was first broached among American Methodists in 1876 and became mandatory for them in 1988.[18] The practice was made possible by the invention of a special pasteurization process by the dentist and lay Methodist minister, Dr. Thomas B. Welch (1825-1903).[19] The impetus for using grape juice was the nineteenth-century movement against the

---

[18] "Word and Table I," UMBW, 33. I note, however, that the United Methodist Church's sacramental practices document states that "in accordance with Scripture and Christian tradition, the historic and ecumenical church uses wine in celebrations of Holy Communion" (*This Holy Mystery: A United Methodist Understanding of Holy Communion* [Nashville: General Board of Discipleship, United Methodist Church, 2004], 30.)

[19] James F. White, *Protestant Worship: Traditions in Transition* (Louisville: Westminster John Knox Press, 1989), 159.

consumption of alcohol in the United States that culminated in the Eighteenth Amendment to the United States Constitution (1919) which banned the production, transportation, and sale of alcoholic beverages.[20] Besides Methodists, churches that commune with grape juice include Baptists, Pentecostals, and a few other evangelical bodies. Positively, its use allows children to receive the cup, since any parental concerns about giving alcohol to children are eliminated. Additionally, its use can be a way of identifying with those struggling with addiction to alcohol and promoting abstinence among church members. Even some churches that regularly use wine offer grape juice to communicants with alcohol dependency issues or allergies, just as they might provide non-wheat bread to those allergic to wheat or gluten products.[21]

Responding to the food and beverage difficulties of church members requires careful thought and planning. Those suffering from alcoholism may not want to be identified as such publicly, in which case announcing that a certain minister will be serving grape juice may or may not encourage the alcohol-dependent to go to that minister. A somewhat better solution is for the communicant to request the juice upon arriving at the table area for communion. Communion ministers might occasionally partake of the juice as an encouragement to others and so that more than a few certain assembly members are identified as grape juice users. Worship leaders should ensure that the provision of alternatives to traditional bread and wine do not lead to cumbersome announcements, confused communicants, and embarrassed feelings all around. It is questionable whether providing alternatives is necessary at all, since some churches consider the reception of one element only to constitute full sacramental participation.[22] To suggest that some communicants receive only the bread or only the cup is not to deny the validity of the traditional Protestant insistence on communion in both kinds. It was one thing for the medieval church to abrogate the example of

[20] This measure was repealed in 1933.

[21] UMG, 44C, 44D.

[22] UMG, 44D.

Christ and impose communion under one kind on all Christians, but quite another if the contemporary church seeks to modify that example in the case of a few persons for pastoral reasons.

In some parts of the world (e.g., Africa and Asia), bread and wine (or grape juice) are unavailable either because wheat and grapes are not grown or because there is not a viable commercial market for bread and wine. For churches in these areas, it is legitimate to seek alternative local foods to serve as the communion elements. The selection of such foods, however, must be done with care and sensitivity because not all foods and beverages are culturally adequate. Following the method of liturgical contextualization known as *dynamic equivalence*, any alternatives should be the local culture's equivalents of bread and wine. This means a cake or loaf made from the local staple grain (e.g., rice), and the local festive or ceremonial drink, preferably one made using a fermentation process, e.g., Japanese sake. Such cultural correspondence is necessary in order to celebrate the Lord's Supper at an appropriate cultural level, one that does not demean the Supper. The early church attempted to achieve this by modeling the Supper on the *symposium*, which was a kind of "supper club" for religious and other societies in the ancient world.[23] The structure and customs of the symposium not only clothed the Lord's Supper in a culturally recognizable form, but gave it cultural respectability. Such respectability would be impossible if the Supper used cheap, ubiquitous street foods (e.g., Coca-Cola and pizza), or modeled itself on the Western television talk show with its frothy, banal content. The Lord's Supper has to rise to a more serious level than suggested by mass-produced food and low-level entertainment if it is to qualify as a sacred meal. This is of special importance in Africa and Asia where a sense of sacredness was never diminished by the Western world's Enlightenment of the seventeenth and eighteenth centuries.

---

[23] In the symposium, a meal was a followed by musical entertainment, a short drama, a reading of poetry, or a (religious) discourse with the consumption of wine. We can see the two-fold structure of the symposium in John 13, where a supper is followed by the dramatic footwashing action and Jesus' discourse on mutual love.

But is this inculturation of the elements really necessary? Couldn't churches in developed countries simply supply churches in mission lands with bread and wine? First, we might wonder whether this solution would foster an unhealthy dependence. Second, it may also assume an uninterrupted supply of bread and wine from the foreign donor to the local recipient. Yet, many lands are affected by wars and other political upheavals that could slow or prevent the supply of bread and wine from reaching the intended recipient. Third, and most importantly, the use of local elements makes an important theological statement, namely, that the gospel seeks to be incarnated in the flesh of local culture. When the local equivalents of bread and wine are used, the implication is that God and the church are not against local culture, but desire to use the best of culture for proclaiming the gospel.

The issue of inculturation is somewhat more complicated in the case of non-Western societies where bread and wine are commercially available, e.g., Japan and major urban areas of China. On the one hand, it does not seem appropriate to expect Asian cultures to use Western staple foods for communion. But, on the other hand, if these are readily available, their use might be expected. Although contextualization has a certain urgency, biblical fidelity is also important. Bread and wine are used because the Lord instituted the Supper as a meal with bread and wine, both of which have strong biblical resonance that shape our understanding of the Supper. Bread was part of the Passover observance that celebrated Israel's deliverance from slavery; thus we eat bread in our Supper recognizing it as a meal of salvation. In certain Old Testament narratives (1 Sam. 21:1-6; 1 Kings 17:1-6, 7-16), bread serves as an image of God's sustenance. The feeding of the masses in the gospels makes bread a symbol of the Messiah's provision for God's people. When we eat the bread of the Supper, we know ourselves to be fed and sustained by Christ himself. Wine is an image of salvation from death (Is. 25:1-6) and of joy and festivity in which the Lord himself is present in a transformative way (John 2:1-12). When we drink wine, we participate in our future deliverance now and experience joy in the presence of Christ.

(Although Christians do not always think of these things, it would be good if they were reminded of them occasionally from the pulpit!) If elements with little or no resemblance to bread and wine are used regularly, we might wonder whether biblically literate Christians can connect the Supper with the great biblical narratives of feeding, sustenance, and salvation. Churches that take historical continuity and ecumenicity seriously will not whimsically seek alternatives to wheat bread and grape wine for their celebration of the Supper. Only in contexts where bread and wine (or their ingredients) are unavailable should alternative forms of the communion elements be sought.

Of course, the contextualization of the communion elements is not necessarily an either-or proposition. In some cases, the bread can be a uniquely local *kind* of wheat bread, as one might find in a traditional bakery in China, Taiwan, or Singapore. Such breads would be truly local (contextual), and yet still be recognizable as a wheat bread, with all of its biblical connotations. Admittedly, grape wine may be more difficult to contextualize, since grapes require specific growing conditions that are not duplicable in every region. Yet, we might note the growth of wine production and consumption in both Japan and China at the present time.

Vessels

The diversity of communion practices among Protestants means a diversity of communion vessels. Fidelity to biblical imagery would suggest the use of a single *chalice* (ceremonial cup) and a single loaf during the eucharistic prayer (Great Thanksgiving). The single cup and loaf make the most visual impact when as few vessels as possible are placed on the table. Extra chalices for serving the wine or juice can be brought to the table just before the communion of the assembly and filled from a *flagon* (pitcher) of wine or juice that is on the table during the eucharistic prayer. Even when pre-filled trays of bread and wine/juice are on the table for the consecration, it is still desirable that the presider use a chalice and a loaf (or larger presider's host), so that (1) the imagery of 1 Cor. 10:7 is not completely obscured;

and (2) those seated at a distance can clearly see the bread and cup during the minister's actions at the Words of Institution (i.e., the manual acts).

The vessels used for bread will depend on the type used. Wafers might be placed in special stacked bread trays that are set on the altar-table before the service and covered with a large cloth. A presider's host is placed in the top tray or on a separate plate for the minister's use during the eucharistic prayer. Lutherans and Anglicans might place the presider's host on a *paten* (bread plate) that fits on top of the chalice, which is vested in cloths of the liturgical color and placed on the table at the beginning of the liturgy. Alternatively, a vested chalice/paten or one covered only with a *pall* and *purificator* may be placed on a *credence table* (see below for descriptions of these items). A bowl-like vessel known as a *ciborium* may be filled with wafers and likewise set on the credence table. The chalice/paten and ciborium are brought to the table during the preparation (i.e., during the offering). If a large loaf is used, it may be placed on the table (Methodists, Presbyterians) or credence table (Lutherans, Anglicans) prior to the service. If the offertory involves a procession of the elements, the loaf is placed on a table in the back of the liturgical space. A loaf requires either a metal or ceramic paten of about 25 cm in diameter, or a wicker basket. An extra bread vessel is needed if more than one minister distributes the bread.

Generally for Methodists, Presbyterians, and various free-churches, trays of small glasses containing the wine or juice are also placed on the table prior to the service. Lutherans and Anglicans bring the wine to the table during the offertory, the former in a large, pitcher-like flagon and the latter in a small vessel called a *cruet*. Only then is the wine poured into the chalice. Traditionally, Anglicans will mix a little water into the chalice.While Anglicans distribute the elements by means of *intinction* (dipping the wafer into a chalice of wine), Lutherans generally pour the wine into individual cups held by the communicants. This practice requires a special chalice with a pouring lip and the distribution of individual (plastic) cups to the communicants. Some Lutheran and Anglican churches also offer the option of a chalice from which the communicants may drink directly – the *common cup*.

While all of the bread and wine must be on the altar for the eucharistic prayer (i.e., the consecration), the same is not true of the vessels. Indeed, because they can otherwise give the table a cluttered appearance, extra chalices and bread containers are brought to the table immediately prior to the distribution, e.g., during the singing of the Agnus Dei in the Lutheran or Anglican communion liturgies, which is normally the first communion hymn.

Just as a festive banquet requires a special table cloth and napkins, so the Lord's Supper requires special cloths. Nearly all Protestants cover the communion table with a *fair linen*, which is a cloth of fine material slightly narrower than the width of the table and overhanging the short sides of the table by several inches. Its purpose is to protect the table from dirt and stains. Extending down in front of the table might be an *antependium*, a vestment in the seasonal liturgical color which may be adorned with eucharistic or other symbols. Alternatively, the table might be entirely covered with a floor-length Jacobean or Laudian frontal in the seasonal color with or without liturgical symbols.[24] The special *eucharistic linens* needed for the Lutheran and Anglican liturgies are as follows:

1. Corporal – a square measuring 46 × 46 cm or larger, but never wider than the table's *mensa*. Spread on top of the fair linen during the preparation at the offering (not before), the corporal serves to keep bread crumbs from falling on the fair linen and the wine from staining it. Corporals are usually folded four times in order to form a smaller square and then unfolded on the table such that an embroidered cross is immediately in front of the presider.
2. Purificator – a fine linen measuring 30.5 × 30.5 cm that is used for wiping the rim of a chalice and the lip of a pouring

[24] This vestment received its name from James I, King of England (1603-25) and William Laud, Archbishop of Canterbury (1633-45).

chalice, or for wiping up wine or juice spills. One of these is placed between the chalice and paten to prevent scratches.

3. Pall – a plastic square usually measuring 18 × 18 cm that is covered with fine linen and placed on top of a chalice to keep out dirt and foreign objects.
4. Veil – a vestment in the liturgical color, with or without liturgical symbols, that covers the chalice (and pall). A vested chalice is placed either on a credence table or on the communion table itself from the beginning of the service.
5. Burse – a stiffened envelope covered with colored fabric and often adorned with symbols. It sits on top of the vested chalice and holds the corporal and purificators.

In Methodist and Presbyterian churches, the stacked trays containing the bread and wine/juice, are usually covered entirely with a simple white cloth that is sometimes embroidered with symbols.

Hygiene and Cleanliness

The rise of medical science and public health in the nineteenth and twentieth centuries created new social attitudes about germs, health, and personal contact. The use of grape juice and individual glasses are examples of how these attitudes have impacted communion practices.[25] In more recent years, the outbreaks of AIDS and SARS have led to reservations about the use of the common cup and to greater concerns about the cleanliness of the communion ministers' hands. It certainly is possible to take cleanliness too far with measures that draw attention to themselves, disrupt the liturgy, or imply that certain actions (e.g., ministers cleansing their hands) are of theological and liturgical importance. Yet, concerns that church members have about the cleanliness of communion food and vessels need to be addressed, regardless of how rational or well-informed these might be. Maintaining a sufficient level of cleanliness helps to address these concerns and allay fears, but the measures taken need not be extreme.

[25] For a fine discussion of this topic, see Frank C. Senn, *A Stewardship of the Mysteries* (New York/Mahwah, NJ: Paulist Press, 1999), 138-54.

The standards of cleanliness for Holy Communion and the resulting procedures are related to local concerns and conditions, e.g., weather, the presence of insects, the susceptibility of the population to disease, which means that there will be variation from region to region.

A loaf of bread should be freshly made or defrosted in the hours prior to the service, and remain in plastic wrapping until pre-service preparations are made. It is then wrapped in a cloth and placed on a paten or into a basket. The bread vessel is then set on the table, credence table, or, if there is a procession with the elements, on a table in the back of the worship space. At the preparation of the table (during the offering or communion hymn), the cloth cover is removed, and once uncovered the bread need not be covered again. (Keeping the loaf in plastic wrapping throughout most of the service is unnecessary and potentially creates a distracting spectacle when ministers try to remove it.) Only the presiding minister need touch the loaf, and in many cases, he or she will have already engaged in hand cleansing. Following the service, any leftover pieces from the loaf are completely consumed by the ministers (or perhaps assembly members); a few small pieces for the sick or homebound should be retained for distribution later that same day.

Wafers should be stored in airtight containers and perhaps even refrigerated. Prior to the service, they are placed in the stacked bread plates or in a ciborium where they remain covered until the preparation at the offering or communion hymn. Likewise, a presider's host is kept covered until that time. What to do with leftover communion wafers is problematic both hygienically and theologically. It is questionable whether wafers that have been exposed and possibly handled should be returned to their original container. It also seems inappropriate to store something that has been set aside for a holy use, i.e., consecrated. If bread is a means of communion with the Lord Jesus Christ, then it is contradictory to treat it like ordinary table bread. Leftover communion wafers are best retained (reserved) for the communion of the sick or homebound following the service or later during the week. Otherwise, the assembly will need to find a way of providing a number of wafers that approximately equals the number communicants (e.g., asking each communicant to place a wafer into a ciborium at the beginning of the service using special tongs).

Wine or juice from newly-opened containers is poured into vessels that have been thoroughly washed. Plastic communion cups are taken either from a newly-opened container or one that has been tightly sealed while in storage. At the preparation time just before the Great Thanksgiving (offertory or communion hymn), the covers on the stacked cup trays are removed. The chalice remains vested until the preparation at the offering, and the purificator or pall need not be replaced after the chalice is filled with wine. Other chalices are covered until filled in preparation for the distribution. During the service, a flagon is covered or closed until the wine is poured into the chalice, and it remains open during the eucharistic prayer. If the flagon has a removable stopper, it need not be replaced once removed. Following the service, used plastic cups are discarded. If a common cup is used during the distribution, it is sufficient if the rim is wiped with a purificator after each communicant drinks from it; concerns about the chalice's spreading germs through contact with the mouth should not be exaggerated.[26] All wine or juice not used for the communion should be consumed by the ministers (or others) following the service, rather than returned to containers for future use.

Those who prepare the elements prior to the service (an altar guild or committee) should be encouraged to wash their hands thoroughly before handling elements and vessels. The surfaces on which the elements are prepared should be cleaned regularly and used for no other purpose.

Any hand cleansing by communion ministers in the service is carried out discreetly. There is nothing particularly edifying about watching a minister wash his hands or seeing a group of ministers use hand-sanitizing gel as they stand in full view of the assembly. The traditional hand washing or lavabo carried out by Anglican or Roman Catholic priests was originally a private devotion with no

[26] See Senn, *Stewardship of the Mysteries*, 141-46.

hygienic purpose in mind at all. It is recommended that any hand-cleansing take place out of the assembly's sight, perhaps in a sacristy or other room located near the table area. If nothing else, ministers can cleanse their hands while seated on the front row of pews or chairs. If the bread is distributed by serving elders, as in some Reformed churches, these ministers need only cleanse their hands prior to the distribution; it is not necessary for them to wear protective plastic gloves, the sight of which is unedifying and distracting.

Mindful that hands easily obtain and spread germs, some practices are not recommend:

- Allowing communicants themselves to break off pieces of bread from a loaf held by the presiding minister
- The minister pressing the hand of the communicant when giving the bread (theologically unnecessary, liturgically ambiguous, hygienically suspect).

Although it has a long history and eliminates the need for individual communion cups, intinction is probably one of the least hygienic communion practices in Protestantism. In many cases, fingers contaminate the wine and chalice as communicants reach into the cup. The practice is forbidden by the Roman Catholic Church.

Other Physical Requirements

Several other items are necessary for the celebration of the Lord's Supper. The minister needs a stand for a worship folder so that his/her hands can be free during the eucharistic prayer. *Missal* or *altar book stands* come in a great variety of styles and materials including wood and brass. Many missal stands are designed to match the other liturgical appointments (e.g., candlestick holders). An elaborate, expensive stand is not essential, and a simple wooden one usually works well. Recommended is one with an adjustable angle to fit ministers of different heights. Alternatively, a special cushion could be used to prop the folder up at an angle for the presider. If the stand is not too heavy, it may be placed elsewhere and brought to the table during the preparation of the elements.

Anglicans (and some Lutherans) require a set of vessels for the ritual hand washing known as the *lavabo*. Included in the set are: (1) a small bowl over which the minister holds his/her hands; (2) a small pitcher from which an assistant pours the water; (3) a towel for the minister to dry his/her hands; and (4) a tray upon which these items are placed. Normally made of glass (sometimes metal), the lavabo vessels are small and inconspicuous since the washing of the minister's hands is really his/her own private devotion and a sign of spiritual purity, rather than an essential liturgical action.

A *credence table*, usually found in Lutheran and Anglican churches, is used to hold the various items needed for communion, including chalices, plates, ciboria, burse, linens, lavabo set, missal stand, and perhaps a small wafer container known as a *pyx*, which is used for the communion of the sick and homebound. Usually small and narrow, the credence table is placed against a wall close to the communion table so that vessels need only be carried a short distance. Alternatively, some churches have shelves built into the chancel walls for the communion vessels.

Other items found in the table area are those with a symbolic and decorative purpose. Although not so common in Asia, many churches place candles on or near the altar to symbolize the "fire" of the Holy Spirit and/or the light of God's Word. Originally, candles were meant to illuminate the priest's altar book, but this need is now met by electrical lighting. Candles are placed at opposite ends of the *mensa,* or processional torches may be placed at convenient locations near the table. Recommended are candles with a bee's wax content of 50% or more, since these burn cleanly and efficiently. To be avoided are so-called "oil candles" because of their propensity to emit smoke and because as imitation candles, they belie the Christian virtues of honesty and integrity. It would be better to use real oil lamps on or near the table if ritual fire is desired. Freshly-cut flowers add beauty to the service and symbolize life and growth, but are never placed on the *mensa* itself, lest they create clutter and secondary visual foci. Instead, flower containers are placed on special pedestal stands near the table or perhaps on the floor. Similarly, offering basins, bags, or trays, which need not be kept in the assembly's sight during the service, are left on a credence table or on special stands. A processional cross may stand near the table during the service, or a large cross (or crucifix) may be permanently suspended over the altar. A profusion of crosses, however, will only draw attention away from the table.

Vessels, vestments, paraments, linens, flower vases, candles, and other liturgical items are stored in a special room known as a *sacristy*. Because some vessels are made from costly metals, some of the sacristy cupboards require locks. Besides storage space, the sacristy needs to be equipped with a sink for washing vessels and perhaps a small refrigerator-freezer for the bread and wine. There should also be a countertop (as in a normal kitchen) for the pre-service preparation of the elements, flowers, and other items. The sacristy is located as close as possible to the worship space for convenience. A sacristy is best included in the architectural plan of a new worship space, otherwise the retrofitting of a building with a sacristy could prove difficult and yield unsatisfying results.

Conclusion

In a way, the church is a banquet facility. It is here that a great event with an honored guest occurs each Sunday when God's people gather for the Lord's Supper. Like the overseers of a secular banquet hall, the worship leaders of a church must see to the physical requirements of the Meal, making sure that all of the necessary items are present, well-maintained, and used for their purposes. All of these tasks may seem burdensome, and there is always a temptation to be careless. But the grace-filled presence of the honored guest transforms our burden into joy, and a cavalier attitude into a deeper sense of Christian stewardship. So it is hoped that worship leaders will attend to the matters discussed in this chapter with both faith and love, as part of their self-offering to the God of Grace.

For Further Reading

Galley, Howard E. *The Ceremonies of the Eucharist: A Guide to Celebration.* Cambridge, MA: Cowley Publications, 1989.

Michno, Dennis G. *A Priest's Handbook: The Ceremonies of the Church.* 3rd Edition. Harrisburg, PA: Morehouse Publishing, 1998.

Stauffer, S. Anita. *Altar Guild and Sacristy Handbook.* 4th Revised Edition. Minneapolis: Augsburg Fortress, 2014.

CHAPTER 13

The Lord's Supper and its Participants

It seems that participation in the Lord's Supper during the earliest years of Christianity was a simple matter: Christians gathered in private homes, prayed, studied the Scriptures, and "broke bread," i.e., celebrated the Lord's Supper (Acts 2:42, 46). The New Testament furnishes few details about (1) who led or presided over the eucharistic actions; (2) whether any qualifications other than baptism were necessary for admission to the Supper; and (3) whether persons from other Christian communities could receive communion. But issues of presidency, qualifications for admission, and hospitality eventually took on importance and have even become divisive. We might therefore wish that we could return to the apparent simplicity and informality of the primitive church's eucharistic celebrations! Yet, it is never possible to turn back the hands of time, and attempting to do so may even be irresponsible and escapist. A better approach is to try to understand why certain procedures and teachings developed and then reflect on their value for today's church. This chapter will focus on the pastoral and ecclesial issues surrounding the persons who participate in the Lord's Supper, both as leaders and assembly members. While readers may not agree with the positions taken, it is hoped that they will at least be motivated to research the teachings of their own traditions in order to develop a pastoral practice that is consistent and theologically sound.

Age of First Communion

Nothing is said in the New Testament about the age for admission to the Lord's Supper. It is apparent that the first converts to Christianity were adults who heard and responded to the apostolic message with repentance and acceptance of baptism. These persons subsequently took part in celebrations of the Lord's Supper (cf. Acts 2:41-42), the only apparent qualification for admission to the Table being baptism. As time progressed, the baptism of infants became more prevalent and eventually normative by the sixth century. There is evidence that in some ancient churches baptized infants received communion soon after their baptism, even at the same service as their baptism. In the early sixth-century, a Roman deacon named John responded to a series of questions about Roman baptismal practice posed by a nobleman of the name Senarius. John indicates that *all* baptismal rites are bestowed on infants, and this included the first reception of communion, since a newly-baptized person was arrayed in white "so that clad in a wedding garment he may approach the table of the heavenly bridegroom as a new man."[1] The *Ordo Romanus XI*, a set of rubrical instructions from the late–seventh century, states that: "After this [i.e., the conferral of postbaptismal gestures] they go in to Mass and all the infants receive communion. Care is to be taken lest after they have been baptized they receive any food or suckling before they communicate."[2] Although the communion of infants at the time of their baptism continued in Eastern churches, the practice slowly died out in the West. But this development had nothing to do with the question of whether infants were fit to receive communion; rather, it reflects the development of eucharistic theology and practice. From

[1] John, *Letter to Senarius* (ca. 500) (see DBL, 211).

[2] *Ordo Romanus XI* (ca. 700) (see DBL, 251).

about the tenth century on, a growing sacramental realism that identified the elements with the actual body and blood of Christ led to an exaggerated scrupulosity about the elements. Cloths were placed under the mouths of communicants so that crumbs of the precious body of Christ would not fall to the floor. But the cup was completely withdrawn from the laity, because any spillage could not be re-collected and disposed of reverently. The withdrawal of the cup from the laity effectively excommunicated infants who, unable to digest the bread, could only receive a small amount of wine placed into their mouths by the priest's finger which had been dipped into the chalice. Additionally, the requirement of the Fourth Lateran Council (1215) that confession precede communion ruled out infant participation in the cup. Yet, the practice did continue in some areas for a while, and there was even a revival of infant communion among the Hussites in what is now the Czech Republic.[3] But in an effort to uphold the requirement of confession before communion, the Council of Trent (1545-63) declared that the communion of children "before the years of discretion" (approximately age 7) was unnecessary.[4] (We might note that the Council's declaration actually witnessed to the survival of infant communion, since church officials do not discourage what is not actually practiced.) Thus, after a history of nearly one thousand years, infant communion more or less ceased.

The Protestant Reformers saw no reason to advocate infant communion. They were committed to providing catechetical teaching that prepared children for participation in the Supper, and this meant that children had to be intellectually capable of receiving instruction and training (see ch. 8). Luther called on the heads of households to instruct children in the basic Christian teachings so that they could participate (intelligently) in the Lord's Supper.[5] Martin

---

[3] David R. Holeton, *Infant Communion – Then and Now*, Grove Liturgical Study No. 27 (Bramcote, Nottinghamshire: Grove Books, 1981), 9.

[4] *The Canons and Decrees of the Council of Trent*, trans. H. J. Schroeder, O. P. (Rockford, IL: Tan Books and Publishers, Inc., 1978), 134.

[5] Martin Luther, *Large Catechism* (1529), BC, 476.87.

Bucer also emphasized catechetical instruction for children, but, unlike Luther, he produced a service of confirmation that included a formal admission to communion. Yet, this service was only used by Lutherans and never found usage among Reformed churches. The first Anglican Prayer Books stipulated that only those confirmed by a bishop could be admitted to communion, and confirmation required (1) the ability to recite the creed, the Lord's Prayer, and the Ten Commandments; and (2) the spiritual maturity to profess the faith for one's self.[6] Thus, Anglicans made catechetical knowledge and a personal confession of faith the primary requirements for receiving communion. John Calvin, like Luther, envisioned a process whereby those baptized in infancy receive catechetical instruction, make a public confession of faith (usually on the Sunday before communion), and then take their first communion.[7] Neither Calvin nor Zwingli produced a rite of confirmation or one of admission to communion. In early Methodism, communion was restricted to adults who demonstrated repentance and holiness of living and could produce evidence of their good standing in the church (a communion "ticket"). Although John Wesley believed that baptism (and not confirmation) admitted one to communion, children were not given communion in Methodist churches until they could understand the spiritual meaning of the Supper and demonstrate their faith.

The late-twentieth century saw a number of mainline Protestant churches lower the age for first communion. While traditionally confirming and giving first communion to teenagers, Lutherans in North America[8] and Europe[9] all began allowing children (ages 7-10) to receive communion prior to their confirmation. Lutheran

[6] "Confirmation," BCP 1549, CIRP, 236-38, 243. See also "Confirmation," BCP 1552, CIRP, 251-52.

[7] Hughes Oliphant Old, *The Shaping of the Reformed Baptismal Rite in the Sixteenth Century* (Grand Rapids: Eerdmans, 1992), 220.

[8] Jeffrey A. Truscott, *The Reform of Baptism and Confirmation in North American Lutheranism* (Lanham, MD/Oxford: Scarecrow Press, 2003), 142.

[9] *...and do not hinder them: An Ecumenical Plea for the Admission of Children to the Eucharist,* ed. Geiko Müller-Fahrenholz, Faith and Order Paper No. 109 (Geneva: World Council of Churches, 1982), 73-76.

Churches in Asia followed suit a few decades later.[10] Currently, some Lutheran churches permit the communion of *infants* at the service of their baptism, although communion on a regular basis will not begin until a child can eat and drink and understand the theological meaning of the sacrament.[11] Presbyterians in the USA similarly began lowering the age for first communion during this same time period.[12] The current *Book of Order* states that

> Baptized children who are being nurtured and instructed in the significance of the invitation to the Table and the meaning of their response are invited to receive the Lord's Supper, recognizing that their understanding of participation will vary according to their maturity.[13]

It is noteworthy that no specific age is mentioned by the Presbyterian document. Anglicans began discussions about admitting children to communion in the late 1960s. Believing that baptism admits to Holy Communion, some Anglicans have been willing to allow the baptized to receive communion *regardless* of age, while others, stressing the same theological principle, have said that admission could occur in the early school-age years, and still others have continued to require confirmation before communion.[14] This third category includes the Church of England itself and most Asian dioceses.[15] Methodist churches in the latter part of the twentieth century have generally been open to the communion of children. Officially, the United Methodist Church (USA) admits children to the Table, including

---

[10] Lutheran Church in Singapore, *A Promised Feast for Children: First Communion for Children* (Singapore, 2011).

[11] UMG, 37C, 37D, and 37E.

[12] *...do not hinder them*, 78.

[13] "Directory for Worship," in *The Constitution of the Presbyterian Church (U.S.A.) Part II: The Book of Order* (Louisville: Office of the General Assembly, 2013), W-2.4011b.

[14] *...do not hinder them*, 77.

[15] *Canons of the Church of England* (London: Church House Publishing, 2000), B15a.

infants, although it stresses the need for instruction.[16] Many Methodist churches around the world today lack any standard of admission to communion, with local custom and pastoral discretion determining any preconditions.[17]

The lowering of the age of first communion and the setting aside of the requirement of confirmation in Protestantism seems to have been influenced by several factors. First, liturgical scholarship made churches aware that catechetical instruction and a public confession of faith were not a precondition to communion at all times and in all places. We noted above that the practice of infant communion lasted for nearly a millennium in Western Christianity, and, in some cases, there was a "catechizing" of infants that consisted of no more than short expositions of the gospels, the creed, and the Lord's Prayer in the presence of infant baptismal candidates.[18] Second, liturgical scholarship also highlighted the unity of baptism, the laying on of hands (confirmation), and first communion, which underscores the inherent relationship between baptism and communion. Simply put: Christian liturgical history teaches us that baptism admits to communion and communion is the culminating act of Christian initiation. Third, ecumenical discussions with the Roman Catholic and Orthodox churches brought to light the communion of younger children (age 7) in the Catholic Church and infants in Orthodox churches. Fourth, Christians re-discovered the essence of the church as "the whole people of God," as opposed to a collection of individuals who come together for the sake of convenience.[19] This renewed ecclesiology helped Christians to see baptized children as true members of the church, which naturally raised the question of their participation in the Lord's Supper. Thus, the lowering of the

[16] *This Holy Mystery: A United Methodist Understanding of Holy Communion* (Nashville: The General Board of Discipleship of the United Methodist Church, 2003), 16.

[17] Karen B. Westerfield Tucker, *American Methodist Worship* (Oxford: University Press, 2001), 143-48.

[18] *The Gelasian Sacramentary* XXIV-XXVI (seventh century), ed. H. A. Wilson (Oxford: 1894) (see DBL, 218-25).

[19] *...do not hinder them*, 6.

age for first communion reflects a greater awareness of Christian history combined with a more profound ecclesiology.

Admitting younger children to communion brings both challenges and benefits. The former include (1) ensuring adequate instruction of children; (2) helping congregations to understand changes in long-standing practices; and (3) dealing with pastoral difficulties caused by a lack of uniformity, e.g., when a family with young children who receive communion transfers membership to a congregation that only permits confirmed (teenage) youth to commune; and (4) redefining the meaning and purpose of confirmation. Yet, the communion of children (including infants) affords the opportunity to better appreciate the meaning of baptism. Admitting baptized children to the Supper clarifies that baptism is full and complete initiation because it leads to communion. The practice also sheds light on the meaning of the church. Receiving communion with the "least" members of the church reveals the diversity and inclusiveness of the church as a community of both old and young (a reality that is obscured when children's activities take place concurrently with the main worship service).When people of all ages gather at the Table, we can better appreciate the "many" in Paul's statement that "because there is one loaf, we, who are many, are one body, for we all share the one loaf" (1 Cor. 10:17).

Decisions about the age (or timing) for admission to communion are best made on a denomination-wide basis. Although Protestantism has traditionally affirmed diversity in practice, a lack of uniformity in this area is potentially problematic since children who commune in one congregation might be barred from doing so in another. Such situations could lead to conflict between congregations and perhaps even a sense of competition that undermines church unity. It would be preferable for local churches to come together at denomination-wide gatherings to discuss the age of admission to communion and to develop policies for entire national or regional church bodies. As it happens, the question of the age for first communion mostly affects mainline Protestant churches that have a strong sense of denominational identity and are therefore quite amenable to cooperation with other local churches at a national or regional level.

As noted above, most churches that admit younger children to communion insist that they receive basic instruction on the meaning of the sacrament. Accordingly, local churches are challenged to find or develop instructional materials to meet this need and devise an instructional program to prepare children for communion. It might be best if the instructional materials were developed by a denomination-wide body with expert input to help ensure theological soundness.[20] Also, it is desirable that parents participate in the pre-communion instruction of their children so that they can reinforce learnings at home and answer questions posed by their children. Parental participation will have the collateral effect of renewing parents in their own understanding of the Supper and deepen their participation in the sacrament. Besides children and parents, it is likely that local congregations will also require instruction and explanation concerning any policy of admitting younger children to communion and the rationale behind it, especially if there has been a long-standing practice of requiring confirmation prior to participation in communion.

Because admission to the Lord's Supper is granted by baptism itself, there is no need for any special rite of admission to communion; such a rite would only obscure the role of baptism as the gateway to the Supper. When several children receive their first communion, the worship leader (pastor) might announce this fact to the assembly at the beginning of the service, informally welcome the children, and then offer a brief prayer.[21] At the appropriate time, the children simply receive communion with their families, or with members of the assembly who have provided them with Christian care and nurture in lieu of their (non-Christian) families. Nothing more needs to be said or done.

---

[20] See Lutheran Church in Singapore, *A Promised Feast.*

[21] For an example of such an announcement see "Notes on the Liturgy," LBW, 32.

Eucharistic Hospitality

Frequently, an assembly's communion service will be attended by visitors who are members of other Christian churches. Can such persons be admitted to the Table, i.e., be shown eucharistic hospitality? Protestants vary in their approaches, and the range of policies may be categorized as follows:

1. No hospitality
2. Hospitality on the condition of formal ecumenical agreements allowing "Table fellowship" among assemblies that belong to the signatory churches
3. Hospitality on the condition that guests at the Table be baptized and confirmed members of their own churches
4. Hospitality to *any* persons, regardless of whether they have been baptized and confirmed.

Some Lutherans believe that because Christ himself is present in the sacrament, the invitation to receive communion comes directly from him to the baptized (only).[22] Other Lutherans admit only visitors who are members of their own denomination or of Lutheran churches with whom there is "pulpit and altar fellowship." Lutherans who practice this type of "closed" communion generally ask visitors to notify the pastor prior to receiving communion for the first time. Anglican churches generally extend hospitality to baptized and communing members of other churches that accept traditional trinitarian doctrine.[23] Stressing the invitation of Christ, Presbyterians extend eucharistic hospitality to the baptized while emphasizing the need for repentance and reconciliation.[24] Most Methodist churches permit other Christians to receive communion, in some cases without stipulating baptism.[25]

---

[22] UMG, 49A.

[23] *Canons of the Church of England*, 15A, 1b.

[24] "Directory for Worship," *Book of Order*, W-2.4011.

[25] *This Holy Mystery*, 17.

Although a somewhat neuralgic issue, eucharistic hospitality is desirable for a number of reasons. First, by permitting members of other churches to receive communion, the assembly visibly manifests the unity which the Supper both signifies and effects (1 Cor. 10:17). Second, eucharistic hospitality dispels any sense of intra-Christian rivalry that might scandalize the world. Third, welcoming other Christians to our tables reflects the inclusivity of the kingdom of God as manifested in the life and teaching of Jesus Christ (cf. Matt. 9:10, 8:10-12). Fourth, eucharistic hospitality affirms that baptism is the basis of Christian unity.[26] While critics might contend that hospitality does not allow for church leaders to properly discern the worthiness of potential communicants, it could be argued that such discernment falls on the communicants themselves (cf. 1 Cor. 11:28) and any attempt to discern the disposition of another can be far from perfect. Even if church authorities "examined and absolved" communicants during the Reformation-era,[27] (1) this examination may have reflected a need to instill correct doctrine among the local faithful; and (2) the Reformers were not living in religiously pluralistic societies like modern Christians. It is questionable whether the principle of "examining and absolving" really applies to the modern issue of eucharistic hospitality.

Eucharistic hospitality has a number of practical requirements. First, a written statement or verbal announcement is needed to clarify who exactly is welcome to receive communion. A verbal announcement is best made immediately prior to the distribution, or the same information could be screened using PowerPoint just before communion. An example is the following: "All baptized Christians are invited to commune. Please proceed down the center aisle to collect your communion cup. Put the used cup in the tray as you return to your seat via the side aisle. If you are not baptized yet, you may come to the table for a blessing. Please cross your arms in front

---

[26] Cf. *Baptism, Eucharist and Ministry*, Faith and Order Paper No. 111 (Geneva: World Council of Churches, 1982), which states that baptism is "the basic bond of unity" (3.6).

[27] See *Augsburg Confession* (1530), Art. XXIV, BC, 258.1.

of you." Second, visitors also need to receive practical instructions about how to receive the elements, e.g., how to proceed to the place of communion and whether communicants drink the wine (from a chalice or individual cups) or whether intinction is practiced. It may be advantageous to offer a welcome and instructions in both spoken and written forms in order to accommodate hearing-impaired persons and those not present during any verbal announcement. In some cases, the unbaptized might be invited to the Table to receive a blessing during the communion; ideally, they would be invited to receive baptism.

Eucharistic hospitality becomes challenging in a service of Christian marriage. On the one hand, it seems an appropriate occasion for the Lord's Supper, since every wedding service is an anticipation of the marriage Supper of the Lamb (Rev. 19:9). As husband and wife begin their life together, it is fitting that they should share in the church's meal of unity. On the other hand, there are many social contexts in which a significant number of attendees at the service may not be Christian, e.g., Asian countries. In that case, it seems inhospitable and detrimental to mission to engage in a communal ritual that will, in principle, exclude many. Communing the bride and groom only is an inadequate solution, since that would reduce the Supper to a nuptial rite and obscure its communal character. A number of official documents recommend that communion be offered to *all* baptized Christians present at a marriage service, not only to the couple and their families.[28] Indeed, that practice is here recommended; the presence of non-Christians need not deter the celebration of the sacrament.[29]

Finally, we must note that eucharistic hospitality is not the same as ecumenical eucharistic sharing, which means services planned and attended by persons of several Christian denominations. In

---

[28] UMG, 49B; *This Holy Mystery*, 17; "Directory for Worship," *Book of Order*, W-4.9003.

[29] See the section "Life Passages: Healing and Funeral" in ch. 16 for a discussion about celebrating the Lord's Supper when many non-Christians will likely attend the service.

these services, the sharing of the Lord's Supper among a diversity of Christians is intentional, rather than ad hoc. Normally, there would be ecumenical agreements among churches represented at such gatherings, i.e., formal declarations of pulpit and altar fellowship. Thus, a service of ecumenical eucharistic sharing at the local level should not occur unless there have been discussions at the broader, church-wide level that have established a theological basis for the sharing. Churches that take seriously their denominational identity and relationship to the broader church will avoid unilateral moves that bypass denominational structures. Currently, Lutheran, Anglican, Methodist, and Presbyterian Churches have agreements that are the basis for ecumenical services of the Lord's Supper.[30]

Open Table

"Open Table" refers to inviting all worshippers, whether believers, seekers, or indifferent guests, including those who might be unbaptized, to partake of communion. Churches that have such a policy include the United Methodist Church (UMC) and the Christian Church (Disciples of Christ or CCDC). The former views communion as a means of evangelism and therefore desires to avoid making the Table an obstacle to seekers:

> Invitation to partake of Holy Communion offers an evangelical opportunity to bring people into a fuller living relationship with the body of Christ. As means of God's unmerited grace, Holy Baptism and Holy Communion are to be seen not as barriers but as pathways.[31]

---

[30] Information about such agreements can be found at the following denominational web sites: Lutheran: http://www.elca.org/en/Faith/Ecumenical-and-Inter-Religious-Relations/Full-Communion; Reformed-Presbyterian: http://oga.pcusa.org/section/ecclesial-and-ecumenical-ministries/ecumenical-and-agency-relationships/; https://www.rca.org/partners; Anglican: http://www.episcopalchurch.org/page/ecumenical-interreligious; Methodist: http://www.episcopalchurch.org/page/ecumenical-interreligious [all accessed 27 August 2014].

[31] *This Holy Mystery*, 15.

(Both UMC and CCDC view the communion of the unbaptized as a step that leads to baptism.) In some churches, unbaptized adults will be permitted to commune, while baptized children are not. Although the underlying pastoral intentions may be good, this anomalous situation suggests a muddled theology of the sacraments.

Arguments for open Table appeal to the hospitality exhibited by Jesus in the mass feeding miracles (Mark 6:30-44, 8:1-10). In these gatherings, food is shared in the presence of Jesus without any stipulations about the recipients' spiritual state or personal commitment to Jesus. Access is open, inclusive, and even indiscriminate. Thus, if the church's eucharistic meal is centered on the risen Christ and offers fellowship with him, it, too, should have an open and inclusive character, such that those who respond positively to the gospel may commune even if they are unbaptized. Without that "openness" the meal takes on an exclusive and possibly oppressive character.

A further basis for the open Table might be found in the words of Jesus during the meal in the upper room with his disciples. There Jesus shared a loaf of bread and a cup that he identified with his body and blood. These things became the means of sharing in the very reality of the risen Lord. Because the Lord himself is present in the Supper, he is the host and the meal is open to all whom *he* invites. Additionally, since Jesus attached words of promise to the bread and cup ("given and shed for you for the forgiveness of sins"), the primary qualification for participation in the Supper is a faith that will trust in these promises. In other words, the Supper is founded not on human worthiness or qualifications, but rather on Christ's command and promise. Consequently, requiring baptism may be an unnecessary qualification for receiving communion.

Indeed, it might be noted that the New Testament does not explicitly relate baptism and the Supper such that the former is a prerequisite to the latter. In other words, there is no direct statement in the gospels or epistles commanding that communion be given only to baptized church members. In that case, the church is free to admit those who are at least capable of responding in faith to Christ's promises.

Nevertheless, the New Testament presupposes that those who accept Christ's promises are to approach the Table by way of baptism. The gospels and other New Testament writings were prepared precisely for Christian worship (eucharistic) assemblies and hence the promises of Christ at the Last Supper are not directed to just anyone but to the *baptized.* The Lord's promises reminded second and third generation Christians of the late-first/early-second century that the fellowship of the church, epitomized and enacted in the Supper, is open even to Gentiles, albeit those who submit to baptism (cf. Acts 10:48). It is noteworthy that the meal of the upper room was the culmination of three years of instruction that Jesus gave to the disciples, and this time period may be a reference to the baptismal *ordo* (structure) whereby instruction – in some places perhaps lasting up to three years – precedes baptism and first reception of communion. Another hint of the presupposition of baptism before communion is found in Acts, where the mention of a mass baptism in 2:41 is followed in v. 42 by a description of early Christian worship assemblies and their "breaking bread" (i.e., celebrating the Lord's Supper). The miraculous meal stories involving Jesus also have baptism in the background, as liturgical scholar Gordon Lathrop argues:

> ...Jesus' meals with outsiders have also been misinterpreted when they have been taken to imply that baptism is not needed or that participation in the Supper has no consequences. To read the stories of Jesus without thinking of the context of the churches in which they were told is naive and misleading. The stories of Jesus' meals were probably indeed recounted in the gospels with the intention of reforming the meal-practice of the communities of the late-first and early-second century, among other things with the intention of urging the inclusion of Gentiles and other outsiders. But, for example, the Markan Jesus has compassion on the crowd and urges the disciples to feed them after "they have been with me now for three days" (Mark 8:2), an old symbolic shorthand for being with Christ in his death and resurrection, the very content of baptism. In the time of

> the church, these outsiders and Gentiles are of course to be baptized and so gathered into the community of the cross and resurrection, so brought to be with Jesus for "the three days." Just so, the young man who is stripped at the outset of the passion in Mark (14:51-52) – stripped like an ancient candidate for baptism – three days later appears as witness to the resurrection for the community, clothed in a white robe (16:5). It is as if he has been immersed in the cross of Jesus and so clothed with the gospel. The very meaning of baptism is so symbolized. And throughout Mark, Jesus being with the sinners and outsiders is a down payment on and image of the cross as well as a promise of the resurrection, of his continued presence with these same people.[32]

Even if there is no explicit biblical teaching on the relationship between baptism and the Lord's Supper, baptism and baptismal instruction are assumed by New Testament writers who addressed their writings to churches – fellowships of the baptized. For this reason, the New Testament actually makes the case *against* an "open" Table.

From the time of the early church onward, the connection between the sacraments and their sequential order does become more explicit. The *Didache* directs that "...no one eat or drink of your thanksgiving but those who have been baptized in the name of the Lord. For about this also the Lord has said, 'Do not give what is holy to dogs.'"[33] Dating from the middle of the second century, Justin the Martyr's description of a baptismal service appears to show that participation in the Lord's Supper is the culminating act of one's Christian initiation, implying that one could not approach the Table before baptism.[34] Although the precise dating of the so-called *Apostolic Tradition* has been subject to scholarly debate, the baptismal

[32] Gordon W. Lathrop, "Welcome to Life in Christ: Reflections on Baptism and Hospitality at the Table of the Lord," http://download.elca.org/ELCA%20 Resource%20Repository/Lathrop_Gordon_W.pdf [accessed 1 September 2014].

[33] The *Didache* 9.5 (late-first or early-second cent.).

[34] Justin the Martyr, *First Apology* 65.1 (ca. 150).

material in chapters 15-21 parallels the practices seen in other third- and fourth-century church orders, including the eucharistic completion of the initiatory process.[35] A number of ancient sources likewise indicate that the Lord's Supper was the culminating act of Christian initiation: Tertullian,[36] Cyprian,[37] *The Acts of Judas Thomas* (third century),[38] Egeria,[39] John Chrysostom,[40] Theodore of Mopsuestia,[41] and Ambrose of Milan.[42] Throughout the medieval period, it was simply taken for granted that all who communed – even infants – had been baptized (see the section above on the age of first communion). The Protestant Reformers of the sixteenth century similarly assumed that communion was for the baptized. Indeed, on the basis of baptism, Luther urged Christians to be diligent in providing pre-communion catechetical instruction for children:

> ...let all heads of a household remember that it is their duty...to teach their children or have them taught the things they ought to know. *Because they have been baptized* and received into the people of Christ, they should also enjoy this fellowship of the sacrament so that they may serve us and be useful.[43]

Although John Wesley spoke of communion as a "converting" ordinance, he was referring to the weak in faith, not to the unbaptized. It would have been inconceivable for Wesley, an Anglican priest, to consider giving communion to unbaptized persons since the Prayer

---

[35] *The Apostolic Tradition ascribed to Hippolytus* 21 (ca 217). See Maxwell E. Johnson, *The Rites of Christian Initiation: Their Evolution and Interpretation*, rev. exp. ed. (Collegeville: Liturgical Press, 2007), 101.

[36] Tertullian, *De Resurrectione Carnis* 8 (ca. 200).

[37] Cyprian, *Letter* 70, *to Januarius* (ca. 256).

[38] *The Acts of Judas Thomas* 27, 50, 121 (ca. 200).

[39] *Egeria's Travels* 46 (ca. 381-84).

[40] John Chrysostom, *Baptismal Homilies* 27 (ca. 390).

[41] Theodore of Mopsuestia, *Baptismal Homily* 3.29 (early-fifth cent.).

[42] Ambrose of Milan, *Concerning the Sacraments* 3.11 (ca. 390).

[43] Martin Luther, *Large Catechism*, BC, 476.87. Emphasis added.

Book tradition assumed that all those admitted to the Supper were baptized and confirmed. A number of current denominational documents explicitly state that communion is for the baptized.[44] Thus, most of Christian history witnesses to the understanding that the Supper is the meal of the baptized and that baptism admits Christians to communion.

We might therefore think of the sacraments as belonging to a single "sacramental economy."[45] Specifically, in baptism, we are made members of the (Christian) family, and at the Supper we take our place at the "family" meal. First communion serves as the completion of a person's Christian initiation, because in taking communion one is fully incorporated into the fellowship of the church. Ritually, meals are the epitome of family or community life because they identify the group and strengthen the social bonds among members (see ch. 3). It makes little sense for an uninitiated seeker to engage in the culminating act of a ritual process (a rite of incorporation) without having participated in the preceding steps of the process (separation, experience of liminality).

Indeed, the very process that leads to the eucharistic culmination of Christian initiation is vital. Participation in the Lord's Supper has to do with coming to the Table hungry for the grace and mercy of God in Jesus Christ who offers his body and blood for our forgiveness. To be "hungry" is nothing other than to recognize our sin, brokenness, and fallen nature as well as our need for the grace, mercy, and forgiveness that Christ offers at the Table. This recognition requires a conversion from a worldly self-confidence that imagines our relationship with God is made and sustained by our personal and religious efforts, rather than by God's mercy for broken sinners. In short, we can only approach the Table after having died to the old person who justifies him/herself before God, and after having been born anew to a way of living before God based on the acceptance of his grace and mercy offered in Jesus Christ. This conversion – a death and resurrection in imitation of Jesus' own death and resurrection – is precisely what

[44] E.g. UMG, 7; "Directory for Worship," *Book of Order*, W-2.4006.

[45] Lathrop, "Welcome to Life in Christ," 2.

occurs in baptism. In the Christian ritual bath, the old self, the sinner, the Self-Justifier, the Old Adam (Luther) is drowned and is empowered by the Spirit to live a new life of faith and trust in the gospel of forgiveness for Christ's sake alone. At the same time, baptism symbolizes and empowers us for an ethical conversion whereby we die to self-centeredness and are born anew to lives lived for others. Having died and been raised with Christ in baptism, we can now come to the Table ready to eat and drink because now we know that we are beggars who need the mercy offered in the bread and cup. *Now* we are truly hungry for these things! Yes, the gospel which calls for conversion is inherently contained in the meal and invites the response of faith. Still, without having experienced the "conversion therapy" of baptismal preparation (the liminal phase of the ritual process) and without having received the new life that baptism grants, a seeker is unprepared for the Supper. Further: even though the Supper constitutes and defines the church, it does so only insofar as it sustains the fellowship in the new life given in baptism. The Supper does not make one a Christian; baptism does. Analogously: a person takes his/her place at the family Table only after being born into the family. Coming to the church's Table apart from the experience of baptism and all that it means, risks sharing in the meal of a family whose ways and mores one has not fully understood nor fully accepted for one's self. Such a lack of understanding is what Paul encountered at Corinth, where some Christians had not completely died to self and to worldly ways, nor embraced the self-giving way of Christ. Accordingly, they are reprimanded for their behavior and for celebrating a meal that is the antithesis of the Lord's Supper. In that case, trying to make our meals into "entry points" for the church risks raising up new generations of Corinthians.

Because baptism and the Supper are components of one sacramental economy rooted in the gospel of Jesus Christ, we must avoid thinking that the Supper "requires" baptism in a legalistic sense. The call and challenge of the Christian gospel is to believe that Jesus is Lord and Messiah, God and Savior of Israel, and, in believing, to have new life. New life is only possible when the old life passes away. The ultimate fellowship with Jesus ritualized in the Supper and the new life it gives calls for the death of the old person. Thus, baptism is not really a requirement, but a *gospel imperative* (cf. the aorist imperative passive in Acts 2:38, βαπτισθήτω ["be baptized"]), as if the gospel says to us: "Come, die in baptism that you might live!" So churches need not be legalistic about the relationship between baptism and the Supper; there may be occasions when a seeker comes to the Table and receives communion not fully informed about a church's normal procedures and expectations. This person hardly deserves a stern reprimand and a condescending lecture on the history and theology of Christian initiation! But neither is it appropriate to omit baptism either for the sake of convenience or in the name of a false hospitality that distorts and cheapens the gospel by setting aside the imperative to die and be born again. The way to the Table is open to one and all who accept the gospel, and the personal appropriation of that gospel inevitably leads to the font. Thus, let the hospitality begin at the font. Let us practice an *open font* by calling each and every seeker to the waters!

Finally, we might consider how hospitality could be expressed in ways other than the reception of communion. In those churches where communion is distributed to worshippers gathered around the table, seekers might be invited to come forward to receive a blessing. Another possibility is to imitate the Orthodox practice of giving the *Antidoron* (bread that is offered but not consecrated) to all worshippers following the eucharistic liturgy. A Protestant version might look like this: bread that is offered at the eucharistic table (during the offertory) is placed on the credence table during the Great Thanksgiving (consecration) and then distributed to all (including children) after the service. This practice would enable the assembly to tangibly express hospitality to seekers while preserving the traditional initiatory order.

Excommunication

Very early on, the church perceived a need to expel from its fellowship those who sinned with impunity and a lack of repentance (cf. Matt.

18:15-20). However, expulsion from the church occurred only after attempts to correct the person failed. Over time, the church came to view some actions (e.g., murder, adultery, apostasy) as "mortal sins," or those that imperiled one's eternal salvation. Persons who did not confess such sins were denied communion ("excommunicated"), and were not received back into the eucharistic fellowship until they had completed a long penitential process. Excommunication was viewed as a way of encouraging appropriate repentance and ensuring that no unrepentant or unworthy person received communion.

All of the Protestant Reformers retained the practice of denying communion to open, unrepentant sinners (the "wicked") and those who "despised" the sacrament or refused to receive instruction in its meaning.[46] Calvin recognizes a three-fold purpose for excommunication: (1) to remove persons whose behavior profaned the Lord's Supper; (2) to prevent the moral corruption of the church; and (3) to lead the sinner-excommunicant to repentance.[47] Anabaptists not only excommunicated those who committed serious sins, but, taking Matthew 18:17 literally, completely shunned such persons, making them into social outcasts.[48] John Wesley oversaw the expulsion of those who did not live up to the moral standards of the Methodist societies.[49]

Today, one rarely hears of any Protestant Christian being excommunicated. Church leaders may be reticent about admonishing even open sinners, for fear of losing such persons and their families to other churches. Indeed, it is easier for people to join other churches rather than admit to sin and submit to the discipline of their own churches. Because of not wanting to turn away potential new

---

[46] *Apology of the Augsburg Confession* (1530), Art. XI, BC, 186. 4; John Calvin, *Institutes of the Christian Religion* IV.12.5 (1559), ed. John T. McNeill, tr. Ford Lewis Battles, in LCC XXI (Philadelphia: Westminster Press, 1960), 1232 (cf. John Calvin, *The Form of Church Prayers* [1542], PEER, 216); "The Supper of the Lord" (1549), BCP *Texts*, 19.

[47] Calvin, *Institutes* IV.12.5, LCC XXI, 1232-33.

[48] See Menno Simons, *A Clear Account of Excommunication* (1550), CWMS, 455-85.

[49] John Wesley, *Journal* (March 12, 1743), WJW, 318.

members, church leaders might readily receive the unrepentant into their churches with "no questions asked." Denominationalism and competition for members – an unfortunate legacy of Protestantism – are ultimately impediments to church discipline and Christian repentance.

Yet, the steps and procedures for excommunication remain on the books of many churches. In some cases, a minister (acting according to his/her church's law) may suspend an open sinner from participation in the Supper until there has been amendment of life.[50] In other cases, constitutions and books of discipline lay out an entire legal process which may culminate in the excommunication of a Christian.[51] Space does not permit a full discussion of these procedures and their intricacies; church leaders are therefore encouraged to familiarize themselves with their church's theology and discipline of excommunication.

The exclusion of a Christian from the Lord's Table is never to be undertaken lightly. Excommunication is inappropriate in the case of minor sins or personality flaws that can be corrected through admonition and/or pastoral counseling. Exclusion from the Table is also inappropriate in the case of persons who disagree with or otherwise are in conflict with church leaders, unless there is behavior that is publicly scandalous and unbecoming of a Christian. Excommunication should not be used as a form of political retribution in the church.When a sin does rise to the level of public scandal, the individual should be encouraged to repent by church leaders (cf. Matt. 18:15-17), and excommunication is imposed only when there is a refusal to acknowledge the sin and to seek reconciliation with wronged individuals and with the church. Excommunication must be considered a measure of last resort.

Abstinence from the Table might well be a discipline for all Christians. Since the Supper signifies and effects fellowship with Christ and with fellow members of his body, any rift in the church's

---

[50] See "Additional Directions," BCP 1979, 409.

[51] See *The Book of Discipline of the Methodist Church in Singapore* (Singapore, 2009), 716.4, 265.

fellowship is a denial of what the sacrament signifies. Receiving communion when one is in a seriously impaired relationship is a sin before God and a scandal to the community. Ministers might therefore encourage all Christians to refrain from participation in Supper when they know themselves to be in a fractured relationship and they have failed to seek reconciliation prior to coming to the Table (cf. Matt. 5:23-24). But encouraging this awareness and need for reconciliation should not lead to a scrupulosity whereby Christians refrain from the Supper unduly or for long periods. Rather, the point is to help Christians reflect on the meaning of the Supper and to realize its serious ethical implications.

Presidency at the Table

Because there is no standard ecclesial leadership in the New Testament, it is not entirely certain who presided over celebrations of the Lord's Supper in the first century. Since the Lord's Supper took place in a domestic setting, the leader was probably the host and owner of the home, i.e., the "patron." But by the second century, Christian liturgical assemblies were increasingly under the leadership of groups of presbyters ("elders"), bishops, and deacons. By the middle of this century, monepiscopacy, or bishops serving as heads of local churches, was the norm. The ministry of Word and Sacrament was the chief work of bishops and presbyters, both of whom came into their positions by a communal selection process ritualized in an official rite of ordination (cf. 1 Tim. 4:14). Presbyters or priests were ordained by bishops who were themselves ordained by other bishops. This pattern whereby those who presided over the sacraments were intentionally chosen and set apart for this ministry remained in place throughout the Middle Ages.

Despite strong criticisms of the ecclesiastical hierarchy and its manifold abuses, the Protestant Reformers nevertheless retained the pattern whereby only ordained ministers presided at the Lord's Supper. None of the magisterial Reformers was willing to allow laypersons to preside. The basic principal articulated in official Reformation-era documents is that no one shall preach the Word or celebrate the Lord's Supper without a regular call by the proper authorities (e.g., bishops, superintendents, presbyteries, etc.), which of course included ordination.[52] Even Anabaptists had bishops and intentionally chosen pastors whose duties centered on preaching and presiding at the sacraments.[53] Although John Wesley's ordination of men for ministry in North America was outside the authority of the established (Anglican) church, his overall intention was to ensure that eucharistic presidency would be undertaken only by those with a regular call and ordination. For the Christian Church (Disciples of Christ) lay presidency at the Supper is an intentional policy meant to reflect the equality of laity and clergy and was undoubtedly influenced by the political egalitarianism of North America.[54]

Those churches that restrict presidency at the Lord's Supper to ordained ministers do so because they recognize the special demands of this ministry. First, those who preside at the Supper must possess the historical, theological, and practical knowledge necessary for this ministry, which requires a program of theological education. Second, they must be able to integrate a theology of the Lord's Supper with pastoral practice in order to (1) make decisions about when to admit or deny access to the Table; (2) select theologically appropriate liturgical texts and songs; (3) provide guidance on proper sacramental celebration to the assembly; and (4) give adequate instruction on the Supper to new communicants and provide ongoing formation to long-time church members. If ministers do not possess these abilities, sacramental orthodoxy is in jeopardy, and the church's public witness is potentially undermined. Thus, one who presides at the Supper must be recognized as possessing the qualifications needed for sacramental ministry. Additionally, a minister must be given official authority to

[52] *Augsburg Confession*, Art. XIV, BC, 47.3; AR XXIII, BCP 1979, 872; *Westminister Confession of Faith* (1646), Art. XXVII.IV, http://www.reformed.org/documents/wcf_with_proofs/ [accessed 24 August 2014]; John Calvin, *Institutes* IV.3.10, LCC XXI, 1062.

[53] *Schleitheim Confession* (1527), Art. V, http://www.anabaptists.org/history/the-schleitheim-confession.html [accessed 24 August 2014].

[54] James F. White, *Protestant Worship: Traditions in Transition* (Louisville: Westminster John Knox Press, 1989), 175.

preside at the Supper so that the local assembly knows him/her to be a legitimate representative of the church and its traditions. The public affirmation of a person's calling and gifting for eucharistic presidency, as well the conferral of authority to preside at the Table, is precisely the purpose of ordination. Those churches that limit presidency to the ordained do so not as a way of building an ecclesiastical hierarchy, but as a way of ensuring pastoral oversight that serves both the local worship assembly and the denomination as a whole. Since ordination is essentially an act oversight, the rite of ordination is presided over by the minister of oversight, which in some churches (e.g., Anglican, Lutheran) is a bishop (cf. Gk, *episcopos*, or "overseer"). In Presbyterian churches where there is collective oversight, ordination to the ministry of Word and Sacrament ("teaching elder") is carried out by the local or regional presbytery, with the moderator or other designated presbytery member presiding.[55]

Additionally, ordained presidency at the Lord's Supper has a symbolic dimension. Every local church celebrates the Supper in union with the broader, wider church (the "church catholic"), since the same Lord is present in the Supper and invites all the baptized to the Table. In that case, the Supper is a sign of the church's catholicity. This catholicity is highlighted and made manifest when the person presiding is one who has been ordained by a representative of the broader, wider church, e.g., a bishop, regional superintendent, or moderator of the presbytery, who him/herself is a symbol of the broader church. Ordained presidency signifies union with all churches of the assembly's communion (denomination) and with all churches that celebrate the Lord's Supper (fellowship or communion in the "holy things"), and also points to the local church's accountability to the denomination and to the universal church itself. Ideally, an ordained minister who presides at the Table helps the assembly to appreciate these relationships and guides it to work cooperatively with the denominational hierarchy, sister churches of the same denomination, and with churches of other denominations, especially those with whom there are ecumenical agreements.

[55] *Book of Order*, G-2.0701, W-4.4005b.

Other Ministers in the Lord's Supper

Once liturgical leadership became regularized, ordained ministers (presbyters, priests) were assisted by other ministers at the Lord's Supper. Considered one of the "major" orders along with presbyters and bishops, *deacons* read the gospel, set the table, and administered the cup. Like presbyters, deacons received ordination from a bishop. *Subdeacons*, for a time one of the major orders, read the Epistle and assisted the deacon in the setting of the table. They were ordained but without the laying on of hands. *Acolytes*, one of the "minor" orders, traditionally carried torches and also assisted by bringing the eucharistic elements to the presiding minister as well as by performing other duties at the table. As Reformation churches abolished the minor orders and, in some cases, even the major orders of deacons and bishops, the writings of Luther, Zwingli, and Calvin do not indicate anyone other than ordained pastors (presbyters) preparing or distributing the elements at communion. However, the BCP 1549 did allow for a deacon to serve the cup.[56] Wesley presumed that only ordained elders would handle and distribute the communion elements. Today, ordained deacons of the Anglican,[57] Presbyterian,[58] and Methodist[59] churches may assist in the distribution of the communion elements.

Greater lay involvement in the Lord's Supper was a hallmark of liturgical renewal among Protestants in the late-twentieth century. The use of lay eucharistic ministers reflects a theology of the church as the "whole people of God" and a greater emphasis on the priesthood of all believers. The ministry of laypeople in the Sunday service, both during the word and meal, points to and symbolizes the understanding that all of God's people are called to minister in daily life. Some Lutherans in the USA permit lay ministers to set the table

---

[56] "The Supper of the Lord," BCP 1549, PEER, 242.

[57] "The Holy Eucharist: Rite I (Concerning the Celebration)," BCP 1979, 322; "The Order for the Celebration of Holy Communion also called The Eucharist and the Lord's Supper (General Notes)," CW 158.

[58] *Book of Order*, G-2.0202.

[59] *Book of Discipline*, 545.

(like deacons in other traditions) and to assist the presiding minister in the distribution of the elements.[60] Some Anglican dioceses and provinces also permit trained and licensed laypersons to administer the cup,[61] and in some circumstances they may allow (adult) acolytes to handle eucharistic vessels before and after the distribution.[62] Among churches of the Reformed-Presbyterian tradition, (elected) lay elders of the congregation prepare and distribute the elements, often by passing the elements to the seated assembly. A similar practice is found among many Baptist and independent churches. In Methodism, ordained deacons may prepare and assist in the distribution of the elements, and lay participation through the preparation of the table, as well as the provision, preparation, and distribution of the elements is encouraged.[63] Lutherans, Anglicans, and Methodists also encourage lay representatives of the assembly to bring the elements forward at the offertory to symbolize the assembly's provision of human-made things that will be used for God's divine service.[64]

Lay eucharistic ministers require training in the following areas:

1. How to handle the eucharistic vessels
2. How to distribute the elements to the assembly
3. How to replenish a vessel
4. What to do if a spill occurs
5. The path of movement from the table to the place of distribution
6. When to receive the elements themselves

---

[60] UMG, 41. See Lorraine S. Brugh and Gordon W. Lathrop, *The Sunday Assembly*, Using Evangelical Lutheran Worship, Vol. 1 (Minneapolis: Augsburg Fortress, 2008), 75-99.

[61] BCP 1979, 408.

[62] Howard E. Galley, *The Ceremonies of the Eucharist: A Guide to Celebration* (Cambridge, MA: Cowley Publications, 1989), 35.

[63] *This Holy Mystery*, 27-28.

[64] "Notes on the Services," ELW, 22; "Holy Eucharist," BCP 1979, 361; *This Holy Mystery*, 28.

7. What vestments to wear, or otherwise what the "dress code" for eucharistic ministers is
8. Where to sit during the service.

Normally, deacons and laypersons only distribute the cup, while the (ordained) presiding minister distributes the bread; the latter, as the chief pastor of the church, would be aware of persons who inappropriately present themselves for communion, and so could withhold the bread from such persons and then direct the deacon or layperson to likewise withhold the cup.

Conclusion

Who may receive at the Table? Who may be denied admission? Who may preside at the Table? Some of these may seem like very troublesome questions, ones that we would rather avoid. But, as we have demonstrated above, they are important questions that relate to sacramental theology, the nature of the church, and the church's mission in the world. Leaders are encouraged to be fully aware of denominational policies and their practical implications so that the Lord's Supper might be celebrated with an orderliness that allows us to focus on the gifts of Christ offered in the Meal.

For Further Reading

Dalby, Mark. *Infant Communion: Post-Reformation to Present-Day.* Alcuin/ GROW Liturgical Study 67. Cambridge: Grove Books, 2009.

Luther, Donald J. *Ministers of Communion from the Assembly: A Worship Handbook*. Minneapolis: Augsburg Fortress, 2001.

Talley, Thomas J., ed. *A Kingdom of Priests: Liturgical Formation of the People of God.* Alcuin/GROW Liturgical Study 5. Bramcote, Nottingham: Grove Books, 1988.

CHAPTER 14

The Lord's Supper Liturgy

Since the time of the Reformation, Protestants have insisted that the Sunday liturgy be one of both Word and Sacrament. The proclamation of God's Word followed by the celebration of the Lord's Supper are the principal means by which the risen Christ gives himself to us, and these two means of grace belong together. The Word exposes our sin and spiritual neediness, and promises God's grace for the truly repentant. By leading us to repentance, the Word makes us aware of our need for the Supper, and, by offering the good news of forgiveness, it awakens the faith that receives the Supper as a gift. While the Word is a public proclamation for any and all to hear, the Supper offers Christ to each one of us in a personal and intimate way – as food that we take into our bodies – thereby confirming that what is promised in the Word is truly *for us*. At the same time, the act of sharing a common loaf forms us into a community that proclaims and enacts God's Word in the world. Through participation in the Supper the church comes to fulfill the very purpose of the Word that is proclaimed in worship.

Thus, the Word leads us to the Supper, and the Supper completes the proclamation of the Word. Without the Word, the Supper has no theological or spiritual context to make it meaningful; without the Supper, the Word is incomplete. Accordingly, the Supper will always follow the proclamation of the Word – otherwise the meaning and relationship of Word and Supper are distorted.[1] Because I have written elsewhere about those parts of the liturgy that precede and follow the Supper, viz., the word and the sending,[2] this chapter will focus on the words and actions of the Lord's Supper.

The Shape of the Lord's Supper Liturgy

Like the entire service, the liturgy for the Lord's Supper has a "shape" or structure, which developed over time and is shared by the various Protestant churches. In broad outline that shape is:

Preparation of the table
The Great Thanksgiving
Breaking of the bread (fraction)
Distribution of the elements
Post-communion prayer

To state it narratively: we prepare the table, give thanks for the bread and cup, share the bread and cup, and then give thanks for the gifts received in communion. Within this structure, there are variations, yet there is probably more agreement than disagreement among (mainline) Protestants about what is said and done in the liturgy of the Lord's Supper. Understanding this shape helps us to plan and select the prayers and music that accompany each part of the eucharistic liturgy.

---

[1] See Jeffrey A. Truscott, *Worship: A Practical Guide* (Singapore: Genesis, 2011), 29-30, and Simon Chan, *Liturgical Theology: The Church as Worshipping Community* (Downers Grove, IL: IVP Academic, 2006), 63-70.

[2] Truscott, *Worship: A Practical Guide*, 123-74 (chs. 9, 10, and 11), and 195-202 (ch. 13).

Preparation of the Table and Offering

For some Protestants, the preparation of the table is a significant ritual action, while for others the preparation is relatively simple. Many Lutherans and Anglicans bring vessels and other needed items to the table as the offerings are collected (see ch. 12, "Vessels"). If a vested chalice has been on the table, its veil is now removed. The corporal is removed from the burse and spread on the table, and the chalice, paten, ciborium, flagon (with bread and wine), and purificators are arranged on the corporal (see ch. 12 for a description of these items).[3] A larger presider's host is already on the paten, or, a loaf and its vessel (plate or basket) is placed on the table, either to the left of the chalice or behind the chalice which is set in the middle of the corporal. Since the purpose of the corporal is to prevent crumbs from falling on the fair linen, it is placed on the table at the preparation, rather than before the beginning of the service. The burse is placed flat on the table; if stood upright it becomes a secondary focal point drawing attention away from the bread and cup.

The bread and wine may instead be brought to the table either at the very beginning of the offering, as the money is collected, or presented along with the money offering at the offertory. The offered elements are given to the minister who places them on the corporal. In the ancient church, bread and wine to be used for communion were offered at the table along with other food items following a grand procession. From the offered items, the priests selected the bread and wine to be used for communion, and what remained was used by the clergy or given to the poor. The ceremonial presentation of the communion elements highlights the fact that things of creation fashioned by human hands are placed into the service of God, which counters the Gnostic presupposition that God disdains matter. The action therefore affirms the goodness of creation and, indirectly, the Incarnation. On occasion, a food offering for the poor may also be

[3] For an illustration, see Lorraine S. Brugh and Gordon W. Lathrop, *The Sunday Assembly: Using Evangelical Lutheran Worship*, Vol. 1 (Minneapolis: Augsburg Fortress, 2008) 194-200; cf. Howard E. Galley, *The Ceremonies of the Eucharist: A Guide to Celebration* (Cambridge, MA: Cowley Publications, 1989), 101.

presented in order to draw a connection with the church's care of the needy.

For Presbyterians, Methodists, and others, the elements have been placed on the table since the beginning of the service in stacked trays that are covered with a cloth. The cloth and top covers for the trays may be removed at one of the following times: (1) during the offering (if it occurs prior to the communion); (2) during a communion hymn that precedes the eucharistic liturgy; or (3) in the case of Presbyterians, just before the invitation to communion.

Anglicans may begin the offertory action with one or more biblical sentences, a practice that goes back to the Prayer Books of the sixteenth century.[4] One of these may be 1 Chronicles 29:11, although some assemblies use it at the presentation of the gifts.[5]

As the money offering is collected, instrumental or choral music may be presented. Such music should be appropriate for the liturgical season and underscore the themes of the biblical readings and sermon for the day. The use of recorded music discourages musicians in the assembly from sharing their gifs and therefore undermines the local, contextual nature of the liturgy. The collection may also be accompanied by assembly songs which express the meaning of the offering (e.g., "We Give Thee But Thine Own") or serve as an invitation to communion (e.g., "Come, Sinners, to the Gospel Feast").[6] The assembly may stand or sit during this song.

When the money offering (and eucharistic gifts) are presented, the assembly stands because of the solemn nature of the action. Assisting ministers receive the money offering and place it on the credence, while the bread and wine (if brought forward) are set on the table or given to the minister who prepares the table. In many Protestant churches, the offertory is punctuated with the traditional doxology

---

[4] "Holy Eucharist: Rite One," BCP 1979, 333 (see 343-44).

[5] "Holy Communion," DSSB, 36.

[6] "Notes on the Services," ELW, 22; "Holy Eucharist One," BCP 1979, 333; "The Order for the Celebration of Holy Communion also called The Eucharist and the Lord's Supper (One)," CW, 175; "An Order of Sunday Worship Using the Basic Pattern," UMBW, 26.

"Praise God from Whom All Blessings Flow" to affirm that what is given comes from God. Lutherans and Anglicans have traditionally not sung a trinitarian doxology at the offertory.[7] Lutherans usually sing a short canticle connected with the Lord's Supper or offering (e.g., "Let the Vineyards be Fruitful" or selected verses of Ps. 116, "What Shall I Render to the Lord").[8] Continuing the ancient practice of singing psalmody at the offertory, some Lutheran books provide "proper offertory" verses based on Psalms and other scripture texts to be sung by a choir as an alternative to the offertory canticle.[9] Lutheran, Anglican, and Methodist worship books are generally amenable to two patterns of using music in connection with the offertory, either (a) one musical form, whether choral, instrumental, or assembly song, that accompanies all of the actions, or (b) one form that accompanies the collection of the gifts and another (usually assembly song) that accompanies the presentation of the gifts. The manner in which music is used to accompany the offertory could vary throughout the liturgical year.

In Anglican (and other) churches, the presiding minister might engage in a ritual washing of hands or *lavabo* after the eucharistic vessels have been prepared and just before the Great Thanksgiving. The presider goes to the side of the table where a lay assisting minister pours water over his/her hands and into a small bowl held by the assistant. The presider then dries his/her hands using a towel that is draped over the assistant's left forearm. The two ministers then go to their places for the offertory or eucharistic prayer that follows. Rather than utilitarian in nature, the action symbolizes the ideal purity of heart needed by the minister who prepares to offer the eucharistic prayer.[10]

---

[7] For a description of various musical possibilities within the Anglican liturgy, see Galley, *Ceremonies of the Eucharist*, 104-5.

[8] *Evangelical Lutheran Worship* (Pew Edition) (Minneapolis: Augsburg Fortress, 2006), #181-188.

[9] "Propers," LBW, 121-70.

[10] Galley, *Ceremonies of the Eucharist*, 107.

In some liturgical books, a prayer concludes the offering.[11] Offertory prayers express thanks for what has been collected.[12] Because the gifts are not merely for the upkeep of the church building, the prayer might also dedicate the gifts for their use in the world (e.g., to feed the hungry).[13] Since the presentation of the eucharistic gifts is an affirmation of creation, some offertory prayers thank God for these and for all the gifts of creation. Other themes include the dedication of our lives to God's service,[14] which is what the offering symbolizes, or the dedication of the bread and wine for the eucharistic action.[15] The prayer is most appropriately given by an assisting lay minister, who speaks on behalf of the assembly whose gifts have been presented. Standing behind the table facing the assembly, the minister prays with hands uplifted, in the *orans* position. Some liturgical books provide offertory prayers that reflect the different liturgical seasons.[16]

The Great Thanksgiving: Words

The Christian worship assembly gathers around the table of the Lord recognizing its great need, but also believing that the risen Lord comes to it through the bread and cup offering forgiveness, life, and salvation – the gifts which satisfy our spiritual needs. Appropriately, we want to acknowledge the gifts of God in the Supper and to praise and thank God for them. Hence, the ancient church referred to the Supper as the Eucharist or "thanksgiving." To speak of the action in this manner is not to imply a purely human action, but to use terminology that captures the sense of praising and thanking God as we receive benefits from God. Paul reminds us that God's gifts

[11] "Holy Communion," ELW, 179; "The Service for the Lord's Day," BCW, 68; "Supplementary Texts," CW, 291-93.

[12] "Service for the Lord's Day," BCW, 68.

[13] "Holy Communion," ELW, 179 ("Blessed are you, O God…").

[14] "Holy Communion," ELW, 179 ("Blessed are you, O God…"); "Supplementary Texts," CW, 291.2.

[15] "Supplementary Texts," CW, 291.4.

[16] "Prayers for Worship," ELW, 138.

are received and dedicated to their intended purpose precisely with thanksgiving and prayer (1 Tim. 4:4-5). In giving thanks at the table we "follow the Lord's example and obey his command" to "do this for the remembrance of me." Because thanksgiving involves the acknowledgement of God's merciful and loving deeds in the past and God's promises for the future, the eucharistic action is also one of *proclamation.* Since Christians cannot tell the story of God without reference to Jesus, giving thanks at the table finds its focus in the life and saving deeds of Christ; it is for him that we give thanks, remembering him as we bless the bread and cup that will become the very means of participating in his saving death and resurrection.

As noted in ch. 10, the Lord's Supper was a matter of controversy during the Reformation era, and the Reformers radically altered the manner in which the assembly gave thanks at the Supper. We noted how some of the earliest Protestant eucharistic prayers preserved many traditional elements while expunging language and actions that muted the gospel character of the Supper. The liturgical renewal movement of the twentieth century sought to renew eucharistic praying by recovering both the earliest examples of Protestant eucharistic prayers (e.g., from the BCP 1549), as well as examples from the early church. What eventually emerged among modern Protestants was a consensus about the shape of the Great Thanksgiving, which might be outlined as follows:

Dialog
Preface
Sanctus
Remembrance of salvation history
Institution Narrative
Anamnesis
Epiclesis
Doxology
Lord's Prayer

Some variations occur, but the similarities in Protestant eucharistic prayers today are striking. Below we shall consider the various components of the Great Thanksgiving and offer suggestions for practice.

The Preface Dialog. To understand why the Great Thanksgiving begins with three exchanges between the minister and the assembly, we need to recall that the liturgy is more than a long monolog by the minister with the assembly merely listening in. It is the whole people of God offering prayer, praise, and thanksgiving to the Father, for the saving deeds of the Son, in the power of the Holy Spirit. The *entire* assembly prays the eucharistic prayer, to which the presiding minister gives voice. Fittingly, the minister invites the assembly's participation in that prayer, beginning with a traditional biblical greeting ("The Lord be with you"; cf. Ruth 2:4) that bids the Lord's presence to be with the assembly as this important liturgical act commences. The assembly reciprocates ("And also with you"), suggesting that the Lord's presence and help is needed to lead the Great Thanksgiving. Normally, this will be the second instance of a mutual greeting, the first occurring at the beginning of the service of the Word. This parallel greeting in the Great Thanksgiving is a cue that a significant stage in the liturgy begins. For Christians, "Lord" is not simply God in general, but the *risen* Lord Jesus (cf. Luke 24:34), and we can only give thanks to God if and when the risen Lord is truly with us. Some books use a declarative statement "The Lord is here!" although the subjunctive ("The Lord *be* with you") is more suggestive of prayer.[17] "Lift up your hearts," a somewhat obscure phrase, probably means to stand and lift hearts and minds to God in prayer. The assembly's response ("We lift them to the Lord") clarifies that hearts are lifted to *God*, which probably refers to the Father, to whom the Great Thanksgiving is directed.[18] The Latin for "lift up your hearts" (*sursum corda*) serves as another name for the entire dialog. The final exchange, "Let us give thanks to the Lord our God/

[17] Uncertainty lies in the fact that the English is a translation of the Latin *dominus vobiscum*, which has no verb. In favor of the subjunctive (prayer) translation is the traditional formula *Pax Domini sit semper vobiscum*, which uses the subjunctive verb (Philip H. Pfatteicher and Carlos Messerli, *Lutheran Book of Worship Manual on the Liturgy* [Minneapolis: Augsburg, 1978], 234).

[18] Brugh and Lathrop, *Sunday Assembly*, 201.

It is right to give him thanks and praise" constitutes the minister's requesting and receiving permission to give thanks in the name of all. Thus, we affirm that the action is one of thanksgiving or *eucharisteo* (from which the sacrament derives its name) and is communal in nature ("let *us* give thanks").

A number of liturgical books provide music for the dialog and preface based on ancient Gregorian chant melodies,[19] a fitting practice for this act of praise. Throughout the centuries, sacred liturgical texts have been sung by peoples of all religions as a matter of course, much like they all have public worship gatherings that include commentary on sacred texts (preaching). Thus, when Christian ministers sing (chant) sacred texts, the action is innocuous and hardly supports syncretism. Both the minister and the assembly sing their parts or speak their parts of the Great Thanksgiving dialog. It makes little sense for the assembly to respond in song if the minister speaks the words of the dialog.

The *preface* is the initial proclamation and praise that culminates with the singing of the Sanctus. It is not merely an explanatory introduction to the praise of the Great Thanksgiving, but *is* that praise, the very beginning of it. In some cases, the preface consists of a short and invariable proclamation of Christ's saving work,[20] or a brief (and invariable) recital of salvation history that mentions creation, the prophets, and the coming of Christ.[21] Some liturgical books provide proper prefaces for the liturgical seasons, which express the christological and soteriological significance of the season and so provide a reason for praising God with the Sanctus.[22] A proper

---

[19] "Holy Communion," LBW, 207; "Holy Communion," ELW, 179; *The Hymnal 1982* (New York: The Church Hymnal Corporation, 1985), S112, S120; *Common Worship: Festivals* (London: Church House Publishing, 2008), 372.

[20] "Order for Holy Communion," CW, 196.

[21] "Service for the Lord's Day," BCW, 69-71; "Order for Holy Communion," CW, 198; "A Service of Word and Table I," UMBW, 36.

[22] "Holy Communion," LBW, 208-20; "Holy Communion," ELW, 180-93; "Additional Texts for the Service of the Lord's Day (Great Thanksgivings B and C)" BCW, 133-37; "Holy Eucharist One (Proper Prefaces)," BCP 1979, 344-49; "Holy Communion," DSSB, 37-39; "A Service of Word and Table IV," UMBW, 46-47.

preface for Advent, for example, might speak of God comforting his people with the promise of the redeemer who will renew the earth at his Second Coming.[23] It is possible for the minister to sing the entire preface,[24] which is the most logical approach if the dialog has been sung.

The Sanctus. While the Gloria in Excelsis serves as the principal assembly song of praise in the service of the Word, the Sanctus (Latin, "holy") is the central act of sung praise in the eucharistic liturgy. The opening lines "Holy, holy…full of your glory" echo the cry of the angels during Isaiah's vision in the Temple (Isaiah 6:3b), and so the assembly, in a sense, joins its praise to that of heaven as it stands in the presence of God. The second part, "Hosanna in the highest. Blessed is he…", which quotes the words of the people as Jesus entered Jerusalem on Palm Sunday (Matt. 21:9; cf. Ps. 118:25-26), is the assembly's greeting of the risen Lord and a plea for his saving mercy ("Hosanna" in Hebrew means "save, we pray"). Thus, the assembly's Supper becomes a place of encounter with God who is holy and awesome, and yet humble and merciful. Traditionally, many assemblies sing the Sanctus, recognizing that its words of praise are appropriately rendered in song. Many simple settings are available, and are easily taught to the liturgical assembly.[25]

The Post-Sanctus and Institution Narrative. Depending on the content of the preface section, this section continues the praise with either (1) a full recitation of salvation history from creation through the story of Jesus;[26] or (2) a proclamation that begins with christological

[23] "Holy Communion," ELW, 181.

[24] "Holy Communion," LBW, 208-20; "Holy Communion," ELW, 180-93; *Common Worship: Festivals*, 372-459.

[25] An especially popular setting by Franz Schubert (1797-1828), can be found in ELW (Pew Edition #190) and *United Methodist Hymnal* (Nashville: United Methodist Publishing House) "Musical Setting C" (21). See also ELW (Pew Edition) #191-193, and the other musical settings in *United Methodist Hymnal*, 17-20 and 23-25.

[26] "Holy Communion (eucharistic prayers I and II)," LBW, 221-24; "Holy Communion (eucharistic prayers III and IV)," ELW, 196-97; "Holy Eucharist Two (eucharistic prayers B and D)," BCP 1979, 368, 373-74.

material.[27] Since the mystery of Jesus' death and resurrection is at the heart of the Christian faith, Christians cannot rightly praise God without reference to Jesus Christ. Normally, this christological praise culminates in the "Words of Institution" or "Institution Narrative" (cf. Matt. 26:26-29; Mark 14:22-25; Luke 22:15-22; and 1 Cor. 11:23-26), which is not a biblical reading in any sense, but the church's way of telling the story of Jesus.[28] Lutherans understand the Narrative as a proclamation of the gospel, while Reformed liturgies treat it as a warrant for the whole eucharistic action ("do this"). The Narrative expresses the church's central beliefs about Christ and the Lord's Supper, namely, that the one who died and was raised is made known in the breaking of *this* bread and the sharing of *this* cup. Although some very ancient eucharistic prayers likely did not contain the Institution Narrative, and in some traditions it was actually added to the eucharistic prayer, for theological and liturgical reasons it is difficult to think of the Lord's Supper liturgy without it today. We noted previously how Luther pruned away much of the existing canon of the Mass, leaving only the Institution Narrative, which he believed to be a summary of the gospel. Not all liturgies use the Narrative in the same way; in most cases, it will be incorporated into the eucharistic prayer, as part of the prayerful proclamation addressed to God (as in Luther's *Formula Missae*), while in others, it is read (to the assembly) just before the distribution to connect the command and promise of the Supper with the actions of eating and drinking, as in Luther's *German Mass*,[29] Martin Bucer's "Order for the Lord's Supper,"[30] and the BCP 1552. In some Reformed-Presbyterian services today, the Institution Narrative serves as the invitation to communion or as the formula at the breaking of the

---

[27] "Service for the Lord's Day," BCW, 70; "Service of Word and Table I," UMBW, 37.

[28] Pfatteicher and Messerli, *Manual on the Liturgy*, 236.

[29] Martin Luther, *The German Mass and Order of Service* (1526), LW 53, 80-81.

[30] Martin Bucer, *The Psalter with Complete Church Practice* (1539), PEER, 211.

bread.[31] Some liturgical books use the older translation of Jesus' command, "do this *in remembrance of me*,"[32] while others use "*for the* remembrance of me" (perhaps even better is "for the *remembering* of me").[33] The latter (newer) translation better captures the idea that the eucharistic action is the very means by which Jesus is remembered – the remembrance is an embodied action. The older translation might give the impression that the remembrance is merely a mental action, rather than mental-physical-ritual in nature.

Traditionally, some Christians have held that it is during the Institution Narrative that the elements are "changed" into the body and blood of Christ or that the pronouncement of these words brings about that change. But this understanding is not helpful, because it reduces the Lord's Supper to a magical incantation and undermines the sense that our action is one of prayer, praise, and thanksgiving. With a similar focus on a "moment" of consecration, Orthodox Christians hold that the bread and wine become the body and blood of Christ by the action of the Holy Spirit, which is ritually expressed in the *epiclesis* or invocation of the Spirit that takes place in the Great Thanksgiving. It would be better, however, to think that our participation in the body and blood of Christ is signified by the *whole* liturgical action of thanksgiving, which is done in obedience to Christ's command and empowered by the Holy Spirit.

In most services, the Institution Narrative is followed immediately by the *memorial acclamation* which consists of three short phrases that summarize what the church believes about Christ ("Christ has died. Christ is risen. Christ will come again."). In some books, the memorial acclamation is made after the act of remembrance or *anamnesis*.[34] In either case, the point is that Christ's

---

[31] "Service for the Lord's Day," BCW, 68-69, 74; cf. *The Presbyterian Church of Singapore Book of Worship* (Singapore, 1984), 63, 67.

[32] Presbyterian Church in Singapore, "The Lord's Supper" (1994), 4; "Service for the Lord's Day," BCW, 71; "Holy Communion," DSSB, 41; "Holy Eucharist One," BCP 1979, 335, 342; "Service of Word and Table I," UMBW, 37.

[33] "Holy Communion," LBW, 222; "Holy Communion," ELW, 195; "Holy Eucharist Two," BCP 1979, 363, 368.

[34] "Service of Word and Table I," UMBW, 38.

death, resurrection, and Second Coming are the chief things that we remember and proclaim concerning him. The progression is from the past ("has died") to the present ("is risen") and into the future ("will come again"). The acclamation may be either spoken or sung, the latter giving greater emphasis and meaning.

The Anamnesis. Usually translated as "remember," this Greek word means more than simply "calling to mind." In the context of the liturgy, anamnesis means to remember a past action that is truly present now in all its power and efficacy. It is not a magical action of bringing the past into the present, but rather a manifesting of the continuing power of a deed that took place in the past. Traditionally, the language of the eucharistic anamnesis is "remembering…we offer/set forth this bread and cup," as in the eucharistic prayer of the *Apostolic Tradition* attributed to Hippolytus (early-third century)[35] or the Egyptian Anaphora of St. Basil (late-third century).[36] Sensitivities about offering eucharistic elements to God – as if the Lord's Supper were a *quid pro quo* proposition – led Protestants to remove offering language from the eucharistic liturgy and/or to focus instead on Christ's offering of himself or the church's offering to God.[37] However, some books have maintained more classical language that speaks of the offering of the bread and cup (or "gifts") to God as the

[35] *The Apostolic Tradition attributed to Hippolytus* 4 (ca. 217), PEER, 35.

[36] "The Egyptian Anaphora of St Basil," PEER, 71.

[37] See "Holy Communion," LBW, 222 ("…with this bread and cup we remember the life our Lord offered for us."). In a rather creative turn, LBW eucharistic prayer IV transforms Hippolytus' "offer" to "lift this bread and cup before you" (226). The eucharist prayers of ELW avoid "offering" language, but do speak of remembering Christ's saving acts with or by means of the bread and cup (194-206). BCW speaks of taking things from creation (bread and wine) and joyfully celebrating Christ's death and resurrection, as well as the assembly's self-offering to God (71). The Presbyterian Church in Singapore's service of the Lord's Supper (1994) simply omits the anamnesis and moves directly to the epiclesis after the memorial acclamation (4). DSSB speaks of celebrating Christ's "one perfect sacrifice" with the bread and cup rather than of offering these things (41). CW eucharistic prayer C speaks of the offering of the church's praise and thanksgiving (193). UMBW speaks of the assembly's offering of itself to God "in praise and thanksgiving in union with Christ's offering for us" (38).

memory of Christ is made.[38] The meaning is this: we now explicitly remember Christ which leads us to obey his command to have a meal that remembers and manifests him. "Remembering" in the liturgical context therefore is a concrete action using tangible objects, not merely a matter of abstract thinking.

The Epiclesis. The invocation of the Holy Spirit or *epiclesis* (Greek, "calling down") is a liturgical formula that invites the Spirit to transform the elements, the assembly, or both. It is appropriate to do this because Christians connect the person and work of the Spirit with the giving of new life (cf. Gen. 1:2) or with transformation (Titus 3:5). It is only by the work of the Spirit that bread and cup can become a means of communion with the risen Lord. The epiclesis is not a magical formula, but a very *trinitarian* way of praying for the Supper to become and to do what God promises. It is now, only after praising and thanking the Father for the life and work of the Son, that we petition (request, ask) the Spirit's presence and the fruits of his work.

In the Reformation era, only the BCP 1549 contained a eucharistic epiclesis: "Hear us, O merciful Father, we beseech thee; and with thy Holy Spirit and Word vouchsafe to bless and sanctify these gifts and creatures of bread and wine, that they may be unto us the body and blood of thy most dearly beloved Son Jesus Christ...."[39] Undoubtedly influenced by Orthodox rites, this formula seeks the consecration of the elements such that they are received as Christ's body and blood. Sixteenth-century Reformed and Lutheran liturgies made no use of the epiclesis. Since his sacramental theology rested on Augustine's idea of the Word of God "making" a sacrament, Luther could not have envisioned an invocation of the Spirit for the consecration of the elements.[40] But less understandable is the lack of

[38] "Holy Eucharist Two," BCP 1979, 363.

[39] "The Supper of the Lord, and Holy Communion, Commonly Called the Mass," BCP 1549, PEER, 239; cf. "Holy Eucharist One," BCP 1979, 342; "Order for Holy Communion (eucharistic prayer C)," CW, 192.

[40] However, Luther affirmed the Spirit's role in the transformation of the elements into the body and blood of Christ. See Martin Luther, *The Sacrament of the Body and Blood of Christ – Against the Fanatics* (1526), LW 36, 341.

Spirit language in the old Reformed liturgies, given Calvin's idea that the Spirit lifts hearts and minds to heaven where worshippers enjoy communion with the body and blood of Christ.

Much later, the liturgical movement of the twentieth century brought about the recovery of the eucharistic epiclesis. In some cases, the epicletic language in eucharistic prayers is no more than a rather mild, general request for the Spirit to grant worshippers participation in the fullness of salvation.[41] In other cases, the Spirit is explicitly invoked upon the people and/or the elements that there may be a communion in the body and blood of Christ.[42] Still other prayers contain robust consecratory language (e.g., "Sanctify them by your Holy Spirit to be for your people the Body and Blood of your Son… "[43] or "Sanctify them by your Holy Spirit to be the Body and Blood of Jesus Christ our Lord"[44]).

Following the Roman and Orthodox pattern, Anglican prayers sometimes include epicletic language both before and after the Institution Narrative.[45] Usually, the first of these invokes the Spirit on the elements (a consecratory epiclesis), while the second requests the fruits of the Spirit for the participants. Perhaps the advantage of this double epiclesis is that it avoids the impression given by a single consecratory epiclesis following the Institution Narrative, namely, that the elements are not truly consecrated until the Spirit is invoked – one reason, perhaps, why some prayers avoid using a consecratory epiclesis after the Institution Narrative. But if the whole

[41] "Holy Communion," LBW, 223; "Holy Communion (eucharistic prayers III through XI," ELW, 169-205; cf. "Order for Holy Communion (eucharistic prayer B)," CW 190.

[42] "Service for the Lord's Day," BCW, 72, 126-56; cf. "Order for Holy Communion (eucharistic prayers C and D)," CW, 192, 195.

[43] *The Presbyterian Church in Singapore Worship Book*, 65 (cf. Presbyterian Church in Singapore, "The Lord's Supper" [1994], 4); "Holy Communion Two (eucharistic prayer A)," BCP 1979, 363; "Order for Holy Communion (eucharistic prayers A, E, F, G and H)," CW, 185, 196, 199, 203, 205; "Service of Word and Table I," UMBW, 38.

[44] "Holy Eucharist Two (eucharistic prayer C)," BCP 1979, 371.

[45] See for example "Order for Holy Communion," CW, 189-90.

prayer is understood as setting aside the elements for their intended purpose, any debate about when and by what words the elements are consecrated is entirely moot. This question would not have occurred to Christians prior to the fourth century, who focused more on the fact that the Supper is a participation in the risen Lord, whose person and presence are manifested in the breaking of the bread.

In ancient eucharistic prayers, the epiclesis might be followed by various intercessory petitions (for the church and world) and the commemoration of saints.[46] Some contemporary eucharistic services incorporate intercessory material in the eucharistic prayer,[47] while others might have slight references to the commemoration of saints.[48]

The Doxology. Because the eucharistic prayer is a trinitarian act of praising the Father for (or "through") the Son, in the power of the Holy Spirit, it fittingly concludes with a trinitarian summary of that praise. In some cases, the wording of the doxology emphasizes the mediatory role of the Son, Jesus Christ, and the empowering work of the Spirit: "Through him, all glory and honour are yours, Almighty Father, *with* the Holy Spirit, in your holy Church both now and forever."[49] In other eucharistic doxologies, the praise is given not only *through* (or "by") the Son, but also (1) "with" him, i.e., the church's praise is joined to Christ's own praise of the Father; (2) "in" him, i.e., praising the Father as part of the "total Christ" joined in essential unity to Christ who is in the church leading its praise of the Father; and (3) "in the unity of the Holy Spirit," i.e., offered as the act of Christians who are united by the Holy Spirit

---

[46] "The Egyptian Anaphora of St Basil," PEER, 72.

[47] "Holy Eucharist Two (eucharistic prayer D)," BCP 1979, 375; "Order for Holy Communion (eucharistic prayer G)," CW, 203.

[48] See "Holy Communion," LBW, 223: "Join our prayers with those of your servants of every time and every place and unite them with the ceaseless petitions of our great high priest until he comes as victorious Lord of all."

[49] "Holy Communion," LBW, 226; "Holy Communion," ELW, 205; "Additional Texts for the Service of the Lord's Day (Great Thanksgiving H)," BCW, 152; "Service of Word and Table I," UMBW, 38.

who is also the bond of unity between the Father and Son.[50] In still other eucharistic doxologies, the praise is to "God, Father, Son, and Holy Spirit," so as to emphasize the equality of all three divine persons of the Trinity.[51]

The doxology concludes with the assembly's "Amen." Since this word essentially means "yes, let it be so," it is the assembly's assent of faith to what has just been proclaimed and its commitment to living out the implications of the prayer. The Orthodox terminology of "Great Amen" suggests its importance to the liturgy. The assembly may speak the Amen, but, as with other parts of the liturgy, singing serves to heighten its importance. Given the trinitarian character of the prayer (praising the Father, remembering the Son, invoking the Spirit for the fruits of the sacrament), a (sung) three-fold amen is an especially fitting way of punctuating the prayer.

The Great Thanksgiving is led by a single presiding minister, rather than by different ministers speaking different parts, which tends to obscure the unity of the prayer. When several ordained ministers are present, they may assist with the distribution of the elements. Some liturgical traditions permit a *concelebration* in which a group of ministers participate in the Great Thanksgiving, but even then the recommended manner of participation is gestures only.[52] It is only appropriate for the assembly to sing or speak the Sanctus, memorial acclamation, and Amen; for it to speak other parts of the eucharistic prayer is to obscure the ordained minister's calling to proclaim the Word and celebrate the sacraments, which is made visible through eucharistic presidency. The assembly participates by

---

[50] "Holy Communion," LBW, 224; "Holy Communion," ELW, 199, 202; "Service for the Lord's Day," BCW, 73 (cf. 152); "Holy Communion," DSSB, 41-42; "Order for Holy Communion," CW, 187, 197.

[51] "Holy Communion," LBW, 225; "Holy Communion," ELW, 195; "Order for Holy Communion," CW, 195. See also "The Byzantine Liturgy of St. Basil," PEER, 123; *Service Book and Hymnal* (Minneapolis: Augsburg Publishing House; Philadelphia: Board of Publication, Lutheran Church in America, 1958), 34.

[52] "Holy Eucharist Two," BCP 1979, 354. See Galley, *Ceremonies of the Eucharist*, 23-26.

listening to the eucharistic prayer – just as it listens to the gospel and other readings.

Today, liturgical leaders have many eucharistic prayers available to them from a great variety of sources. Most official liturgical books provide several prayers, and some of these are intended for use during specific seasons of the liturgical year.[53] Careful use of these prayers gives variety to the praise and proclamation at the table as well as added depth to the assembly's experience of the liturgical seasons. Worship leaders might evaluate a particular eucharistic prayer based on how well it (1) expresses the trinitarian character of Christian thanksgiving at the table; and (2) affirms the gift character of the Supper.

The Great Thanksgiving: Actions and Postures

During the dialog, the minister may use a series of gestures that convey the meaning of the words. In one pattern, the minister may extend open hands toward the assembly at the words "The Lord be with you..." as if to welcome a guest into the home. This action is referred to as either the greeting or invitation gesture. As the assembly responds ("And also with you."), the minister joins the hands together and may bow slightly toward the assembly to acknowledge its presence and response. At the words "Lift up..." the minister opens the hands and raises them – as if to visually portray the "lifting up." An upward circular motion may also be used. Finally, the (open) hands may be extended again toward the assembly at the words "Let us give thanks...." During the congregation's responses, the minister's hands are brought together (palm against palm) in front of the minister.[54] A simpler pattern is to raise the opened

[53] "Holy Communion (eucharistic prayers III and IV)," LBW, 224-26; "Holy Communion (eucharistic prayers III and IV), ELW, 196-97; "Additional Texts (eucharistic prayers)," and "Resources for the Liturgical Year," BCW, 126-55, 165-400; "Great Thanksgivings," UMBW, 54-80. See also *Chinese Lutheran Book of Worship* (Minneapolis: Augsburg Fortress, 2005), 152-60.

[54] Peter J. Elliot, *Ceremonies of the Modern Roman Rite: The Eucharist and the Liturgy of the Hours* (San Francisco: Ignatius Press, 1995), 281. Cf. Galley,

hands into the *orans* position at the words "Lift up your hearts" and to leave them in that position until the Sanctus, when they are lowered.[55] Neither pattern of gesturing is absolutely essential to the meaning or efficacy of the Lord's Supper; these gestures are meant to visually engage the assembly and draw it into the proclamation of the eucharistic prayer. The *orans* gesture is appropriate because it is the biblical posture of prayer (cf. Pss. 134:2, 141:2). Even if no gestures are made, it is still recommended that ministers memorize the words of the dialog so that eye contact can be made with the assembly during this act of invitation.The minister's hands remain in the raised *orans* position during the Preface and are then lowered and brought together during the Sanctus, otherwise, the minister will find the posture too physically taxing and awkward. During the Sanctus ("Holy, holy, holy"), the minister may cross the arms over the chest and make a profound bow to the presence of Ineffable Divinity. The sign of the cross may be made by the ministers (and assembly) at "Blessed is he who comes…." Throughout the Great Thanksgiving, the minister's hands need to be free, which means that any book or folder containing the liturgical texts should rest on a stand (a *missal stand*) that is placed on the table near the center.

Traditionally, the Institution Narrative is accompanied with actions and gestures involving the bread and cup, the so-called "manual acts." Some ministers do not use these, perhaps to avoid the impression of magical actions or of "sacrificed" items being offered to God. Yet, Jesus himself obviously handled the loaf and cup, and physical actions with bread and cup serve to connect the words of thanksgiving with the elements: we are blessing *this* bread and *this* cup. It is these things that are now the bearers of God's saving promises in Jesus Christ. The manual acts might be undertaken as follows:

- At the words "took bread," the minister lifts the bread off the table so that it can be seen by the assembly. A large loaf will be taken in both hands, while a *presider's host* is held

Ceremonies of the Eucharist, 156, and Brugh and Lathrop, *Sunday Assembly*, 208-9. See also Pfatteicher and Messerli, *Manual on the Liturgy*, 234-35.

[55] "Service of Word and Table I," UMBW, 36-37.

with two fingers of one hand while the paten is raised with the other hand.

- At the words, "took the cup," the cup (chalice) is raised from the table. One hand grasps the cup under its bowl, while the other hand supports the base of the cup. If there is a flagon on the table, the minister might touch it to associate it with the proclamation.

When holding the bread and then the cup, the minister may turn slightly to the left and to the right, to insure that all in the assembly may see the bread and cup. The bread and cup need only be raised to the height of the presider's chest and never in front of the face. The bread is not broken during the words "he broke the bread" of the Institution Narrative because that action occurs later in the service (at the fraction). Memorizing the Institution Narrative will help the minister perform the actions effortlessly and confidently. The matter of where to direct the eyes depends on how the Narrative is used in the liturgy. If the Narrative is incorporated into the prayer addressed to God, then the eyes are not directed to the assembly. Instead, they are fixed on the bread or cup as a way of directing the assembly's attention to these things. If the Narrative functions as an invitation or as a proclamational formula accompanying the fraction (as in the Reformed-Presbyterian tradition), the minister's eyes may focus on the assembly since the words are spoken to the assembly. During the memorial acclamation, the minister's hands are joined in front.

Gestures may also accompany the epiclesis. The BCP 1549 directed the minister to make the sign of the cross at both the words "bless" and "sanctify," as if to identify the elements with the crucified Christ who, in the power of the Spirit, blesses them with his presence.[56] With the right arm extended over the table, finger tips pointing toward the assembly, and the palm facing to the left, the cross is made from top to bottom and then left to right. The area in which the action takes place is no larger than the corporal. In other types of epicletic formulas, the hands are placed palms down

[56] "Supper of the Lord," BCP 1549, PEER, 239. Cf. Galley, *Ceremonies of the Eucharist*, 115-16.

just above the elements at the invocation of the Spirit.[57] This gesture of conferral suggests the coming of the Holy Spirit to the elements, much like the laying on of hands suggests the conferral of the Spirit to a candidate for ordination. Alternatively, ministers might remain in the *orans* posture during the epiclesis, since it is still prayer.

Because the bread and cup embody the praise and thanksgiving offered over them – indeed were understood to be the "eucharist" by ancient Christians – the chalice and paten may be lifted together during the doxology of the eucharistic prayer. Luther, who advocated an elevation during the Sanctus, understood the action to suggest adoration and praise of the present Christ;[58] others view it as a gesture of offering, which is part of Christ's own offering to the Father.[59] Traditionally, the chalice is raised with the left hand to the height of one's head, while the presider's host is held over the chalice. If a loaf of bread is used, the paten may be raised with the right hand while the chalice is elevated with the left hand.

Many assemblies stand from the Preface dialog through the Lord's Prayer (Lutherans); others kneel after the Sanctus (Anglicans), and still others might be seated throughout the Great Thanksgiving or for parts of it (Methodist). Standing conveys joy and thanksgiving, the mood suggested by the words "lift up your hearts" in the opening dialog. Although suggestive of prayer, kneeling connotes repentance and introspection, attitudes that may obscure the joyful character of the Supper. The practice of standing for some parts of the Great Thanksgiving while kneeling for others interrupts the flow and unity of the prayer. The *orans* position may also be assumed by assembly members during the eucharistic prayer since nothing suggests that its use be limited to presiding ministers.

The Lord's Prayer

The Great Thanksgiving continues through the Lord's Prayer, the prayer taught to the church by the Lord Jesus himself. Because this

[57] Pfatteicher and Messerli, *Manual on the Liturgy*, 239.

[58] Pfatteicher and Messerli, *Manual on the Liturgy*, 239.

[59] Galley, *Ceremonies of the Eucharist*, 113.

is the church's model intercessory prayer and a summary of the Lord's teaching about God, the kingdom, and forgiveness, it has traditionally been a centerpiece of catechetical formation. Ancient catechumens were required to learn it, and Protestant catechisms (e.g., Luther's *Small Catechism*) provided short explanations for youth preparing for confirmation and first reception of communion. The prayer's relevance to the Supper is readily apparent: in this Supper, God's kingdom of love and mercy is made known to the assembly when bread and cup are shared. The church feasts on its daily bread, which is Christ himself. In receiving Christ's body and blood, God's forgiveness is given. Insofar as the Supper anticipates the final victory of God's kingdom, we can taste our deliverance from sin, death, and evil even now. It is fitting for the assembly to pray the prayer given to it by the Lord, as it prepares to experience communion with him in the Lord's Supper. In a way, the Lord's Prayer is the assembly's "table prayer" for the Supper.

The Breaking of the Bread (Fraction)

In the Jewish sacred meal tradition, the breaking of the bread signaled the start of the meal. The gospel accounts of the Last Supper report that Jesus broke the bread after giving thanks, prior to sharing it with his disciples. A number of early eastern liturgies contain a fraction that was followed immediately by the words: "Holy things for holy people," to which the people responded "One is holy, one is Lord, Jesus Christ, to the glory of God the Father, with the Holy Spirit; to him be glory to the ages of ages." This formula connects the breaking action to the distribution, suggesting that the bread is broken not in order to imitate Jesus, but to invite the people to communion.[60]

Protestants vary as to how much importance they attach to the fraction. Luther makes no mention of it in either his Latin or German Masses and early Lutheran liturgies had no fraction. Among the early Reformed theologians, only the Scottish Reformer John Knox mentions the breaking of the bread prior to its distribution

[60] See the following in PEER: "The Liturgy of St Mark" (66), "The Egyptian Anaphora of St. Basil" (73), "The Liturgy of St James" (99).

to the assembly, but he provided no formula.[61] The *Westminster Directory* calls for the bread to be broken as the minister speaks these words: "According to the holy institution, command, and example of our blessed Savior Jesus Christ, I take this bread, and having given thanks, I break it, and give it unto you."[62] The breaking of the bread was a point of contention between Reformed and Lutheran churches in the seventeenth century, with the action serving as a mark of identity for the former, and refusing to do it a characteristic of the latter. For Anglicans, it was only the BCP 1662 that directed the minister to break the bread during the Words of Institution,[63] a practice retained by John Wesley in his version of the Prayer Book communion service.[64]

The bread is broken immediately before the communion of the people. For most Lutherans, the action is optional and may or may not be accompanied by words.[65] Reformed-Presbyterian liturgies permit the action to be accompanied by the Institution Narrative in keeping with the old Reformed practice of juxtaposing the Narrative with the communion of the people, as if to provide the biblical warrant for communion immediately beforehand.[66] Other options are also available for Reformed worship assemblies. A typical Anglican fraction formula is this: "We break this bread to share the body of Christ. Though we are many, we are one body, because we all

---

[61] John Knox, *The Form of Prayers and Ministration of the Sacrament* (1556), PEER, 256.

[62] *The Directory for the Public Worship of God throughout the Three Kingdoms of England, Scotland and Ireland* (1645), PEER, 269.

[63] "The Order for the Administration of the Lord's Supper or Holy Communion," BCP 1662, PEER, 281.

[64] "The Order for the Administration of the Lord's Supper," JWPB, 136.

[65] "Notes," LBW, 29; "Notes," ELW, 23.

[66] See Ulrich Zwingli, *Action or Use of the Lord's Supper* (1525), PEER, 187; Martin Bucer, *The Psalter, with Complete Church Practice* (1539), PEER, 211.

share in one bread."[67] Methodists use similar words.[68] Some liturgical books provide collections of fraction formulas, and usually some of these are meant for particular liturgical seasons.[69]

If a larger loaf is used, the minister tears or breaks the loaf in view of the assembly. If wafer bread is used, a larger *presider's host* is needed for the fraction. In both cases, the bread is taken from its container and raised no higher than the presider's chest and broken in an unhurried manner. The action need not be exaggerated. Since the breaking of the bread parallels the Jewish action that signals the start of the meal, any parallel action with the cup is unnecessary.

The Communion of the Assembly

The words that accompany the breaking of the bread could function as the invitation for the assembly to receive communion. If (additional) words of invitation seem necessary, appropriate ones are either "The gifts of God for the people of God," or "Taste and see that the Lord is good." If a loaf is used, it is now broken into smaller pieces, and any additional vessels (e.g., chalices, paten) needed for communion are brought to the table. Verbal instructions to visitors might be made at this time, but these should be kept brief.

In one pattern of distributing the elements, the people come forward to the table (*altar communion*). In many churches with this tradition, especially Anglican and Lutheran, the people are invited to kneel around the altar-table. This posture suggests reverence and adoration, not so much of the elements but of Christ who gives himself to his people in and through the elements. For the sake of those with physical disabilities or limitations, some assemblies have made kneeling optional, that is, for those "who are able." But the resulting diversity tends to undermine the belief that communion is an expression of the church's unity. Assemblies might therefore

---

[67] "Holy Communion," DSSB, 42; "Order for Holy Communion," CW, 179; cf. *The Occasional Services Book*, 2nd ed. (New York: The Church Hymnal Corporation, 1988), 15.

[68] "Service of Word and Table I," UMBW, 39.

[69] *Occasional Services*, 15-19.

consider whether a better approach is to have all standing while receiving the elements.

The bread is distributed first and then the cup (wine). Normally, the presiding minister distributes the bread followed by an assisting communion minister with the wine (juice). It is somewhat odd if the minister who gives thanks over the bread and cup does not participate in the distribution, since the bread is blessed in order to be shared with God's people. Other ordained ministers present may help in the distribution of the elements as a way of affirming their calling to the ministry of Word and Sacrament. Traditionally, the bread is given with the words "The body of Christ, given [broken] for you."[70] Anglicans use the formula "The Body of our Lord Jesus Christ keep you in everlasting life" or a variation of this.[71] Other words are possible.[72] The communicants respond by saying "Amen." These words announce the gift of Christ in and through the elements, just like the baptismal formula declares that a person is washed into the life of the triune God. The same distribution formula is spoken to each communicant. The bread is placed into the hands of the communicants, and assembly members should be taught to extend the hands to the minister, the right hand (palm up) resting in the open left hand. Grasping at the bread should be discouraged because it risks having the element dropped to the floor.

The wine/juice is distributed with the words "the blood of Christ shed for you" or "the blood of our Lord Jesus Christ keep you in everlasting life." Four methods are possible: (1) distributing pre-filled cups to the communicants; (2) intinction (communicants dipping a wafer into a cup of wine/juice); (3) offering a common chalice from which all drink (i.e., the "common cup"); or (4) pouring the wine into small communion cups that the communicants received on the way to the table. Because the use of individual communion cups

[70] "Holy Communion," LBW, 227; "Holy Communion," ELW, 206; "Supplementary Texts," CW, 295; "Service of Word and Table I," UMBW, 39.

[71] "Holy Eucharist Two," BCP 1979, 365; cf. "Holy Communion," DSSB, 44.

[72] See the five optional distribution formulas in "Supplementary Texts," CW, 295.

seems to contradict the communal import of the Supper, assemblies might consider recovering the practice of offering a common chalice – at least as an option.[73] Method (4) requires the use of special pouring chalices that are used this way: the minister holds the stem of the chalice with one hand and the bowl of the chalice with the other hand just under the lip using a purificator to catch any drips. While saying the appropriate words of distribution for the wine or juice, the minister slowly fills the cup of the communicant to about three-quarters full. To facilitate the distribution, the communicants leave the table area after consuming the elements; a table blessing for each group of communicants is unnecessary and prolongs the distribution.

Because the distribution of elements blessed in the name of Jesus Christ is a powerful action in and of itself, embellishments are unnecessary. The minister need not say the name of the recipient, who has already been named before God and the church in baptism. This practice risks awkward delays and embarrassment when the minister does not know or forgets the communicant's name. Neither is it necessary to break a piece of wafer bread while placing it in the hand of the communicant since there has already been a breaking at the fraction. These little "fractions" individualize the sacrament and detract from its communal nature. Squeezing the hand of the communicant is painful to those with arthritis and draws undue attention to the minister when the focus should be on Christ's gift of himself in the bread.

Communion ministers are required to deal with a number of contingencies. The minister with the cup may need to be alert to situations when the presiding minister does *not* give communion to a person or when a person has come to receive a blessing rather than the elements themselves. When there is uncertainty as to whether a child receives the elements, the minister may simply ask a parent or accompanying adult: "Does your child commune?" In the event that pouring chalices need refilling, a minister bearing the flagon with wine/juice brings it to the communion minister in order to

[73] See ch. 12.

refill the cup. If convenient, the communion ministers may go to the flagon bearer for replenishment. If the flagon itself appears to be running low, one solution is to pour water into the remaining wine/juice to increase the volume. Some traditions require that when the bread and wine prove insufficient, the presiding minister return to the table and consecrate new elements, using formulas such as the following:

> Father, giving thanks over the bread and the cup according to the institution of your Son Jesus Christ, who said, Take, eat; this is my body (and/or Drink this; this is my blood) we pray that this bread/wine also may be to us his body/blood, to be received in remembrance of him.[74]

Or

> Hear us, O heavenly Father, and with your Word and Holy Spirit bless and sanctify this bread (wine) that it, also, may be the Sacrament of the precious Body (Blood) of your Son Jesus Christ our Lord, who took bread (the cup) and said, "This is my Body (Blood)." Amen.[75]

In the event that a piece of bread or a wafer falls to the floor, a minister simply picks it up and places it on the table, and gives a new one to the communicant (the old wafer is later placed on the ground outside). Wine spills are wiped up with purificators, which are laundered after the service. Because accidents are inevitable, there is no need for embarrassment, but communion ministers should be trained to deal quickly and calmly with such situations.

The other manner of distribution, common among Presbyterian, Reformed, and many independent churches, is a *pew communion* in which the elements are taken to the people who remain in their seats. This practice requires recruiting and training a cadre of servers, who in many cases are elected leaders of the local church. Details to be worked out include when the servers come forward to receive

---

[74] "Holy Communion," DSSB, 44.

[75] "Additional Directions," BCP 1979, 408.

the communion vessels, how (what order) they receive them, which part of the assembly is served by which servers, and the manner of distributing to the people – whether handing the elements to the people or allowing them to take the elements from the trays. Usually churches that distribute in this manner have the practice of all eating/drinking together, which means that visitors must be informed to refrain from consuming the elements until directed to do so by the presiding minister. The re-collection of used communion cups has no theological or spiritual meaning and arguably extends the time of the service. If at all possible, a small shelf could be installed on the back of pews for the used cups – although this solution might rule out the use of chairs or other kinds of flexible seating.

The most appropriate time for the communion of the ministers themselves is a matter of some debate. In keeping with the cultural custom whereby the host serves others before partaking him/herself, the ministers (including the presider) might take communion after the assembly.[76] Yet, this custom may not offer the best model for the church's Supper, since Christ, rather than the presiding minister, is the true host. Indeed, by receiving communion before the assembly as some books direct,[77] the ministers model the idea of "being fed in order to feed others." It is also appropriate and less distracting if the presiding minister gives the elements to him/herself, perhaps with another minister saying the words of administration.[78]

The celebration of the Lord's Supper may be accompanied by songs in the following ways:

1. Songs of invitation (during the preparation of the table)[79]
2. Songs that interpret the meaning of the Supper (during the communion of the assembly), and

[76] "Notes," ELW, 23.

[77] "Holy Eucharist Two," BCP 1979, 365; UMBW, 30.

[78] Galley, *Ceremonies of the Eucharist*, 121.

[79] A number of invitational hymns are listed in UMBW, 26.

3. Songs that give thanks for the gifts received in the Supper (after all have received communion).[80]

If the assembly goes forward to receive the communion elements, it may be advisable to use one or more songs that are short and memorizable ("Jesus, Remember Me," "Let Us Break Bread Together on Our Knees") or songs with a refrain ("You Satisfy the Hungry Heart") so that those making their way to the table can participate in the singing. Assembly song makes the event joyful and imparts the church's theological understanding of the Lord's Supper. In fact, for many members of the assembly, the singing of communion songs may be the only means of ongoing sacramental formation and catechesis. At times it may be appropriate not to sing at all, but instead to reflect quietly on the meaning of the Supper.

As an alternative to assembly song, choral or instrumental music may accompany the communion, but the emphasis is always on assembly song. Since singing during the sacrament symbolizes unity in Christ, it is appropriate that members of the assembly unite their voices in one song at this time. Some traditions (Lutheran, Anglican) consider the Agnus Dei (Latin, "Lamb of God") hymn, based on John 1:29, as a fitting initial song for communion. Like John the Baptizer, the assembly knows itself to be in the presence of the one "who takes away the sin of the world," whose atoning work is now shared in this communion Meal.[81]

Following the communion, the altar-table is cleared. When stacked bread and cup trays are used, they will be restacked and covered with a large cloth. Lutheran and Anglican assisting ministers will cover extra bread plates and chalices and either place them on a credence table or take them to a sacristy, if it is conveniently located. The corporal is refolded and with the purificators is returned to the burse. The pall is placed on top of the chalice. Then the pall and chalice are covered with the veil, and the burse is put on top of the

[80] For examples of each type of song, see my *Worship: A Practical Guide*, 191.

[81] "Holy Communion," LBW, 227; "Holy Communion," ELW, 206; cf. "Order for Holy Communion," CW, 179.

vested chalice. Any remaining elements may be (1) consumed by the ministers, or (2) set aside for the communion of the sick during the coming week. Recognizing that the elements have been set aside for a holy purpose, it is inappropriate to treat them as one would common leftover food items by returning them to their original containers. Such a practice is also questionable for hygienic reasons, since the elements may have been handled by various ministers.[82]

The Post-Communion

Following the communion of the people, there may be words and actions that conclude the communion liturgy. Lutheran books provide a final communion blessing, but this formula tends to duplicate the distribution formula and so is best considered optional.[83] Lutherans and Presbyterians often conclude with the Song of Simeon (Luke 2:29-32) or another song,[84] which is also possible for Methodists.[85] Nearly all Protestant eucharistic services have a post-communion prayer, which is considered mandatory. This prayer gives thanks for the Supper and asks for the gifts of the sacrament. Themes of unity, mutual love, and service to neighbors are common and so serve to place the Supper in the wider context of Christian living and the church's mission in the world. The post-communion prayer may therefore be considered a transitional element that leads to the sending. If the assembly stands for a preceding song or post-communion blessing, it stands for this prayer. The minister leading the prayer may use the *orans* posture.

Other Liturgical Shapes to Thanksgiving and Communion

The shape of the Great Thanksgiving described above is by no means the only shape or the only theologically valid one. Following Luther's

---

[82] UMG, 47; "An Order of Sunday Worship Using the Basic Pattern," UMBW, 30.

[83] "Holy Communion," LBW, 228; "Holy Communion," ELW, 207.

[84] "Holy Communion," LBW, 228-29; "Holy Communion," ELW, 207-8; "Service for the Lord's Day," BCW, 77.

[85] "Basic Pattern," UMBW, 30.

Formula Missae, Lutherans might give thanks at the table using the traditional dialog, Preface, Institution Narrative, Sanctus, and Lord's Prayer.[86] Even though this order is greatly abbreviated compared to the more "classic" eucharistic prayers, it is still essentially prayer that thankfully remembers Christ and praises the Father. This form of thanksgiving, with its emphasis on the Institution Narrative, makes the gifts of Christ's body and blood obvious and apparent. As noted above, Reformed-Presbyterian services might proclaim the Words of Institution in connection with the breaking of the bread rather than during the eucharistic prayer.[87] A Baptist or "free-church" communion liturgy might consist of the following:

Introduction to the meaning of the Supper
Scripture reading
Prayers for the bread and cup (extempore)
Invitation to the assembly
Partaking of the bread (bread words of the Institution Narrative)
Partaking of the cup (cup words of the Institution Narrative)
Proclamation: "When you eat this bread…"
Closing song[88]

We might note that the Baptist shape also contains prayer and proclamation, and so is similar to the other traditions described above.

Conclusion

With the Great Thanksgiving and communion of the people, the Sunday liturgy reaches a second high point, the first being the proclamation of the Word. Christ comes to us in his Word, and then gives himself to us in bread and cup. Because the gifts of the Supper are so great, it is both a high duty and privilege to serve at

[86] "Holy Communion," LBW, 224; "Holy Communion," ELW, 194.

[87] "Service for the Lord's Day," BCW, 74.

[88] Choon Sam Fong, Field Education Group Session, Semester 2, 2007/2008, Conducting the Lord's Supper (unpublished lecture paper).

the Lord's Table. Communion ministers need practical training to help them serve with confidence. At the same time, they need study and reflection on the meaning of the Meal in order to serve with a reverence that helps the assembly to focus on Christ and his gifts in the Supper.

For Further Reading

Bouyer, Louis. *Eucharist: Theology and Spirituality of the Eucharistic Prayer.* Translated by Charles Underhill Quinn. Notre Dame: University Press, 1968.

Bradshaw, Paul F., and Maxwell E. Johnson. *The Eucharistic Liturgies: Their Evolution and Interpretation.* Collegeville: The Liturgical Press, 2012.

Dix, Gregory. *The Shape of the Liturgy.* London: Dacre, 1945.

Mazza, Enrico. *The Origins of the Eucharistic Prayer.* Collegeville: The Liturgical Press, 1995.

Reed, Luther. *The Lutheran Liturgy*. Revised Edition. Philadelphia: Muhlenberg Press, 1947.

CHAPTER 15

The Lord's Supper and Justice

The great contribution of the Protestant Reformers was their recovery of the *grace* character of the gospel: in Jesus Christ, God has taken the initiative to save humanity from sin and death, and all of Christian life is a response to God's saving work. Although the theology and biblical interpretation of the Reformers offered a fresh perspective on the individual's relationship to God, they did not neglect the individual's relationship to the Christian community or to society in general. Their work had implications for both spirituality and ethics. Unfortunately, the Enlightenment with its stress on reason and rationality, egalitarian political movements with their emphasis on individual liberties and rights, and evangelical revival with its concern for "saving souls," shifted the focus of Christian thought to the individual's relationship with God. The result has been a reductionism whereby the liturgy and the sacraments are viewed mainly in terms of "what they do for me," and little attention is given to the relationship between sacraments and the ethical life.

But the latter half of the twentieth century saw a renewed interest in ethics, due to two world wars, revolutions, militant movements, environmental degradation, and economic exploitation. While Christians of earlier periods were mainly concerned about the individual's relationship to God, twentieth-century Christians have stressed the church's relationship to society and the natural environment. "Liturgy and ethics" and "liturgy and justice" have emerged as important scholarly themes in recent years. Perhaps the latter category has captured the Christian imagination more since justice is a central biblical theme, particularly in the prophetic literature of the Hebrew Scriptures. This chapter will explore the relationship between the Lord's Supper and justice. The basic assumption is that participation in the Supper defines and shapes our relationship with others and with the world itself in a way that embodies God's justice.

What is Justice?

Justice might be defined as giving people what is rightly their due. If the ethical requirements contained in the Ten Commandments are an expression of divine justice, then justice seeks to ensure that nothing is taken from a person by force or violence. For the prophets of the Hebrew Scriptures, the enrichment of one's self at the neighbor's expense and the perversion of the legal system for one's own benefit are not commensurate with divine justice:

> You levy a straw tax on the poor
> and impose a tax on their grain.
> Therefore, though you have built stone mansions,
> you will not live in them;
> though you have planted lush vineyards,
> you will not drink their wine.
> For I know how many are your offenses
> and how great your sins.
> There are those who oppress the innocent and take bribes
> and deprive the poor of justice in the courts.
> Therefore the prudent keep quiet in such times,
> for the times are evil. (Amos 5:11-13)

Yet, justice means more than simply helping people to maintain what is rightfully theirs; the community of Israel is to aid those who are economically deprived so that they, too, can share in the abundance of the land that was given by God:

> Do not go over your vineyard a second time or pick up the grapes that have fallen. Leave them for the poor and the foreigner. I am the LORD your God. (Lev. 19:10)

> At the end of every three years, bring all the tithes of that year's produce and store it in your towns, so that the Levites (who have no allotment or inheritance of their own) and the foreigners, the fatherless and the widows who live in your towns may come and eat and be satisfied, and so that the Lord your God may bless you in all the work of your hands. (Deut. 14:28-29)

In making provision for the "have-nots" of society, God's justice is flavored with *mercy*.

In the gospels, Jesus advocates mercy not only for the poor and oppressed, but for those who would persecute his followers:

> You have heard that it was said, "Eye for eye, and tooth for tooth." But I tell you, do not resist an evil person. If anyone slaps you on the right cheek, turn to them the other cheek also. And if anyone wants to sue you and take your shirt, hand over your coat as well. If anyone forces you to go one mile, go with them two miles. Give to the one who asks you, and do not turn away from the one who wants to borrow from you.

> You have heard that it was said, "Love your neighbor and hate your enemy." But I tell you, love your enemies and pray for those who persecute you, that you may be children of your Father in heaven. He causes his sun to rise on the evil and the good, and sends rain on the righteous and the unrighteous. If you love those who love you, what

> reward will you get? Are not even the tax collectors doing that? And if you greet only your own people, what are you doing more than others? Do not even pagans do that? Be perfect, therefore, as your heavenly Father is perfect. (Matt. 5:38-48)

Jesus himself offered mercy to those who persecuted and killed him:

> Two other men, both criminals, were also led out with him to be executed.When they came to the place called the Skull, they crucified him there, along with the criminals – one on his right, the other on his left. Jesus said, "Father, forgive them, for they do not know what they are doing." And they divided up his clothes by casting lots. (Luke 23:32-34)

Paul interprets the crucifixion as God's way of being reconciled to people who are, in fact, turned against God:

> You see, at just the right time, when we were still powerless, Christ died for the ungodly. Very rarely will anyone die for a righteous person, though for a good person someone might possibly dare to die. But God demonstrates his own love for us in this: While we were still sinners, Christ died for us (Rom. 5:6-8).

God's justice is all about giving people *more* than they deserve; it is giving them what they *do not* deserve, so that they might experience God's goodness and seek to live in right relationship with God. In other words, God's justice seeks to maintain and restore relationships that have been fractured by sin. The proper response is the living out of this merciful justice so as to witness to the goodness and glory of God and create harmonious relationships within the human community. As a locus of God's merciful and reconciling justice, the Lord's Supper becomes the nexus from which the church's execution of justice arises and spreads forth into the world.

Eucharistic Justice and Reconciliation

Reconciliation between estranged parties (enemies) is at the heart of the New Testament gospel. Jesus encouraged his followers to love their enemies and pray for their persecutors (Matt. 5:44; cf. Rom. 12:14). While suffering on the Cross, Jesus asked his Father to forgive those who crucified him (Luke 23:34). Indeed, Christ's sacrifice on the Cross is the very means by which God reconciled to himself a humanity that has constantly been at enmity with him (Rom. 5:9-11; cf. Eph. 2). Thus, God's justice involves the reconciliation of humanity with God and reconciliation within the human community.

Reconciliation within the Corinthian church is central to Paul's discussion of the Lord's Supper in 1 Cor. 11. At the heart of Paul's critique of the Corinthian church's meal practice is the "individualized suppers" (v. 21), i.e., the preparation of different menus for different classes of guests, according to the social customs of the Greco-Roman *symposia* (dinner banquets). It appears that the rich brought their own sumptuous fare from home and then dined without leaving anything (or very little) for the poor.[1] In Paul's view, this practice only exacerbates social differences and creates disunity, since poor members go hungry while richer ones gorge themselves. This situation represents nothing less than a despising of the church and the humiliation of the church's humbler members (v. 22). More importantly, the divisive practice of individualized meals signals a failure to discern the body of Christ in the community, and thus constitutes an "unworthy" eating (v. 27) that garners God's judgement. The solution is to eat together (v. 33) so that unity at the Table is maintained.

Since Paul's time, the need for unity within the eucharistic fellowship has led to the church's insistence that Christians avoid partaking of the Supper if there are unresolved conflicts with fellow Christians. This understanding is based on Jesus' words about being reconciled to another before offering a gift at the altar of the Temple (Matt. 5:23-24) and Paul's emphasis on the unity of the assembly

---

[1] Gerd Theissen, *The Social Setting of Pauline Christianity: Essays on Corinth*, ed. and tr. John H. Schuetz (Philadelphia: Fortress Press, 1982), 147-63.

during the Lord's Supper (cf. 1 Cor. 11:21, 29, 33). The *Didache* directs that no one involved in a "quarrel" with another partake of the Supper until there has been reconciliation.[2] In the early church, bishops held special courts that sought to resolve disputes within the Christian community precisely so that unity at the Supper could be preserved. The *Didascalia Apostolorum* ("Catholic Teaching of the Twelve Apostles and Holy Disciples of Our Savior") instructs bishops to hold such sessions on the second day of the week so that there is sufficient time to resolve disputes and reconcile conflicted parties before the Sunday celebration of the Lord's Supper.[3] This practice continued throughout Christian history.

Unity and reconciliation as a condition for participation in the Lord's Supper was also important to the Protestant Reformers. In one of his earliest writings on the Lord's Supper, Luther states that the very thing signified in the Lord's Supper is the "fellowship of the saints."[4] He then admonishes the Christian communicant to "...give yourself to everyone in fellowship and by no means exclude anyone in hatred or anger. For this sacrament of fellowship, love, and unity cannot tolerate discord and disunity."[5] In Calvin's eucharistic service, the minister is supposed to bar from communion those who "break the unity of the Church," and who are "quarrelsome."[6] According to the BCP 1549, those at enmity with others are to abstain from communion, and only receive the sacrament again after reconciliation has occurred.[7] A similar idea is expressed in the exhortation that preceded the offertory. The exhortation to

[2] The *Didache* 14 (late-first or early-second cent.), PEER, 24.

[3] The *Didascalia Apostolorum* 11(ca. 230), http://www.earlychristianwritings.com/text/didascalia.html [accessed 14 January 2015].

[4] Martin Luther, *The Blessed Sacrament of the Holy and True Body of Christ, and the Brotherhoods* (1519), LW 35, 50.

[5] Luther, *Blessed Sacrament*, LW 35, 61.

[6] John Calvin, *The Form of Church Prayers and Manner of Celebrating the Supper* (1542), PEER, 216.

[7] "The Supper of the Lord, and the Holy Communion, Commonly Called the Mass," BCP 1549, LWC, 245.

confession (and communion) serves as a final admonition to unity before approaching the Table:

> You that do truly and earnestly repent of your sins to Almighty God, and be in love and charity with your neighbors, and intend to lead a new life, following the commandments of God, and walking from henceforth in his holy ways: draw near and take this holy sacrament to your comfort, make your humble confession to Almighty God, and to his holy church here gathered together in his name, meekly kneeling upon your knees.[8]

John Wesley retained this invitation to confession in his Sunday communion service for American Methodists, but omitted the disciplinary rubrics and long exhortations of the BCP 1662 presumably because Methodists would have been receiving disciplinary instructions about communion within the meetings of the classes and bands.[9]

Protestants today continue to emphasize the importance of reconciliation in relationship to the Lord's Supper. The ELCA's *Use of the Means of Grace* states that "helpful forms of personal preparation [for the Lord's Supper] may include self-examination, prayer, fasting, meditation, and reconciliation with others through the exchange of peace."[10] The PCUSA *Book of Order* states that "reconciliation with Christ compels reconciliation with one another…Coming to the Lord's Table the faithful are actively to seek reconciliation in every instance of conflict or division between them and their neighbors."[11]

---

[8] "Supper of the Lord," BCP 1549, LWC, 259.

[9] "The Order for the Administration of the Lord's Supper," JWPB, 131.

[10] UMG, 42A.

[11] *The Constitution of the Presbyterian Church (U.S.A.) Part II: The Book of Order* (Louisville: Office of the General Assembly, 2013), W-2.4006.

Furthermore:

> The invitation to the Lord's Supper is extended to all who have been baptized, remembering that access to the Table is not a right conferred upon the worthy, but a privilege given to the undeserving who come in faith, repentance, and love. In preparing to receive Christ in this Sacrament, the believer is to confess sin and brokenness, to seek reconciliation with God and neighbor, and to trust in Jesus Christ for cleansing and renewal.[12]

In contemporary Anglican churches, priests are still required to bar members who are at enmity with fellow Christians, although those members who are repentant and desire reconciliation can be admitted to the Supper.[13] Similarly, United Methodists in the USA affirm that:

> Communing with others in our congregations is a sign of community and mutual love between Christians throughout the church universal. The church must offer to the world a model of genuine community grounded in God's deep love for every person. As we eat and drink, we are motivated to act compassionately for those whose physical, emotional, and spiritual needs are unmet.[14]

The peace is the quintessential ritual of reconciliation within the liturgy of the Lord's Supper. Various New Testament passages (e.g., 1 Cor. 16:20; 2 Cor. 13:12) suggest that a ritual "kiss of peace" was a regular part of communal life in the apostolic era. In the early church, the newly baptized were greeted with the kiss of peace, and thereafter could take part in this ritual act at every communion

---

[12] *Book of Order*, W-2.4011.

[13] *Canons of the Church of England* (London: Church House Publishing, 2000), B16A. See BCP 1979, 409.

[14] *This Holy Mystery: A United Methodist Understanding of Holy Communion* (Nashville: The General Board of Discipleship of the United Methodist Church, 2003), 36.

service. Prior to baptism, catechumens were dismissed before the kiss of peace, because their kiss was not considered holy. Thus, the action was a sign of inclusion into the community of the redeemed and baptized people of God, a mark of the church's fellowship and a sign of its unity. Coming at the conclusion of the prayers of intercession, the greeting of peace is an enactment of Mark 11:25 ("And when you stand praying, if you hold anything against anyone, forgive them, so that your Father in heaven may forgive you your sins") and thus the means by which the assembly embodies the shalom that it prays for in the intercessions. At the same time, the peace is a proclamation of the peace of Christ that is the fruit of his death and resurrection (cf. John 20:19, 26); the peace (shalom) that the risen Christ offered his disciples is now present and available to our fellow assembly members and to the entire world.[15] Because the peace expresses the gospel and signifies the unity that is enacted at the Table, the gesture serves best when placed after the prayers of intercession and before the offering, as a kind of bridge between the word and meal movements of the Sunday liturgy. As a conclusion to a rite of confession in the gathering it also serves as an act of reconciliation – we forgive as we have been forgiven. Admittedly, however, when placed in the opening part of the service, the peace could be confused with a mere gesture of welcome.[16]

The reconciliation enacted in the liturgy through the greeting of peace and fellowship at Table finds expression outside the Sunday liturgy. Christians who are reconciled with God at the Table seek out those in the church or the community whom they have wronged and offended, admit their wrongdoing without qualifications, ask forgiveness, and make any appropriate restitution. For their part, those who have been wronged forgive wrongdoers who ask for forgiveness. Churches might provide opportunities for conflicted parties to

[15] See Lorraine S. Brugh and Gordon W. Lathrop, *The Sunday Assembly: Using Evangelical Lutheran Worship*, Vol. 1 (Minneapolis: Augsburg Fortress, 2008), 172-173.

[16] For a discussion of the peace, see Jeffrey A. Truscott, *Worship: A Practical Guide* (Singapore: Genesis, 2011), 171-72.

gather for guided dialog and a liturgy of confession and forgiveness that leads to more informal words and gestures of reconciliation. Such a gathering might even culminate in a celebration of the Lord's Supper in order to confirm the reconciliation that has taken place. Local churches might encourage reconciliation and dialog between groups in the community that are at enmity. The Truth and Justice Commission in South Africa offers a model of reconciling severely conflicted parties by allowing the offended to share their pain and giving offenders the opportunity to apologize without fear of reprisals.[17]

Eucharistic Justice and Creation

From a biblical perspective, food is bound up with God's creative work because God provides food in order to sustain life. In the garden of paradise, God planted trees so that the first humans could eat (Gen. 1:29, 2:9), although this easy provision was taken away due to their disobedience (Gen. 3:17-19, 23). The Psalms acknowledge God as the provider of food for all living creatures (Ps. 104:27-28), and wheat in particular symbolizes God's gift of food to humanity (Pss. 81:16, 147:14). When people of faith thank God for food at meals, they acknowledge God's provision as well as their own dependence on God. When Jesus gave thanks over the bread and cup during the meal in the upper room and identified these things with his own body and blood, he essentially made things of creation to be bearers of God's saving grace.

At each celebration of the Lord's Supper, creation and God's sustenance of creation are symbolized by the bread and wine, the fruits of creation. To thank God for the gifts of food in the Lord's Supper is to give thanks that things of creation are now bearers of God's grace, since the bread and wine offer participation in the body and blood of Christ. In other words, the Lord's Supper – particularly the act of thanksgiving – proclaims that God's messiah was not ashamed to use created things as a means of self-giving! To receive the grace and mercy of God through these gifts of creation and then

---

[17] See Desmond Tutu, *No Future Without Forgiveness* (London: Rider, 1999).

participate in the wanton destruction of creation or involve ourselves in practices and lifestyles that are wasteful and insensitive to creation suggests a failure to comprehend how the Lord's Supper *sanctifies* creation in general and food in particular.

Indeed, recognizing the presence of creation in the Lord's Supper leads Christians to reorient themselves to creation in redeeming ways. For example, churches might participate in gathering up litter from areas along highways and coastlines. Such projects not only benefit the land and sea, but also serve as an encouragement to individuals, families, and communities to refrain from behaviors that harm the environment (e.g., littering, unlawful dumping). Furthermore, Christian communities might adopt recycling policies for their own facilities and encourage members to recycle paper, glass, and plastic items in their own homes. Churches may want to rethink the use of "two-in-one" prepackaged communion elements, since the packaging of elements for each individual is inherently wasteful; it is ironic to think that the Lord's Supper could be a means for Christians to contribute to environmental degradation. Finally, because fossil fuels pollute the air and crude oil in particular has been a source of ecological endangerment (e.g., through spills in the ocean), Christians might consider alternative energy sources for homes and automobiles, in order to reduce reliance on fossil fuels.

Justice for creation that flows out of the Lord's Supper also challenges Christians to consider their eating habits. Feeding the world is hard work for people and the creation itself, and both human beings and soil can experience exhaustion. In that case, we might ask whether it is right for people to eat more than is necessary and thereby create a greater demand for food and put more pressure on the earth to produce. While most men only need to consume 1,800 calories per day and women 1,200 calories to survive, many people eat in excess of these amounts, and the worldwide problem of obesity seems to bear out the problem of overeating.[18] Christians might be encouraged to eat only as much as they need and to avoid

[18] See http://win.niddk.nih.gov/statistics/index.htm#b [accessed 1 December 2014].

overeating.[19] Although Christians believe that feasting on abundant amounts of food is an appropriate way to give thanks for a harvest or other events, feasting is by no means normative on a daily basis. Christians have also practiced fasting, particularly during the Forty Days of Lent, and have considered moderation and self-control to be important virtues. Indeed, fasting and abstinence are meant to help people acquire control over physical appetites so that time and money can be available for serving God and the neighbor.

Christians might also think more carefully about *what* they eat. Many foods are highly processed, often with added salt, white sugar, and fats, which increase blood pressure and cholesterol levels. If we value our own bodies as creations of God and desire not to harm them, then limiting or avoiding highly processed foods is wise. Such an alteration of habits could be viewed as a way of honoring the God who provides the food. If an item of food is good in and of itself as provided by God, then adding to it or otherwise altering it seems to deny its natural goodness. For the same reason, we might also question the use of genetically modified food, which in a way represents a manipulation of (or perhaps tampering with) one of God's creatures to the point that it is no longer recognizable as God's original creation. While higher production yields and greater resistance to pests and disease might be laudable goals, for humans to arrogate the role of Creator to themselves possibly opens the door to unimaginable evil, especially if the human gene is altered to serve the purposes of evil. Human fashioning of creation should not obscure God's creative role, and what is fashioned should serve God's creative and redeeming purposes, rather than human intentions.

If the Lord's Supper implies a proper stewardship of food by Christians, then the matter of food wastage must also be addressed. It has been estimated that one-third of the food produced for human consumption every year (1.3 billion tons) is lost or wasted. Such wastage also means that resources used for the production of food such as land, water, and energy are squandered, and there is a needless

[19] Singaporean folk wisdom holds that a person should only eat until he/she is "80% full."

production of greenhouse gasses that contribute to global warming.[20] While wastage in developing countries is related to factors involving harvesting, storage, infrastructure, and packaging, food wastage in developed countries is related to standards that reject items that are less than perfect in appearance. "Best-before-dates" and the failure to plan purchases adequately also lead to wastage by consumers.[21]

Thus, individuals can do much to stem the problem of food wastage. Possible measures include (1) purchasing some or all fresh produce at farmers' markets that do not have high grading standards that promote the disposal of edible food that is considered "inferior"; (2) planning purchases more carefully, e.g., by not purchasing such a large amount of fresh food that it will spoil before it can be eaten; (3) practicing proper storage of foods (e.g., freezing) that will help prevent spoilage. In order to help minimize waste at the societal level, individuals and local churches might (1) advocate the redistribution of unused food to individuals and organizations that can use it; and (2) use caterers and food retailers who give away unused or unwanted food to those in need. Local churches might educate members about the problem of food wastage and provide their membership with print and electronic resources pertaining to this problem. In doing all these things, Christians witness to the sacredness of food that is implied in their own sacramental meal of the Lord's Supper.

Eucharistic Justice and the Hungry Poor

In the Hebrew Scriptures, God provides the essentials of human existence: land, water, and food. God gives the first humans food and a place for living (Gen. 1, 2). God promises to give the dispossessed Hebrew slaves their own land, and then provides them with food and water during their perilous journey to the promised land. The people of Israel are commanded to ensure that all people in the community receive adequate food and water, especially the poor, downtrodden,

[20] Jenny Gustavson, et. al. "Global Food Losses and Food Waste: Extent, Causes and Prevention" (Rome: Food and Agriculture Organization of the United Nations, 2011), v.

[21] Gustavson, "Global Food Losses," v.

and the dispossessed in the community. Thus, vineyards and fields are not to be harvested down to the last grape or grain, but some of the produce is to be left for the hungry poor to glean (Lev. 19:10), and some is to be stored for those who might go hungry (Deut. 14:28-29).

That same concern for the hungry poor is also expressed in the New Testament. The Magnificat, or Song of Mary (Luke 1), speaks of the hungry being filled with good things (v. 53), and Jesus himself provided food for hungry people (Matt. 14:13-21) as a sign of his divine messiahship. In Paul's view, the Corinthian practice of the Lord's Supper is invalid because poorer, working class Christians go hungry, which implies that they are despised by their wealthier Christian brothers and sisters (11:22). The Letter of James states that anyone who fails to provide a hungry person with food has a "dead" faith (2:14-26).

From early on, the celebration of the Lord's Supper has been bound up with aiding the hungry and others in need. Justin the Martyr reports that in his community a collection is deposited with the "president" of the liturgical assembly who uses that money to aid those in need (widows, orphans, the sick, imprisoned, sojourners).[22] Presumably, this meant providing food. In the patristic era, significant amounts of food, including cheese, olives, and honey, were brought to the Sunday service and presented at the offering along with the bread and wine. Any of these items not given to the clergy or used for the Eucharist were given to the poor.

The very manner in which the eucharistic food is shared witnesses to a kind of economic egalitarianism. All participants receive the same food; there is not one fare for wealthier members and another for poorer members. Additionally, all receive the *same* amount: one sip of wine and one piece of bread. This equal distribution of food in the Lord's Supper draws attention to and challenges the unequal distribution of food in the greater society and invites Christians to work for a more equitable distribution of food.

[22] Justin the Martyr, *First Apology* 67 (ca. 155), PEER, 30.

In order to highlight the relationship between the Lord's Supper and providing for the hungry, churches today might consider the following steps. First, an offering of canned and boxed foods is taken at Sunday liturgies when the Lord's Supper is celebrated. In those churches with a weekly Eucharist, one Sunday a month could be designated for this purpose. (Given the early church's commitment to aiding the hungry poor, it is hardly defensible if the Sunday offering is always monetary and only used for the maintenance of the church!) Second, eucharistic services might occasionally be followed by communal meals to which the hungry poor of the local community are invited. Third, services of the Lord's Supper could end with the commissioning or blessing of those who go to work in soup kitchens or feeding centers following the service. This action symbolizes the idea of being fed (at communion) in order to feed others.

Eucharistic Justice for the Poor and Oppressed

A recurrent theme in the Hebrew Scriptures is mercy for the oppressed. The prophets constantly pronounce judgement against Israel and Judah for oppressing those who have no one to depend on economically, e.g., widows and orphans, and those whose opportunities for a livelihood are limited, e.g., foreign sojourners (cf. Jer. 7:6; Zech. 7:10). Specific acts of oppression include the levying of unfair taxes on the poor and depriving them of justice in the courts by bribing witnesses and officials (Amos 5). The call for just treatment of the poor and the oppressed is rooted in Israel's own experience of God as the One who delivered them from oppression in Egypt. The confession of God's merciful deliverance of Israel from slavery leads to a call for justice in the Israelite community that will witness to the mercy of God (cf. Deut. 10:14-19; Lev. 19:36). Justice for the poor and oppressed is therefore a means of glorifying a merciful God. Conversely, not to seek justice for the poor and oppressed suggests a blindness to God's mercy and amounts to a repudiation of the covenant (Is. 59:1-11).

Early Christians affirmed the idea of showing mercy to the poor and oppressed. Jesus' Sermon on the Mount assumes that his followers give alms to the poor (Matt. 6:3-4), but emphasizes the idea that charity has to do with one's relationship with God and is not for self-aggrandizement. Elsewhere, relief of the poor is considered a Christian virtue (Acts 2:45, 9:39), as is generosity toward those local Christian communities that are suffering deprivation (2 Cor. 9).

In the Lord's Supper, the church participates in Jesus' identification with the afflicted and God's plan of justice for all the oppressed. The cup of wine symbolizes Christ's shed blood and thus his identification with all human suffering. Similarly, the bread, made from crushed grain, symbolizes Christ's broken body, and his unity with all of those who are crushed by oppression. Thus, the acts of eating the bread and drinking the cup become the very means for Christians to identify with those who suffer oppression, whether social, economic, or physical. But this eucharistic identification with the oppressed in no way constitutes a glorification or justification of oppression; participation in the Lord's Supper means that Christians commit themselves to struggling against all forms of oppression, for ultimately God overcame the oppression experienced by the Israelites, and Christ's resurrection represents God's victory over the oppressive forces of sin and death.

Like early Christians, Protestants of the Reformation era were concerned to aid the poor. Upon the advice of Luther, the city of Leisnig, Germany, drafted an ordinance for the creation of a common chest which was to be administered by the civil authorities. This common fund provided for the regular disbursement of funds to the aged poor and infirm.[23] Influenced by the Leisnig ordinance, which was published with a preface by Luther himself, many other evangelical communities in Germany established a common chest for the poor. In England, the BCP 1549 directed that those who desired were to place donations into a poor box during the singing of the Offertory.[24] This practice underscored the connection between the offering and the relief of the poor.

---

[23] Martin Luther, *Ordinance of a Common Chest* (Preface) (1523), LW 45, 189.

[24] "The Supper of the Lord," BCP 1549, LWC, 254.

Christians today might consider how to demonstrate the connection between the Supper and the struggle against injustice and oppression. One way is to revive the Anglican poor box. Going somewhat further, food, clothing, school kits, blankets, and quilts might be received along with the money and eucharistic gifts in order to suggest that donations for the world's suffering ones are also part of the church's offering. During the sending rites, special prayers might be offered for persons who will be going to work with the poor and suffering immediately following the liturgy (e.g., hospice volunteers) or later as part of a long-term mission effort (e.g., disaster relief). Churches might consider holding eucharistic services in places where suffering is keen: hospitals, palliative care centers, etc., as a further reminder that the Supper leads the church to an identification with the world's suffering ones in order to offer them the hope of God's deliverance.

Eucharistic Justice for the Imprisoned

Deliverance for captives is another important justice theme in the Scriptures. God liberates the Hebrews from slavery in Egypt (Ex. 3:7-10) and orchestrates the release of those held in captivity in Babylon (Ezra 1:1-11, 2:1). God's justice for the oppressed is closely connected with the release of prisoners:

> He upholds the cause of the oppressed
> and gives food to the hungry.
> The LORD sets prisoners free,
> the LORD gives sight to the blind. (Ps. 146:7-8)

The prophet Isaiah envisions God's anointed one proclaiming release for captives (61:1b), and Jesus' life and ministry are understood as the fulfilment of Isaiah's prophecy. If courts and government officials were corrupt, as suggested in prophetic literature, then it is probably a safe assumption that many innocent persons were imprisoned unjustly, in which case their release would be a vindication of divine justice.

In the early church, imprisonment and aid for the imprisoned are associated with righteousness. Leading figures of the New Testament, such as John the Baptizer (Matt. 14:3; cf. Mark 1:14, 6:17), Peter (Acts 12:5), and Paul (cf. Phil. 1:7), all suffered imprisonment, as did many early Christians. The nations are judged according to their willingness to minister to imprisoned followers of Christ (Matt. 25:36, 43). Not surprisingly, Christians are encouraged to pray for fellow Christians who suffer imprisonment. The earliest example of a prayer mentioning the imprisoned is found in Clement of Rome's *Letter to the Corinthians* (ca. 95-98 CE):

> Save the afflicted among us,
> have mercy on the lowly.
> Raise up the fallen,
> show yourself to those in need.
> Heal the sick
> and bring back those who have strayed.
> Fill the hungry,
> give freedom to our prisoners,
> raise up the weak,
> console the fainthearted.[25]

With roots in the fifth century, the anaphora (eucharistic prayer) of the Liturgy of St. James, likewise intercedes for the imprisoned:

> Remember, Lord [Christians at sea, on the road, abroad], our fathers and brothers in chains and prisons, in [captivity and] exile, [in mines and tortures and bitter slavery] for a peaceful return home for each of them.[26]

Because the Lord's Supper unites the church with the One who became a captive in order to free humanity from its captivity to sin and death, the Supper leads to a ministry to the imprisoned. The church

---

[25] Lucien Deiss, *Springtime of the Liturgy* (Collegeville: The Liturgical Press, 1979), 82-85.

[26] "The Liturgy of St. James," PEER, 95.

prays for those unjustly imprisoned, especially those imprisoned because of their faith, and advocates for their release. For those justly imprisoned for crimes, the church prays and seeks to bring about their reconciliation with God, their families, victims, and society. The church offers compassion to such persons while calling them to repentance and amendment of life. Ministry to the imprisoned does not involve excusing or justifying crimes, although ordained ministers have the prerogative to offer absolution to those who are genuinely repentant. Additionally, ministry to the imprisoned is distinct from legal advocacy, which is best left to lawyers.

Participation in the Lord's Supper following imprisonment is an important part of an ex-offender's rehabilitation. To be welcomed to the Lord's Table following imprisonment is a powerful experience of reconciliation both with the local church and with the local community that the church represents. Reconciliation at the Table becomes an impetus for the former inmate to work for reconciliation with victims and with society as a whole. Churches might intentionally welcome former inmates into their Table fellowship – perhaps even inviting them to become servers or sacramental lay ministers to further highlight inclusion into the church's eucharistic fellowship. As a sign of its ministry of reconciliation to the imprisoned, churches pray for and bless those involved in prison ministries when they depart from the Sunday Eucharist, in order to demonstrate the connection between the Supper and justice for the imprisoned.

Conclusion

Justice is about the restoration of relationships to what God intended. The Supper of the Lord, in a sense, is *pure* justice, for it is the means for God's people to be in right relationship with God through the reception of the saving body and blood of Christ and the living out of the justice that is implied by that experience. The Supper is therefore like a pebble which, when thrown into a body of water, generates a ring of ripples going out from a center point. The Christian community that gathers around the Lord's Table each week is called to be ripples of justice for the world's suffering ones, the creation, and for the imprisoned.

For Further Reading

Anderson, E. Byron and Bruce T. Morrill, eds. *Liturgy and the Moral Self: Humanity at Full Stretch Before God.* New York: Pueblo, 1998.

Morrill, Bruce T. *Anamnesis as Dangerous Memory: Political and Liturgical Theology in Dialogue.* Collegeville: Liturgical Press, 2000.

Smith, Harmon. *Where Two or Three are Gathered: Liturgy and the Moral Life*. Cleveland, OH: Pilgrim Press, 1995.

CHAPTER 16

The Sacramentality of Other Rites

As stated previously in this book, sacraments are ritual actions of the church that are bound up with the saving activity of God in Jesus Christ. Baptism and the Lord's Supper most aptly fit this definition, since baptism is union with Christ in his death and resurrection (Rom. 6) and the Lord's Supper is participation in the body and blood of Christ (1 Cor. 10). These two actions of the church are uniquely related to the person of Christ and his work of delivering people from sin, death, and the power of evil. To use language associated with the Dominican Edward Schillebeeckx, bath and meal offer an encounter with Christ. Other actions of the church – marriage, ordination, healing, and the funeral service – possess a sacramental *character* because they announce and signify the saving work of Christ at particular occasions in the human life cycle. Some of these are *rites of passage*, but they do more than merely ease anxiety because they renew our faith by drawing us back to the holy mystery of Christ crucified and raised from the dead. *Rites of vocation* do more than signify changed status; they point to the mystery of Christ and his living presence among us. Thus, the rites of the Christian life cycle have an integral relationship to baptism and the Lord's Supper.

The purpose of this chapter is to describe how rites of vocation (marriage, ordination) and rites of passage (healing, burial of the dead or funeral) possess this deeply christological character and yet are subordinate to and dependent on baptism and the Lord's Supper for their meaning. In keeping with the title of this book, some suggestions for practice will be offered.

Vocational Rites: Marriage and Ordination

A *vocation* (Latin, *vocare*, to call) is a particular state of life or office to which a person is called by God. Any vocation is more than a matter of the human will or a human decision, and the rites for entering into a new vocation clarify God's role in calling a person to that particular state of life.

Christians speak of marriage as a vocation because it was founded by God from the very beginning of human existence for the sake of companionship and the propagation of the human species (Gen. 2:20b-25). Because marriage is a universal human vocation, there is nothing particularly Christian about it. Thus, we can only say that there is marriage by Christians in their churches. Central Christian affirmations are that marriage (1) is indissoluble (cf. Matt. 19:6); (2) involves mutual love and obedience (cf. Eph. 5:21-25); and (3) is a *mystery* reflective of Christ's love for the church (Eph. 5:32).

Very little is said about marriage in the early church, except that Christians are strongly encouraged to marry other Christians. In the Middle Ages, marriage comes to be regarded as a Christian sacrament. Peter Lombard states that it was instituted before the fall for the sake of procreation; after the fall it serves as a way of curbing lust. The sacramental status of marriage in medieval thinking owed to the biblical understanding that it is a sign of Christ's union with his church.[1]

While denying the sacramental status of marriage, the Protestant Reformers nevertheless held marriage in high esteem. Luther regards

---

[1] Peter Lombard, *The Sentences* 4.26.1-2, 6 (ca. 1152).

it as a matter both secular and sacred. It was not instituted by Christ and so cannot be considered a sacrament. As a human universal, it is entirely a secular matter, and so all of the legal details should be left to the civil authorities. Yet, because it was instituted and blessed by God, it possesses a sacred character and should therefore be treated with all seriousness. The challenges and difficulties of marriage make prayer and the church's blessing necessary.[2] Luther prepared a rite with a tripartite order:

1. The banns, or official announcement of the marriage read out during a public service prior to the marriage;
2. The marriage rite proper at the church door, consisting of
   a. Consent ("Dost thou desire to have *Name* as thy wife/husband?")
   b. Matt. 19:6 ("What God has joined together…")
   c. Pronouncement of the marriage;
3. Scripture reading, exhortation, and prayer for the couple before the altar.[3]

Luther took the Matt. 19 text literally, and so refused to sanction the divorce of a German prince who was forced to marry young and frequently resorted to adultery. Calvin believed that marriage is a "good and holy ordinance of God," but rejected the sacramental designation because marriage does not confirm any promises of God.[4] Neither he nor Zwingli produced a marriage rite.

The BCP 1549 listed three purposes for marriage: (1) to produce children who will be raised as God-fearing people; (2) to serve as a remedy for fornication; and (3) to offer mutual companionship.[5]

---

[2] Martin Luther, *The Order for Marriage for Common Pastors* (1529), LW 53, 111-13.

[3] Luther, *Order for Marriage*, LW 53, 113-15.

[4] John Calvin, *Institutes of the Christian Religion* IV.19.34 (1559), ed. John T. McNeill, tr. Ford Lewis Battles, in LCC XXI (Philadelphia: Westminster Press, 1960), 1480-81.

[5] "The Form of Solemnization of Matrimony" (1549), BCP *Texts*, 64.

The order of the service, which began in the nave and moved to the choir for the prayers, was:

Admonition
Wilt thou have this man/woman…?
Who gives this woman…?
Vows
Exchange and blessing of rings
Matt. 19:6
Declaration of marriage
Blessing
Prayers
Final blessing
Gospel
Sermon

The bride and the groom were to receive Holy Communion the same day as their marriage ceremony.[6] The basic structure of the rite remained the same in the BCP 1559 and BCP 1662. Wesley's version of the marriage ceremony from the BCP 1662 left out the "giving" of the bride, the ring ceremony (objectionable to Puritans), the Psalms, and the final exhortation. Wesley makes no mention of the couple receiving Holy Communion. Much of the BCP 1662 rubrical material also disappeared from Wesley's rite.[7]

Pentecostal Christians believe that marriage is sacred, and this view is undergirded by three biblical motifs: (1) God's institution of marriage at creation; (2) Jesus' attendance at the Cana wedding; and (3) marriage as a reflection of Christ's union with the church. Many, but not all, Pentecostal marriage services stress the man's role as head of the family and the indissolubility of marriage. Ordained ministers are not bound to use a particular marriage service, but many

---

[6] "Solemnization of Matrimony" (1549), BCP *Texts*, 64-71.

[7] John Wesley, "The Form of Solemnization of Matrimony" (1784), JWPB, 149-55.

published manuals provide sample services that contain most of the elements found in the services of other Protestant denominations.[8]

In Protestant services today, most of the traditional ritual/ceremonial elements are retained (viz., consent, vows, rings, declaration, and blessing). In some cases, the marriage rite is structured as the first part of a full service of Word and Sacrament.[9] The consent ("Will you have *Name* as your wife/husband?") is treated as a preliminary, since the marriage cannot even take place unless both parties willingly agree to it. The vows are placed after the biblical readings and sermon as a response to the Word. Generally, a blessing by the family replaces the "giving" of the bride by her father, which reflects the modern sense of gender equality. Another newer development is a stress on marriage as a *covenant* rather than a contract. While a contract can be broken if either party fails to live up to the conditions of the agreement, a covenant is an unbreakable and unconditional relationship. In entering into the marriage covenant, a man and a woman pledge mutual love and support, no matter the failings of the other or the hardships that life together brings. The marriage covenant is modeled on God's covenant with Israel, where God's love is constant despite the people's waywardness and sin. If marriage is in some sense sacramental, it is because in experiencing the unconditional love of another, a person experiences something of God's unconditional love for his people. The selfless love of the marital relationship ultimately points to the selfless love of God revealed in the death and resurrection of Jesus. Yet, marriage possesses no salvific implications since there is no promise that it conveys the saving grace of God in Christ or constitutes a personal encounter with Christ. Rather, marriage images these realities.

An understanding of the sacramental character of marriage is our best guide to its celebration. Many weddings today revolve around the tastes, experiences, and lifestyles of the couple (love of gardening,

---

8 *The New SCM Dictionary of Liturgy and Worship*, s.v. "Marriage, Pentecostal."

9 "Marriage," LBW, 328-330; "Marriage," ELW, 675-86; "Christian Marriage: Rite II," BCW, 853-81; "Celebration and Blessing of a Marriage," BCP 1979, 423-32; "A Service of Christian Marriage I," UMBW, 115-27.

horseback riding, etc.) – in short, marriage services tend to celebrate the couple and their love, rather than the unfailing love of God. But, if God created and blesses marriage such that it becomes a sign of Christ's love for the church, then all things that point to God will be made strong and central in the service: readings, vows, homily, and blessing – rather than flowers, costumes, sentimental songs, and expressions of the couple's personalities. In a word, we allow *God* to speak to the assembly and couple, with words of promise that will sustain the marriage and make it a true sign of Christ's love. When a minister perceives that a couple merely wants the church as an elegant backdrop for the wedding and is not open to discovering and living out the meaning of marriage as Christians, he or she rightly declines the request to preside at a couple's marriage service.

As ministers of Word and Sacrament, ordained pastors have a duty to ensure that couples understand what a Christian marriage service is. Ministers stress that in requesting a "church wedding," couples imply that hearing the Word of God, having the church pray for them, and receiving God's blessing are important to them. Ministers therefore discourage actions, gestures, and music that are irreverent, vulgar, or overly-sentimental – things that are best done during the festivities following the service (if at all!). A good way of encouraging reverence and thoughtfulness is to remind couples that marriage points to the mystery of Christ's love for the church, as revealed in his sacrificial death, a narrative that resonates with baptized Christians. It is desirable to stress that their marital union is actually a living icon of Christ's love for his church. If ministers habitually fail to stress the sacredness of marriage in premarital counseling, there can be little wonder that marriage services become human-centered events.

If indeed marriage is a sacred thing that witnesses to Christ, is not every wedding ceremony an "evangelistic opportunity" to win people for Christ? Would it not be desirable, then, for ministers to perform the marriage services of any and all who request such a ministry? While there can be no denying the power of the Word to transform lives, wise pastors recognize how simplistic this argument really is. Furthermore, they know that (1) the gospel can only be received by those who hunger for what it offers, namely, the grace and mercy of God; and (2) in the busyness and excitement of a wedding, many participants (especially a bride and groom) are probably not attuned to their deepest spiritual needs. Nor are persons in the best position to respond to the gospel with a life-long commitment while focused on beginning a new life with another person. Given these realities, sensible pastors are realistic about what a Christian service of marriage can accomplish and accordingly are judicious about accepting requests to perform weddings.

***

All Christians are called to ministry in daily life, meaning that they are to pray with and for others, offer them spiritual encouragement, and teach them about the Christian faith. Beyond this ministry in daily life, the church needs leaders with the special skills, knowledge, and gifts for a *public* ministry of proclaiming the Word and administering the sacraments. While ministry in daily life is common to all Christians, only a few Christians are called to public ministry. Persons judged to be suitable candidates for the latter undergo a period of ministerial formation that includes advanced theological education and careful ecclesiastical oversight. Candidates who successfully complete this process and are officially called by the church are then set apart for their public ministry in a rite known as ordination.

In the New Testament, there are indications that churches consecrated or designated persons for ministry through ritual acts. In Acts 6, those chosen by the apostles for the ministry of distributing food to the needy were prayed for and received the laying on of hands (v. 6). Paul and Barnabas were consecrated for their missionary work by similar actions (Acts 13:3). Paul himself mentions a laying on of hands that imparted the gifts of ministry to Timothy (1 Tim. 4:14).

Documents from the early church speak of leaders being appointed and then set apart for their ministries. The *Apostolic Tradition* gives details that may represent practices from the late-fourth and early-fifth centuries. When a bishop has been chosen by the people, the whole church gathers on a Sunday with all the priests and other bishops present. Following the assembly's assent, all the bishops lay hands on the candidate. After a period of silence, one of the bishops lays hands on the candidate's head and prays for the granting of the "spirit of leadership" which was given to the apostles.[10] The ordination of presbyters (priests) involves a laying on of hands by a single bishop along with the local presbyters. The bishop prays for the imparting of the Spirt who will help the candidate to "govern" God's people.[11] The diaconal laying on of hands is administered by the bishop only, since a deacon's role is to serve the bishop. The accompanying prayer speaks of the candidate being given the Spirit of "grace and caring and diligence" to serve the church.[12]

In the Middle Ages, ordination gained sacramental status. Lombard speaks of the "sacrament" of the seven-fold Spirit in which there are seven ecclesiastical degrees (doorkeeper, lector, exorcist, acolyte, subdeacon, deacon, and priest).[13] Only the diaconate and the presbyterate are "sacred orders," since these were the only two known by the ancient church. Ordination into these two orders is sacramental because grace is conferred on the recipients.[14]

The Reformers denied not only the sacramental status of ordination, but also the idea that it conferred a spiritual order or ranking. For Luther, ordination lacks sufficient scriptural warrant to be called a sacrament. Since God's promises make the church, rather than vice versa, the church cannot invent rites that only appear to have a divine warrant and authority behind them. Ordination can certainly be considered a churchly rite, like the consecration of an item used by the church (e.g., vessels, buildings, water, salt), an action that no one would consider to be a sacrament. Thus, ordination, like a rite of consecration, is merely a preparation of something for service

---

[10] Paul F. Bradshaw, Maxwell E. Johnson, and L. Edward Phillips, *The Apostolic Tradition: A Commentary* (Minneapolis: Fortress Press, 2002), 24, 30.

[11] Bradshaw, et al., *Apostolic Tradition*, 56.

[12] Bradshaw, et al., *Apostolic Tradition*, 62.

[13] Lombard, *Sentences* 4.24.1.

[14] Lombard, *Sentences* 4.24.12.

in the church.[15] Luther suspects that the traditional sacramental view of ordination had a role in exalting the clergy over the laity, which led to various ecclesiastical abuses. In reality, Luther argues, all Christians are by virtue of baptism priests, and clergy possess only a ministry, one that is delegated to them by the consent of the whole church. Because this ministry centers on the preaching of the Word of God, ordination is essentially a rite for the "selection" (designation, commissioning) of preachers. Any ordained person who does not preach or teach cannot really be considered a Christian priest (pastor) at all.[16] Since Luther understood ministry in relationship to the Word and its proclamation and rejected a sacrificial understanding of the Mass and its implication for priesthood, both he and Melanchthon deny that ordination places a person into a priestly caste, like the priesthood of the Old Testament.[17] Yet, Melanchthon was willing to consider ordination a sacrament precisely because of its connection to the proclamation of the Word, for preaching has both the command and promise of God (cf. Rom. 1:16; Is. 55:11).[18]

In 1539, Luther prepared a rite of ordination that eventually received wide acceptance in Lutheran territories.[19] The rite had seven parts: (1) a public examination of the candidates followed by prayer for them; (2) the singing of *Veni Sancte Spiritus* while the ordinands and other ministers kneel before the altar; (3) Scripture readings (1 Tim. 3:1-7; Acts 20:28-31); (4) an admonition to the ordinands; (5) the imposition of hands on the ordinands by the clergy accompanied by the Lord's Prayer (and possibly an additional prayer for the Holy Spirit to make the new preachers faithful to their calling); (6) the reading of 1 Peter 5:2-4; and (7) a blessing.

---

[15] Martin Luther, *The Babylonian Captivity of the Church* (1520), LW 36, 106-109.

[16] Luther, *Babylonian Captivity*, LW 36, 112.

[17] Luther, *Babylonian Captivity*, LW 36, 114; *Apology of the Augsburg Confession* (1531), Art. XIII, BC, 220.7-10.

[18] *Apology of the Augsburg Confession*, Art. XIII, BC, 220.12-13.

[19] Martin Luther, *The Ordination of Ministers of the Word* (1539), LW 53, 124-26.

Like Luther, Calvin holds that any candidate for ordination must have the approval of the people (i.e., laity) and that clergy should preside over the election process.[20] Although there was no definitive command to lay hands on ministers at their ordination, apostolic usage legitimated the action, which is administered by clergy only. The action gives dignity and gravity to the ministerial office and reminds ministers of their accountability to God and the church.[21] Ordination services in most Reformed churches focussed on prayer and the laying on of hands, actions prescribed by the First and Second Helvetic Confessions.[22]

On the basis of Scripture and the early Fathers, Anglicans concluded that there were three orders of ministry: bishop, priest, and deacon. Because of the importance of these offices, only those who are duly called, examined, approved, and ordained by the church can assume them. Ordination is to be celebrated on a Sunday or festival during a public worship service. Without consecration/ordination, no one can be considered a "lawful" holder of a ministerial office.

Anglican liturgical books of the sixteenth and seventeenth centuries provided services for the "consecrating" of archbishops and bishops and the "ordering" of priests and deacons.[23] All of these included scripture readings, prayer, admonitions, examination of the candidates, and the laying on of hands. While the handlaying formulas for bishops and priests used strong pneumatic language, the diaconal formula spoke only of taking the authority of the office without any reference to the Holy Spirit. The handlaying formulas for priests and bishops were altered slightly in the BCP 1662 so as to clarify that the Spirit is given for a particular office ("Receive the

[20] Calvin, *Institutes* IV.3.15, LCC XXI, 1066.

[21] Calvin, *Institutes* IV.3.16, LCC XXI, 1066-67.

[22] *The New SCM Dictionary of Liturgy and Worship*, s.v. "Ordination, Reformed."

[23] "The Form for Consecrating an Archbishop or Bishop," BCP 1549 (1550), 1552, 1559, http://justus.anglican.org/resources/bcp/1549/Bishops_1549.htm [accessed 8 February 2015]; "The Form of Ordering Priests," BCP 1549, http://justus.anglican.org/resources/bcp/1549/Priests_1549.htm [accessed 8 February 2015]; "The Form and Manner of Ordering Deacons," BCP 1549, http://justus.anglican.org/resources/bcp/1549/Deacons_1549.htm [accessed 8 February 2015].

Holy Ghost for the office and work of a priest/bishop in the Church of God...").[24]

John Wesley provided simplified versions of the BCP 1662 ordination rites in the *Sunday Service* for American Methodists, retaining most of the prayers, Scripture readings, and the laying on of hands with accompanying formulas. To reflect the ecclesial situation in America, Wesley substituted "elder" for "priest" and "superintendent" for "bishop."[25]

Pentecostal preachers, like all members of their churches, are expected to evidence conversion of life and baptism in the Holy Spirit. The call of Pentecostal ministers is understood as a prophetic call to preach the Word publicly.[26]

The rite of ordination for all Protestants essentially accomplishes five things:

1. Recognition – affirming the candidates' calling to public ministry
2. Intercession – beseeching God to "stir up" or strengthen the Spirit's gifts for ministry[27]
3. Consecration – setting the candidates apart for public ministry
4. Authorization – conferring authority from the church to publicly preach the Word and administer the sacraments
5. Commissioning – sending forth to a ministry.

Ordination takes its meaning from the sacraments, since men and women are ordained to public ministry in order to be servants of Word and Sacrament. This relationship gives ordination a certain sacramental character. Because God calls men and women to public

---

[24] "The Form and Manner of Ordering of Priests" (1662), BCP *Texts*, 642; "The Form of Ordaining or Consecrating of an Archbishop or Bishop" (1662), BCP *Texts*, 650.

[25] The Form and Manner of Making and Ordaining of Superintendants, Elders, and Deacons," JWPB, 208-305.

[26] *The New SCM Dictionary of Liturgy and Worship*, s.v. "Ordination, Pentecostal."

[27] Cf. BEM 42, 44.

ministry, endows them with the gifts needed for this ministry and promises that their work will be fruitful (cf. 1 Cor. 15:58), there is a parallel to baptism and the Lord's Supper where God likewise acts in the lives of his people in a grace-filled way. Like the sacraments, ordination signifies the grace of God. Yet, it does not convey grace in the same way that baptism and the Lord's Supper do; to be ordained is not to obtain personal union with Christ and the assurance of salvation. Rather, it is to assume a role in proclaiming the saving grace of Christ and making the means of grace available to God's people.

Ordination services today contain many of the same actions as ordination rites of the Reformation era. Candidates are presented to the assembly which is asked to support them in their ministry. The candidates are examined as to their faith, Christian life, and commitment to the church and its teachings. They then receive the laying on of hands accompanied by a prayer that uses Spirit-language. In some cases, a Bible and possibly other objects (e.g., a clamshell for baptizing and a communion cup for pastors and priests) may be presented to the newly ordained as symbols of their new office. Modern worship books place more emphasis on celebrating ordination within a service of the Lord's Supper in order to highlight the connection between ordination and the means of grace.

If confusion or misunderstanding surrounds any aspect of the ordination rite today, it is the laying on of hands. In some churches, the laity join with the bishop and clergy in this act. However, since the laying on of hands symbolizes the conferral of gifts for the office of public ministry, it makes little sense for those not serving in the office of public ministry and possessing its charisms to participate in the symbolic conferral of these charisms. One cannot "give" what one does not have. Any argument that laity need to be included in the handlaying in order to symbolize how the call to ministry comes from the church is weak, since this call comes from God through the church. The Reformers held that ministry is primarily a divine calling.[28] Furthermore, if inviting the laity to lay hands on ordinands is seen as a way of "including" the laity, it needs to be pointed out that the laity already performs a crucial function at the beginning of the service by affirming the candidates' worthiness for ordination. Without that affirmation, the ordination could not even happen! In reality, lay participation in the handlaying demeans the laity, because it suggests that their participation is not valid unless it is done in conjunction with the clergy. A sound theology of ordination dictates that only the clergy lay hands on the candidates.

Unfortunately, ordained ministers themselves may be confused about the nature of ordination, specifically, what it empowers them to do. While most ordination rites point to the centrality of preaching the Word and celebrating the sacraments, many ministers today seem preoccupied with everything *except* the means of grace. When ministers increasingly take on the tasks of community organizers, therapists, and activities directors, it is apparent that many have never reflected on the meaning of their denomination's theology of ordination, especially as it relates to the ministry of Word and Sacrament. It might therefore be advisable for regional church bodies to celebrate services for the renewal of ordination vows on occasion in order to reinforce the theology of ministry and ordination. This practice would help to ground ministerial identity in the means of grace.

Life Passages: Healing and Funeral

A *passage* is a transition from one place to another. The Israelites made a passage from Egypt to the Promised Land, which was also a passage from slavery to freedom. Jesus' life and ministry culminated in his passage from death to life, from being the despised, crucified One to becoming the resurrected Lord. Sometimes people pass from health and wholeness to sickness and, in many cases, back to health again. Death is a passage from this world to the next. Like other

[28] *Augsburg Confession* (1530), Art. V, BC, 40.1; see also Calvin, *Institutes* IV.3.2, LCC XXI, 1055.

religions, Christianity has its own perspectives on these life passages and rituals for proclaiming its beliefs about God's role in them.

Healing has found very little place in the liturgical life of most Protestants. Traditionally, the sick were prayed for and given communion at home or in the hospital room during pastoral visits, and were mentioned in the intercessory prayers of the Sunday service. Other than intercessory prayer, ministry to the sick within a public worship service is practically unknown among Protestants. Pentecostals are the exception. Yet the twentieth century saw the development of special healing services that included anointing and the laying on of hands. This revival reflects a more holistic understanding of salvation as a reality that affects the entire person, mind, spirit, and *body*.

The Hebrew Scriptures connect healing with God's saving activity. God is the source of healing, no matter the means by which it is accomplished, for God declares that "I am the Lord, who heals you" (Ex. 15:26). Physical healing therefore serves as a sign of God's sovereignty and power (2 Kings 5:1-15). Job is afflicted with sores as God's way of testing him (2:7), while his physical healing is part of God's restoration of Job following the various afflictions (Job 42:10). In the Psalms, healing is a sign of God's graciousness (103:3).

Jesus healed people with various afflictions and diseases (Mark 1:29-34), and this action bore witness to his messianic identity and served as a visible manifestation of the kingdom of God (Mark 1:15; cf. Luke 11:20). Even when other "miracles" were lacking, Jesus still healed (Mark 6:5). Jesus also instructed his disciples to heal (Matt. 10:8; Luke 10:9), and that action also testified to the kingdom of God. In Acts 3, the healing of a lame man in the name of Jesus confirms that Jesus is the messiah whom God raised from the dead (v. 16). The healing "miracles" of Jesus and his disciples were therefore not ends in themselves, but were meant to point to God's saving mission that Jesus himself witnessed to in word and deed.

The Letter of James offers a glimpse of both the rituals and theology surrounding healing.

> Is anyone among you sick? Let them call the elders of the church to pray over them and anoint them with oil in the name of the Lord. And the prayer offered in faith will make the sick person well; the Lord will raise them up. If they have sinned, they will be forgiven. Therefore confess your sins to each other and pray for each other so that you may be healed. The prayer of a righteous person is powerful and effective. (5:14-16)

We might note three things concerning this text. First, sin and sickness go together: to be healed is to be forgiven, and vice versa. Thus, a body-spirit dualism is lacking here. Second, the passage does not support the idea that sickness is a "punishment" for sin, for it is not assumed that the sick person has sinned ("*If* they have sinned…"). Third, *prayer* rather than anointing is seen as the effective agent of healing. In that case, it is difficult to suggest that oil is somehow the "element" of a "sacrament" of healing.

In the early church, special oils for the sick and other items (e.g., bread, water) were blessed at the Sunday Eucharist and then taken home for administration to sick persons. But increasingly, anointing of the sick became the domain of the clergy. By the Middle Ages, anointing was considered the sacrament of dying, and was referred to as *extreme unction.* According to Lombard, the sacrament is given both for the forgiveness of sins and for healing, although it may be "expedient" for the person to receive only spiritual healing.[29] Thomas Aquinas, however, states that the purpose of this sacrament is to cure the sickness of *sin*, and consequently its main effect is the forgiveness of sins and the remission of guilt.[30]

The Protestant Reformers completely rejected extreme unction. Luther denies that healing has both a sign and promise (based on James 5), arguing that even if the apostle James himself composed the epistle attributed to him (which Luther doubted), no apostle had the authority to institute a sacrament since a true sacrament has a

[29] Lombard, *Sentences* 4.23.3.

[30] Thomas Aquinas, *Summa Theologia*, Suppl. XXX, 3:2671-72.

divinely-given promise with its accompanying sign. Furthermore, the gospels do not speak of a sacrament of "extreme unction." In practice, extreme unction does not follow the apostolic institution, since it has been made into a special anointing for those nearing death, whereas the apostle meant the anointing more generally for the sick. Thus, extreme unction has been arbitrarily made into a sacrament, and the benefits of the anointing have thereby been denied those who truly need them. Luther notes the irony that while extreme unction is for those approaching death, the James 5 passage envisions the recipient of the anointing being restored to health – "raised up" (v. 15) – which rarely happens with extreme unction! In that case, the sacramental promise of extreme unction fails.[31] Calvin argues that healing was given only to the apostles, and that even if it were a sacrament it has nothing to do with the church of the post-apostolic period.[32] Like Luther, he notes the discrepancy between the anointing of the sick in James 5 and the anointing of those nearing death, and also argues that the apostle's anointing was to have a much more general use than for only the dying.[33]

Although Anglicans had rejected the sacrament of healing, the BCP 1549 contained an order for the "Visitation of the Sick" that included psalms, prayers, exhortation, confession and absolution, anointing, and communion.[34] Objections from Martin Bucer led to the removal of the anointing from subsequent editions.[35] The BCP 1549 viewed sickness as a chastisement from God meant to benefit the sick person by leading him/her to greater holiness of life and faith. Many aspects of the BCP 1549 rite served as a preparation for death, e.g., the confession sin whose purpose is to acknowledge sins

---

[31] Luther, *Babylonian Captivity*, LW 36, 117-20.

[32] Calvin, *Institutes* IV.19.18, LCC XXI, 1467.

[33] Calvin, *Institutes* IV.19.21, LCC XXI, 1468-69.

[34] "The Order for the Visitation of the Sick, and the Communion of the Same" (1549), BCP *Texts*, 72-79.

[35] Arthur Roberts, *A Review of the Book of Common Prayer, Drawn Up by Martin Bucer, Briefly Analyzed and Abridged* (London: James Nisbet and Co., 1853; repr., Nabu Public Domain Reprints, 2014), 36-37.

and faults and thus avoid condemnation at the final judgement. Sin and sickness were linked together, although not necessarily in a causal relationship; the two appear to be symptoms of human mortality and brokenness. While the sick person was encouraged to trust in a merciful God, deliverance is left to God's sovereign will: "Visit him, O Lord, with thy salvation; deliver him in thy good appointed time from his bodily pain, and save his soul for thy mercy's sake. That if it shall be thy pleasure to prolong his days here on earth, he may live to thee…or else receive him into those heavenly habitations…."[36] John Wesley's version of the Prayer Book's "Communion of the Sick" consisted of only a collect, Scripture readings, confession of sins, and communion.[37]

In Pentecostalism, healing is viewed as a visible manifestation of the Holy Spirit's work for the benefit of sick persons and the whole Christian community. The ability to heal is regarded as a special gift, and is frequently exercized in public worship. Pentecostals regard healing as a normal part of the liturgy, rather than an occasional rite. Those seeking healing come forward to a "minister of healing" who prays for and lays hands on them. Anointing is often included in Pentecostal healing.[38]

Perhaps due to the influence of Pentecostalism, as well as the development of a more holistic view of humanity, modern Protestant churches devised corporate services of healing, although these may be adapted for use in private.[39] Most of these services assume the celebration of Holy Communion. Common features include scripture lessons, confession and absolution, intercessory prayers

---

[36] "The Order for the Visitation of the Sick" (1662), BCP *Texts*, 445-46.

[37] John Wesley, "Communion of the Sick" (1784), JWPB, 155-56.

[38] James White, *Protestant Worship: Traditions in Transition* (Louisville: Westminister/John Knox Press, 1989), 202.

[39] "Service of the Word for Healing," *Occasional Services: A Companion to* Lutheran Book of Worship (Minneapolis: Augsburg Publishing House; Philadelphia: Board of Publication, Lutheran Church in America, 1982), 89-98; "Healing," ELW, 660-65; "A Service for Wholeness for Use with a Congregation," BCW, 1005-15; "Ministration to the Sick," BCP 1979, 453-57; "A Service of Healing I," UMBW, 615-21.

with a special focus on healing, laying on of hands, and anointing. The theological emphasis is on comfort, strength, and hope. Hand laying formulas can vary from those that ask God to "drive away" sickness to more ambiguous ones that speak of the recipient simply knowing "the healing power of [God's] gift of love."[40] The BCP 1979 stands alone in providing a prayer "For the Sanctification of Illness" which asks that the experience of illness strengthen a person's faith and add seriousness to his/her confession.[41]

It appears that a good case could be made for considering healing a sacrament. Among the reasons are:

1. Jesus commanded his followers to heal (Matt. 10:8; Luke 10:9)
2. The apostles healed in the post-resurrection era (Acts 3:1-10)
3. Oil is a biblically-appointed element for healing (James 5:14)
4. Healing rituals carry a promise (James 5:15).

However, against the sacramentality of healing is the inconsistency between the gospel accounts of the sending of the Twelve in Matthew versus the Seventy-Two in Luke. Luke's account suggests that the ministry of healing was limited to the "lost sheep of Israel," which raises doubts as to whether there is an imperative for the church of all times and places. Furthermore, in the two gospel narratives above there is no commanded sign, whether the laying on of hands or anointing with oil. As mentioned, the Letter of James does speak of an anointing, but *prayer* (rather than anointing) is the efficacious agent of healing. In reality, nothing in the New Testament suggests that healing unites a person with Christ. The most we can say is that healing and healing rituals are signs of the kingdom of God and the saving work of Christ. Even if the disciples mediated divine healing, those healed would still have death in front of them. Only baptism and the Lord's Supper contain promises that deal with life on the other side of death and offer participation in that life. Thus, healing

[40] "Ministration to the Sick," BCP 1979, 456; cf. "Healing," ELW, 664.

[41] "Ministration to the Sick," BCP 1979, 460.

cannot be said to share the same sacramental status as baptism and the Lord's Supper. This is certainly not an excuse for the church today to eschew services of healing; on the contrary, a service of healing can address a significant pastoral need in proclaiming the grace of God for the whole person, body, mind, and soul.

Churches that celebrate healing services are advised to be clear on four points. First, such services do not offer *cures*. While it is appropriate to pray for relief from bodily infirmity, how and when that relief comes about must be left to the sovereign will of God. Similarly, the church baptizes in the hope that recipients will become true and faithful Christians, but it makes no guarantees to this effect. Rather, it recognizes that true faith is a gift from God and so obediently baptizes and teaches while leaving the outcome of baptism to God's sovereign will. Second, reception of the church's healing ministry is not to be construed as a substitute for professional medical treatment. The church believes that God calls people to the medical professions for the purpose of restoring and preserving health and life. Indeed, nothing in the New Testament should prevent a Christian from seeking help from doctors and other medical professionals. There is no dichotomy between the church's healing ministry and medical healing. Third, the use of oil to anoint the sick is to be considered a matter of freedom, whether in the context of a private or public rite. Perhaps more essential is prayer for the sick. Yet, if the relief of physical suffering is sought, it is only appropriate that a physical element be used. Fourth, when physical healing takes place, it must be understood as penultimate – as a sign that a greater healing and restoration awaits all Christians on the other side of death in Christ's eternal kingdom.

***

Like people of other faiths, Christians ritualize death in order to comfort the bereaved and to proclaim its beliefs in the face of death. Although Christians have never viewed their burial service as a sacrament, it can nevertheless be a time to rearticulate the sacramental promises of baptism.

The New Testament provides no material on the ritualization of death in early Christianity, although it does speak of the disposition of the faithful departed. Amid doubts in the Corinthian community, Paul emphatically states that the dead will be raised. If the dead are not raised, then Christ himself is not raised and Paul's preaching is useless. Since Christ is the firstfruits of the resurrection, Christians can be assured that the dead will be raised (1 Cor. 15:12-32). Indeed, the dead will be united with Christ and with the faithful who remain (1 Thess. 4:13-18). Christian creeds affirm that the living and the dead will be judged by Christ at his return and receive their due reward.

In the early church various burial customs began to emerge. It is clear from a number of liturgical books, such as the prayer book of Sarapion of Thmuis (Egypt), that prayers were made for the dead, especially for their rest, resurrection from the dead, and forgiveness of sins.[42] God was also asked to comfort mourners. Augustine knew of the celebration of the Lord's Supper in connection with funerals.[43] Normally, early Christian funerals were held during the day (rather than at night according to the pagan custom), and the overall tenor was one of joy and hope in the resurrection. It was also customary to observe the anniversary of a person's death with a eucharistic service at the grave. Eventually, the faithful departed were remembered at every celebration of the Mass in the prayer petition known as the *Momento etiam* ("Remember, also, O Lord…").[44]

The tone of Christian funerals changed during the Middle Ages. The fear of judgment and hell replaced the joy and hope of heaven. The focus was on pleading with God to forgive the sins of the deceased and to deliver him/her from judgement. While the Introit and Gradual of the Requiem Mass petitioned eternal rest and the perpetual light of heaven, the sequence hymn known as the *Dies Irae* ("Day of Wrath") speaks of fierce divine judgement, and the Offertory pleads: "O Lord, Jesus Christ…free the souls of all

[42] *The Prayers of Sarapion of Thmuis*, SW, 336.

[43] Augustine, *Confessions* IX.7.32 (ca. 400).

[44] *The Roman Canon* (late-fourth cent.), PEER, 165.

the faithful departed from infernal punishment and from the deep pit."[45]

Protestant Reformers, most notably Martin Luther, sought to shift the focus back to joy in the resurrection. Luther provided no funeral rite, but he did comment on how to reform funeral services.[46] Deploring the hopelessness and mournfulness of funerals in his day, Luther advocates the singing of comforting hymns that speak of forgiveness, rest, sleep, and the resurrection of the faithful departed. Every funeral, he says, should witness to the church's faith in the resurrection, as articulated in its creed. Only this faith can comfort and provide hope in the face of death's terrifying finality. Funeral songs should be scriptural verses in order to praise and glorify God, and to comfort mourners.

The funeral rite in the BCP 1549 was quite simple.[47] The body of the deceased was carried into the church (or to the grave) accompanied by the singing of scripture verses pertaining to the resurrection. At the grave, earth was caste on the corpse (casket) and the deceased was commended to God. Psalms and 1 Cor. 15 were read either before or after the graveside rites. A final prayer was followed by a celebration of Holy Communion. Overall, death is viewed as a deliverance from the wretchedness of this life, and the final judgement is still in view, although God is imaged as merciful. A simplified and revised version of the rite appeared in the BCP 1559 and BCP 1662, although both the final petition for God to forgive the sins of the deceased and communion were omitted.[48] Wesley's order for the burial of the dead makes no mention of the deceased at all,[49] which suggests that Protestants were becoming increasingly

---

[45] http://en.wikipedia.org/wiki/Music_for_the_Requiem_Mass#Offertory [accessed 16 February 2015].

[46] Martin Luther, *Preface to the Burial Hymns* (1542), LW 53, 325-31.

[47] "The Order for the Burial of the Dead" (1549), BCP *Texts*, 82-90.

[48] "The Order for the Burial of the Dead" (1559/1662), BCP *Texts*, 171-74, 451-56.

[49] John Wesley, "The Order for the Burial of the Dead" (1784), JWPB, 156-61.

uncomfortable with intercessory prayer for members of the church triumphant.

Funerals in other branches of Protestantism (Baptists, Pentecostalism) have traditionally shared the concern for comforting mourners, while placing less emphasis on commending the deceased to God. More distinctively, evangelical Protestants have viewed the funeral as an opportunity to convert unbelievers precisely through the sharing of a message of hope in the resurrection to eternal life. Liturgical uniformity is eschewed, although songs, prayer, sharings by friends and family, scripture readings, and the sermon are central elements.

For the most part, funeral services in mainline Protestantism today follow a four-fold structure of gathering, word, meal (or response), and sending.[50] Opening words and the minister's greeting to the assembly may be followed or preceded by singing. An opening prayer asks God for the grace to face the finality of death and/or gives thanks for the life and witness of the deceased. Biblical readings focus on God's faithfulness (Is. 40:1-8) and promise to destroy death (Is. 25:6-8). Selections from 1 Cor. 15 and John 14 are frequent recommendations since the resurrection to eternal life is the basis of Christian hope in the face of death. Acts of response following the sermon include a memorial statement about the deceased, sharing by family and friends, and the creed. The sending includes prayer and other words that commend the deceased to God's loving care. Recognizing that the Lord's Supper offers fellowship with the resurrected Lord and with all of God's faithful ones, communion might follow in many services. Additional prayers, songs, a benediction, and a dismissal conclude the service. Most liturgical books assume that the committal follows either at the graveside, crematorium, or other place of interment and therefore provide appropriate prayers and lessons.

---

[50] "Burial of the Dead," LBW, 331-39; "Funeral," ELW, 666-74; "The Funeral: A Service of Witness to the Resurrection," BCW, 911-38; "The Burial of the Dead: Rite Two," BCP 1979, 491-505; "Services of Death and Resurrection," UMBW, 141-57.

When planning, it is helpful to remember the two-fold purpose of a Christian funeral: to comfort mourners and to commend the deceased to God. The basis of this comfort is the promises of God's Word, and the sharing of Scripture and a biblically based homily (message) are essential. The proclamation of the Word is all the more effective when the funeral takes place in the church of the deceased, the very place where his/her family and church have heard that Word proclaimed many times before. Appropriate closure is made when a faithful Christian's funeral is held in the same place where he/she was baptized, confirmed, married, and worshipped for years. Commending the deceased to God's eternal care requires naming the person and applying the message of the resurrection to that individual. Death is another stage in the baptismal journey that culminates with the resurrection, so a baptized Christian is most appropriately named again when commended to God for the final phase of that journey. Without such a naming, the funeral service is little more than an abstract, cold statement about death.

Here, a word of caution is due. It is appropriate to remember the life and gifts of the deceased, particularly his/her service to the church. But "celebrating" the deceased's life, to the extent of providing a service "themed" around one of his/her interests or hobbies (e.g., football, classic movies, motorcycles), has no place in the Christian church. Rightly speaking, the theme of any funeral is the resurrection of Jesus Christ, rather than the interests and tastes of the deceased. The life of a Christian finds its ultimate meaning in service to the God whose love is stronger than death. Additionally, tributes to the deceased or displays of devotion and affection must be restrained in order not to overwhelm or overshadow the Word of God. It must be remembered that God's baptismal promises to the deceased carry far more importance and meaning that anything that we can do or say. It may even be advisable to restrict tributes to a wake service held prior to the funeral.

Perhaps one way to ensure that God's promises shine through in all their brilliance is to reclaim the sacramental connections of the Christian funeral. As mentioned, the Christian funeral has never been considered a sacrament, and yet it points to both baptism and the Supper. Paul reminds us that we are baptized into the death of Christ, and so the death of every Christian is an opportunity to remember the promises made to us in baptism. That happens when the funeral is held in the deceased's church and when the opening rites are led from the baptismal font. Indeed the service could even begin with a "Thanksgiving for Baptism."[51] Such a rite might even include the sprinkling of the casket and the liturgical assembly with water from the baptismal font. The celebration of the Lord's Supper is a fitting way of participating anew in the life of the risen Christ who feeds us now and on the other side of death. Along with reminders of baptism, the Lord's Supper speaks powerfully to those who need a token of God's faithfulness during a time of loss and mourning.

Although significant numbers of non-Christians are often present, this fact alone should not deter the celebration of the Lord's Supper at funerals. There is no reason why an announcement or note cannot state who is and is not welcome to receive Holy Communion – something that is done in many Sunday services. To begin with, Protestantism has a long history of "fencing the table"[52] (i.e., excluding those deemed inappropriate communicants) because it takes baptism, faith, and discipleship very seriously and knows that without these things no person can rightly participate in the Supper. Additionally, Roman Catholic and Orthodox churches today are forthright in stating that non-members (and non-Christians) should not receive communion. Finally, thoughtful followers of other faiths will appreciate churches that set boundaries rather than appear to have none at all. A sensitively-worded statement saying that the Lord's Supper is for the baptized will not offend non-Christians, who can probably intuit that a sacred meal is what mourners need.

---

[51] See "Funeral," ELW, 667.

[52] See John Calvin, *The Form of Prayers and Manner of Ministering the Sacraments According to the Usage of the Ancient Church* (1542), PEER, 216.

Conclusion

The occasional rites of the church – marriage, ordination, healing, and funeral – are not sacraments, and yet they are related to baptism and the Lord's Supper. Indeed, as we have seen, the occasional rites take their meaning from the two sacraments, and so participate in the whole sacramental economy of the church's liturgical life. Failure to understand this vital connection and to work out its implications in practice will impoverish the occasional services theologically and the church spiritually. Ministers and other church leaders are especially encouraged to draw out the baptismal implications of the occasional rites so that each and every Christian may learn to wear baptism as a daily garment.[53]

For Further Reading

Private Confession and Forgiveness

Jennings, Theodore W. *The Liturgy of Liberation: The Confession and Forgiveness of Sins*. Nashville: Abingdon Press, 1988.

Morton, Mark. *Personal Confession Reconsidered: Making Forgiveness Real.* Bramcote: Grove Books, 1994.

Oden, Thomas C. *Corrective Love: The Power of Communion Discipline*. St Louis: Concordia Publishing, 1995.

Healing

Alexander, Kimberly Erwin. *Pentecostal Healing: Models in Theology and Practice*. London: Deo Publishing, 2006.

Evans, Abigail Rian. *Healing Liturgies for the Seasons of Life*. Louisville: Westminster John Knox Press, 2004.

Weddings and Funerals

Malphurs, Aubrey. *Contemporary Handbook for Weddings and Funerals*. Grand Rapids: Kregel Publications, 2003.

Webber, Christopher L. *The Art of the Homily: Including Homilies for Baptisms, Marriages and Funerals*. Harrisburg, PA: Morehouse Publishing, 1992.

[53] For the idea of baptism as "daily garment," see Luther, *Large Catechism*, BC, 466.84.

Ordination

Bradshaw, Paul F. *Ordination Rites of the Ancient Churches of the East and West.* Collegeville: Liturgical Press, 2000.

Harnish, John E. *The Orders of Ministry in the United Methodist Church.* Nashville: Abingdon Press, 2000.

Holeton, David R. *Anglican Orders and Ordination.* Cambridge: Grove Books, 1997.

Smith, Ralph F. *Luther, Ministry, and Ordination Rites in the Early Reformation Church.* New York: Peter Lang, 1996.

Index of Subjects

T

V

W

Y

Index of Authors